# This Just In

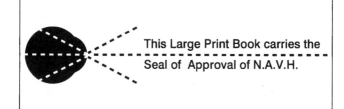

This Large Print Book carries the
Seal of Approval of N.A.V.H.

# This Just In

## WHAT I COULDN'T TELL YOU ON TV

## Bob Schieffer

**Thorndike Press • Waterville, Maine**

Published in 2003 by arrangement with G. P. Putnam's Sons, a member of Penguin Putnam Inc.

Thorndike Press® Large Print Americana Series.

The tree indicium is a trademark of Thorndike Press.

The text of this Large Print edition is unabridged.
Other aspects of the book may vary from the original edition.

Set in 16 pt. Plantin by Warren S. Doersam.

Printed in the United States on permanent paper.

**Library of Congress Cataloging-in-Publication Data**

Schieffer, Bob.
    This just in : what I couldn't tell you on TV / Bob Schieffer.
      p. cm.
    ISBN 0-7862-5327-4 (lg. print : hc : alk. paper)
    1. Schieffer, Bob. 2. Journalists — United States —
Biography. 3. Large type books. I. Title.
PN4874.S32A3 2003b
070.92—dc21
  [B]                                   2003040660

*For Susan and Sharon*

# Acknowledgments

Some years back, Dan Rather was off in some godforsaken corner of the world and I was in New York anchoring a special report, when a young desk assistant named Jill Rosenbaum approached the anchor desk during a break and handed me a piece of copy.

In my best TV voice, I said, "Ah . . . this just in?"

"No," she said in all seriousness, "this was just sitting there on the desk. I didn't think you saw it."

That's sort of how it was with this book. Most of these stories had just been sitting there, waiting until I had a place to put them down on paper. Over the years, I've told some of them on Don Imus's radio show. Imus has been on my case for years to publish a collection of the commentaries that I do each Sunday on *Face the Nation*, and when I resisted one day, he said, "Well, you should talk to Esther about it," Esther being Esther Newberg, the literary agent (super-agent, I've come to understand) who represents Imus. Nothing stops Imus when he gets on a project, and when I called Esther later that morning, she said, "Oh, he's already called.

The problem is, journalism collections don't sell very well. Why don't you just do a book?" So I did. I wrote the first four chapters, sent them off to Esther, and she sent them to several publishing houses, including Penguin Putnam, where Neil Nyren saw the makings of a book and has proven to be a wonderful editor. So first thanks go to Imus, Esther and Neil. Without them, this book wouldn't have happened and these stories would still be sitting there. (Note to Imus: We're working on that collection of commentaries.)

Nor would this book have been possible without the cooperation of the eighty-five people who allowed me to interview them on the record. Nearly all of them are quoted by name. Others, such as Brent Scowcroft, George H. W. Bush's national security advisor, and historian Michael Beschloss, gave me valuable context and background and guided me to others who had the answers I was seeking. Only on several occasions was I forced to resort to anonymous sources, and in those cases, the information they gave me usually amounted to no more than minor detail. What I set out to do when I began this book in January 2001 was to write about my experiences in covering some of the big stories of the past forty years, but as I jogged my own memory, I began to wonder how the people involved in many of those events felt about them with the passing of time. So I decided to call as many as I could find. Over the next eighteen months, I talked to two former presidents, Jimmy Carter and Gerald Ford. During the Middle East crisis in the spring of 2002, the current president, George W. Bush, found time to talk to me about his feelings on 9-11. I had hoped to interview former president Bill Clinton as well, but his office informed me that his publisher has forbidden him to give book interviews until his own book is published. Former Secretaries of State Alexander Haig and James A. Baker, III, were especially generous with their time, as were former Defense Secretaries Melvin R. Laird and James Schlesinger. I spent a delightful afternoon with Eugene McCarthy, now eighty-six, talking about campaigns past and present, and had two long interviews with George McGovern. Many of those in Lyndon Johnson's inner circle, especially George Christian and Joseph Califano, spoke candidly to me about Johnson's decision not to seek reelection in 1968, and his later regret about withdrawing from the race. Senator Edward M. Kennedy, former Senator Bob Dole and Senator Tom Daschle gave me new insight into the Washington of more recent years. Dr. Frank Stanton, who along with William S. Paley shaped CBS into the Tiffany network, spoke candidly about those days, as did Arthur Taylor, the man Paley chose to replace Stanton. During a long telephone conversation, former CBS owner Lawrence Tisch gave me new insight into his side of the turbulent period when control of CBS shifted from Paley to Tisch and eventually to Westinghouse and later Viacom. To each of them, my thanks for helping me to have a better understanding of what I had remembered and, in some instances, for reminding me of things I had forgotten.

Several books proved especially helpful, first among them Theodore White's *The Making of the President* series. They remain the indispensable guide to American politics in the 1960s and 1970s. Richard Reeves's books *President Kennedy* and *President Nixon* were good reference points for me as I wrote about my own experiences during the enrollment of James Meredith at Ole Miss and during the early days of the Nixon administration. Corydon B. Dunham's book *Fighting for the First Amendment: Stanton of CBS vs. Congress and the Nixon White House* provides the best compilation yet of the once secret memos, tapes and other White House documents that detail Nixon's war with the press. As I wrote about my own experiences during those years, I found myself referring to it constantly to trace the things that Nixon's people were doing that I later learned of but could not have known about at the time. I am also indebted to my CBS News colleague Eric Engberg, who shared his extensive files of

Nixon White House documents that have been released over the years by the National Archives. Thanks also to Karen Hughes and Christa Ritacco of the Bush White House, Penny Circle of President Ford's staff, Faye Purdue of the Carter Center, and Harry Middleton of the LBJ Library.

In Fort Worth, Phil Record helped me remember things I had forgotten from the police beat and Jani Torrence pored through back issues of the *Fort Worth Star-Telegram* to track down many of the early stories I had written about Vietnam.

At CBS News in New York, it was Bonney Kapp's diligent search of the CBS News archives that produced a long-ago interview I had done with Bill Clinton. (We used only ten seconds of it at the time.) Toby Wertheim, who has spent a career at CBS tracking down obscure facts and statistics that seem to elude others, knew just where to track down hard-to-find details about Ground Zero, and CBS News president Andrew Heyward gave me leads on several good stories. Dan Rather and I have been friends for more than forty years, no small feat in TV land, and we had fun remembering details of many past adventures together.

In the Washington bureau, Charlie Wilson provided expert help on pictures, and Mary Hager read sections of the manuscript and, as she has so many times over the years, discov-

11

ered what could have been embarrassing er-
rors. In addition to being a terrific journalist,
Janet Leissner is the most caring bureau chief
I have ever worked for. I appreciate her help
and treasure her friendship.

My daughters, Susan and Sharon, have
made me proud a thousand times over. I
hope this book will help them understand
where I was during those times when I wasn't
home. And then there is my wife and best
friend, Pat. Most of what I have done in life,
including this book, she has helped me do a
little better. If they ever pick a wives' All Star
team, she's my choice.

— Washington, D.C.
April 30, 2002

# Contents

# One

## *Oswald's Mother*

In those days, I was the night police reporter at the *Fort Worth Star-Telegram*, the newspaper in the town where I grew up. I was twenty-six years old, made $115 a week and worked the late trick, 6 P.M. to 2:30 A.M.

I hung out with cops, emergency-room nurses, barmaids and other creatures of the night. Like most young reporters who covered crime, I considered myself a superb investigator, more cop than journalist. I wore a snap-brim hat, hoping I'd be mistaken for a detective, and when someone made that mistake I never corrected him. The stories I covered were an endless series of car wrecks and murders, the hours were awful, the pay was low, even by Texas newspaper standards, and I thought it was about the best job anyone could ever have.

But when I heard that President Kennedy was coming to Fort Worth, I wasn't entirely happy about it. In those days, presidents didn't travel nearly as much as they do now, so it was big news for my hometown, but bad

15

news for me. Kennedy's visit would cause no interruption in my regular schedule. The political reporters would handle Kennedy. They would not need any help from me. For a reporter, there's nothing worse than being in the middle of a big story that someone else is covering, and I was more than a little irritated.

Kennedy and his entourage flew into Fort Worth late on a Thursday evening and, assignment or no assignment, once we put the paper to bed early Friday morning, I hustled over to the Press Club, which was being held open after-hours to accommodate the traveling White House press corps. The party was well under way when I got there around 2 A.M., and for me this was as good as it got. There I was, chatting up reporters I had known only for their bylines, Merriman Smith of UPI, Tom Wicker of the *New York Times*, Bob Pierpoint of CBS and a dozen more.

Kennedy had come to Texas to heal some quarrels in the Democratic Party and to raise money for the '64 campaign, and the tour had started in Houston and San Antonio. After a Thursday-night speech in Houston, he had flown to Fort Worth to spend the night and attend an early-morning Chamber of Commerce breakfast before taking a ten-minute flight to Dallas for a parade and luncheon speech. The tour was to end with a

16

huge fund-raising dinner in Austin. Governor John Connally had convinced Kennedy that only in Austin, the state capital, could you count on getting people from the rest of the state to come to a fund-raiser. People from Houston wouldn't go to San Antonio for a fund-raiser, Connally told Kennedy, and people from Fort Worth damn sure wouldn't go to Dallas. He was right about that. When Amon Carter was running the *Star-Telegram*, he made a point of taking a sack lunch when he had business in Dallas, claiming he did not care for the city's restaurants. Dallas repaid the courtesy when Fort Worth built an airport between the two cities and named it Carter Field. Dallas residents declined to use the airport, in large part because of the name, and the airport eventually failed. (There was and is such a rivalry between the two cities that the only project they ever cooperated on is the current airport. Planners were careful not to name it after anyone from either city.) The visiting reporters had no interest in our airports, of course. What they did want to know about was a local after-hours joint called the Cellar. The Cellar had no liquor license, but if you were a friend of the owner, a former stock-car racer named Pat Kirkwood, the drink of choice, Kool-Aid spiked with grain alcohol, was on the house. It was not the drinks, but the fact that the Cellar's waitresses wore only underwear, that had given the place some notoriety and the notoriety had apparently spread as far as Washington. Hippies and free love would descend on San Francisco, and Kirkwood always claimed his place was a forerunner of what was to come. Whatever the case, Phil Record, the *Star-Telegram* night city editor, and I were appointed to guide our visitors to it.

It seemed a good idea at the time and must have been quite an evening. I remember that we stayed long enough for some of the easterners to see their first Fort Worth sunrise. A group of off-duty Secret Service agents joined us, and in months to come, there would be congressional hearings into whether the visit had left them as alert as they should have been the next day in Dallas.

Having no assignment the next day, I could afford to sleep late, which was my normal practice, anyway. I was the oldest of three children and my father had died when I was in college, so I still lived in my mother's house, helping her to make a home for my brother, Tom, and my sister, Sharon. Tom had been ten when Dad died and Sharon fifteen, but by the time Kennedy came to Texas, Tom was in high school, and it was Tom who shook me awake, shouting, "Kennedy has been shot — you'd better get to work!"

Tom had been allowed to miss school that

day, and he and Mother had driven into town early to see the president as he emerged from the Chamber of Commerce breakfast. As Kennedy walked out of the Texas Hotel and toward his car, Tom had been one of the last people in Fort Worth to shake his hand. Within hours and before they had returned home, Kennedy had been shot.

I dressed as quickly as I could, grabbed my black felt snap-brim Dick Tracy hat, and roared off in my two-seater Triumph TR-4 sports car. As I parked in the lot near the *Star-Telegram* office, the radio confirmed the worst: The president was dead. It was as if someone had hit me with a hammer. At once, I was stunned, hurt and embarrassed. Stunned, because such violence was unthinkable in those days; hurt and embarrassed, because it had happened in our home state. Why did something like this have to happen, and why did it have to happen in Texas?

As I made my way inside, lines of people two and three across were already surrounding the *Star-Telegram* building. The Kennedy assassination would be the first story that the entire nation would watch together on television, and because of it television would soon replace newspapers as the place where most Americans got their news. But when Kennedy was shot, people still really didn't believe the news unless they saw it written down in black and white, so hundreds waited outside the Star-Telegram for the special editions that rolled off the presses. "The truth was, we couldn't print them fast enough," said one of our editors later. "People would stand in line to buy one edition, then go to the back of the line to buy a copy of the next one." They were the last of the great newspaper Extras and they would come to symbolize the end of the newspaper era.

Inside the city room it was bedlam. When the flash that Kennedy had been shot had hit the wires, an editor had dispatched so many reporters to Dallas that there was no one left on the city desk to answer the phones, and they were all ringing. Nonetheless, one of the editors told me to get to the police station. A man carrying a load of dynamite in his car had been arrested leaving Dallas County and was being brought to the Fort Worth jail. He was the best suspect so far in the Kennedy shooting.

I managed to get to the police station just as he was being brought down the back stairs. Early in my police reporting days, I learned a trick from the cops. People will sometimes blurt out the truth if they are surprised by the question, so I jumped in front of the handcuffed suspect, who was between two detectives, and shouted, "You son of a bitch, why did you do it?"

"Well, I didn't," he said, as the cops hustled him into the lockup.

In a matter of hours, it would become clear that the poor man had done nothing and knew no more about the assassination than the rest of us. He had stopped for gas at a service station between Dallas and Fort Worth and mentioned to the attendant what he had heard on the radio, that the president had been shot. The attendant hadn't heard about it and called the cops, figuring the only person who could have known about the shooting was the one who had done it. When police stopped the man's car and found the trunk loaded with dynamite, it was enough for them, too. As the afternoon wore on, it was determined that the man was exactly who he said he was, a demolition contractor who was en route to a construction job. Had it happened today, it would have triggered dozens of lawsuits against the city and the police and at least the threat of one against me; but the police apologized, and the man said no problem and went on his way.

When I got back to the city room, the confusion was worse than ever. By now, a dozen *Star-Telegram* reporters were on the scene in Dallas, but when they called in, there was no one on the city desk to answer the phones and take down the stories they were trying to call in.

I hadn't even removed my hat when I settled behind a typewriter and picked up one of the ringing phones. In all my years as a reporter, I would never again take a call like that one.

A woman's voice asked if we could spare anyone to give her a ride to Dallas.

"Lady," I said, "this is not a taxi, and besides, the president has been shot."

"I know," she said. "They think my son is the one who shot him."

It was the mother of Lee Harvey Oswald, and she had heard on the radio of her son's arrest.

"Where do you live?" I blurted out. "I'll be right over to get you."

Why she called the *Star-Telegram* that day remains a mystery. She had lived a vagabond life during most of Oswald's childhood, but she had eventually settled in Fort Worth, and when Oswald had defected to the Soviet Union, *Star-Telegram* reporters had interviewed her. We would also later learn that sometime before the assassination, she had worked briefly as a governess in the home of *Star-Telegram* founder Amon Carter's son. The family had had no idea she was the mother of a defector, but had discharged her because the children complained that "she was mean."

Whether those connections prompted her call, we never knew, nor did I know any of that as I began to think about how I was going to get her to Dallas. Somehow, taking her there in a two-seater open sports car just didn't seem quite right. Which led me to the desk of Bill Foster, the paper's automotive editor. For years, local car dealers had furnished the auto editor with a new car and gas to fuel it. It was offered and accepted without embarrassment, with the understanding that the auto editor would "road-test" the car and write up the results in his Sunday column. Not surprisingly, the reviews were usually favorable. When Bill told me he was driving a Cadillac sedan that week, I said, "Come on, I'll explain as we go and you're gonna like it."

We found Mrs. Oswald on the lawn of a small home on Fort Worth's west side. She was a short, round-faced woman in enormous, black horn-rimmed glasses and a white nurse's uniform. She carried a small blue travel bag. I got into the backseat with her and Bill drove. She was distraught, but in an odd way. I would later come to believe she was mentally deranged, but for most of the trip she seemed less concerned with the death of the president and for her son than with herself. She railed about how Oswald's Russian-born wife would get sympathy while no one would "remember the mother" and that she would probably starve. I marked it off to understandable emotional overload and I couldn't bring myself to use her self-serving remarks in the story I filed later that day. I probably should have. She would later be so brazen as to tell a reporter for *Life* magazine that "Mama wants money," and years later she was still saying the same things. As she had predicted, the world showed her little sympathy and she supported herself in the end by selling Oswald's clothing to souvenir hunters.

The drive to Dallas took about an hour, and when we reached the police station, Bill let us out and said he would join us later once he had parked the car. Hundreds of reporters had converged on the station, most of them in a hallway where the detective offices were located. Since I was wearing the Dick Tracy hat, it was easy for me to pass for a plainclothesman. There was a uniformed cop behind a counter in one of the offices so I approached him and said, "I'm the one who brought Oswald's mother over from Fort Worth. Is there someplace she can stay where she won't be bothered by all these reporters?"

The officer guided us to a small space that seemed to be some kind of interrogation room and said, "How about this?" I said thanks, settled Mrs. Oswald in and went into the hallway to see if I could help our guys. By then, there were seventeen of us on the scene, but the problem was finding phones to call in what we had found out. Other reporters were having to walk several blocks to find phones. I began to gather up what our team had collected, and called it in from the office the police had given to Mrs. Oswald and me. Never once did anyone ask me who I was. As the evening wore on, Oswald's wife was brought to the police station and an officer asked me if we would mind if they let her share the room. I told them I saw no problem. The only difficulty for me was that she seemed to speak no English, only Russian.

Toward dark, Oswald's mother asked Detective Captain Will Fritz if they could visit Oswald. Fritz agreed, and led us into a holding room below the jail. The group included Oswald's wife, his mother, an FBI agent and me. I couldn't believe it. Oswald was being brought down from his cell. I would soon be face-to-face with the man who was being charged with killing our president. Whatever Oswald said, this would have to be the story of a lifetime. An exclusive interview with the man who had just been charged with killing the president. We had only been there a few minutes, but to me it seemed an eternity and I could feel my heart beginning to beat faster, when the FBI agent casually asked, "And who are you with?"

I had watched veteran interrogators bluff their way with a suspect by answering a question with a question, and in my best imitation I sort of half snarled, "Well, who are you with?"

The agent seemed a little edgy now. "Are you a reporter?"

25

Now I was really pushing it: "Well, aren't you?"

It was at this point that I believe I received my first official death threat. The embarrassed agent said he would kill me if he ever saw me again. Or at least that seemed to be what he was saying. I was already leaving as he said it.

It would be the biggest story I almost got but didn't, and I went back to the crowded corridor and blended in with the rest of the reporters. For the next two days, I would just be part of the crowd.

That night, I had dinner at one of Dallas's largest steak houses with Roger Summers, another *Star-Telegram* reporter, and except for a man and woman at another table, the restaurant was empty.

My interview with Mrs. Oswald came too late for the Friday-evening Extra, but it made the Saturday-morning paper and I spent that Saturday at Dealey Plaza where Kennedy had been shot. Hundreds of people had gathered there, the nation was in shock and nowhere was it more obvious than in the plaza where he had been shot. People seemed to wander aimlessly, occasionally talking to anyone who happened by. Some left flowers, some just stared. I talked to one man who had come to Dallas to see Kennedy but had seen only a motorcade racing toward a hospital after the

26

shooting. It was as if he had lost a friend. He could not understand how it could have happened. His grief became the heart of a story that I filed for the Sunday paper, a story that began, "Today, I walked with a man named Gregory Pontes and for a moment he seemed to speak for all America." I've written thousands of stories since that day, but I never forgot the lead to that one.

Oswald was still being held in the police station, but was to be transferred to county jail the next morning to await trial. We had begun to scale back our coverage and our photographers were sent home. One of our reporters would watch Oswald as he was brought out of the city jail and placed in a car for the trip to the county jail nearby. I was to watch him arrive there. It was a trip he would never make. As two detectives brought him to the loading dock, the man we would later know as Jack Ruby walked from the crowd of reporters and onlookers, stuck a small pistol in Oswald's side and killed him.

How could it happen? I have been asked that question many times, and when I explain that it was a different time, the answer seldom seems to suffice. But those were the days before metal detectors, identification cards and concrete barriers — all the security precautions that we have come to accept as a part of modern life. America was yet to be scarred by the violent acts that led to the security checks. We didn't shoot our presidents, we didn't know much about terrorists, and the only people who used bombs were gangsters, and as long as they confined their killings to each other, we didn't really mind. In those days, if you looked as if you belonged, you could usually get in most places. I had walked into the Dallas police station and secured the use of an office on the strength of nothing more than wearing a hat that made me look like a detective. Ruby had been a hanger-on at the police station. Because he looked as if he belonged there, no one had questioned his presence.

For the reporters, Oswald's shooting meant it was time to go back to work. Our managing editor, Lorin McMullen, decided to put out a Sunday-afternoon Extra, something that had never been done. This was no simple task. When the paper had churned out those Extras the day Kennedy was shot, the presses were already rolling with a complete newspaper that only needed to be updated. McMullen was talking about starting from scratch, a complete newspaper, including want ads, to be on the streets early Sunday afternoon. Somehow, McMullen and his team of editors managed to do it. We were so proud of the accomplishment that when the first copies were trucked over from Fort Worth, I grabbed a bundle and sold them myself at Dealey Plaza. I guess I still owe the paper some money. I don't remember turning in my profits, but in truth, I gave away more papers than I sold.

It was a sweet scoop. We had managed to get our papers to Dallas before the *Dallas Morning News* had printed its first edition, and it was even sweeter because McMullen found a way around having no photo of the shooting. The Dallas paper had a graphic shot of Ruby just as he rammed the gun into Oswald's stomach and had moved it as a copyrighted photo on the Associated Press wire shortly after the shooting. McMullen grabbed it off the wire, blew it up and spread it across the front page. Beneath the photo, in six-point agate type (the tiny type used in baseball box scores), was the line "Copyright 1963, *Dallas Morning News.*"

We had beaten the *Dallas News* to the streets of Dallas with the paper's own photo.

*Newsweek* and *Time* picked up my quotes from Mrs. Oswald and both sent me checks for fifty dollars, and later that week I got a phone call from Dan Rather, the young CBS News reporter who had flown in to cover the story. He was trying to reach Mrs. Oswald and wondered if I might have her phone number. I didn't, but I gave him her address. It was the beginning of a friendship that would last more than thirty years, but the information proved to be of no help. A New York–based *Life* magazine reporter named

Thomas Thompson, who also happened to be from Fort Worth, had managed to put the Oswald women under exclusive contract to his magazine and had secreted them away in a Dallas hotel. My brief quotes from Marguerite Oswald would be her only comments to appear in print for weeks.

I was sent back to Dallas the next week to cover the funeral of J. D. Tippitt, the policeman Oswald had killed as he fled the Texas School Book Depository. As hundreds of police officers from all over America paid their last respects to Tippitt, Oswald was being buried quietly in Fort Worth.

Fearing violence, officials gave no public notice of the Oswald funeral. His mother, wife and brother attended, but there were not enough people to act as pallbearers, so three *Star-Telegram* reporters, Jon McConal, Jerry Flemmons and Ed Horn, helped the funeral-home workers carry the casket.

It would not be until weeks later that I realized the emotional toll those days had taken on me. I have heard of people who experienced traumatic events that left them so drained of all emotion they were unable to feel pain, but for me the overpowering shock of trying to work in the midst of it left me so exhausted mentally that for a while I somehow became immune to emotion.

Several nights later, back on the police beat, I was in the emergency room of Saint

Joseph Hospital when the bodies of a family that had been fatally injured in a car wreck were wheeled by on gurneys. They had been beheaded when their car had slammed into the rear of a truck loaded with metal pipes. A police reporter sees many sights, and death and injury were nothing new to me, but only after I had watched the bodies pass by did I realize the sight had provoked no reaction at all. It was as if I had no emotion left to express.

It would take me a long time to get over those days. But I would not be the only one. That day in Dallas would be a turning point for America. It was the first time that virtually the entire nation had come together to witness and share a national tragedy and we had shared it on television. The scenes of that week, the killing of Oswald and the hour upon hour of the live coverage of Kennedy's funeral, the cortege, the black-veiled young widow, the dead president's tiny son saluting the flag, all those sad pictures would be burned into the national psyche. No more would Americans have to see something written down in the newspaper to believe it. For the first time, Americans were seeing what the reporters saw; no longer would they have to wait to read what the reporters had written about it. From then on, they would compare their own observations to those of the reporters. From that day on, it would be the imprimatur of television that made events official. The change in the way Americans thought about the presidency and the men who occupied it would be even more profound than the shift from newspapers to television as the medium most Americans now turned to for news. Before Dallas, we had come to believe our presidents were somehow invincible. It was not so much that we considered them bulletproof, but it was inconceivable that someone would try to kill a president. Or even want to. Presidents had bodyguards, to be sure, but they rode in open cars and mingled freely with people. After Dallas, all that would change, and because they seemed more vulnerable, we would no longer see the invincibility of the office itself in the same way.

The next four decades would bring great change to America, but none more dramatic than the changes that would come to pass in journalism and politics. America lost its innocence that day in Dallas, and we would never look at government and our politicians in the same way. As a young newspaperman in those days when most Americans got their news from newspapers, I saw it begin to happen that day in Dallas. Later, in Vietnam, I saw the awful war that caused many young Americans to lose all faith in government and our leaders. As a network television correspondent in Washington, I would see the nation's confidence in government and the media shattered even further. I would see other national leaders cut down in their prime, another president shot and still another survive impeachment. And I would finally see the country come together once more after the terrorist attacks in 2001.

I got to see most of it and came to know many of the major figures of those four decades because I am a reporter. I became a reporter because I always wanted to see things for myself and make my own judgments about them. The lucky thing for me was that I found people to pay me for doing it, and it is what I have done over and over at CBS News in more than ten thousand interviews, stories, special reports and radio and television reports, as well as in thousands of newspaper articles. Those events I covered have become part of our history and you already know most of them. But I want to tell you about the parts that didn't get on television or in the paper, the serious parts and the not-so-serious parts, the good times I had, and the presidents, senators, correspondents, big-time crooks and small-time swindlers I came to know in the four decades since that day in Dallas. Here are the stories I tell my friends, and they are the stories I want to share with you.

# Two

## *The Johnson City Windmill*

When my daughters were young, they loved to ask me if I wanted to be a TV reporter when I was a little boy, and they always giggled when I told them, "There was no TV when I was a little boy. We didn't have a TV until I was in the eighth grade." A world without television was so incomprehensible to them, they would ask me the question over and over, as children do when they want to hear the same bedtime stories because they love the endings. I have come to understand their disbelief. Television has become such an overwhelming part of our culture, it is sometimes hard for me to believe there was a world before the tube and that I was a part of it. But even in those long-ago days before I knew about television, I knew I wanted to be a reporter, a reporter who covered politics.

I can't pinpoint just when I decided on journalism, but like so many of a certain age who grew up in Texas, my political awareness, my starting point for politics was Lyndon Johnson. In the years after World

War II and on into the 1960s, Johnson didn't just dominate Texas politics; he *was* Texas politics. His name was attached to everything that came from Washington, whether it was money for a highway or a new contract for the defense plant on the edge of Fort Worth. He was the giver of all good things, the defender against those who would take away from Texas, and he was the first politician I ever saw.

The year was 1948. Harry Truman was campaigning across the country by train and that fall he would score his famous upset over Tom Dewey, but if you were eleven years old and living in Fort Worth, Truman and Dewey were just names. We weren't thinking much about presidential politics that summer. From daylight to dark, all we thought about was baseball. There was no Little League. We organized our own games, and that's how we heard about Johnson. Word spread through the neighborhood that he was coming to the vacant lot where we played ball, so we all went down to see him.

Several hundred people had already gathered there when we arrived, and all at once we heard this great whirring noise and there was this thing in the sky: an airplane with no wings, the helicopter that would become known that summer as the Johnson City Windmill.

This would be tame stuff for today's Little Leaguers, but we had never seen a helicopter or anything like this, and from out of the sky we heard this booming voice:

"This is your candidate for the United States Senate, Lyndon B. Johnson, and I'll be down there to talk to you in just a minute . . . go tell all your neighbors."

We didn't go tell anyone. We were transfixed in terror. As Moses must have felt when he realized the burning bush was SPEAKING TO HIM, we didn't know what to think. God, Lyndon Johnson, whoever it was, we were frozen in awe or fear or just frozen, as we watched this contraption make its way to the ground and shut down its engines.

As the dust settled, the helicopter doors opened and there he was: Lyndon Johnson, who remains in my memory to this day as the most imposing man I ever saw.

I have no idea what Johnson said that day, but everyone clapped and hollered, and as he turned to board the helicopter, he grabbed the Stetson cowboy hat he was wearing and threw it into the crowd.

And then he was gone, up, up and away like Superman. We just stood there. It took us a while to believe what we had just seen. Even the grown-ups were amazed.

Many years later, I told this story to long-time Texas congressman Jake Pickle, who said, "Oh, I know all about it. My job was to catch the hat."

Johnson campaigned all over Texas that summer, sometimes making as many as sixteen stops a day. As Pickle told it, he had been a young volunteer in the campaign and his main job was to be in place at each rally site before Johnson's helicopter landed. He would position himself in the front of the crowd as Johnson spoke, so that when Johnson threw his hat, Pickle was in place to catch it.

"It was all worked out in advance," he said. "Lyndon wasn't about to throw away a hat. He was too tight. He'd throw the hat to me and I would run around to the other side of the helicopter and put it on board. If I didn't get back there in time, I'd have to drive like the dickens to the next stop to give it to him there, and if I didn't make it, he'd start asking people where the hell his hat was."

The national political reporters in 1948 wrote most of their stories about Truman's whistlestop campaign by train, but in Texas, Lyndon Johnson's every move was what we wanted to know about. The rest of the campaign, I checked the *Fort Worth Star-Telegram* every day to see where that helicopter was. Johnson went on to win the election in a run-off, but it was a race that would haunt him all his political life. Out of a million votes cast, he won by a mere eighty-seven, and then only after a bundle of ballots that had gone un-counted turned up several days later. If voter registration rolls were to be believed, two hundred of the people who had cast the newly found ballots had voted in alphabetical order and many of them appeared to have the same handwriting!

This mysterious action was never ex-plained, and his opponents claimed the elec-tion had been stolen, but we were too young to understand any of that. We just remem-bered Johnson and the helicopter and the day he came to our neighborhood. As we came of age, Johnson was as much a part of our cul-ture as the Alamo, and we couldn't imagine politics without him. From the day I saw Johnson, I was hooked on politics. The jour-nalism part would take a little doing.

In junior high, I served as sports editor of the school newspaper, did the same in high school, and was also editor in chief of the yearbook, so my friends assumed I would be a reporter of some kind, but it was an as-sumption my mother did not share. She was a child of the Depression, and to her genera-tion it was the mother who spoke of "my son, the doctor" who was considered the real suc-cess.

So it was that when I enrolled as a fresh-man at Texas Christian University in Fort Worth, I declared my major to be premed. I had been an A student in high school, but I had no interest in science or the healing arts and it was soon apparent they had no interest in me (or any other student who refused to study and thought a biology test could be aced with a little creative writing). Thus, when students ask me today how I got into journalism, I usually give them the truth: "Comparative anatomy made me do it."

After fooling around with premed for two years, I switched my major to journalism and I never regretted it. My plan was to become a newspaper reporter. Even then I had no plan to get into television. For one thing, my first try at TV had been a total disaster. During high school, I had been invited to participate in a student talent show broadcast every Saturday on the local NBC affiliate. The host was a local college student named Pat Boone. Boone would soon record a song called "Hearts Made of Stone" and go on to stardom. My career, it is fair to say, stalled. The show was sponsored by Foremost Milk, and Boone emceed it from behind a soda fountain. I was to give the commercial, which required me to pour myself a glass of milk, take a sip, smile and say, "That Foremost Milk is suuurrre good."

I did it perfectly, except to say, "That Vandervoort's Milk is sure good," which did not please the Foremost people, since Vandervoort's was their chief rival. I was never asked back, until many years later, when I became the station's news anchor.

But I digress. A week after I switched my major to journalism at TCU, a student named Bruce Neal told me he had just gone to work at a small radio station and that there might be an opening for another reporter there. Two days later, I got my first paying job as a reporter working the night shift in the news department of KXOL, a 5,000-watt radio station. At night, KXOL carried the games of our minor-league baseball team, the Fort Worth Cats. The play-by-play man was Bill Hightower, an old NBC staff announcer who doubled as news director. I went to see Hightower. The station was across the street from Farrington Field, the high school football stadium. Hightower took me to the station's front door and asked me what I saw. "A football stadium," I replied. "No," he said. "Give me a word picture of what you see." I remember babbling on to the effect that it was big and gray. It still looked like a football field to me, but my words seemed good enough for Hightower and I got the job, after assuring him I could type. (I couldn't but I learned in a day, proving a variation of Sam Snead's old adage about golf: "If you don't know how to putt, play for a hundred dollars a putt. You'll learn soon enough." Moral: We learn what we need to learn when we need to learn it.)

The job paid the grand sum of one dollar an hour and featured an overtime payment system that, as far as I know, remains unique to this day. We received ninety cents for the first hour of overtime, eighty cents for the next hour, seventy cents for the hour after that, and so on. If you worked ten hours overtime, that last hour was worth a dime. None of that mattered; I was to be paid for being a reporter, and it was big stuff for a twenty-year-old kid. I went to school in the mornings and worked a split shift at the station: 1 P.M. to 4 P.M., followed by a four-hour break and then a return to the station for another four-hour shift from 8 P.M. to midnight. It left little time for study, which was excuse enough not to. Miraculously, my grades did improve after I went to work, and even with the switch in majors I was able to take extra courses and graduate on time, if not with honors. In reality, college life for me ended the day I went to work. I wanted nothing from the university but the degree. I put little into it and got little in return. I have always been a voracious reader. Books are my greatest pleasure, and I have since read most of the books I should have read in college, so I consider myself largely self-educated. My great regret is that I never gave college a chance and it took many years for me to realize what I had missed. In those days, I just didn't have time for it. I was too busy being a reporter. It was what I had always wanted to do and I was being paid to do it.

Radio was in a transition in the late 1950s. The programs that we had grown up with — Bob Hope, Burns and Allen, *Your Hit Parade* — had all moved to television, and radio was groping to fill the void, not always with success. Local stations no longer wanted network programming. Station managers discovered they could build bigger audiences with a new format that featured music and local news. KXOL was a "top forty" station. Over and over, the disc jockeys played the same forty most popular rock-and-roll records. On the hour and half hour, those of us in the news department read a five-minute newscast. But only when we weren't out covering what we came to call the "three R's — wrecks, rapes and robberies." We monitored police radios constantly, and when we heard of a convenience-store robbery or car wreck (when police radio identified wrecks as "Signal Twos," that meant injuries), we raced to the scene in brightly painted panel trucks that we called "mobile units." We left the disc jockeys to read the newscast, while we reported on the latest calamity by two-way radio from on the scene. Our reports were preceded by a recorded ambulance siren that the disc jockey played as he switched to us. We signed off by reminding our listeners that KXOL was the station that "pioneered and developed on-the-scene news coverage in the Great Southwest." Well, perhaps *one* of the stations that pioneered such coverage would have been more accurate, but we probably should also have added, the station that had "turned its news department over to three college students who knew nothing about reporting but were being paid a dollar an hour for the chance to learn." News Director Hightower soon moved to a higher-paying job in the sales department, which meant the station that "pioneered and developed on-the-scene news coverage in the Great Southwest" had a news department staffed entirely by students: me; Roy Eaton, who later became a newspaper publisher and remains a lifelong friend; and the late Bruce Neal, who went on to become one of the area's most successful public-relations executives. Bruce had been the student who led me to the job. Of the three of us, he had the most experience and was the only one of us old enough to buy beer. In truth, we had no idea what we were doing, but we learned by doing it, over and over, which is the best way to learn reporting, and if we were inexperienced we weren't about to tell it. The second week on the job, I was covering a horrible auto accident on a county road northeast of Fort Worth. With no hesitation, I described it on the air as "the worst accident I have seen in all my experience as a reporter."

Some weeks later, my "experience" would be challenged when I heard the police radio alert that an East Fort Worth nightspot called the Penguin Club had been bombed. Fort Worth was a fairly wide-open town in those days, gangsters were always ambushing one another and the explosion had all the earmarks of an underworld hit. I raced to the scene in the mobile unit, but a uniformed cop stopped me at the door of the bombed-out building and asked for identification. I proudly flashed my new press card.

"Sorry," the cop said, "I need to see your driver's license or something with your date of birth on it. This is a beer joint. Nobody gets in here unless they're twenty-one." I didn't even bother to show him the license. I was only twenty, the only reporter I ever heard of who was carded at a gangland bombing. Surely, there was a First Amendment issue there somewhere.

For a kid who wasn't old enough to buy beer, chasing wrecks and robberies was far more exciting than sitting in a college classroom. It was a seamy side of the world to be sure, a world of cops and crooks and various lowlifes of the night, but I loved it. I just liked being where the news was, knowing about it before other people did and telling them about it before someone else could. What I remember most about those days are the rookie mistakes I wanted to forget at the

44

time: walking into a death scene and asking in my most official voice, "Where's the body?" only to discover that I was standing in it. A shotgun suicide can spread a body over most of any room. Or the time I followed the cops to a lake outside town where they had been tipped that another of our gangsters had been buried by his killers. It was a fairly routine crime story, except the part where I accidentally stepped backward into the grave. The cops couldn't have been more pleased, but the smell was so overpowering I didn't even try to wash it off my pants. I just threw them away.

If we learn by our mistakes, I was learning a lot. I've always believed the police beat to be the best training ground at any news organization, for the simple reason that wherever the police reporter goes, he's not wanted. He is always intruding on someone who is probably experiencing the worst moment of his or her life. Police reporters show up at tragedies and no one wants them there. Contrast that to the sportswriter who is welcomed wherever he goes. (Except the losing team's locker room, or in the presence of the spoiled multi-million-dollar athlete who's in a slump.) Even so, the sportswriter is usually given the best seat in the house, free food if he chooses and help if he asks. People run when they see police reporters, and the police reporter must use his wits to get even the bare facts. If a young reporter can learn to do his job in a businesslike way in the circumstances a police reporter finds himself, he can do his job anywhere.

The only thing I didn't like about KXOL was the wife of station manager Earle Fletcher. It wasn't that I didn't like her personally, but she couldn't pronounce Schieffer. So Fletcher decreed that I should be called Shafer. Go figure. At school, I was Schieffer. At work, I was Shafer. Schieffer or Shafer, the two years until graduation passed quickly. Between crime stories, I covered everything from the opening of the new toll road between Fort Worth and Dallas to an unscheduled visit from Louisiana's erratic Governor Earl Long. Long would later gain national notoriety when he had a torrid and very public affair with stripper Blaze Starr.

We trailed Long around Fort Worth for several days, but never quite got his reason for dropping in. We had been tipped he was coming, and when he stepped from the plane at the old Carter Field, we knew this was no ordinary visit. He had removed the pillowcase from one of the plane's pillows, cut eyeholes in it and pulled it over his head. Atop all this, he was wearing a Western hat.

"I wish to remain anonymous," he announced grandly, and said later he had only come to "buy some watermelons." After several days, he left, and we still didn't understand why he had come. Except that he was crazy.

I had graduated earlier that summer and the Long visit was the last story I would cover before heading to Travis Air Force Base, north of San Francisco. Because I had been in the ROTC, I owed the Air Force three years of active duty. It was a pleasant interlude for me, and once again Lyndon Johnson would be a part of my life. Not long after he and Kennedy took office, he passed through Travis en route to Asia and a goodwill tour.

During refueling, he left his plane to shake hands with the military people who had come out to see him, and when he got to me, I told him I had been born in Austin. He ordered one of our base photographers to take our picture, and it was such a fine shot, I had a dozen copies printed. I sent one to my mom and took the liberty of signing another, "To Bob, good friend and fine officer. All the best from his friend, LBJ." It looked terrific on my desk and I kept it there throughout my three-year tour of duty. No officer who outranked me ever commented on it, but I noticed more than one giving it the eye. It really was a fine photograph.

These were the days of the Cold War, civil defense shelters and the "Sino-Soviet threat," but as I headed to the Air Force, none of that bothered me much. We had been living with the nuclear buildup and the threat of nuclear war for so long, since the early days of the Eisenhower administration, that we seldom thought of it. As it must be with Californians who know they live with the constant threat of earthquakes, we couldn't bring ourselves to believe nuclear war would ever come. Nor would I ever see or hear a shot fired in anger during my Air Force years. Like many Cold Warriors of the day, I flew what we called the LSD, the "Large Steel Desk," and I spent most of my time editing Air Force publications and serving as a public-information officer. It was not until my assignment was all but completed that the war interfered with what had been, for me, a chance to travel the world and, for the first time in my life, live alone outside my mother's house. I was to finish my three years of active duty in early September, but that summer a mysterious Soviet buildup appeared to be under way in Cuba, and those of us due to be released were told we might be "frozen," that is, kept on active duty until whatever the trouble was had passed. Not until the last week in August did I get word I would be released on time. A friend at the *Seattle Post-Intelligencer*, a newspaper I had dealt with as public-information officer for McChord Air Force Base, offered me a job as the paper's real estate editor, an offer I politely declined. KXOL had saved a job for me back home, and the day the Air Force issued its official thanks for my service, I headed back to Texas. It took me three hard days of driving, but I was back in Fort Worth on a Sunday night and reported for work at KXOL on Monday morning, stipulating only one condition: no more Shafer; this time I would be Schieffer. An hour into my first day back, it was as if I had never been away. Same wrecks, same robberies, and I couldn't wait to start covering them.

# Three

## *Mississippi Burning*

The summer and fall of 1962 was a dangerous time, more dangerous than those of us who had come of age during the Cold War had realized. Kennedy had almost gone to war with the Soviet Union over Berlin, and the situation remained so tenuous that as I was driving back to Texas in late September, Kennedy's secretary of defense, Robert McNamara, issued yet another warning to the Soviets: If war came over Berlin, the United States was prepared to use nuclear weapons. And now there was that Soviet buildup in Cuba. The young officers at my level had no idea of the scope of it, but the notification that we might be held on active duty beyond our scheduled release date was more than enough to get our attention.

What I had not understood as I drove home that September was the intensity that was building in the civil rights movement. Military people lead a somewhat cloistered life, and during the three years I spent on West Coast air bases, the civil rights demonstrations were something we saw only on television. Montgomery, Alabama, was a long way from San Francisco and Tacoma, Washington, where I had spent the last three years, and the demonstrations neither touched our lives nor did they provoke much comment at the Air Force bases where I was stationed. To be sure, I thought of myself as someone who believed in equality. My mother had been somewhat ahead of her time for Texas. As the child of a poor family growing up during the Depression, she had known what it meant to be different, even if the difference was that your clothes were not as fine as those of your schoolmates, and she taught us that all people were to be treated with courtesy. The word *nigger* was still so commonly used in Texas that when dispatchers broadcast alerts on the police radio, they routinely described black suspects as "young nigger males . . ." But it was not a term used at our house. My mother thought the people who talked that way only showed their ignorance. We were told the polite terms for black people were *colored* or *Negro*, which usually came out "Nigra" because of the southern tendency to substitute an "ah" sound for words that end in a hard *o*. In college, I had also come to believe in "integration," which put me at odds with some of my contemporaries, but I considered myself an enlightened person. In truth, I hadn't given racial questions much

51

thought. I had gone to segregated schools, ate in segregated restaurants and went to segregated movie houses. When I read my hometown newspaper, the *Fort Worth Star-Telegram*, I read only about white people. The paper took notice of Negroes only when they were arrested for crimes against whites. White women were referred to in the newspaper as Mrs. or Miss. In the rare instances when black women got their names in the paper, they were given no title but were referred to as "the Jones woman" or "the Smith woman." Male Negroes were never referred to as "Mr." It was easy for me to say I had never had a problem with Negroes. I didn't know any, with the exception of the occasional housekeeper my mother hired to help with spring cleaning. They lived on their side of town; we lived on ours. The only time we really ever saw them in groups larger than two or three was on June 19, called "Juneteenth," the anniversary of the day the slaves in Texas learned they had been emancipated by Lincoln. On Juneteenth, Negroes were allowed to use the Fort Worth parks and visit the zoo. As a child, I can remember driving through the park with my parents and hearing them comment on what a nice thing it was that the colored people were being allowed to use the park on their holiday. It never occurred to us that they might feel short-changed, since their taxes helped pay for the park just as ours did. It was not until I was in the Air Force and shook hands with a black sergeant that it occurred to me I had never shaken a black hand. It wasn't that I had anything against it; the opportunity had never presented itself. Like many young white men and women in Texas, we thought of people in the Deep South as the ones who "hated Negroes." We had no problems with Negroes because we seldom came in contact with them. Somehow, we never got around to asking why. After the Supreme Court ruled on *Brown* v. *Board of Education*, Fort Worth adopted a stair-step plan starting at the lower grades to integrate its schools, but since the neighborhoods were strictly segregated, blacks continued to go to black schools and whites to the schools they had always attended. It was some years after I had graduated from college that any black person could say he or she had attended any school that I had attended. As it was in most communities across the Sun Belt, we knew changes were coming, but the Negroes did not push for action and Fort Worth remained as it had always been. It would be well into the 1970s before schools, movie theaters, restaurants and other public places were truly integrated, and when it happened, it happened quietly and without incident.

Across the Deep South, the situation was far different. The Freedom Rides had begun in the summer of 1961. These stories did not always get the play in our newspapers that they did in the East, but the week I returned to Fort Worth, the papers were filled with stories about Edwin Walker, a retired right-wing Army general from Dallas, who had been arrested for trying to raise an army of white militia to block integration at the University of Mississippi. Acting on orders from a federal court, U.S. marshals had tried four times to enroll a young black man named James Meredith there, only to be turned back by mobs that had numbered 2,500 at one point.

Not much had changed in my hometown, but one thing that was different was little KXOL. It had become a real news organization. Roy and Bruce had enlarged the staff, raised reporters' pay to respectable levels, and the station had begun to win awards. (The staff of disc jockeys who spun the records had also enlarged. Rod Roddy, who went on to become the announcer on *The Price Is Right* on television, had joined the announcing staff, as did a young George Carlin, who was just beginning to put together a stand-up comedy act. Station manager Earle Fletcher thought it unseemly for one of his disc jockeys to be working after-hours in nightclubs and fired him.) In any case, the place where Roy and Bruce and I "played radio" as college students had become a station people respected and depended on for news. No longer did we cover just the wrecks; Bruce had established a beat covering City Hall, and my main job would be to cover trials and county government. Still, I was a little surprised the station had begun to take its commitment to news so seriously that Roy told Bruce to fly to Mississippi and cover Meredith's enrollment at Ole Miss. The next day, I was even more stunned when Roy told me to take one of the mobile units to Oxford and help him.

By now, the wire service news tickers were clicking out a steady stream of reports from Mississippi and there was little doubt that the situation was becoming serious. Playing to the crowds, Mississippi's Governor Ross Barnett vowed never to allow Meredith to enroll. As a group of white U.S. marshals approached him during one attempt to enroll the black man, Barnett asked sarcastically, "Which one of you is Meredith?"

The rabble-rousing Edwin Walker, the retired Dallas general, had been among the military troops Eisenhower had dispatched to Little Rock to enforce integration five years earlier. Now, he was telling followers he "was on the right side." In vitriolic language on a Louisiana radio station, he told listeners, "We have listened and waited and been pushed around too long by the anti-Christ Supreme Court. It is time to move. Ten thousand strong from every state in the union, rally to the cause of freedom, descend on Oxford and stand with the governor.

"Bring your flag, your tent and your skillet."

Asked if the volunteers should bring guns, Walker said that would be left to the individuals. Walker's crackpot views would have been laughable, but he was dead serious.

I drove all night and pulled into Oxford on Sunday afternoon. The red-and-white panel truck with radio antennas whipping in the wind and KXOL, THE STATION THAT PIONEERED AND DEVELOPED ON-THE-SCENE NEWS COVERAGE IN THE GREAT SOUTHWEST emblazoned across its sides was quite a sight for its day. It had drawn appreciative honks and waves (or at least I thought they were appreciative) along the highway and when I had stopped for gas.

But there were no cheers in Oxford. Rough-looking gangs of men were roaming the streets, and as I tried to make my way through them, they booed and shouted, "Go home, nigger lover." Suddenly, I was under attack. Rocks, and what appeared to be the weapon of choice, long-neck beer bottles, hit the sides of my truck with thuds.

I couldn't believe it. Having announced no allegiance, I assumed a truck with Texas splashed across its sides would have received a friendlier greeting. But this mob didn't seem all that impressed with the "station that pioneered and developed on-the-scene news coverage." To them, I was an outsider. I retreated to a calmer place, hoisted the suitcase-sized tape recorder from the back of the truck and made my way on foot to find Bruce, who'd left word he was somewhere near the campus.

I found him easily enough, but the next twelve hours would be among the most terrifying experiences of my life. There would be close calls in the future in Vietnam, but nothing like the terror I felt that night on the campus of Ole Miss. We had no idea when Meredith was to be enrolled. There were reports he would be brought to the campus the following morning. But it was obvious something was about to happen. The center of the Ole Miss campus is a beautiful grassy area. The main gate to the campus is situated at one end, brick dormitory buildings line its sides and at the far end sits the school administration building called the Lyceum, a lovely brick structure with six white columns across its front. Bruce and I had wandered to the Lyceum and were making idle talk with the students. They were friendly enough, but when word spread that federal marshals were on the way, the crowd began to swell and it was obvious that the new additions were not all students.

Within minutes, the crowd grew to several

hundred people. Most of them seemed more curious than angry, but I did see several of the hooligans who had pelted my truck.

A convoy of military vehicles turned from the highway and onto the campus and when the students saw them, the mood changed. Still, the crowd was not altogether unfriendly. Like us, the students didn't know what was happening and had come out to see what the commotion was about.

The trucks drove on to the Lyceum building, and more than a hundred helmeted men — the marshals we had been told about — emerged from the trucks and took positions around the building. They carried clubs and some had tear gas guns.

Within an hour, another convoy had brought more marshals, a force that Bruce and I estimated to be around three hundred. By now, five or six hundred students and townspeople were milling about, and at one incongruous moment, they chanted football yells.

Then we heard it. From the main gate behind us, there was a sudden scream, and it was no football yell. This was a scream of pure hatred and it came rolling toward us, growing louder, a cascade of screams and boos. Rumors had spread through the crowd that Meredith had been brought onto the campus. What had been a swarm of curious students had become an angry, screaming mob. The rumors were right. Meredith was being brought in. Marshals had originally planned to bring him onto the campus the following Monday morning. What was not known publicly was that Governor Barnett had been talking by telephone with Attorney General Robert Kennedy. Barnett suggested Meredith be brought onto the campus secretly on Sunday night. That way, Barnett had told Kennedy, Mississippi officials could claim they had been blindsided and could not be blamed for Meredith's presence. Kennedy took Barnett's advice, and marshals brought Meredith into one of the dorms, Baxter Hall, by a back road. Seeing the marshals surrounding the Lyceum, the crowds mistakenly thought Meredith was there. At first they shouted jeers and insults, then pelted the marshals with rocks and bottles and several Molotov cocktails, gasoline-filled bottles that exploded on impact. What triggered the first violence remains in dispute. At the time, Mississippi officials blamed it on provocative actions of "inexperienced marshals," and in fact when the marshals responded to the pelting with the first rounds of tear gas, a canister struck the back of a highway patrolman who was trying to push the mob back. As night closed in on the campus, the marshals fired tear gas again and again into the mob, and through the early evening managed to hold their own. Then, without warning the state patrolmen who had been ringing the campus returned to their patrol cars and drove away and a rougher crowd poured onto the campus. What police call "a situation" became a war, and the area around the Lyceum the main battleground. What those of us caught on campus wouldn't know until the next day was that as President Kennedy had gone on television that evening to report that Meredith had been brought on campus to be enrolled, he was unaware that the riot had broken out and that the Lyceum was already under siege. The first tear gas was apparently fired as he began his speech. From the fringe of the crowd, Bruce and I watched a grim pattern develop. Groups of people would form behind men waving Confederate flags and charge the marshals, throwing rocks and bottles. The marshals would drive them back with tear gas and then another mob would form and charge again. Before it ended, two people would be killed, 166 marshals would be injured, one of them shot through the neck by a sniper, at least forty soldiers would be hurt and two hundred people would be arrested.

William Geoghegan, a young Justice Department lawyer who had been left to man Kennedy's secure phone line at the Justice Department when the attorney general moved to the White House to set up a Washington command post, told me the afternoon had been as confusing in Washington as it had been on the Oxford campus. "We kept getting reports from our people that the Mississippi highway patrol had left the campus, then the White House would get a report from the highway patrol or the governor that they were still there," he said. "It was total bedlam. And that night when the president decided he had no alternative but to send in the federal troops to restore order, it was so disorganized we couldn't get the troops to move." The troops had been flown to the Naval air station near Memphis, but orders for them to move would be given and then countermanded. No one seemed to know what was going on. Finally the president sent word to "tell the Army to get those troops to Oxford, now!"

For years, there have been questions about what took the Army so long to get to Oxford from Memphis and nearly four decades later, as I was doing research for this book, I uncovered one factor. Incredibly, the first troops to arrive in Memphis had no idea how to get to Oxford! Washington lawyer Henry T. Gallagher was a twenty-three-year-old second lieutenant in the 716th Military Police Battalion that had been flown to the naval air station near Memphis that Sunday morning. When the first federal troops were dispatched to Oxford after the rioting began, Gallagher was told to lead the one hundred-military-vehicle convoy.

"The problem was we didn't know where it was, and we had no maps," Gallagher told me. "There was a Navy guy on the front gate as we drove out, so I asked him if he knew where it was. He said he did and he had a southern accent, so I figured he was telling the truth. I ordered him to get in my jeep. He didn't want to go, but I told him I was acting on orders of the president and he got in. Once we were out on the highway, I pulled into a Phillips 66 station and got a map. That's how we knew where to go."

Gallagher said the entire afternoon had been one of total confusion. "First they sent orders telling us not to take ammunition to Oxford, then they reversed that and told us not to leave without ammunition. Then when we asked if the Mississippi highway patrol was with us or against us, we were told their loyalty was uncertain and they gave us authority to shoot their dogs if they attacked us.

"The worst thing was they pulled our black guys out of the ranks and told them they had to stay in Memphis. It really hurt morale. One of our sergeants said he was refusing to step down, and we had to get one of the black officers to intervene."

It was well past midnight when Gallagher and his troops finally got there and others would begin to arrive within the hour. Once the federal troops were deployed, order was finally restored.

"Bobby [Kennedy] didn't want to send federal troops. He thought the uniforms would remind everyone of the Union Army occupation after the Civil War. That's why he put together that force of marshals in civilian clothes," Geoghegan told me. "What we learned that night was that the people of Mississippi respected the military uniforms and were much more reluctant to attack the federal troops than the marshals."

That the soldiers were carrying loaded military carbines may have also been a factor. In any case, the marshals had managed to keep the mob at bay until the federal troops arrived.

The most terrifying part of the evening for Bruce and me had come earlier when a sniper opened fire from a dorm roof. I had spent the three previous years in the Air Force and never heard a shot fired in anger. Now, two weeks out of the Air Force, I thought someone was shooting at me. I hit the dirt as a bullet whistled by, but it was apparently aimed far from me. Other shots cracked through the night. Lights were shot out. An Associated Press newsman was wounded when hit by bird shot fired from another gun. In one of the evening's more bizarre episodes, students commandeered a bulldozer from a nearby construction site, revved the motor to full throttle and drove it toward the Lyceum and jumped clear. Fortunately, the huge machine stalled and no damage was done. Other students brought a fire truck onto the campus and were unfurling fire hoses across the grounds and using the truck as a moving platform from which to throw rocks. By this time, most of the streetlights had been shot out or broken by rocks. The rioters had brought in cans of gasoline and were beginning to torch parked vehicles. The acrid smell of burning rubber cut into the tear gas that hung over the Lyceum lawn, and with the only light coming from the glow of the burning cars, the area took on an eerie orange cast. I watched as Gordon Yoder, an NBC cameraman from Dallas, was pulled from his car before the mob torched it. I was still lugging the enormous, suitcase-sized tape recorder, and when I tried to record some of the sound, the crowd turned on me. I was pushed back into a tree and fell, but a noise diverted the crowd's attention and no one harmed me as I lay on the ground. Toward midnight, Bruce and I had had enough. We were covering the story of our lives, but we hadn't called in a report in hours and we were choking on tear gas. The sound of sniper fire overhead may have had something to do with our decision to take a break. In any case, we retreated to safer territory, filed our reports, and when we returned, the campus had been sealed off by the federal troops.

We got back onto the campus at daybreak to find a scene out of a World War II movie. The Lyceum looked like the German headquarters after the GIs had stormed it. Burned-out cars littered the grounds.

We got there in time to see the marshals escort Meredith from Baxter Hall to the Lyceum, where he was formally registered for class. I got close enough to shout a question, but he looked straight ahead and gave no sign of hearing me. What struck me was how perfectly groomed he looked that morning and what a striking contrast he was to the wire service reporter who was jogging beside him trying to ask a question. The wire man was wearing a porkpie straw hat, slacks and a seersucker blazer, but somehow in the confusion of the night he had lost his shirt. Only a hairy chest showed through beneath his coat.

More than sixteen thousand troops had taken up positions on campus overnight. Later in the week, the number of troops in Oxford would grow to more than twenty-four thousand, and the town of ten thousand residents was turned into a military fort, but the court orders had been carried out and Meredith had been enrolled. If I had not understood before what blacks were going through in the South, I was beginning to understand now. Live gunfire has a way of bringing abstract arguments into sharper focus. Meredith attended two classes that day, one in colonial American history, the other in Spanish, and was correctly, if not warmly, received. But the only official recognition of his presence was a notice posted on the door of the trustees' conference room that read, "Pursuant to the mandate of the federal courts, the orders for the registration of Meredith have been followed."

Meredith was a twenty-seven-year-old Air Force veteran when he decided to transfer from Jackson State to Ole Miss to complete his college work. As historian Richard Reeves would later write, the Kennedy administration had been dubious about supporting him in the beginning. Kennedy had his hands full with the Soviet buildup in Cuba and November midterm elections were six weeks away. He had no interest in a civil rights blowup just then, but as he would later tell Governor Ross Barnett in one of those secret phone calls, "I don't have the power to call off Meredith." Nor did he, and one reason federal officials finally decided to back Meredith was his age and the fact that he had done well at Jackson State and would need only one year on campus to graduate.

Second Lieutenant Gallagher, who had led the first federal soldiers onto the campus, became chief of Meredith's guard detail and remained on the campus until spring. Governor Barnett spent the next year trying to block Meredith's graduation but despite

66

that, and despite the fact that Meredith never left his dorm without his security detail, he was a model student and graduated on time. His graduation became a turning point in the civil rights movement, but his own life later took a strange twist. He declared himself to be a "Conservative Republican," and at one point endorsed former Ku Klux Klan leader David Duke's candidacy for president.

Neither of the men who died the night Meredith was brought to Ole Miss had been participants in the battle. One was a jukebox repairman who had been hit by a stray bullet when he had come from behind a building to see what had caused all the noise.

The other fatality was Paul Guihard, an Agence France-Presse reporter and budding playwright based in New York. He had been sent to Oxford on his day off because the bureau was shorthanded. Earlier that year, Guihard's first play, a one-act comedy, had been produced in an off-Broadway theater.

It was a story about a shipwrecked sailor who lands on what he thinks is a deserted island only to discover a deck chair there and a policeman who has no one to police. The policeman won't let the man sit in the deck chair because it is against the island rules and they argue. Then a tidal wave sweeps the chair and both men away. A friend said Guihard meant the play to be about man's revolt against the absurdity of life. Guihard was twenty-nine when he wrote it, thirty when he died on the Oxford campus, shot in the back.

Kennedy, despite initial fears that the situation in Oxford would harm him politically, went up in the polls.

# Four

## *The Night Beat*

As I look back on Meredith's enrollment, the most incredible part to me is that Kennedy dealt with it in the midst of the Cuban Missile Crisis. Over the years, countless stories have been written about how the two superpowers came so close to nuclear war in those tense weeks, but it was not until Kennedy went on television the night of October 22 that we really understood the gravity of the situation. As for Meredith, once he began attending classes, the story was over for me. I drove the mobile unit back to Fort Worth and settled into a routine of covering wrecks and murders, but the Cuba situation was always in the background and continued to get more and more play in the papers. We had known something was going on in Cuba, but we had no idea it would be anything as serious or as threatening as what Kennedy told us in the October 22 TV address: that there were missiles ninety miles offshore with the range to drop nuclear bombs on every American population center except Seattle! He told us that

American ships had already blockaded Cuba, and would enforce a quarantine on offensive weapons. In the most ominous passage, he warned the Soviets that ". . . should these offensive military preparations continue, thus increasing the threat to this hemisphere, further action will be justified. I have directed the armed forces to prepare for any eventuality . . ." This was it. We had heard our president threaten to go to war and we understood that meant nuclear war.

The next week would see a blizzard of events unlike anything that America had experienced since World War II, and to those of us who had grown up in Fort Worth, we understood this was not a war that would be fought in some faraway place. Our Carswell Air Force Base was home to the Strategic Air Command, the American strike force of long-range nuclear bombers. As kids, we had taken some hometown pride in knowing that if war ever came, our hometown was so important we would be a priority target, a point of pride that did not seem nearly so important once we understood that war was a real possibility.

In New York, Ambassador Adlai Stevenson pilloried his Soviet counterpart with questions about the buildup, a fact the Soviet man refused to confirm even when confronted with the photos. In Moscow, the Soviet press blamed it all on American warmongers. Official and unofficial emissaries carried secret messages between world capitals. In Fort Worth, we bought extra canned goods and talked of the best escape routes if war came. In public, neither side was backing off, but as we would later learn, Khrushchev was secretly writing a long, rambling personal letter to Kennedy that proposed a way out. If the United States would pledge not to invade Cuba, "the question of armaments would disappear, since if there is no threat, then armaments are a burden for every people." The next day, the Soviets publicly released a more strongly worded message that proposed removing the missiles in Cuba only if the United States removed the missiles it had installed during the Eisenhower administration along the Soviet border in Turkey. Kennedy weighed both messages and decided to answer the private one. He made no specific mention of the Turkish missiles, but said the reduction of tension that would come about with the removal of the missiles in Cuba "would enable us to work toward a more general arrangement regarding other armaments."

He released the message publicly on the Voice of America, and that night, a Saturday, he signed an order mobilizing 140,000 Air Force reservists and went to bed. With the rest of the world, he waited for Khrushchev's reply.

By chance, I was working the early shift at KXOL the following day when the crisis finally ended. Sunday was normally my day off, but I had traded shifts with another reporter and got to the newsroom early. Sunday morning was the one time of the week when we deviated from our strict format of rock-and-roll records and five minutes of news on the hour and half hour. Sunday mornings were set aside for religious broadcasts, the one time of the week we could not, under any circumstances, sound the siren and break in with news bulletins. Our star Sunday attraction was the Reverend Charles R. Jones, pastor of Bethel Temple, an evangelical church on Fort Worth's East Side. His thirty-minute program mixed calls to repentance with recorded gospel music and occasional interviews with guest speakers who appeared at his church from week to week. His guests ranged from reformed alcoholics who had seen the light to a man who claimed to have memorized the entire Good Book and immodestly called himself "The Walking Bible." The Reverend Jones had no guest that Sunday, however, and I had the volume on our on-the-air monitor turned low and was reading the newspaper about Kennedy's latest offer when the bulletin bell dinged on the Associated Press wire machine behind me. I had hardly turned around as the machine began to print out: BULLETIN: SOVIETS AGREE

TO DISMANTLE MISSILES.

Subsequent paragraphs explained that Radio Moscow had reported that Khrushchev had notified Kennedy that work would be stopped on the missile sites and the weapons dismantled if the United States pledged not to attack Cuba. Rules or no rules, I had to break into the Reverend Jones's program and report this news. The crisis was over. We were not going to war. I buzzed him over the intercom and told him I had to break in immediately with news that just couldn't wait and I put the bulletin on the air.

"Well, praise the Lord," the Reverend said, as I turned off my mike. If my memory is not playing tricks, I think I actually responded, "Amen."

For the first time in weeks, tensions relaxed and shortly after, my own life would take an unexpected turn. Phil Record, the *Star-Telegram*'s night-shift police reporter, was being promoted to night city editor. He wondered if I would be interested in taking his place covering the night police beat for the paper? It took me about thirty seconds to say yes. If you lived in Fort Worth and wanted to be a reporter, the *Star-Telegram* was your goal. Fort Worth was still a two-newspaper town then. The Scripps Howard chain operated a tabloid afternoon paper called the *Fort Worth Press*. It had a fine sports department that included future novelists Dan Jenkins, Edwin Shrake and Gary Cartwright, as well as the legendary Blackie Sherrod, who became the model for one of the characters in Jenkins's book *Semi-Tough*. The *Press* also had some crack police reporters, Harold Williams and Jack Moseley, and gave the *Star-Telegram* fierce competition on the news beats. But for the most part it was a ragtag operation that couldn't match the well-financed *Star-Telegram*, which was packed with ads and had twice as many reporters. The *Star-Telegram* was owned by the Amon Carter family. Carter was a multimillionaire who had made his first money selling chicken sandwiches along the tracks of a railway station in the small North Texas town of Bowie. He'd parlayed those early dollars into a financial empire built around the *Star-Telegram*, a radio and television station, a large stake in American Airlines and a multitude of other businesses. He became a confidant of FDR, Eisenhower, Lindbergh and Will Rogers, and even his enemies conceded that he "ran Fort Worth." No project happened there without his blessing and with his help all things seemed possible. One year, during the Gridiron show, an evening of satire put on by local journalists, a reporter playing Fort Worth mayor Edgar Deen had only one line. Each time a voice from offstage would call out, "Edgar," he would dutifully answer, "Coming, Amon." That more or less summed up the relationship between Carter and Fort Worth.

Carter envisioned the newspaper first as a vehicle to promote Fort Worth and West Texas and second as, well, a newspaper. But it was still the best paper in town and on a par with the better southern newspapers of its day. Carter died before I came to the paper, but his son, Amon, Jr., and daughter, Ruth, continued to run it in his spirit. For a reporter, working at the *Star-Telegram* carried such prestige that I thought nothing of going to work there for $115 dollars a week, twenty dollars less than I made at the radio station. I had taken the job at KXOL because the news director was willing to take a chance on someone with no experience, but I had never thought of broadcasting as a career. So when Phil cleared the way, I gave a week's notice and reported to the *Star-Telegram* for work. The pay may have been lousy and the hours even worse (6 P.M. to 2 A.M.), but I would be replacing the man who had become my role model, Phil (the Hat) Record. Phil was known as the Hat because he always wore a felt snap brim. It was the standard uniform for police reporters, for one reason: it made it easier for them to pass themselves off as detectives. We had an informal code of ethics then; we never lied about who we were. But if people mistook us for the police, that was their problem, not ours. If they thought they

75

were giving confidential information to an investigator, well, that was their problem, too. As we understood the First Amendment, everyone had a right to talk to the *Star-Telegram*, even if they didn't know they were talking to the *Star-Telegram*. At KXOL, we had learned by doing, but at the *Star-Telegram*, I would have a chance to learn from people who knew more about reporting than I did. It was Phil who would teach me how to capture the essence of a story in the lead sentence, how to cover a beat and, the most important thing a reporter needs to know, how to listen. On every beat I ever worked, there was always one reporter like Phil the Hat who set the tone, had the best sources, knew the historical context for every story and framed the unwritten rules the other reporters followed. Phil looked more like a cop than Dick Tracy and the first thing he told me to do was get a hat. Phil's hat had become such a trademark that when he freelanced articles in *True Crime* magazine, he wrote under the name L. E. Chapeaux. He believed the first rule of reporting was to blend in. Looking like you belonged would get you into most places, he told me, and when Kennedy was shot, I would understand how right he was. The detectives — we called them dicks, which is what they called themselves — all wore felt snap brims. Because they did, Phil did, and because Phil did, I did.

Every new reporter gets a certain amount of hazing, but Phil let the cops know I was his guy and I was soon accepted. I realized it the night I came barreling around a corridor near the dispatcher's office and thought I had been attacked by a dog. I felt a tugging at my ankle and heard a sharp "Arf, Arf, Arf." In fact, it was not a dog, but Detective Captain Chick Matlock, whose favorite trick was to sneak up behind an unsuspecting person, grab an ankle and bark. It seemed odd to me, but when I told Phil about it, he said, "Oh, that just means you're one of the guys now. Don't blow it."

No situation remains exactly the same when a working reporter is present. People either are more guarded or try to impress the visitor. This is never more true than when TV columnists are brought into the CBS newsroom in New York to watch us put together the *Evening News*. Suddenly every conversation becomes a seminar on the First Amendment. But during those nights in the Fort Worth police station when I would be the only reporter in the building, I was as close as any reporter can ever get to going unnoticed. I trusted the cops and they trusted me and we took care of each other. I realized just how much they expected from me after a convenience store holdup that occurred one night just as the detectives were finishing their shift. A detective told me the incident didn't sound like much and decided to put off investigating it until the next day. When I wrote it that way in the morning paper, it caused a real stink. For me it had been a throwaway three-paragraph story, but the chief of police had seen it, roasted the detectives, and one of them accused me of unfair treatment. His complaint? "I didn't know you were going to tell some newspaperman." I am sure he was sincere.

The night-side denizens of the Fort Worth police station were some of the oddest and, in their own way, most likeable characters I would ever know. There were no security checkpoints in those days. My desk in the press room was directly across from the detective office, and I roamed the station at will, as did people who wandered in off the street. Some would have legitimate complaints, some didn't and the dicks had their own methods of crowd control. Detective Grady Haire was a proper old gentleman nearing retirement. He would listen with sympathy to a visitor's complaint, but if it was something he didn't want to deal with, he would say, "Oh, that's not our department. That's a matter for the police," and he would politely shoo them away. Others used cruder methods. Captain Matlock's favorite tactic for getting rid of unwanted visitors was to sidle up beside them and let go a thunderclap fart. He would then threaten to arrest the unsuspecting soul for violating the city's anti-fart ordinance. Matlock carried more gas in his tanks than a 1950 Cadillac, and few visitors stayed to argue after these window-rattling events. One person who did protest was Gil Strickland, a rookie *Star-Telegram* reporter who was sent to the station one afternoon. Strickland was a deeply religious person, and as he was engrossed in checking through some arrest reports, Matlock came ambling by and let one go. Strickland was outraged. He jumped to his feet and shouted, "You can't do that to me. I'm a Christian!"

Matlock was so taken aback, he called Phil at the city desk and reported the incident.

To the crowd on the night shift, nothing was out of bounds. One evening, a man and woman appeared at the detective office and asked if this was where people came to get married. I watched openmouthed as one of the detectives said, "It certainly is," and picked up a black loose-leaf notebook where investigative reports were kept. Clearing his throat, he opened the loose-leaf binder, pretended to read from it as if it were the Bible, and pronounced them man and wife. To his credit, he declined the offered tip. I always wondered if the marriage lasted.

One of the first things a police reporter learns is that real-life crimes are not solved the way they are in the movies or on TV. Police catch most criminals because someone tells on them or a witness sees them commit a crime. Even so, Fort Worth detectives checked out every lead. On one occasion, a detective brought a parrot into the detective office and set the cage on his desk. The parrot had witnessed a murder, but it was never clear whether the detective had brought in the bird for questioning or just left it there while he filled out some paperwork. If the parrot did talk, it must have been later. It said nothing in the detective office.

These were great days for me. I was twenty-five, single, and this was a side of life I had never seen. I couldn't get enough of it and it wasn't just the characters I was meeting. It was also the bylines, seeing my name on top of stories that were splashed across page one with a huge headline. For me, there has always been something almost magic about that, to write a story on deadline, or to be in the middle of a chaotic crime scene or disaster, and an hour later, see that newspaper come off the press with my name over a story. I loved it then and I still do. Radio reports had been fun, but they floated off into the air. The newspaper was something real. Something you could hold in your hand. Something that had to be taken seriously. My mentor Phil was now my boss. As night editor, he edited every story I wrote and he taught me to write in the direct, punchy style of the day. I learned how to put a "hook" into the lead sentence that would draw the reader deeper into the story, and how to drive home the essence of the story with a pithy quote in the second paragraph. When a student committed suicide by jumping in front of a train, I wrote that she jumped only after "clasping her hands in a prayerful position." When the district attorney emerged as the chief suspect in a gangland murder, the female assistant district attorney who was suspected of being the D.A.'s love interest would be described in my story as "a willowy redhead." When I discovered bricks falling off the sides of the new jail in what would prove to be a major construction scandal, I described the structure's walls as "Jericho-like." An armed bandit who laughed at his victims became the "Jolly Robber" in my stories, and when a teenager killed his younger brother and hid the body in his family's garage, I quoted the youth as saying, "I killed him because he tore up my Bible."

(My wife, Pat, also grew up in Fort Worth, but we would not meet until several years later. As she was reading an early manuscript of this book one evening, she looked up and said, "Why, I remember the Jolly Robber — I didn't realize you had named him!")

In many newsrooms, the police reporter seldom writes the stories that appear under his byline. Instead, he calls in the basic facts to the rewrite desk, where an editor shapes them into a finished report. But our big boss, city editor Bill Hitch, didn't want it done that way. He wanted all his reporters to dictate their stories. A rewrite man on the other end of the phone was there to help, but Hitch said the flavor of the story could only come from the man on the scene. When a reporter called in, Hitch didn't want a list of facts; he wanted to know what the news was. What was the lead? Why should our readers care? What he was really doing was teaching us to think as reporters, to collect facts, but as we were doing so, to assemble them in order of priority. Years later, when I was covering White House news conferences, I would constantly ask myself, "What's the lead here?" And by the time the news conference had concluded, I could go to the lawn of the White House and immediately say to Walter Cronkite, "What's important here, Walter —" During those White House years, I developed something of a reputation for being able to find the lead, what the news was, fairly quickly, and I always thanked Phil and Bill Hitch for it. The ability to sort out a story quickly before you sit down to the typewriter is one of the most valuable skills a reporter can have. If you know what you're trying to say, the story writes itself, but it's a skill that can only be learned with practice. Hitch's order to dictate when there was no typewriter available also helped me in another way: I was learning to write the way people talk, which is the clearest and best writing.

What I also came to learn in those years was that the *Star-Telegram* was a newspaper for white people. Pictures of blacks would not appear on the front page until the Vietnam War. Only years after that would black faces appear in the society columns. We disregarded nearly all crime stories that involved blacks, unless there was a white victim. The first crime story involving blacks that made the front page was Phil's account of a black man who killed his brother at the dinner table in an argument over the last French fry, and it would remain the only black-on-black crime to make page one for many years. After my experience covering Meredith's enrollment at Ole Miss, I was more sensitive to the black struggle for equality. But as it was with so many of us in the South in those days, as long as the Negroes in our community didn't push for change, we didn't push it for them, and we really saw no reason to provoke trouble. To its credit, when Fort Worth schools and public places finally integrated in the next decade, the *Star-Telegram* would be a driving force with its editorials and work behind the scenes, and it would be praised for helping in the peaceful transition; but when I covered night police, we just looked the other way. The force had no black policemen, and black homicides were still referred to by detectives as "misdemeanor murders," a phrase used so often it had no more meaning to us than "Hello" or "How's it going?"

After I had been on the beat for a while, the detectives let me ride with them to the scenes of crimes that had the promise of making a good story. In police-station shorthand, a tragic shooting would be described as a "good murder," as in "Looks like we got a good one here." Even the uniformed police on the scene would sometimes assume I was a detective. Who could have known? An unmarked car arrives at the scene of a crime, and three men wearing snap-brim hats emerge from the car instead of two. The detectives might identify themselves; I remained silent and took notes. Sometimes, I did get a little carried away. One night I had just left the Harris Hospital emergency room, where I had gone to check on victims of a terrible car wreck, and was heading back to the office, when the police radio called for "the closest available officer" to investigate a shooting at a nearby nursing home. It was no more than six blocks away, and as I pulled to the curb, a patrolman was just getting out of his police cruiser and heading toward the front door. The door was open and there was screaming and general confusion inside and someone said, "They're in the back." I followed the patrolman in and told a man in a white coat nearby to "lock the door and don't let anyone in until the official photographer arrives." I had no idea what the official photographer was, nor did he, apparently, because he did as I ordered. The young patrolman was already in the back room, and, glancing up, he saw me and assumed I was a detective. He said it looks bad, and it was, but it was a whale of a story. A dead man on the floor with half his head blown away had been the husband of what was left of an elderly, equally dead woman who lay on the bed. An attendant told me the woman was dying and was in excruciating pain. It was her birthday, so her husband told attendants he had brought her some chocolates. But when he'd approached the bedside, he'd taken a pistol from the chocolate box, performed a mercy killing and then turned the gun on himself. I had just gotten this down in my notebook when I heard a commotion at the door. Another attendant approached and said there was a Mr. Harrison there, who demanded entrance. I blanched. Archie Harrison was a homicide detective. "Of course," I said. "Let him in." As I was making my way out, I couldn't help but brush by Archie. "Hi, Archie," I said. "This is a good one." Archie didn't respond, but I knew he was steaming, and I got out of there. I could only pray he didn't know I was the one who had ordered the door locked. It all blew over in a few days, but years later, as I reread the story I had written that night, I noticed that the detective I quoted in the story was Archie's partner, Willie Taylor. I left Archie alone for a while.

*Star-Telegram* reporters had such a close working relationship with the police that we often took confessions from criminals. This was long before the days when suspects had to be warned of their rights and told they were entitled to a lawyer. Allowing us to take the confessions had practical benefits for the police and for us. We could type and most of the police couldn't, and once we signed the confessions as witnesses, we could testify that the police had not beaten the suspects. That was the advantage for the cops. The advantage for us was that libel laws at the time prevented us from using a suspect's name unless he had been formally charged in a court of law, or had confessed the crime to us face-to-face. Since ours was a morning paper, that meant I couldn't use a suspect's name until the next day, when he had been taken to the courthouse. But once the criminal had dictated his statement to me and signed it, I could not only use his name, but also write into the story that he had "told a *Star-Telegram* reporter . . ."

Taking confessions was the one instance when we told suspects exactly who we were. But I don't remember going into a lot of detail about the rest of it.

# Five

## *Courthouse Days*

Several weeks after President Kennedy's assassination, I got my first promotion. I was moved from the police beat to covering the county courthouse. It was a great beat, a mix of county politics, local government and trials, and since it was also my responsibility to cover the sheriff's office, plenty of crime news still came my way.

Politics and crime had always been my main interests. This was the best of both worlds, and any way you cut it, the hours were a lot better than the 6-P.M.-to-2-A.M. regimen I had followed on the night police shift. As courthouse reporter, I checked in at noon, made my rounds of the various courts and elected officials, returned to the paper around 5:30 or 6 in the evening, wrote my stories and was at the bar of the Press Club by 8:30. I never covered a beat where there were more stories just waiting to be reported. I uncovered a scandal or two, one of which literally fell into my lap. Or would have, had I been sitting. I was walking past the county's new jail and criminal courts building one afternoon, when I noticed some dust had fallen on my jacket. I glanced toward the building and realized it had come from there and quickly understood why. It was mortar dust from the building's brick walls, which seemed to have developed huge bulges several stories up. It was as if something behind the bricks was pushing them away from the structure, in the way that an inner tube or a balloon will bubble out at a weak point when pressure is applied. It didn't take long to confirm that embarrassed county officials were already aware of the problem, but had not made it public. Once the bricks started falling, the scandal would have become known anyway, but I got credit for an exclusive, and eventually every brick on the building walls had to be taken off and relaid with new mortar at taxpayer expense.

The courthouse itself was a majestic old red granite building that had been built in 1894. Above the dome flew (if that's the word for it) the most unusual flag I ever saw. It was tin. The Stars and Stripes had been painted onto the tin and it was bolted to a flagpole. At night, the entire contraption was lit up in red, white and blue neon. The creation had been the brainchild of the county commissioners. "It can be seen for miles," one of them said. Unfortunately, that was true. The flag was the object of constant derision, and during the Gridiron show one year, it was parodied in a song that began "It's a grand old flag . . . it's an old tin flag." Finally, the commissioners grew tired of the jokes and voted to haul it down, perhaps the only flag ever taken down with socket wrenches. I was sorry to see it go. To me, it had been the perfect symbol for the wackiness going on below.

The courthouse was like a small town within the city of Fort Worth. It had its own rules and its own social hierarchy. The center of the courthouse community was the telephone switchboard. The entire courthouse telephone system went through one central board, which was presided over by a delightful, hardworking woman who had only one drawback, a speech impediment that made it impossible for her to pronounce "county courthouse," which meant that when you called, you heard her say "Cow-Co-How." I always wondered what an out-of-state caller must have thought, but the woman's great talent for locating people far outweighed her inability to speak clearly. She couldn't say courthouse, but she had an uncanny knack of knowing where everyone in the courthouse was, whether they were sick, whether they had taken a break or whether they were at their desk. She could track down anyone, and if my boss called, she knew where to find me. But she never put the boss through unless I told her it was okay. She would first ask,

"Stagram wan yew? Okay if I connea yew?"

For reporters, the great thing about the courthouse beat was the constant squabbling that went on among the county's elected officials. At City Hall and the police station, everybody worked for the mayor and the police chief. They were all on the same team. At the courthouse, all the judges, the district attorney and the other officials were elected in their own right, so the sheriff was always in a fight with the D.A. or the county commissioners, and the judges operated their own individual fiefdoms. It was a fine mix for a reporter on the lookout for news. It was at the courthouse that I learned the first rule for covering politics: The best stories about the sheriff came from the county commissioners; the best stories about the commissioners came from the sheriff. As I would later learn, if you substituted Air Force for sheriff and Army for commissioners, you had the key to covering the Pentagon. And as I always tell young reporters, it works on every beat: Figure out who is in competition for the same tax dollar and you have yourself a source — two sources, actually.

Of course I had one advantage modern reporters don't: direct access. The layers of public-relations experts and staffers who come between a reporter and public officials these days were unknown then. I had direct access to every official just by walking into his office. If they weren't listed in the phone book, I had their private numbers, and we were all on a first-name basis. It was a reporter's dream. One day, I would be writing about a district judge who had held some carpenters in contempt of court for "hammering too loud" near his office, the next day there would be an "exposé" of some hapless county worker who had used taxpayer-owned machinery to spread gravel in a neighbor's driveway. In one instance, the district attorney's chief investigator called me to say he "had nothing to do" with a recent homicide.

It was all very informal. The euphemisms and the issues of political correctness that we spend so much time worrying about today had not yet appeared on our radar screens. When I would call the office of County Clerk W. C. (Red) Cowen, who had lost his legs in World War II and moved through the courthouse in a wheelchair, his receptionist would sometimes say, "Sorry, Bob, he just rolled out for coffee. I'll tell him you called."

Since I had sometimes typed criminals' confessions and signed them as a witness during my nights on the police beat, I would occasionally see the same people brought into court for trial. I thought nothing about it when I was covering a trial one day and was summoned to the courtroom next door. There I took the witness stand, was sworn in, and testified that I had witnessed the confession of the defendant in that case and that he had given the confession voluntarily. The judge excused me and I returned to the courtroom next door, sat down at the press table there and resumed covering that trial.

My daily routine seldom varied. I would drop in on trials that might be under way, check with the commissioners and the D.A.'s office and spend at least an hour going through court records to see what lawsuits had been filed. At midafternoon, I would drop by the courthouse coffee shop, where Sheriff Lon Evans would be holding forth. Evans had been a TCU football star in the leather-helmet era and had been elected sheriff after a long football career, first with the Green Bay Packers and later as a referee in the National Football League. He was the best and maybe the toughest lawman I ever knew, the best source I ever had and a friend until the day he died. If you missed the afternoon coffee break with Lon, you probably missed a story that day. He knew everybody in the county and the choicest courthouse gossip, so the other reporters who covered the beat — Roger Summers from the afternoon *Star-Telegram*, Jack Mosely and Carl Freund of the Scripps Howard *Press* — usually joined us. We called him the "High Sheriff," and for us he was a gold mine. Unlike most public officials who try to avoid controversy, Lon seemed to look for it because he seemed to get such a kick out of telling about it later. And he could always give you that quote that cut through the blather and made the story special. When a well-known Fort Worth man killed his father, I asked Lon what the motive was. "He killed him because he thought the old son of a bitch ought to be dead," Lon said, and that about summed it up.

Lon could always maneuver his way around any courthouse controversy. The courtroom bailiffs were deputy sheriffs on Lon's payroll, but judges often treated them like servants. When a bailiff refused to get coffee for Judge A. L. Crouch, Crouch ordered the man jailed for contempt of court. It never occurred to Lon to refer it to a lawyer. He simply made the bailiff a "trusty," which meant he did not have to go behind bars but had the run of the courthouse. That left him free to fetch coffee for Lon.

Carl Freund was the best reporter of us all, but he had an annoying habit of chewing on his notepaper while interviewing, which led Lon to observe that "Carl has eaten more stories than he ever filed." The sheriff may have been right, but Carl had the best instincts of any reporter I ever knew. He also subscribed to the "wouldn't you say" school of journalism. When interviewing someone, his favorite trick was to ask, "Would you say this is the worst wreck you ever saw?" If the person nodded yes, he would be quoted in the next day's paper as saying, "This is the worst wreck I ever saw." When Carl quoted an assistant district attorney named Dutch Winters at length about a hot murder case, I was outraged. When I had asked Winters about the case, he hadn't given me the time of day. Why, I wanted to know, did he tell Carl all that after stiffing me? "I didn't say any of it," Dutch said. "I saw Carl out in the hall and he was telling me about the case and I nodded a couple of times and the next day there it was in the paper." Well, didn't he feel he had been misquoted? "Not really," he said. "Carl seemed to have it about right."

I used the technique myself in those days before tape recorders, and it was amazing, though not surprising, how pithy those quotes could sometimes be. To my regret, I was never able to make it work with the county purchasing agent, whose name was B. O. Lange. I longed to write the sentence " 'This deal really smells,' said B. O. Lange," but try as I might, I could never put those words in B.O.'s mouth. Probably just as well.

Good beat that the courthouse was, when a big story breaks, every reporter wants a piece of it, and the big story breaking in 1965 was Vietnam and I wanted to cover it. In the fall of 1964, Lyndon Johnson had promised not to "send American boys nine or ten thousand miles away from home to do what Asian boys ought to be doing for themselves." That promise and the Great Society legislation that Johnson was ramming through Congress had been enough to crush Barry Goldwater, and in a landslide, Johnson was elected to the presidency in his own right. But within a month, Johnson's advisors had convinced him the war would be lost unless the American role in Vietnam was dramatically expanded. By February, American bombers were pounding North Vietnam. In March, the first ground combat troops — two battalions of U.S. Marines — had been dispatched to guard the air base at Da Nang, South Vietnam, which was home base for many of the bombers. Until 1965, the American military people on the ground had been "advisors," but by April another contingent of Marines followed the first troops in, and Army troops would soon follow them. The airfield "guards" were now moving into the jungles to track down the Viet Cong before the Viet Cong could attack the bases. By the end of the year, the American military presence in Vietnam would swell to more than two hundred thousand, and American boys found themselves doing what Lyndon Johnson had said was the job of Asian boys, fighting in the jungle. America had been sucked into a land war in Asia. As more American troops poured into Vietnam, I began to lobby my bosses to send me there to cover the war.

At first, even my mentor, Phil Record, greeted the idea with some amusement. Our bosses recognized that this story would only get bigger, but they were not sure I could add anything to the coverage. While the story produced headlines in our paper, casualties at that point were low and the war had not created the controversy in our part of the world that was being seen in the big cities and on the campuses of the Northeast. In Texas, we trusted Lyndon Johnson. We didn't understand the "peaceniks" and we generally believed what Johnson believed: that somewhere, some placc, a line had to be drawn that the Communists could not be allowed to cross. It was not a view that originated with Johnson. In so many words, the American foreign-policy establishment had been saying the same thing since the Eisenhower administration. When Lyndon Johnson endorsed that school of thought, it took on added credibility in Texas. If he said Vietnam was the place where the line against Communism had to be drawn, Texans believed him, or at least gave him the benefit of the doubt. As for me, I had no real grasp of Vietnam's strategic significance. I can remember going to our encyclopedia once to see exactly where it was. But I knew enough to know it was a story and I was determined to see it for myself. The first person I had to convince was the *Star-*

*Telegram's* top news executive, our editor, Jack Butler, and I knew it wouldn't be easy. First, because sending a reporter to Vietnam would be extremely expensive and the *Star-Telegram* was not known for spending money foolishly. Second, no other Texas newspaper had a reporter there, and third, the paper saw its main mission as covering Fort Worth and West Texas.

Yet the first time Butler turned me down, I sincerely believe it was for none of the above reasons. Butler was a kindly, rotund man who genuinely liked his reporters and thought of them in the way a caring father might think of his children. I believe he said no because he was concerned I would be hurt. Thus began a series of memos between us that went on for weeks. I argued I could do it in a way that would minimize danger. He said no. I offered to do it on a freelance basis. He said no. Finally, I decided to shame him into it. I offered to resign my job at the *Star-Telegram* and pay for my own ticket to Vietnam if he would agree to hire me once I got there. Maybe he was just tired of arguing with me. But one day he called me into his office and said, "Okay, Bob, we're going to do this, but you've got to promise me you won't take any chances." Perhaps because he thought it would be safer, he told me the paper would use the wire services and our Washington bureau to cover the big picture. (It may also have occurred to him that I knew nothing about Vietnam.) My assignment was to go to Vietnam and track down the Texans behind the lines, especially the kids from Fort Worth. "You tell us what they are saying and we'll tell our readers what the generals are saying," Butler said. I promised him I would do just that.

It was a great day for me. Once committed, Butler decided to go all the way. From the days of founder Amon Carter, reader service had always been a big part of how the *Star-Telegram* promoted itself and Butler pulled out all the stops. The paper ran full-page ads telling readers I was on the way to Vietnam. They were invited to send me the names of their kin so I could visit them. "He won't be talking to many generals," the ads stated. "He'll be looking for your sons and daughters." The local TV station sent a reporter by to interview me. On the day I was to leave, the local Bell Helicopter plant dispatched a helicopter to take me to the airport, where I caught a civilian airliner for the twenty-nine-hour flight to Saigon. Butler had hoped to say I was the first reporter from a Texas newspaper to report from Vietnam, but we learned that Wick Fowler, an Austin chili maker and former reporter who had been a pal of Ernie Pyle during World War II, had been too quick for us. Fowler had been long retired from the *Dallas Morning News*, but had convinced a friend who was running the newspaper in the tiny North Texas town of Denton to make him a special correspondent so he could go to Vietnam. Fowler got there a week ahead of me, so the paper had to say that I was the first reporter from a "metropolitan Texas newspaper to cover the war."

Vietnam would become a national tragedy of unimagined proportions. Even today, the death and carnage it produced are so staggering as to be all but incomprehensible: Four million Vietnamese civilians and soldiers on both sides — ten percent of the country's population — would be killed or wounded. Three million Americans would eventually be sent there and 58,000 of them would die. Historian Stanley Karnow would write that "in human terms at least, the war in Vietnam was a war that nobody won — a struggle among victims." But not for me. It would be the turning point in my life.

# Six

## *The* Star-Telegram *Goes to War*

Vietnam was a war of unending ironies, not the least of which was that throughout the American involvement, it was possible to reach the war zone on regularly scheduled commercial airliners. Though it was occasionally shelled with enemy mortars and a bomb was once set off in the passenger terminal, commercial airliners flew in and out of Saigon's Tan Son Nhut Air Base during daylight. The pilots made only one concession to the occasional riflemen who took shots at the big planes: They landed them on a steeper than usual approach pattern, and once on the ground, reloaded them quickly and departed. I flew in on a Pan Am 707, and as it taxied down the runway I could see that this was a different place. Hundreds of planes painted in green and brown camouflage lined both sides of the runway. Guards carrying rifles or machine guns were posted near most of the planes, and sandbagged bunkers and antiaircraft weapons could be seen on the outer edge of the field. As I stepped down the exit ramp with the other passengers, officious attendants hurried us off the tarmac and into the terminal. It was no more than fifty yards, but the heat was stifling and I had broken into a sweat before I entered the building. I soon located the enormous suitcase I had stuffed with more than eighty pounds of clothing and other gear, and cleared customs with unexpected ease.

I had one problem. I had no idea where to go from there.

When military people arrived (and many came in on commercial charters), there was always someone to tell them where to go. The networks and the big newspapers did the same for their new arrivals. But being the first *Star-Telegram* reporter to set foot in Asia since World War II, I was on my own. I hired a taxi and told the driver to take me to Saigon. He didn't seem to comprehend.

"You Saigon. You Saigon," he kept repeating. It took me a while to realize he was telling me I was *already in Saigon, where in Saigon* did I want to go? I had the address of the place where I had been told I would be issued a press pass, but he seemed to have no idea where that was. In desperation, I flagged down a soldier and told him I was a reporter and asked his advice. He told me he thought there was some kind of press center in town,

101

gave me what he thought was the location and suggested I go there. I passed that on to the driver. He motioned for me to get into the tiny cab, tied my enormous suitcase on top and off we went on a terrifying ride through some of the worst traffic I had ever seen. A half hour or so later, he roared to a stop on a street corner in downtown Saigon, and said, "Three dolla." I was told later the usual fare was about thirty cents in U.S. currency, but I had no way of knowing that, so I paid, added a generous tip and dragged my suitcase off the top of the car. If there was a press center nearby, I didn't see it. I sat down on the suitcase and tried to think. I had been hearing over and over that this was a war with no front lines, but I couldn't find the back lines. I couldn't even find the press center. I was also about to faint. I had been too excited to sleep on the twenty-nine-hour flight and the heat was becoming unbearable. It had been winter in Fort Worth, so I had worn a wool suit and carried my trench coat. Now it was so hot my clothes were soaked through with sweat. I looked at my feet and realized that I had even sweated through the tops of my shoes.

I had the address of the Saigon Associated Press office in my suitcase. Mike Cochran, the AP's Fort Worth correspondent, had urged me to drop by the Saigon AP office, but I hadn't really planned on it. The AP was the headquarters for some of the most famous newsmen covering the war — Peter Arnett, and the photographers Horst Fass and Eddie Adams. I couldn't imagine they would have time to fool with me. But I could think of no place else to go, so I dug out the bureau's address from my suitcase, hailed another American in uniform and asked if he knew how to get there. It turned out to be no more than a block from where I was, so I righted my suitcase and headed in that direction. This was before suitcases had wheels, and dragging an eighty-pound piece of luggage was no small feat. Somehow I got it there, and I was in luck. The building had an elevator. The elevator opened into a long, narrow office with desks and wire machines along one wall. At one end, I could see what had once been a rest room that had been converted into a photo lab. At the other end, there was a small office and a man was typing. I introduced myself and he told me his name was Ed White. That afternoon I would come to believe he was the kindest man I ever met. He was the AP's Saigon bureau chief, Edwin Q. White. I recognized his byline as that of one of the AP's old Asia hands. I told him I had come to cover the war. He asked where I was staying and I told him I had no idea. Did he have a suggestion? To his great credit, he didn't laugh. To his greater credit, he offered me one of the AP's rooms at the Continental

Palace Hotel until I could find a place of my own and he warned me that wouldn't be easy. He also told me to come back the next day and he would help me get started.

Looking back, I think he must have taken pity on a confused young guy in a soaking wet, wool suit. Whatever his motives, I appreciated it. It wasn't as if he had nothing else to do. His bureau was, after all, in the middle of covering a war, and there had been something of a scare the previous afternoon. The bureau was near the Brinks Hotel, which had been leased by the U.S. Command to house American officers. It had been bombed the year before and several Americans had been killed. Yesterday's attack, apparently, had been thwarted only by the would-be bomber's faulty workmanship. The triggering device on the grenade bomb that had been planted in the hotel had failed to work and the grenade had been discovered and de-armed.

The Continental Palace Hotel was one place I had heard about. On the flight over, I had read *The Quiet American*, Graham Greene's melancholy novel about Vietnam during the time of the French Colonial War, and much of it took place in the Continental. Saigon, with its tree-shaded streets and its nineteenth-century European architecture, was called the Paris of the Orient in those days, and the epitome of French Indochina was the Continental Palace. Across the front of the hotel, there was a veranda framed by arches, and beneath the arches, an outdoor cafe. It was as if the whole thing had been designed as a set for a spy movie, and since the time of the French occupation it had been the real-world version of just that, a center of intrigue where hundreds of spies, journalists, military people and others of mysterious background had gathered to trade lies, rumors and the occasional accurate story. I would spend many pleasant evenings there, but not that evening.

Dragging an eighty-pound suitcase around, the heat and lack of sleep left me exhausted. As I checked into the hotel, I felt I would pass out. All I wanted was a shower and some sleep. The room was all I could have hoped for. There were two big double beds. Ed had told me I would be rooming with one of his photographers, and there was a pile of photo gear on one of the beds. After a shower, I took the other bed. The last thing I remembered as I dropped off to sleep was seeing what appeared to be two hand grenades piled in the photo gear. Well, I thought, I guess there is a war going on, but I was really too tired to care. Around 2 A.M., I was awakened from a deep sleep by a low rumbling sound. My first thought was that those hand grenades had gone off. But they hadn't. I dozed back off and was told the next day the noise was just "friendly" artillery on the edge of town. The next morning, I made my way to the hotel veranda, where I had a fine Western breakfast and walked around the corner to the AP office. I was ready to cover the war. If I could find it.

Ed White told me I could use his office as a place to receive mail and showed me where to find the American Military Assistance Command Vietnam headquarters (MACV), which everyone pronounced MAC-VEE. He told me I could pick up credentials there and suggested I buy several sets of fatigues and boots before I headed into the field. Remarkably, he said I would be able to buy any equipment I needed, including weapons, on the street below his office. I've never been all that handy with guns, so I passed on the chance to buy side arms. I did buy several sets of field clothing and boots. All of it was new, U.S. government issue. Black market racketeering was so rampant throughout the war that soldiers and Marines in outlying areas would sometimes get passes and come to Saigon to buy the equipment that had been meant for them, but had been stolen off the docks before it could be shipped to the field. I came to realize just how rampant the thievery was a month later when I visited an Army unit in the Central Highlands. The supply sergeant had posted a sign on his door that read: DON'T ASK FOR THE BOOTS. WE DON'T HAVE THEM. WE DON'T KNOW

WHEN THEY WILL ARRIVE. The kind of boots they were waiting for were the kind I was wearing: U.S. issue, bought with U.S. dollars, a month before on the streets of Saigon, where there seemed to be no shortage. The black market had already become one of the war's great scandals, and when the U.S. pressured the Saigon government to do something about it, a well-known businessman was arrested and put on trial on a charge of hoarding. The man was an enemy of Nguyen Cao Ky, the flamboyant Air Force general who was running the government at the time. To make sure the trial did not go unnoticed, Ky visited the courtroom himself and brought along a military band. At one point, he vowed to have the man shot by a female firing squad, since women were those being hurt most by shortages. He never carried through on the threat, but even while the trial was in progress, the black market continued to thrive and the stalls remained open, including the one across the street from the military command. Some weeks later, I bought a pack of cigarettes from a Saigon street vendor, only to discover the pack had been stamped on the back "Compliments of the Benevolent Order of Elks." After that, I decided to limit my black market purchases.

For all the talk about how the administration and the military tried to control the news, Vietnam was one of the few wars where there was no censorship as such. Reporters were warned they would be expelled if they disclosed U.S. and South Vietnamese troop movements, but otherwise we were free to report what we pleased and we were not required to show our copy to military censors before we filed it. In Saigon, military briefers painted an ever-rosy picture of how the war was going, and berated correspondents who wrote critical pieces, but the only real control the military was able to exercise was over our travel. In the early sixties, correspondents had driven cars or hired taxis to take them from Saigon to various battles in the Delta regions to the south. But by 1965, it was not safe to travel most roads and there were really only two ways out of Saigon, on military aircraft and Air America, ostensibly a commercial airline but in reality run by the CIA. Air America flew creaky old two-engine C-47s, the military version of the first passenger airliners flown by the commercial airlines. The planes were so old and unreliable that correspondents avoided them when possible and hitched rides on military planes. Getting a ride involved checking with the Air Force press liaison in Saigon, who would call the air base at Tan Son Nhut and book the next available fight, usually a transport plane. When a famous correspondent or a friendly columnist came to Saigon, the military routinely laid on helicopters and planes to fly them to areas where they believed progress was being made. The liaison officers were equally vigilant in discouraging or preventing reporters from getting rides into places where the war was going poorly. Still, if a reporter was persistent, he could usually get where he wanted to go.

It was much easier for those of us who worked for regional publications that weren't being read daily in Washington. Since the Pentagon wasn't seeing what we wrote on a daily basis, they never knew exactly where we were. We more or less fell through the cracks and were usually able to travel when and where we wanted to go. During my first days in Saigon, I would check in with the liaison officer at MACV to book a flight, but as the weeks wore on, I would simply go to Tan Son Nhut, hang around flight operations and hitch rides when I could find an air crew going my way. I can't remember ever being turned down. Once in the field, helicopters were usually the best way to get short distances, and if helicopter pilots had room, they were usually happy to give you a lift.

I had gone to Vietnam with two preconceived notions: First, I thought Lyndon Johnson was right. We had to draw the line somewhere. Like so many in my part of the country, I didn't have much use for peaceniks and the antiwar movement, and like so many of my generation, it was inconceivable to me that America could ever lose a war. Second, I knew that the first thing I would have to do in Vietnam was break my promise to my boss, Jack Butler. I knew I wasn't going to find any news in Saigon. The people I wanted to talk to were out in the field, and I had to go there if I was to see them. I still have the copy of *The Quiet American*, the Graham Greene novel that I had read on the flight over, and as I reread it while writing this book, I noticed that I had underlined a passage that read, "The further you get from headquarters, the looser becomes the control, until, when you come within range of enemy fire, you are a welcome guest." If I was to find one true thing about the war in Vietnam, that was it. Relations between the correspondents in Saigon and the military briefers ranged from skeptical to hostile. Once outside Saigon, the troops and soldiers were glad to see you, and the more of the war you were willing to share, the more they welcomed you. I didn't know much about global strategy, but I knew a reporter had to go where the story was and I had come to see the war. There was another reason. I wanted to know if I was a man.

In the ethos of my generation, war was the only real test of manhood. We had heard of the heroic efforts of the men who beat the Nazis and the Japanese and, to be sure, their war had been the turning point of the twentieth century, the greatest work of Tom Brokaw's *Greatest Generation*. We had been children during that war and too young for the war that came later in Korea. For us, courage was defined by the standards we had learned from one man: John Wayne. Of course, he had never actually served in combat, and in his movies, we didn't see arms and legs torn off in combat, or soldiers mistakenly shot by their comrades. The romanticized version of the wars that we saw in movies such as *The Longest Day* told only of deaths that were noble and wounds that didn't bleed. The horrors that later generations would see in *Saving Private Ryan* were unknown to us. As I have grown older, the question that keeps coming back to me is: How many of history's wars were started because men felt as I did, that only in war can manhood be determined? Who can say? But in those first weeks in Vietnam, I came to understand that war can be unparalleled adventure and, for lack of a better word, fun. On one level and in an odd way, it can even be liberating. In war, we are separated from people we know and placed in an environment where the people we care about back home will never know what we do. In a war zone, it is easy to believe that the rules that we have lived by all our lives no longer apply. War can become the ultimate hunting and camping trip, where the thrill is heightened because

111

the animals shoot back. With its planes and tanks and all the other tools of modern warfare, it becomes an adult amusement park, where there are things to be ridden and experiences to be had, experiences to be told about later. Men have been raised to believe that war brings out the best in them, and in many cases it does, but it also appeals to our baser instincts if we allow it, and can also bring out the worst in us.

During his first month in office, I asked George W. Bush what had surprised him about being president, and he said it had been the realization during his first visit to a military base that if young men and women were ordered into combat, it would be his personal responsibility to send them there. It was one thing, he said, to think about that in the abstract, but quite another thing, once he actually had the power, to look into the faces of the young and realize that he alone would be the one to issue the orders. It is a responsibility that must have weighed heavily on every president. But what I came to understand in Vietnam is that sending young men and women into a war zone leaves more than their lives at risk. It also means that every value they have been taught, every belief they hold, will be tested. When we send our young people to war, we are placing them in an environment that appeals to their best and worst sides. I came to believe that training a seventeen-year-old to understand and cope with the temptations of war was as important as teaching him to shoot straight. Those thoughts would not come until much later, of course. In those first days in Saigon, my only aim was to locate as many Texans as I could. I had come to share their war and I set out to find them.

Over the next four months, I located 235 military people from Texas. I flew dive-bombing missions with Air Force pilots and rode on hundreds of Army helicopters, including one day when I made thirty-six landings and takeoffs as chopper pilots moved infantrymen into a battle zone where they believed a unit of North Vietnamese regulars were trapped. I made a D-Day-type beach assault with Marines and went on dozens of ground operations in the flat Delta region south of Saigon, where I watched as U.S. advisors tried — sometimes in vain — to rally their South Vietnamese charges into pursuing the mysterious Viet Cong. Most of the time, we never saw the enemy, but we would often see their work. As was usually the case in Vietnam, the casualties I saw were mostly the result of snipers, or ingenious traps that ranged from land mines to deadly poison-tipped arrows set off by trip wires. Set-piece battles and the infantry firefights we had known in previous wars seldom happened in Vietnam.

I have never compared the chances I took (some were simply foolhardy) with what military men and women faced in Vietnam. I was there by choice. I came and went as I pleased. The "grunts," as the infantrymen called themselves, were entirely under the control of others. When I tired of the war in one place, I could go to another. They couldn't. In time, I would come to understand the futility of what they had been sent to do, and many of them would later come to the same conclusion. But I could move on. They had to keep trying because that was what their government expected of them, knowing all the while, they might be the next person to step on a land mine or be randomly picked to die by a sniper they never saw. Because there were no front lines in Vietnam, soldiers in the field could go for days without hearing shots fired in anger. Yet, they might come to Saigon on a three-day pass and be injured by a hand grenade thrown into a restaurant. Knowing that death might come so randomly causes some men to become more religious, but most of the young people I interviewed had simply become more fatalistic. A Marine told me one night that he never worried "about that bullet that has my name on it. It's the one addressed 'To whom it may concern' that bothers me," he said.

★ ★ ★

During my first weeks in Vietnam, I wrote the kind of offbeat features I had written on the police and courthouse beat back home. I found an Army tank commander named Randy Yeargan who had volunteered for the war zone to be near his wife. (She was a military nurse.) I wrote of a one-eyed Marine named Nelson Busch, who removed his glass eye on the Marine Corps anniversary and inserted a false eye with the Marine Corps emblem on it. I found an enlisted man named Hans W. Doehle who had been in basic training three times: once in the Air Force, before that in the German navy during World War II and before that in the Hitler youth corps. A young Marine named Gary Clodfelter told me, "I never dreamed of being a cook, but the Marines did, and now I am one." I decided a colonel named Tom Kelly had the best excuse for *not* being there. He was the father of eleven children.

Rereading those early stories, I realize how jingoistic many of them were. Most of the soldiers were anxious to criticize the war protestors back home, and I probably quoted them more than I should have, because I had no great love for the protestors, either. But what still comes through in those early stories is what I found over and over in those first weeks. The enlisted people, those who had the toughest and most dangerous jobs, believed in what they were doing. Their government had told them it had to be done and they believed their government. If Vietnam fell, Thailand was sure to be next, then the Philippines and San Francisco wouldn't be far behind. What they didn't understand then, nor did I, was that the French soldiers had been given the same reasons when they had been sent to Vietnam during the French occupation. In one way or another, somebody had always been telling soldiers that.

Many of the reporters had been in Vietnam for several years and had already soured on the war, as had some of the advisors who had been stationed there over the last year to guide the South Vietnamese army. But in late 1965, when the first ground combat troops had been there only a matter of months, they still believed what their government told them: that this was something that had to be done. That attitude would change as the war dragged on. Troops would become disillusioned and turn on their officers, and drug use would become so rampant that by 1971, an official study showed troops were using marijuana on a regular basis and estimated that as many as one-third may have been addicted to opium or heroin. But in 1965, most troops thought they had been sent to fight a just war and believed they were well treated. At that point, African-Americans and white enlisted men believed they were sharing a just, common cause and there was little racial friction. The best quote I ever got and could not find a place to use resulted from a conversation I had with a black Marine. When I asked if he ever felt discrimination, he replied, "Nah, the Marines treat ever'body like niggers."

# Seven

## *"I Can't Never Tell What Happened to Me"*

Two days in Saigon were all I needed to know that I wanted to be someplace else. I soon realized that the Saigon press corps was divided into two distinct groups: those who went into the field and those who stayed in Saigon and fought with the official briefers. The U.S. Command held a news briefing at 5 P.M. each day to give an overall report on the war. Reporters had named the briefings the "five o'clock follies," because they seemed to have more to do with entertainment than usable information. Briefers talked of "body counts," of various enemy headquarters destroyed, and offered all sorts of indecipherable statistics. By the second afternoon, I turned to the correspondent next to me and said, "I don't understand any of this." He responded, "Don't sweat it, it's all lies anyway." I came to understand that some of the story lines being spun by the Saigon briefers *were* false, but more often they were simply irrelevant. They had no bearing on how the war was going. The briefers would report exact numbers of enemy headquarters or warehouses that had been destroyed on a given day, but I would later discover that what Americans at home might call a backyard toolshed could qualify in Vietnam — at least by the briefer's standards — as an enemy warehouse.

I discovered this one afternoon when I went to Bien Hoa, fifteen miles north of Saigon, to do a story about Gail Anderson, an Air Force captain from Waco who was part of an outfit called the 1st Air Commando Squadron. The group flew A1E Skyraiders, propeller-driven fighter bombers that the Navy had flown off aircraft carriers during World War II. The planes had been headed for the scrap heap when the Air Force realized they could carry more bombs than modern jet aircraft and, even better, enough fuel to stay over targets much longer than the jets. There was another advantage: The planes carried none of the modern electronics used by newer planes, so unless a gunner on the ground hit a fuel line or the pilot himself, it was all but impossible to shoot them down. "The planes were not pressurized," Anderson explained. "You can shoot these old birds full of holes and all you wind up with is a plane full of holes. Except for a fuel line or two, there's not much in them that a gunner

could hit that is critical to keep them flying."
He had already flown one mission that morning and had picked up one round from a
fifty-caliber machine gun. It had left a hole in
the tail about the size of a quarter. I was
slated to fly with him that afternoon and wondered if the hole would cause the mission to
be canceled. He said no, none of the tail controls had been hit, so the patchwork could
wait until another day.

I was outfitted in a flight suit and helmet
and, during a flight briefing from the squadron's intelligence officer, I learned where
those statistics that were given out each day
in Saigon originated. Anderson and three
other officers, Major Bernie Fischer of Idaho,
Captain Bruce Wallace of Pasadena, California, and Major Buzz Blaylock of Colorado
Springs, would be bombing a Viet Cong supply line. I wasn't sure what that meant, but
the pilots would be guided to the target by a
forward air controller, another Air Force pilot who flew a small single-engine spotter
plane at low altitude and fired phosphorus
rockets called "Willie Petes" to mark where
the pilots were to bomb.

I was strapped in behind Anderson, and we
were in the air in a matter of minutes. In minutes more, we and Anderson's three squadron mates were over the target area. We flew
in wide-apart formation at five thousand feet
and we could see the forward air controller's

plane below, maybe a thousand feet off the deck. To that point, the flight had been like a joyride in a private plane. Then the forward air controller fired his phosphorus rocket and told us to drop our bombs to the left of it and WHAM! Suddenly we were upside down and seemed to be going straight down. The altimeter was spinning and my stomach was somewhere in the vicinity of my Adam's apple. At 1,100 feet, I could feel and hear a thunk sound and realized Gail had released the bomb, and now we were going up again, pulling four Gs. My flesh felt as if it were coming off my bones and then it was over. We were back at 6,000 feet. As we circled, we could see Buzz and Bruce coming in at treetop level and blasting two sampans out of the water. The old A1Es could stay over a target for hours, and through the afternoon our plane made five more passes at targets. Our plane and Fischer's carried eight bombs. Bruce and Buzz carried two bombs, plus the napalm. As we headed back to the base, the forward air controller told us it had been a successful mission. We had destroyed fourteen buildings, damaged ten more, sunk four sampans and damaged several others. Had it really been an enemy supply line? Were those really Viet Cong boats? We had to take the word of the forward air controller, who was stationed in the area and served as a liaison to the local village chief. The chief said they were enemy craft, so his word was taken. And what was the real strategic value of those buildings? To me, they seemed no more substantial than a thatched-roof lean-to that might be used for shade on an American beach. But American pilots had risked their lives to destroy them, and in Saigon the next day, they would be added to the statistics that the military briefers would release to show that we were winning the war.

Back on the ground, Captain Anderson discovered another hole in his aircraft. During one of the dives, we had apparently been hit just below a fuel line by another fifty-caliber machine-gun slug. Buzz had taken a hit, too, just behind the cockpit. Over dinner that night, the pilots talked as pilots do, not so much about the hits they had taken but about how their planes had performed. Over the previous 90 days, Anderson had flown 90 missions like the one we had flown that day. Wallace had 127 and Fischer, too, had flown scores. Blaylock had only eleven, but he had been there only eleven days. It was the second time Anderson's plane had been hit twice in one day. He had no idea how much ground fire there had been. "In the daylight," he said, "you never know they're shooting until they hit you, but it can get a little hairy at night. When those fifty-caliber rounds start coming at your airplane, it's like somebody down there is hitting red golf balls at you."

The next day, I would be back in Saigon, but Anderson and his squadron mates would be back in those old planes, dodging red golf balls, and they would be there the next day and the next until they had been there a year. Or killed. I wrote a straightforward account of the mission, and the pictures I had snapped from the cockpit were a big hit with my editors. What I didn't write was what was already beginning to trouble me. We seemed to be putting in a lot of effort and taking some enormous risks to destroy some wooden sampans and thatched-roof lean-tos. I was uneasy about it, but I wanted to see more before I wrote that part.

Within two weeks, I had settled into a routine. The ads we had run in the *Star-Telegram* promising that I would visit every Fort Worth boy I could find had begun to pay off. Hundreds of letters had been forwarded to me. I would line up the letters by name and region and set out to find them, a practice I followed over the next four months. Armed with the names of forty or fifty servicemen, I would usually hitch a ride on a transport plane out of Saigon and then bum rides on helicopters and smaller planes to get to the remote outposts. I would generally stay in the field for five to ten days, and then return to Saigon to develop film and write enough stories to fill the paper for two weeks and then head out again. Since the *Star-Telegram* published morning and evening editions, Monday through Saturday, and one paper on Sunday, I tried to write twelve stories, and one longer feature with pictures for the Sunday paper, before I went back to the field. I wrote individual features about most of the Texans I found. If they happened to be from Fort Worth, I included pictures when I could. When I was unable to write individual stories, I grouped names into columns and sent home individual greetings such as "Private Joe Jones says Hi to all the gang at the Su-Su Lounge and wishes he was having a cool one with you right now." Maybe that part wasn't really journalism, but of all the honors I have received in my long reporting career, I have yet to match the thrill I got when I would turn up in some out-of-the-way place in Vietnam and tell a nineteen-year-old kid, "I'm from the *Star-Telegram* and your mom wrote me a letter and asked me to look in on you." One Marine was so taken aback he cried. At that point in my life, at the age of twenty-eight, I had always been the "young man" in the office. But I was usually five to ten years older than these kids, usually a year or two older than their officers, and I would sometimes find myself being looked up to as an older man of experience. That was my first great lesson of Vietnam. These were not men, they were boys, and these were the people governments always send to fight their wars. I came to love those kids, and I still do. If I had let them pop off about war protestors more than I should have in those early stories, so be it. They were a long way from home, doing what they thought was a good thing, and they deserved to be quoted someplace. For sure, the government hadn't asked their opinion when it sent them there. The government just wanted them to do the dirty work and be quiet about it. Later, as the war protests grew more intense, the same soldiers would be spit upon by their contemporaries because they had done nothing more than what their government had asked of them.

Over the next months, I crisscrossed Vietnam in my search for Texans. At every stop, I seemed to find a different war. To the north, in the Marine sector around Da Nang, I found a kid named Leland Meadows who had dug into his foxhole on the perimeter of an airfield and thought he was under Viet Cong attack one night, only to discover a rock ape was throwing stones at him. In the jungle area of the mountainous Central Highlands, I found a helicopter pilot who claimed he had shot an elephant because the Viet Cong were using it to transport supplies. In a Special Forces camp along the Cambodian border, I found a remote Special Forces camp where Green Berets were training

Montagnard tribesmen — the indigenous people of Vietnam — into fighting troops.

The Montagnard culture was similar to that of Native Americans; just how similar the Green Berets had discovered one night as they showed an American Western movie on the camp projector. "It's amazing," Sergeant Robel Reagan told me. "Whenever the Indians rode up in that movie, the 'Yards cheered 'em on."

Every stop may have been different, but at every stop I found the Americans shared the same problem. They couldn't get the Viet Cong or the North Vietnamese soldiers who were supposed to be in South Vietnam to stand and fight. Most of the time they couldn't find them. The Viet Cong fought on their own terms: ambushes, mines, terrorist attacks. Seldom did they show themselves.

Walter Clerihew, an Air Force pilot from Jacksboro, Texas, who was stationed in South Vietnam's southernmost area, knew one way to find them. He was a forward air controller who called in air strikes like the ones I had flown farther north with Gail Anderson and the 1st Air Commando Unit. I went along in Clerihew's single-engine eighty-mile-an-hour spotter plane one hot afternoon as he flew low over the rice paddies and canals south of Saigon on the lookout for Viet Cong. "I figured out the best way to find them is just to fly in low and see if anybody shoots," he said. "If they do, I figure they're the enemy and I call in an air strike." Sure enough, as we crossed one area at 900 feet altitude, we heard the sharp crack of rifle fire from below. "This is where we thought they were," Clerihew said, "and I guess those shots mean we were right." He called air operations and soon we saw F-100 fighter bombers overhead. Clerihew put the little plane in a dive and fired his phosphorus rocket at the target and instructed the bombers to aim to the left of the smoke where his rocket hit. Over the radio he told me to hold on, because "it might get a little tricky." "We're near the Cambodian border," he said, "and the jets can't cross it so they have to turn back toward us as they pull out of their dive." He was right. As one of the F-100s pulled out of its dive and headed back to higher altitude, it seemed to be coming directly at us. "Not even close," Clerihew said later. It was close enough for me, but I supposed Clerihew was used to it. He was halfway through his one-year tour of duty in Vietnam the day I flew with him and had already flown 276 such missions. He expected to fly at least that many more before his tour was up.

I had found Clerihew on my first trip into the vast delta area south of Saigon, where most of Vietnam's rice was grown. He was working out of a small camp where American advisors were headquartered, and I was the first reporter to visit there. At that point, none of the large American units were based there, only advisors to South Vietnamese units, and in that flat region of paddies and canals, I found still another war. One day, an Army sergeant from San Antonio named Rodolfo Salinas invited me to go on a patrol with the South Vietnamese unit he was advising. I agreed, only to discover it was a "popular force" unit, a group of very young teenagers that seemed something of a cross between a Boy Scout troop and a National Guard unit. He was the unit's advisor and he told me I might see some things that morning that I hadn't seen in my travels with American units. Salinas and I were the only Americans in the group, and I soon saw what he meant. I noticed that he spent a good part of his time advising his young charges to turn off their transistor radios, and as we moved into an open area, he told them to spread out, something American soldiers learned by the second day of boot camp. Some of his troops wore sneakers, some were barefoot and one wore a conical straw coolie hat over his metal helmet.

A "company" of Viet Cong was supposedly camped along a canal that fed into the Mekong River and it was to be our mission to find them. I asked Salinas if he really believed we would find them. "If they want us to," he said. Clearly, Salinas had adopted the ground version of the strategy that pilot Walter Clerihew had used. Go into enemy territory, and if they start shooting at you, they must be the enemy. During a day-long march, we found two of the "enemy." As we moved through a small village, a search of one hut turned up hand grenades and a Viet Cong flag. The occupant of the hut said he had found the items and had been trying to turn them in. It was a dubious story at best and our troops arrested him for questioning. As we walked through another village, two shots rang out from a haystack and a man in black pajamas broke out of the hay and ran. Our troops shot him and spent the next half hour posing with the body and taking pictures. The dead man had committed a sniper's ultimate sin. His bad aim had given away his position and he'd paid with his life. The "company" of Viet Cong that had supposedly massed along the canal never materialized, but Salinas thought it had been a good day. "Down here, we don't get many at a time. If we get one or two a day, that's one or two that won't be shooting at us tomorrow," he said. "It's going to take a long time to get them all." I decided he was right, but it was not until some weeks later, when I had joined the Marines on a beach assault, that the futility of finding the enemy really hit me. It was an operation that had been named Double Eagle, and had it been a movie, it would have been the perfect vehicle for John Wayne.

My friend Eddie Adams, the AP photographer, had tipped me that the Marines were planning something big. I checked with the Marine headquarters and was invited to go along. Once we had been helicoptered to troopships offshore, we were told we would be part of the biggest operation of the war thus far, the largest amphibious invasion since the Inchon invasion during the Korean War. I found six sailors from Fort Worth on the troopship, and for two days, we steamed off the Vietnamese coast. Finally, we were told D-Day would begin the next morning. We were roused from our beds at 3 A.M. and fed a big breakfast. At dawn, I found myself climbing over the side of that ship and making my way down its side on a webbed rope ladder. It was a scene that I had seen dozens of times in war movies and so had the young Marines. They were new arrivals who had not yet set foot in Vietnam and were going into their first battle. At that point, I had seen more combat than they had. What struck me during the two days aboard ship was how much their concept of war was based on what they had seen in movies. Again and again, they would mention John Wayne and what he might be doing in a similar setting.

But as we went over the side of those ships, it was not at all like the movies. Commanders had chosen this particular day to launch the invasion because forecasters had predicted good weather and calm seas. We found neither. It was raining and the sea was churning. One minute, the flat-bottomed boats that would take us into the beach would be inches from the bottom of the rope ladders. The next minute, it would be a ten-foot drop into the landing craft. I was lucky, I timed my drop when the distance was about four feet. It was easier for me. I wasn't carrying a seventy-pound pack and a weapon, as many of the Marines were. They were having trouble timing their jumps and three fell into the water, one between the ship and the landing craft. Another froze on the nets halfway down the side of the ship and had to be helped. Our group had been designated the trouble squad.

We would hold back before we hit the beach and go to the rescue of any unit that encountered resistance. But there was no opposition. Our problems were in the water. Our landing craft hung on a sandbar and we were stuck there for an hour. Finally, as the coxswain was working the little craft off the bar, we were somehow caught between two huge swells and the boat stood on its end. One of the Marines who had hit the beach before us told me later he thought we had capsized. Somehow, we all made our way out and started to wade in. But just as we made it out of the boat, the swells began to pound the beach and several of the Marines who were carrying the big packs went down. Other Marines got them on their feet. Miraculously, no one had drowned. The Marines who had fallen from the sides of the ship had somehow separated themselves from their packs and had been fished out of the water, and every Marine who had fallen as we waded in had been pulled to his feet by comrades. My head went underwater once and my Nikon 35-millimeter camera was doused with salt, but most of the film I had shot on the way in survived. Eddie Adams helped me do a little maintenance work on it once we reached land, and forty-plus years later, it's still working. Once on the beach, the Marines set up patrols, but we found little. The first villages we passed through appeared deserted. Apparently, the Viet Cong had been tipped off well in advance of the operation. There was no one home and it appeared they had left well before we got there. This wasn't a case where people had flown in such a hurry they had left meals cooking on the stove. These people hadn't been there for days. Only after dark did we find evidence of the enemy. Snipers from some unknown post shot and killed two of the Marines and wounded seven. The operation had been those young Marines' first taste of combat, and they had died in the first hours they had set foot on Vietnamese soil.

I found a kid from Fort Worth named Colvin Boone driving an armored personnel carrier, and when he offered a ride, Eddie and I climbed on top and helped deliver water to some of the Marines who were digging foxholes along the beach. At one stop, we loaded the body of one of the dead Marines on board and took it to the field headquarters. Colvin said he recognized the body as that of a Marine he had seen the day before on the troopship. We left Colvin and his team at midday and joined up with an infantry patrol. It appeared the whole operation had been a bust and we were trying to figure out a way to get back to Saigon. After our patrol moved through another inland village and found nothing, we stopped for lunch. We had hardly opened our C-rations when we came under mortar attack. Not an attack, really: The mortar man had fired only one round and it landed thirty yards away. But, curiously, the mortar had been launched from the deserted village we had just passed through.

Double Eagle, as advertised, had been the biggest operation of the war and had been executed flawlessly. Watching hundreds of Marines coming down the rope webbing on the sides of those troopships and making their way to shore in dozens of landing craft was one of the most impressive things I had ever seen. Except for a bum weather forecast, it had gone exactly as planned. Unfortunately, we had again failed to find the enemy. A massive operation designed for the set battles of World War II had been a total failure in a war where there were no front lines and the enemy always disappeared to fight another day.

Double Eagle had convinced me World War II tactics weren't going to work in Vietnam, but the longer I was there, the more I came to wonder if any kind of tactics would work. South of Da Nang one night in late March, I joined some Marine advisors who planned a sweep through an area of the Hoi Buc Valley, where the Viet Cong had been stealing rice. Our advisors were worried about security leaks and had given the Vietnamese troops no advance briefing on what was planned. When the troops didn't arrive until a full hour after the operation had been scheduled to begin, we wondered if word of the operation had already leaked. In any case, when the interpreter passed on the plans to the Vietnamese lieutenant commanding the troops, the young officer shook his head no. Apparently, he did not want to take his troops across an open field where they might be picked off by snipers. A Marine gunnery sergeant named Ladale Sampson was becoming more fed up by the minute and told the interpreter to tell the Vietnamese officer to tell his troops to move out or else. But the lieutenant simply shook his head. The interpreter told the sergeant that the lieutenant was sorry, but unless they could cross the clearing in trucks, they weren't going. "He's tired," the interpreter said. "He says his people don't want to walk. Get trucks or they're not going."

"Well, to hell with that," said one of the Americans. "They can either stay here or walk back to town. They're not going with us. If we walk, they walk."

They didn't. We left them there and moved on across the field. The Viet Cong had clearly been tipped off to our operation, and as usual we found nothing. Most of the Marines were delighted that the Vietnamese had been left behind. "Did you see all those transistor radios and tape recorders?" one Marine asked me. "They get out here at night and play that stuff on patrol." Later that evening, we had a big laugh when our radio operator reported what had happened to our reluctant warriors back at the base camp. They had demanded a truck for the ride back to town and it had so infuriated one of the Marine lieutenants that he told a tank driver to chase them off. The radio man said the folks back at base camp reported "those boys really lit out when that tank got after them." It was anecdotal evidence, to be sure, but I concluded that night that if the Vietnamese were not willing to fight this war, there wasn't much we could do to help. I would become even more disillusioned in the coming days when anti-American riots broke out in Da Nang. Suddenly the whole Vietnam scene was taking on a surreal quality. Victor Krulak, the top Marine in the Pacific Command, came to Da Nang to tell us how well the war was going. Krulak was a tough guy who had become a legend in the Corps. It had been a year since the first of his 51,000 Marines had come into I Corps, the region around Da Nang, and Krulak was there to tell us how much the situation had improved. Unfortunately, no reporters showed up for his news conference. We were all in downtown Da Nang to cover the riots. Krulak was about to leave the press center, when several of us trooped back in from town. We were a welcome sight to the Marine public-relations officer who had arranged the press conference for his boss that not a single reporter had attended. He pleaded with us to listen to Krulak, and we agreed.

"We are making progress," Krulak told us. He had the usual bundle of statistics, but unlike the Saigon briefers, we enjoyed interviewing Krulak because he usually gave us a good quote, and he did not disappoint.

"When the Marines landed a year ago, the

boundary between freedom and slavery was the fence that surrounds the American air base here," he told us, with a flourish. "Today, that boundary has been extended many miles."

Two weeks later, Vietnamese premier Nguyen Cao Ky called another press conference and announced that the city of Da Nang was in the hands of the Communists. That was not entirely accurate. But riots continued in Da Nang and it appeared those boundaries of freedom had shrunk again. They had certainly shrunk for the Marines. Da Nang was declared off-limits and the Marines were confined to the base. What had happened was that Ky had decided to dump Lieutenant General Nguyen Chanh Thi, a charismatic warlord who had long ruled South Vietnam's northern provinces. Ky and the other Saigon generals were worried that Thi was plotting to overthrow them. When Ky fired Thi for insubordination, Vietnamese students (carrying signs lettered in English) took to the streets. They were soon joined by radicals in the Buddhist movement. For days, the city was racked by riots that soon took an anti-American tone. The Marines, who had been under the impression they had been sent there to help the Vietnamese, were baffled, and so was I. Outside the base, draft-age Vietnamese carried signs denouncing Americans. The American military PX closed because Vietnamese clerks who worked there had gone on strike to show sympathy for the demonstrators, and American cargo sat on Da Nang docks because Vietnamese truck drivers stayed home. "I came here to help these people and now I don't know what they want," a Marine said. I had no answer, but a Vietnamese cameraman who worked for one of the American networks tried to explain. "They believe the Americans are keeping them from having a civilian government," he said, "and they don't like it." Then should we leave? I wondered. "Oh no," he said. "We know you won't do that. You have to fight the Communists. We just want you to stop supporting the Ky government." I wrote an angry story that reflected the Marines' feelings and my editors spread it across the top of the *Star-Telegram*'s front page under the heading YOU WOULDN'T HAVE LIKED DA NANG ANYWAY, FELLAS.

In a matter of weeks, officials in Saigon were reporting that twenty thousand new troops from North Vietnam had infiltrated into the South, and it was estimated that even though sixteen thousand enemy troops had been killed in the first four months of 1966, the enemy had actually seen a net gain in manpower.

In the coming weeks, the riots would spread to Hue in the Central Highlands and eventually to Saigon. This was not good news to the U.S. Command or to the Johnson administration. After a parade of military leaders had toppled each other in a series of coups, U.S. officials believed the American people were becoming comfortable with the Ky government. Officials worried (rightly) that the demonstrations would cause Americans back home to have doubts about supporting the war effort, and they ordered the briefers to play down the whole affair. I realized just how worried the high command was becoming one night, when I went out to cover a demonstration in Saigon with Eddie Adams and Peter Arnett from the AP and Bob Keatley of the *Wall Street Journal*. Two jeeps loaded with American Military Police pulled up beside us and ordered us to clear the streets. When we said we were newsmen and refused, one of the MPs said, "We know who you are, but that's our orders." Journalists had generally had good relations with the military enlisted men, but the authorities had clearly decided to discourage coverage of the riots and had instructed the MPs to remove newsmen from the area. Peter protested that the MPs had no jurisdiction over civilians. That was the job of Vietnamese police, but the MPs weren't buying, and finally one pulled his pistol. Adams was furious. "Well, you prick," he said, "you've pulled that pistol, let's see you use it." It was a stirring declaration, but I would have enjoyed it more had the pistol not been pointed at me. Calmer heads finally prevailed and we moved on.

The next day, it had all been worked out. Barry Zorthian, the U.S. Information Agency chief who ran the information program in Saigon, told Arnett that if we weren't careful he would charge us with "assault with a pencil and paper" on an armed MP. Zorthian found it amusing, but Arnett never did. Nor did many other reporters who saw it as one more reason to believe the government was more interested in shaping the news than giving an accurate account of what was happening.

The next day, I was back at a Buddhist rally with Adams and the AP's other photographer, Horst Fass, when the demonstrators turned on us. We had no idea why, but all three of us were kicked and punched and there was a lot of shouting about "Americans Go Home." We escaped with scrapes and a few bruises. What irritated me was not the pushing and punching, but in the middle of it all, literally as I was fending off one demonstrator who was trying to kick me, another Vietnamese tugged at my sleeve and begged a cigarette. Back at the AP office, Ed White had put the incident on the wires, and it sounded much worse than it actually was, but when Jack Butler, my editor back in Fort Worth, read it, he had had enough. He had convinced himself that I was taking too many chances and told me to come home. His plan had been for me to stay three months and I had already stayed more than four. I refused to answer his wires for a week, and then wrote letters arguing that I had just begun to understand the situation, and outlined what I thought I could do if I stayed another three months. He was having none of it, and finally told me to come home or else.

Resigned to the fact that I was leaving, I decided not to risk another trip to the field. Instead, I went one day to visit the 93rd Evacuation Hospital at Bien Hoa. It was where they brought the wounded from three airborne divisions. I entered through the emergency room, where seventeen soldiers who had been helicoptered in from various battlefields were awaiting treatment. Some had been burned, some awaited amputation of limbs. Surgery was under way in seven operating rooms, and outside four of them, patients had been prepped and were waiting for surgery. These were the people that the Saigon briefers referred to only as WIAs, wounded in action. But seeing them there on those stretchers, it was hard to think of them as statistics. These were people, young people, and as I stood there, it occurred to me that long after this war was over, long after the arguments about whether the war had been right or wrong had been settled, these people would still have no arms or legs. It is one thing to see the wounded on the battlefield when adrenaline is running high. It was another to see them as I did that day, cleaned up in a quiet setting. Only then did you really understand they would be going home not as God made them, but as war has left them.

I had gone through the ward asking for Texans, but as I turned toward the door, a voice said, "How about a Georgia peach, would you like to talk to a Georgia peach?" I said Georgia guys were my favorite people next to Texans, and asked how he was feeling. "Glad to be alive," he said. "Mighty glad to be alive." He said there had been seventeen in his company on a hill when the mortars had come in. Seven of his buddies had been killed. He said he would be going home soon. I could see by the outline of his body under the sheets that he still had his legs and I asked what was wrong with him.

"You can't tell nobody," he said. "That's the part that really bothers me. I can't never tell what happened to me." He raised the sheet and showed me the bandages between his legs. I put my hand on his shoulder and turned away. I had done it all in Vietnam, but I was never quite so brave after that.

I had gone to Vietnam convinced the government was on the right course, and was coming home convinced the course was hopeless. I was still torn over what impact an immediate pullout would have on American prestige and whether that would tempt the Soviets to launch adventures in other parts of the world. But I was certain of one thing: Our presence there was not helping the Vietnamese. Nor would it ever. I had no sympathy for the Communist cause, but we had attached ourselves to the remnants of an army that had fought on the side of the French colonists and aligned ourselves with a bureaucracy that had become ineffective and corrupt. The Vietnamese people were caught between that army and the Communists in the north. During my last week in Saigon, a Vietnamese newspaper editor named Noc told me that I should remember that, from the time there had been a Vietnam, there had always been foreigners there, trying to exploit the Vietnamese.

"We have seen the Chinese here, the Japanese and the French," he said. "A Vietnamese has to be fairly sophisticated to understand that you are somehow different from the others. I believe the Americans came here because they wanted to help, but the truth is, once you go into the countryside, most of the people have no idea who their own government is. All they know is that people with guns come through and take their men off to fight the war and haul away their rice to pay taxes. Sometimes, the people with the guns are the Viet Cong, sometimes they are the people from the Saigon government. The people in the paddies don't know anything about who they are or who they represent. They are just the people with the guns."

The one feeling that did not change for me in Vietnam was my admiration for the American servicemen and -women. I left Vietnam believing they were just as brave and smart as I had believed them to be the day I arrived. But after going there, I was never able to agree with the generals' argument that the war was winnable if only they had been allowed to make an all-out fight. Of course we could have remained in Vietnam indefinitely, but to what purpose and at what cost? We went there with the military equipment and war-fighting doctrines that had been used successfully in other wars, but like the information that had been given out at the Saigon briefings, the doctrines had had little relevance to what the Army found in Vietnam. We were unable to help the Vietnamese, but almost destroyed our own military and saw our own institutions threatened. From the beginning, we underestimated the resolve and the capability of Ho Chi Minh's forces because we forgot our own revolution. George Washington understood that when you are fighting a much larger, organized army, the goal is not to hold territory or win battles, but simply to keep a viable fighting force together. As long as your army stays together, your revolution lives. Eventually, the conqueror tires of the struggle or decides it is no longer worth the cost. Washington won only two significant battles during the American Revolution, but he kept his army together until the British concluded the battle was no longer worth it. Ho Chi Minh's generals knew that. Our leaders forgot it. Arguing that we could have stayed in Vietnam was the wrong question. The right question would have been whether it was worth the price, and it wasn't. We made a mistake in going there. Our greater mistake was in not recognizing the error sooner. Americans are optimists. They want to hear good news, and when the news from Vietnam was not good, the government found news that was. But it had nothing to do with gauging the progress of the war. We asked repeatedly, Are we winning? What all of us should have realized was that when you're winning, victory is usually apparent. When you have to ask, it probably means you're losing.

As I left Vietnam, the American military force there had grown to 235,000 men and women, another 70,000 were based offshore, and the generals were already saying even more troops would be needed. I left convinced that the Vietnam government would fall in a matter of weeks and American troops would be asked to leave. Unfortunately, I was wrong.

# Eight

## *News at Six*

I wasn't ready to come back to Fort Worth, nor was I prepared for the reception I would receive. I stepped off the plane and was greeted by one of my colleagues from the *Star-Telegram*, who pulled out a notebook and proceeded to interview me. This seemed odd. I couldn't remember ever being interviewed by someone from my own paper, but I would soon discover that the stories from Vietnam had made me into something of a local celebrity. I was told the circulation of the morning and evening papers had gone up by about 7,000 during my absence, and the circulation department attributed the increase to my stories from Vietnam. I was stunned, but over the next week I would realize just how much comment the stories had created. I was besieged with invitations to speak. As the number of American troops in Vietnam continued to rise and casualties had grown, the war had become front-page news, and everyone I saw or heard from wanted to know about it. People would stop me on the street to ask what I really thought was going to happen. If one person stopped me, five or six other people would wander up to join the conversation. When our reporter had interviewed me at the airport on the afternoon I returned, I told him that I believed the situation in Vietnam was dire, that the government would probably fall and the United States would be asked to withdraw its military forces. As for the troops, I told him we could all be proud of what they were doing. He made my remarks about the troops his lead and that was the headline. It wouldn't be the last time I would disagree with what I thought was the lead when someone interviewed me, and I'm sure people who are frequently interviewed often have the same feeling. What I also realized in the coming weeks was that our reporter was more in touch with what our readers wanted to know than I was. Over the next year, I gave more than a hundred fifty talks around the state, and what people wanted to know about were their kids, the young people who had been sent to fight the war. I got few questions about whether we should be in Vietnam. The government said we needed to be there, and at that point, most people in our area still believed the government. Only later, when the casualties began to mount, did people in Fort Worth seriously question the reasons the government had given them. As I would discover so many times in my long career in journalism, Americans want to believe their government is doing the right thing, and they will usually give the government the benefit of the doubt until shown otherwise.

Editor Jack Butler thought the invitations to speak at local civic clubs were a great promotional device for the paper, so he encouraged me to make as many talks as I could. It was great training as well. I hadn't done much ad-libbing during my college radio days, and the talks helped me to think on my feet. It was also somewhat humbling on occasion. Every speech to a Lions Club was an adventure. The Lions had one official called the tail-twister, whose job seemed to be to embarrass guests. The tail-twister's favorite trick was to put a wet napkin in your seat when you got up to be introduced; then when you sat back down you would slowly realize the seat of your pants was soaked through. Another tail-twister trick was to slip a knife or fork into your jacket pocket and then blow a whistle and accuse you of stealing silverware. On one occasion, I showed up at a luncheon club only to discover the audience consisted of the program chairman, the club president and one other person. We waited, and when no one else showed, we repaired to the front of the restaurant, asked for a table for four and had lunch. Even then, the club president did most of the talking. I listened politely, answered several questions and left. At another luncheon club, I arrived only to discover that Bobby Bragan, who had been the legendary manager of Fort Worth's minor-league baseball team, had also been invited to speak. The club program chairman had invited me only when he had thought Bragan would be unable to make it. When he showed up unexpectedly, the program chairman said, "We knew you'd understand, so could you come back another time?" Most of the time, I had better luck, but the program chairman who holds a special place in my memory represented a club in Mineral Wells, a small town west of Fort Worth. He called me one night at the paper and gave me a long spiel about how the club was trying to make its programs more educational. He said his goal was to take the programs to a whole new level, to make them so his members came away feeling inspired and informed about the issues of the day. He was so persuasive that I felt a little guilty when I told him I was booked solid for the next several weeks and would be unable to speak at his event. He didn't lose a beat. "Oh, okay," he said, "but while I've got you on the phone, do you know of any good magicians in Fort Worth?"

I covered several fairly interesting stories over the next few months, but the speeches were taking so much of my time, and Vietnam was still so much on my mind, that it was difficult to concentrate. After Vietnam, the courthouse squabbles no longer held the attraction for me they once had and I decided it was time to move on. I wanted to go back to Vietnam and I wanted to work for somebody who would send me back. I had always held reporters who worked for the big papers in awe, and in Vietnam I had convinced myself that I could be as good as they were. I just needed more practice. They covered stories the same way that I did. They just worked for papers with larger circulations. I would always love the *Star-Telegram*, but I wanted to work for a national publication. I was even beginning to think I might want to work at one of the networks. In Vietnam, I had come to know John Lawrence, at twenty-six the youngest reporter at CBS News. I had discovered that this guy could write. He was a real journalist, not like so many of the TV reporters I had known back home, old dance-band announcers who read copy written by somebody else. So I mailed résumés to every major organization that came to mind, the *New York Times*, the *Wall Street Journal*, CBS, *Time*, *Newsweek* and on and on. Unfortunately, word of my celebrity and the impact of my Vietnam stories had not extended much beyond Fort Worth. I got turndowns ranging from polite to rude, from everyone except Time-Life, where I got through two levels of interviews. *Life*'s people seemed more interested in hiring me as a photographer than a reporter, but other events intervened before we ever came to a deal.

It was when Ray Miller, the news director at a Houston television station, offered me a job that I began to think seriously about switching to television. Ray had an idea for a program about city government that combined film pieces and live interviews. He had seen my stories from Vietnam and thought I could make an easy transition to television. I still remember that he said, "We have to have a reporter to make this work." Miller was a real professional, and I wondered why the head of a news department would say such an obvious thing, but in those days, I didn't know much about television. The job seemed fairly interesting, and I might have taken it or continued to pursue the possible opening at *Life*, but for a fortuitous call I received the following week from Bobbie Wygant, who hosted a noon talk show on WBAP-TV, the NBC outlet in Fort Worth and Dallas. Bobbie invited me to be on her program, show my pictures and talk about the war.

We had a pleasant interview, and afterward I was stunned when the station news director offered me a job as the station's news anchor. The pay was $150 a week, $15 more than I made at the paper. The job wouldn't get me back to Vietnam, but I felt I just couldn't turn down that much money. For the grand sum of an extra $15 a week, I became one of the first print journalists who switched to TV for the money.

WBAP-TV, Channel 5, was the first southern television station west of Richmond, Virginia, and east of Los Angeles, and the reason it wound up in Fort Worth instead of Dallas was a point of some pride to those who worked there. Like the *Star-Telegram*, it was owned by the Amon Carter family. Amon had heard about television during one of his forays to New York and sent his people to check it out. The brass at the *Dallas Morning News* had also gone to New York to see what television was all about. In the Fort Worth version of the story, Amon's people recognized that television was the medium of the future and urged Amon to get a television station. The Dallas people returned convinced the future lay in FM radio and saw no urgency in getting a TV license. Amon lobbied the government, called in chits, and did whatever else was necessary, and in 1948, Channel 5 went on the air. As it was with the *Star-Telegram*'s radio stations, a cowbell was rung to signal station breaks on the hour and half hour. By the time I arrived in 1966, the station had become an NBC affiliate and the cowbell was abandoned. But they still rang it at the radio stations and it was an attention-getter. A deep-voiced announcer would say, "You're listening to WBAP, eight twenty, in Fort Worth"; then you would hear the clang, clang, clang of that bell, which had its own little stand beside the announcer's microphone. I never heard another station break like it.

The station's news department was run by a former *Star-Telegram* editor, James A. Byron, one of the most respected journalists in the Southwest and the first broadcaster to be named president of Sigma Delta Chi, the society of professional journalists. For its time, Channel 5 had one of the best news departments in the Southwest. My job was to anchor the 6 P.M. news, which followed NBC's *Huntley-Brinkley Report*, the network's national news broadcast. My job consisted of reading seven or eight minutes of local news, which included narrating silent film of various local events, and then introducing the weatherman and the station's sports reporter. It was dull stuff by today's standards, and fairly primitive. We had no graphics, and if I wanted to illustrate a story with a still photo, I would often cut out pictures of newsmakers that had appeared on the cover of national magazines, stick them on colored pasteboard, and place them on an easel where they could be photographed by a studio camera. The news department put most of its effort into the feature newscast at 10 P.M., which had a unique format. It resembled one of those old movie theater newsreels, which had become popular during World War II. There was no anchor, but an off-camera narrator. It opened with a dramatic burst of recorded symphony orchestra music . . . a sort of "BOOM, BOOOM, BOOMEDY, BOOM, BOOM, BOOM," and then the announcer would say, "The Texas News." A title card would flash on the screen with words printed out: TWO KILLED IN NASTY FREEWAY WRECK. Silent film of the wreck would then appear, the background music would switch to a funeral dirge and the announcer in somber tones would narrate what had happened. Then the music would become more festive and a new title card would read, ZOO ACQUIRES RARE BIRD, and we would see a bird and the narrator would tell us about it . . . and then it was on to the next title card. There were few interviews and almost no sound. Occasionally, a cameraman would hand a visiting celebrity a microphone and allow him to say something innocuous, but most news conferences were covered with silent film cameras, which couldn't record sound. The narrator would relate what the people being interviewed had said. All the local news was covered in the newsreel. Once that was completed, a sports reporter read a few scores and handed off to the weatherman. Finally, the news "anchor" (we didn't use that term in those days) read a five-minute summary of the national news, said good night and went home. I had never seen a format like it, and one night I asked an old hand named Doyle Vinson how it had come to be. He said they had stumbled onto it. When they had formed the news department, no one there had ever seen a TV newscast. "None of us had been to the East Coast, where the big stations were. The only thing we had seen were those movie newsreels, so we just copied that," he said. "We never dreamed it would be so successful."

It was certainly that. Because the station got on the air first and because of the "Texas News" format, Channel 5 dominated the news for a decade. People in Fort Worth considered it their hometown station, so it got virtually every viewer there, plus enough of the Dallas audience to sometimes get double the ratings of its competitors. Eventually, the *Dallas Morning News* and the *Dallas Times Herald* also acquired television stations and set them up in Dallas, but because the *Star-Telegram* had been first, Channel 5 remained the leading station for many years. By the late sixties, however, the other stations had news departments of their own and the ratings had begun to slip. The station's managers decided the newsreel format's inflexibility was hurting them. That was one of the reasons news director Byron had decided to revamp the format and hire me. Again, Vietnam would be the cause for a major turn in my career.

The war was now dominating the news and Vietnam had become the lead story in the paper almost every day, but because of the local newsreel that played first, Channel 5 found itself locked into a format where news of the war couldn't be broadcast until the end, after the local news, sports and weather. Because I had been to Vietnam, Byron thought I could add credibility to reports from Vietnam, and under the new format, I would appear at the top of the newscast, give the latest on the war and then introduce the local newsreel. After weather and sports, I returned at the end of the broadcast with a wrap-up of national news. As Byron had expected, the new format did cause the ratings to go up and it was well received, except by some of the film editors, who felt it was too "fancy" and took too much time away from their newsreel of car wrecks, murders and the passing parade of movie stars and other visitors.

I enjoyed television, but I had always worked a beat outside the office, and for the first time I found myself stuck behind a desk, rewriting stories brought in from the field by our cameramen. That part I didn't like. And I was surprised at the way we covered the news. In essence, we had no reporters. We sent cameramen to cover city council and commissioners' court. Some of the cameramen were actually good reporters, but I had learned in Vietnam that it is all but impossible to take pictures and take notes at the same time. The cameramen would turn in their notes to a film editor, who would then fashion a script to go with the story they assembled. Too often, it seemed to me, the film editors just fashioned their scripts from information taken directly from the newspaper. I was never comfortable with stories written by someone who wasn't there, but I discovered that was often how television covered the news in those days (and all too often, these days). In any case, sitting around the office drove me nuts. Every time a story happened, I wanted to cover it myself, which I sometimes wound up doing. My hours at the station were from 2 to 10:30 P.M., and on the two mornings a week that commissioners' court met, I began to drop by the courthouse just as I had done when I worked at the paper. When a train carrying toxic chemicals overturned in East Texas, I got up before dawn, drove to the site with a cameraman and interviewed residents who had been evacuated from their homes. This was something of an innovation in those days, but I didn't do it because I was trying to improve the quality of the journalism; I just hated sitting around the office. When news happened, I wanted to see it for myself: a habit I was never really able to break.

When a hurricane hit the Texas coast one weekend, I committed one of the more foolhardy acts of my life. I flew south to San Antonio, then rented a car and drove through the storm. I hooked up with one of our cameramen, who had been sent there ahead of the storm, and we filmed some terrific pictures. We worked through the night and I drove back through the worst of the storm to bring the film back to Fort Worth. It was one of the scariest car trips I've ever taken. The car rocked with the wind, power lines were down, and thousands of snakes had come out of the ground and were trying to flee the storm. I later learned I wasn't the only reporter who had taken leave of his senses during a storm. During a previous hurricane on Galveston Island, young Houston TV reporter Dan Rather had basically tied himself to a palm tree in order to make a series of dramatic reports on a hurricane's progress. Dan's reports were noticed by CBS News brass in New York and he was hired on the spot. It would be awhile before CBS noticed me. I returned from the coast exhausted and broadcast my report on the six o'clock news. The report went well. Unfortunately, by the time the ten o'clock news rolled around, I ran out of gas, and when we went to the first commercial break, I fell sound asleep. Television control rooms are hectic places, and that control room must have been especially hectic that evening, because no one noticed that the anchorman had nodded off. When the commercial ended and the director switched back to me on camera, I just sat there, eyes closed. One of the studio cameramen finally noticed, and in a loud stage whisper said, "Bob . . . Bob . . ." I jerked awake and finished the newscast. I returned to the newsroom mortified and expected the telephone switchboard to be jammed with calls of complaints, but amazingly few of our viewers had apparently noticed. Some of them must have nodded off, too. In any case, we got only one or two calls.

After about six months on the job, I was convinced I was ready for the networks, a view apparently shared by no one, at least not at any of the networks. I sent out letters and tapes to CBS, NBC and ABC. I got a polite turndown from CBS and never heard from the others. The turndowns were for the best. I wasn't ready for the networks by then, and if I had left Fort Worth at that point in my life, I would probably have missed the most important phone call of my life.

The call came one afternoon in January 1967, and I almost jumped out of my chair when the caller said, "Bob, this is George Ann Carter, what are you doing?" George Ann was the glamorous wife of the *Star-Telegram* publisher and Channel 5 owner, Amon Carter, Jr. The Carters had been very nice to me when I returned from Vietnam, and Amon and his sister Ruth had given a coming-home party for me, but I can't remember having passed more than a few words with them before that. For sure, phone calls from Amon's wife were not part of my usual afternoon routine. I couldn't imagine why she had called and I had no idea what to say, so I just responded, "Well, I'm sitting here, Mrs. Carter. What can I do for you?" She asked if I had a girlfriend. The first question had been a shock, but this was like the aftershock of an earthquake. I was so unnerved, I realized I had risen from behind my desk and was standing up. Mrs. Carter went on to explain that she had a friend she wanted me to meet. Since George Ann was the publisher's wife, I figured I really had no choice, and the following Sunday, I made my way to the Carters' home in Westover Hills, Fort Worth's high-rent district. It was a neighborhood of beautiful, stately mansions. I could remember having driven through it as a child with my parents when we took our annual holiday drives to look at Christmas lights and decorations. But as an adult, I had probably been in that neighborhood no more than two or three times. I was still driving my old Triumph sports car, and it had become such a wreck by this time that I had borrowed my mother's car on that afternoon. The Triumph hadn't been good enough to drive Lee

Harvey Oswald's mother to Dallas, and I wasn't about to drive it into Westover Hills.

The Carters' home was a beautiful Georgian mansion, and the woman George Ann wanted me to meet was the daughter of her next-door neighbor Neville Penrose, a well-known Fort Worth civic leader and a fixture in state Democratic politics. Penrose was a colorful character who had run away as a teenager to Mexico, where, among other things, he had been twice captured by the Mexican revolutionary Pancho Villa. He had spent many years in Mexico before eventually settling in Fort Worth, where he became a successful businessman. I knew him by reputation and because of his work in politics, and his daughter turned out to be a cute blonde named Pat who had begun writing a society column at the *Star-Telegram* while I was away in Vietnam. Her aunt had heard me give one of my Vietnam lectures, and on a lark, Pat had asked George Ann to introduce us. If there really is love at first sight, we must have caught it. Pat and I went to dinner that night at a little Italian restaurant on Fort Worth's west side, where as children we had both gone to eat many times with our parents. She liked news as much as I did, and we talked long into the night about Vietnam and politics and the courthouse. It must have been a good conversation. Three weeks later, we decided to get married and, so we would never

161

forget it, set the date for April 15, income tax day.

We were married on that date in a small ceremony at Ridglea Presbyterian Church. Pat had won two airplane tickets to Acapulco in a raffle and we flew there for our honeymoon. It was an outing to remember. On the second night, a minor earthquake rattled the chandeliers in our hotel. (Yes, we thought the earth moved.) On the third day, Pat almost drowned. We had been bodysurfing off the beach when a huge wave swamped her and left her bikini top around her ankles. Instead of swimming, she began groping for her top and went under. I was laughing so hard, I didn't realize she was in trouble until two beach boys raced by me, dived into the wave, fished her out and brought her to shore. Three weeks later, back in Fort Worth, I discovered I had contracted hepatitis from eating Acapulco shellfish, and spent the next six weeks in bed. But at thirty-five years and counting, we're still married. Once we got through the honeymoon, the rest was easy.

As 1967 came to a close, we had purchased a small house and Pat had turned it into the prettiest home I had ever seen. Because I was thirty and she was twenty-eight (old for newlyweds in those days), we wanted to start a family immediately. It was a good time for us, but in Vietnam, the war was going badly and casualties continued to rise. Most nights, I would begin the news with another grim report from Vietnam.

As the war got worse, there were continuing reports that Robert Kennedy, the slain president's brother who had been elected to the Senate from New York in 1964, would challenge Johnson for the presidency, and indeed Kennedy was torn by whether he ought to run.

Many years later, his longtime advisor Fred Dutton told me, "He didn't like Johnson and he was worried about the war, but he didn't want to destroy the party, so he kept putting it off."

One of those who had been watching Kennedy was Eugene McCarthy, a gadfly poet and senator from Minnesota, who was little known to us in Texas. As Kennedy pondered, McCarthy decided something had to be done. He had been among the first senators to speak out against the war, and late in the year he decided if no one else was going to do it, he would. He would challenge the sitting president of his own party.

"People thought Bobby Kennedy was going to run," he told me in an interview for this book, "so I went to see him and he told me he would not run under any foreseeable circumstances. He told me he had his future to consider. I think what he meant was that he did want to run for president someday, but he didn't think he could beat Lyndon, and he thought that if Lyndon beat him he would be finished. So we shook hands and I announced that I would challenge Johnson."

Four months later, when McCarthy stunned the nation (and himself) by nearly beating Johnson in the New Hampshire primary, Kennedy reversed himself and got into the race.

In Texas, it was widely believed, even by the politically astute governor, John Connally, that McCarthy had been a stalking horse for Kennedy. McCarthy was anything but that. He had enjoyed a friendly relationship with Kennedy's older brother John, but, as he told me more than three decades later, he had had no relationship with Bobby. Had Bobby decided to run in the beginning, McCarthy wouldn't have, but when Kennedy decided to run only after McCarthy's showing in New Hampshire demonstrated that Johnson was vulnerable, he created a breach with McCarthy that never healed.

"In politics, when they smell blood, there are no principles," McCarthy told me.

There would be too much blood in 1968. It would be the bloodiest year in America since the Civil War, a year when the country seemed to be falling apart.

# Nine

## *1968*

"When sorrows come, they come not in single spies, but in battalions." Shakespeare had written that some four hundred years earlier, but he could have been referring to 1968. There had never been a year like it in America. Vietnam exploded. Martin Luther King, Jr., was assassinated. The cities burned. Robert Kennedy was killed by a crazed Palestinian. The Democratic Convention in Chicago spawned a riot over the war and Lyndon Johnson shocked the country by announcing he would not seek reelection. As surprise turned to shock, and shock turned to tragedy, serious people wondered if the country was coming apart. "For the first and only time in my life," Walter Mondale told me one day, "I wondered whether the anger and venom that had taken over American life was going to bring it down."

By chance, Pat and I were in New York the weekend that Johnson told the nation on television that he would not seek and would not accept the nomination of his party. We heard the news from a cabbie and couldn't believe it, returned to our hotel, turned on the late television news and called friends at home to see what they knew. The trip to New York had not been altogether pleasant and, for me, Johnson's announcement made it worse. We hadn't been out of town since our honeymoon, so we had taken a long weekend and flown to the Big City. Pat wanted to see some plays and I was making one more stab at getting the networks to hire me. The visit to Broadway had been more enjoyable than my mission to NBC. Jim Byron, my Channel 5 boss, set up an appointment for me with some of the NBC people who would be running the network's convention coverage that summer, and the meeting couldn't have gone worse. In fact, I would rank it among the more humiliating experiences of my life.

In those days the networks hired stringers to cover the state delegations at the national conventions, and I had come to apply for the stringer job covering the Texas delegations. I thought it would be a way to see the conventions and maybe get my foot in the door for a network job. I arrived at NBC at the appointed time and was directed into an office, where I was greeted by two executives who seemed confused about why I had come to see them. I outlined what I had in mind, but about five minutes into the session, it became clear the executives had no interest in me or my ideas, and that the meeting had been set up only because someone at the network's affiliate-relations department had asked them to see me as a courtesy. One of them asked why I had spent my own money on an airplane ticket to apply for such a minor job. When I said the trip also included some vacation, the other said something to the effect that since that was the case, the trip wouldn't be a complete waste. I took it from that remark that I would not be joining the NBC News team that summer, and excused myself.

I had never felt lower, and when we heard later that Johnson had taken himself out of the race, I was even gloomier. With Johnson out, the race would be wide open and the story would be even better. And among those who would not be covering it was young Bob Schieffer of Fort Worth, Texas. So we flew home the next day, dejected because I had been unable to wrangle a way to get to the political conventions, and puzzled by Johnson's decision.

There had been no indication of it publicly, but as I would later learn, Johnson had been contemplating quitting the race for more than six months. He believed that such a grand gesture might convince the North Vietnamese that he was serious about bringing the war to a peaceful conclusion. But it was not until January, his aides told me, when

North Vietnam launched the Tet Offensive, a coordinated attack involving thousands of enemy troops who attacked more than a hundred cities and towns across South Vietnam, that he concluded the war could not be won. The invaders were eventually driven back from all the cities, and the American generals declared victory, claiming the Communist offensive had failed. Johnson knew better. George Christian, who was Johnson's press secretary and one of his closest advisors, said, "The generals tried to tell him that the Communists had lost because so many of the Viet Cong had been killed. But when he saw those attacks on all those villages that the generals had told him were pacified, he knew what it meant and he knew what the country would think of it."

Johnson's private disillusionment reflected the growing skepticism about the war that had begun to settle over the country. After Tet, the war protests became more violent. Walter Cronkite had gone to Vietnam in the days after Tet and returned to report that the war couldn't be won. Cronkite almost never expressed an opinion in his reports, and because he did so on his return from Vietnam, his words had added impact. What he said in essence was that the United States should begin to look for a way out. The broadcast prompted Johnson to make the oft-quoted remark, "If I've lost Cronkite, I've lost the country." Ironically, Johnson never saw the actual Cronkite broadcast. Christian told me Johnson apparently saw some clips of it the next morning, and Christian told him what Cronkite had concluded. "That's when he made the remark about Cronkite. But he knew then, that it would take more time than Americans were willing to give it."

In the weeks before Tet, thousands of college students from the Northeast had invaded New Hampshire, site of the first presidential primary in March. Eugene McCarthy had formally announced he would oppose Johnson on January 3. Johnson had considered McCarthy little more than a nuisance then. He had always been convinced that if anyone challenged him for the nomination, it would be Bobby Kennedy. But after Tet, McCarthy had to be taken seriously. Even so, no one expected what happened next: McCarthy came within 230 votes of defeating Johnson, a sitting president. Little remembered is that Johnson's name had not been on the ballot. All his votes had been the result of a write-in campaign. The press declared McCarthy the winner.

Winner or not, he had made an astonishing showing and presidential politics was turned on its head. For McCarthy, the candidate that neither the press nor the White House had really taken seriously in the beginning, victory was sweet. But it was also short. He returned to Washington the next morning, but before his plane landed, the wire services were already carrying stories that Robert Kennedy was "reassessing" his previous decision not to run. The euphoria that had engulfed the McCarthy campaign the night before evaporated. "It was like Christmas morning for our kids," McCarthy told me. "Santa Claus had come, but before they could get to the tree, Bobby had stolen the presents." Within a week, Kennedy made it official. He, too, would seek the Democratic nomination.

It wasn't like Christmas for Lyndon Johnson. Johnson had loathed Bobby Kennedy since the 1960 convention, when Bobby had tried to block his brother from putting Johnson on the ticket as Jack's vice presidential running mate. Johnson was convinced (and it is hard to argue otherwise) that Kennedy would not have carried Texas and the few southern states that gave him his narrow victory had he (Johnson) not been on the ticket. He had never felt that Bobby Kennedy gave him the credit he deserved, and throughout Kennedy's term, felt that Bobby went out of his way to slight him. Christian says Johnson had always believed Bobby Kennedy would run against him in '68 and, in the beginning, believed he could beat him, but as the war grew worse, Johnson talked more and more about his health, repeatedly saying he did not believe he could live long enough to serve a full term. The more he agonized, the more he became convinced that only by dropping out of the race could he convince North Vietnam's leaders that he was serious about wanting peace. There is also no question that, looming over all this, was the possibility that if he did stay in the race, he ran the risk of being beaten for the nomination of his own party by Kennedy.

Sometime in the two weeks after the New Hampshire primary, Johnson finally made up his mind not to run. Or as finally as Lyndon Johnson ever made up his mind about anything.

"He was hell-bent to get the North Vietnamese to talk," George Christian told me in the spring of 2001. "He always thought there was something he could do that would appeal to them. He thought this would be a way to show them he was serious and get it over with. But the truth was, there wasn't anything that appealed to them."

On March 27, two days before his scheduled television address to the nation, Johnson called Christian, and two other aides, Marvin Watson and Jim Jones (later an Oklahoma congressman and ambassador to Mexico), and told them he had decided not to run. "Marvin urged him to reconsider, and George and I told him he had done the right

171

thing," Jones later told me, "but Johnson himself kept going back and forth.

"The speech was scheduled for ten that night, and at six o'clock Johnson was getting a haircut, and Arthur Krim (a longtime Johnson friend and advisor), was right there, still urging him to run while Johnson was getting his haircut. We really weren't sure he would do it till we stuffed it in the TelePrompTer and he read it on the air."

The announcement caught the nation totally by surprise. No one in the Washington political community had anticipated it; no one across the country had expected it. Nothing more accurately reflected the nation's astonishment than the reaction of a round table that had been assembled by CBS News after the president's announcement. When Walter Cronkite turned to Roger Mudd for analysis, the veteran political correspondent replied, "I'd like to go home and think about it and come back tomorrow and tell you."

In a year when the unexpected became routine, whatever was wrong in America somehow came to a boil in the summer of 1968. Johnson had pushed landmark civil rights legislation through Congress, but the struggle for equality turned increasingly violent. In April, four days after Johnson announced he was not a candidate for reelection, Martin Luther King, Jr., was killed by a sniper. A nation that was becoming accustomed to surprise had been stunned again. And each surprise seemed to get worse. King's death set off rioting in the big cities of the country, including Washington, D.C. Neighborhoods burned within two blocks of the White House. In June, it happened again. On the night that he won his most important primary victory in California, Robert Kennedy was fatally shot by a deranged Palestinian-American who had apparently become enraged when he saw Kennedy wearing a yarmulke during an appearance at a synagogue. Again the nation would sit transfixed before its televisions, watching the Kennedy family, the women in black funeral veils, the men in mourning suits, the children — all those children — in their Sunday best, as they went through the ordeal of yet another funeral.

Despite my mangled attempts to get a job that would take me to the conventions, Pat and I did manage to get to Chicago that summer, and it was Pat's doing. Like her father, she had always been active in local Democratic politics and as a member of the state Democratic executive committee, she was invited as a guest. We decided to go. I wouldn't be covering the story, but neither of us had ever been to a national convention, and at the least I would be able to see one of them as the "spouse of." Since it wouldn't be a working trip for me, we decided to see a little of the country and drive to Chicago. I was still having no luck at finding a job with a national news organization, but I was convinced I would find something eventually, and for us there had been only one real disappointment in our lives. It appeared we would not be blessed with children. So on the Friday before we set out for Chicago, Pat made an appointment for later that year at the Edna Gladney Home to start adoption proceedings.

We arrived in St. Louis about dark, after becoming hopelessly lost in East St. Louis. This led to our first celebration of the ancient marital ritual, "the car fight," but we eventually found our way and had dinner at Stan Musial's restaurant. There I discovered the second great surprise of our young marriage. Pat did not share my enthusiasm for baseball and had no idea who Stan the Man was, but it was a nice dinner and we went on to Chicago the next day. By the time we found the Conrad Hilton Hotel, where the Texas delegation was headquartered, we knew this would be no ordinary political gathering. Protestors were already filling the parks in front of the hotel, police were everywhere and that night a group called the Yippies had their first run-in with the cops. National Guard units could also be seen, but we would later learn that we saw only a small part of the security forces that had been deployed. Eugene McCarthy, who still believes his rooms were bugged, saw all the elements in place for a fascist takeover. The possibility of that still seems remote, but the force that Johnson and Chicago mayor Daley assembled was enormous. Five Chicago schools were commandeered as barracks for more than 7,500 National Guardsmen; nearly 12,000 Chicago police were placed on twelve-hour shifts; 1,000 FBI and Secret Service agents were dispatched from Washington; and 7,500 regular Army troops from around the country were placed on alert for possible Chicago duty. The convention hall itself looked like a military camp. A one-square-mile security area had been set up around it, and the convention hall itself was surrounded by chain-link fences topped by barbed wire.

What happened in Chicago has been well documented and requires little additional description here. The inevitable clash between the enormous security force and the young protestors happened, and in what proved to be a perfect setting for the demonstrators to get maximum exposure — the parks that fronted the hotels where many of the delegates were housed and where the major candidates had set up headquarters. In retrospect, there seems little question the demonstrators wanted a fight and taunted the police, but the police response was inexcusable. Young people were beaten and clubbed, and news reporters had equipment smashed. Under the eerie glare of the TV lights, the demonstrators shouted, "The whole world is watching." Somehow, it was as if all of America's problems and grievances had come to Chicago, put themselves on display, dared the authorities to interfere and asked the country to judge them. It was not just the argument over the war, but the clash between the old politics and the new, the cultural divide the war had created among parents and children, men and women, and the meaning of patriotism.

Pat and I soon realized that those who were watching on television saw more of it than we did. We had gone with the Texas delegation to the convention hall by bus each evening and were inside the hall and unaware of the trouble outside. But when we returned to our hotel on Wednesday night, we understood how serious the situation had become. Glass windows on the hotel's first floor had been smashed. Fire hoses were spread through the hotel lobby, and the air was filled with the smell of tear gas and stink bombs. The next night, I was in the lobby when police rushed into the hotel and broke into the rooms of some of the McCarthy delegates whom they accused of throwing objects from their windows. We saw blood on the hotel carpets that night, and at one point I saw McCarthy confront the police and finally convince them to leave.

I went back to Chicago in 1996 to prepare a report for the *CBS Evening News*, because the Democrats had decided to hold their convention there to nominate Bill Clinton for a second term. I retraced the demonstrators' route on the night of the riots with Tom Hayden, who had been one of the demonstration organizers. He said that, in time, he'd realized that Chicago had been so much more than a war protest. It had become a place where America had tested its long-held core beliefs. "My father's generation was absolutely wedded to the belief that the government always told the truth," he said. "We were saying that's not always the case." The next day, I flew to Minnesota with CBS News producer Bridget Murphy to talk to Walter Mondale, who was home on leave from his post as U.S. ambassador to Japan. By then, Mondale had already served as Jimmy Carter's vice president, and in 1980 had waged his own campaign for president, but as we sat on the deck of his Minnesota vacation home, he told me Chicago in '68 would be with him always. He had been one of Hubert Humphrey's young supporters in those days and had gone to Chicago to help Humphrey get the presidential nomination, but it was a sad mission. Humphrey's support for the war had cost him many of his lifelong friends. "The war had just snapped those relationships," Mondale said. Humphrey was also morose about reports that Johnson had lost confidence in him and was secretly plotting to reenter the race and secure the nomination for himself. Once it became clear that Johnson would not try to engineer the convention into drafting him, Humphrey was confident the nomination was his. But when trouble erupted in the streets, Mondale and the others felt the nomination was all but worthless. It was not just Humphrey's chances that worried Mondale as he left Chicago. He was worried about the country, worried that it was falling apart, and it was a feeling that would haunt him for many years. As we sat there that summer afternoon in 1996, he recalled Lincoln's quote that "with public trust, all things are possible, and without it, nothing is possible."

"I think," he said, "that some of our difficulties today stem from the fact that Americans have never trusted again as fully as they did before that war."

Mondale's revelation that Humphrey had worried about Johnson plotting against him intrigued me. We had heard rumors of such maneuvering during the convention and there was speculation about it over the years, but it was not until I began to retrace the events in Chicago for this book that I learned that the maneuvering had actually begun in the hours after Johnson announced he would not be a candidate in March of 1968.

"I was standing there," said Jim Jones, his young aide at the time. "One of the first people he talked to was Nelson Rockefeller." Nelson Rockefeller? The Republican governor of New York? "Oh yes," said Jones. "Johnson was a great admirer of Rockefeller. He told him, 'you've got to get high and behind . . . you are my first choice.' "

Joe Califano, another of Johnson's aides and later Jimmy Carter's secretary of Health, Education and Welfare, didn't know of the phone call, but he wrote about Johnson's admiration for Rockefeller in his book *The Triumph and Tragedy of Lyndon Johnson*, perhaps the best book about the Johnson years. Califano reported that several times after Johnson dropped out of the race, he had Rockefeller and his wife to dinner at the White House to urge him to seek the Republican nomination. There were several reasons: Johnson believed that only Rockefeller could carry out Johnson's Great Society programs. And, if Bobby Kennedy had gotten the nomination, Johnson thought Rockefeller was the only Republican who could have beaten him.

George Christian, Jim Jones and Larry Temple, the aides who were closest to Johnson that summer, agreed about Johnson's admiration for Rockefeller, but none of them

179

believed he would have openly supported Rockefeller or endorsed him over a Democrat. Califano is not so sure. Had Rockefeller gotten the nomination that year, Califano believes Johnson may well have endorsed him. "I always thought there was a very real possibility he would have done it," Califano told me. "He really admired him." Whatever the case, the story confirms what Humphrey suspected. Lyndon Johnson had little use for him. (Records at the LBJ Library show there was a telephone call between Johnson and Rockefeller on the day of Johnson's withdrawal and that the conversation was taped. It is scheduled to be made public in 2003.)

As spring had turned to summer, Johnson's dramatic withdrawal had not had the intended effect on the North Vietnamese. Not only did it not spark peace talks; the North Vietnamese ignored it. As George Christian had feared, there was nothing Johnson could do that would appeal to North Vietnam. They were winning.

That was when Johnson began to second-guess his decision to withdraw from the race, and as the convention in Chicago opened, it was clear that, while he was not a candidate — at least not publicly — Johnson and his people were in charge. It was Johnson who had selected the convention site, and Johnson's people (in close coordination with Chicago mayor Richard Daley) who controlled every aspect of it. Johnson's people controlled all the phones and all the microphones within the hall, to ensure that no one on the convention floor could speak out unless the Johnson forces approved it. Johnson's sixtieth birthday fell during the convention, and plans were made for a huge celebration. Daley planned to have an enormous cake baked. Huge electric candles were placed behind a barrier below the speaker's podium. The candles were placed on a lift and were to rise into view when the convention sang Happy Birthday to Lyndon. Was it all a cover to get Johnson to the convention and, once there, draft him to be the nominee even though he had pulled out of the race? "I always thought so," Mondale told me. "I always wondered if he didn't want a big birthday celebration followed by a call to run again."

George Christian wondered about that, too. In the weeks before the convention, Johnson had gone to his ranch in Texas. His aides Jim Jones and Larry Temple were at the ranch with him; Christian was in San Antonio, where the White House press corps had been quartered; and Texas governor John Connally was running the Johnson forces in Chicago. His purported purpose was to ensure that the convention platform on Vietnam conformed to White House policy.

There is no question in the minds of Christian, Jones and Temple that Johnson wanted to go to Chicago that summer. But to secure the nomination for himself?

First, Christian: "Oh, he would have loved it. He was very ambivalent about Humphrey and he came to question whether he had done the right thing in withdrawing. Humphrey got started late (and Johnson had told his cabinet, which included many of Humphrey's friends, that they could take no part in the campaign). McCarthy's campaign had petered out. Kennedy was dead.

"He thought he had done the right thing for the country in withdrawing and he was proud of what he had done, but it had no impact on the North Vietnamese and he was just unhappy with the lay of the land. In his own mind he was beginning to believe he was the only Democrat who could beat Nixon," Christian said.

In the meantime, Johnson was taking extraordinary steps to build in "deniability" for a connection to whatever might transpire. He never spoke to Connally directly. When Connally would call the ranch from Chicago, Jones or Temple would take the phone. Johnson would position himself on another extension and put his hand over the mouthpiece. When Connally would ask a question or pass on information, Johnson would tell one of the aides, "Tell him thus and so . . ." Connally would then say, "Is that the president's view?" Johnson would shake his head, yes, and the young aides would then answer, "Yes, sir." The aides said they began to feel like Charlie McCarthy sitting on Edgar Bergen's knee. "They were Johnson's words," Jones said. "But they were coming out of my mouth." For all the maneuvering, Jones is convinced Johnson would never have accepted a convention draft. Christian, Califano and Temple are convinced he wanted to be asked.

"I was in mortal fear that he would do something precipitous," Christian said. "I was afraid that he would go to Chicago, and if he had, it would have been a disaster. Even more riots. But I don't doubt for a minute that he had conjured up in his own mind that if he had gone there, he would have been drafted by the convention to run again."

While Christian, Califano and Temple believe Johnson wanted to be drafted, it's another question whether he would have actually run.

"I think he wanted them to offer it to him," Christian said. "And then I think he would have declined. It would have sort of closed the chapter for him." Califano and Temple agreed.

"Some of his old friends still believe he would have run if asked," Temple told me, "but I don't. He wanted that convention to say we love you, you're wonderful, we need you, and then he would have said, 'No thank you.' He was so worried about his health at that point that he had convinced himself he wouldn't live through another term."

In the end, the riots made a trip to Chicago unthinkable and Johnson watched the convention on television from his ranch.

Political conventions are always places of intrigue, but the 1968 Chicago gathering must have set some kind of record in that department. As I tried to pin down the story of Johnson's purported plan to engineer a draft for himself, I ran across an even stranger tale: that at the height of the trouble in Chicago, one of McCarthy's top strategists tried to strike a secret alliance with Johnson's people that would have resulted in having Johnson's lieutenant, John Connally, run for vice president on a ticket headed by McCarthy. It happened this way: As the police clashed with many of McCarthy's supporters outside the Hilton Hotel, Wayne Gibbens, then a young aide to Connally, took a call in Connally's suite from Richard Goodwin. Gibbens was surprised to hear from Goodwin, who had been with the McCarthy campaign early on and then left and joined Kennedy when he got into the race, and then returned to McCarthy's camp after Kennedy's assassination. Goodwin had authored the proposed peace plank in the convention platform that called for a halt in the bombing of North

Vietnam and a withdrawal of U.S. troops, which Connally had successfully quashed. Gibbens wondered what Goodwin could possibly have to discuss with Connally, but the appointment was arranged. Goodwin arrived in Connally's suite and was joined by Bob Strauss, another Texan and Johnson supporter. What the men had to discuss, as Connally later told Gibbens, was whether Connally could somehow swing southern delegates who were for Humphrey, to McCarthy. Why would Connally want to do that? And what would the demonstrators who were outside being beaten by the police have thought if they had known their hero's emissary was making deals with the friends of the devil they opposed? This was not the new politics that the students had talked so much about. This was the old practical politics, and one of the old pols would have told them that a politician can't accomplish much of anything unless he can get elected. This was a long shot, but it was a way to get the nomination for McCarthy. As for Connally, Goodwin said that if he could swing those southern delegates to McCarthy, McCarthy would be grateful, so grateful that he would see Connally in a whole new way. And surely he would want to reward him. Did Goodwin actually offer Connally the vice presidential nomination? Connally seemed to think so. Or at least that is what he told Gibbens. Strauss thought so, too. And still believes it today.

Goodwin does not deny it. When I asked him about it in 2001, he told me that no direct offer was made, but he could understand how Connally might have drawn that from the conversation. "We talked about how he could be a kingmaker," Goodwin said. "He understood what I was saying. And he didn't turn me down. He said he would think about it. It wasn't until a day or so later that he called and said he couldn't help me. I remember it very well."

McCarthy denied being any part of it. He said he had heard about it after the fact and said Goodwin had been freelancing. He said he wouldn't have offered the vice presidency to Connally under any circumstances.

It was too expensive for reporters of local stations to transmit reports back to their home stations from conventions in those days, and since I was a "guest," it didn't seem appropriate for me to file reports from Chicago. Once we were back in Texas, however, I was soon immersed in covering state and local politics, and when Humphrey made a swing through Texas, I covered him at several stops. At one rally, I struck up an acquaintance with Eddie Barker, the news director at the CBS station in Dallas and my competitor on the six o'clock news. In my never-ending quest to land a job at one of the networks, I asked Eddie if he might know someone I could call. He laughed and said he was always happy to help a competitor move out of the area, and offered to send a tape to CBS. I sent him the tape, but nothing ever came of it. I had a fine job, but as for finding a better one, I was still batting zero.

And then one day, it happened. After I had been trying for more than two years to land a job, one dropped in my lap. I was sitting in the Channel 5 newsroom one day in early December when a woman who identified herself as Shirley Barish called and said she represented a New York head-hunting firm. Metromedia, an independent group that owned television stations around the country, was forming a national news team. The company was planning to merge with an insurance company and had long-range plans to start a fourth network. The company had seen a tape of our newscast and wondered if I would be interested in joining their Washington bureau. We made a deal quickly. Pat said she had always wanted to live in Washington and we were on our way. There were no contracts in those days, and when I told my bosses at Channel 5, they couldn't have been nicer and wished me well. Jack Brown, one of my friends at the station, wrote a story about my new job in the company newsletter and described Metromedia as "one step below the networks, a step up we're sure Bob will make shortly." Brown added, "I'm sure Bob is even more confident that he'll step up shortly." Actually, I was. But then, I was fairly cocky in those days.

## 1968 POSTSCRIPT

Humphrey did lose, of course. As Mondale had feared, America couldn't forget the pictures from Chicago. George Wallace, the segregationist governor of Alabama, would use those pictures to rail against the long-haired hippies and he would capture five states across the South. But even as Wallace cut into the conservative vote that should have gone to Nixon in those states, the Republicans swept the Midwest, running on a platform of "law and order," and beat Humphrey in one of the closest elections ever. Nixon got 43.4 percent of the popular vote, Humphrey 42.7 percent and Wallace 13.5 percent.

Johnson, as he himself had predicted, did not live long. He worked with no success to end the war until the day he left office and returned to Texas, where he brought the same intensity to running his ranch that he had brought to the presidency. "Once a week or so, he would bring in eggs from the ranch and sell them to employees at his television station for sixty cents a dozen," Temple said. Johnson died four years and two days after he had left office, two days after Nixon's second inaugural. Temple believed Johnson would have lived longer had he been reelected. "He started smoking again after he left Washington. He hadn't done that while he was president because of his heart trouble," Temple said. "He felt he owed it to the country not to smoke, but once he left the White House, he said he had always wanted a cigarette, so he started back. He also started drinking more and really got out of shape." The man who had spent so much of his life talking, wheeling, dealing and cajoling had been reaching for the phone when his heart finally gave out. It was a broken heart, many of his friends thought. The war had broken it. Success in Vietnam had been the one deal the great deal-maker had never been able to make.

Gene McCarthy was several months past his eighty-fifth birthday when I interviewed him. He has never really forgiven Bobby Kennedy for running against him in 1968, but he has softened toward many of the others, including Lyndon Johnson.

"Bobby was just too young to run for president," he told me one afternoon. "He had been too young when Jack made him attorney general. Too young for so much power."

McCarthy said he always got on well with Bobby's older brother, whom he recalled as someone who never took himself too seriously. He recalled one day when both had served in the House of Representatives and he came upon Kennedy in a cloakroom, with his feet up. "You know," Kennedy told him, "if you don't want to work, this is as good a place as any to have a job."

The difference between Jack and Bobby? "Oh, if Jack was going to screw you, he would tell you first," McCarthy said. "If he had been the one running against me in 'sixty-eight, he would have called me and given some excuse for doing it."

As for the campaign itself, McCarthy said he could never forgive Kennedy for misrepresenting McCarthy's record. He remains most upset about a remark Kennedy made during a debate before the California primary. McCarthy had suggested that ghettos be dispersed, and Kennedy had responded, "You say you are going to take ten thousand black people and move them into Orange County?"

McCarthy's feelings toward Johnson have mellowed. He makes no apology for his opposition to the war. He believes it was the right thing to do, the only thing to do, and someone had to do it. But he has developed some empathy for Johnson.

"I've been reading some transcripts of his tapes," McCarthy said, "and the more I read about it, I feel kind of sorry for him. He knew he was in an impossible situation and he was beset on every side. He had the Kennedys scaring him, and the Army, and he had his own image of himself to think about. He didn't want to be the one to lose a war."

McCarthy recalled a time in 1963 when Johnson had been vice president. He had little to do and would come to the office that is maintained for vice presidents off the Senate floor. As stragglers came off the floor, McCarthy said, Johnson would corral them and bring them into his office.

"The Democrats had increased their numbers in the sixty-two election," McCarthy said, "and one afternoon he had Muskie, Humphrey, and Phil Hart and me in there, and he started talking about how the Democrats should be picking a fight over civil rights at that moment."

He said the opponents to civil rights legislation were in bad health — Byrd of Virginia was just out of the hospital, Russell of Georgia thought he had cancer, Ellender of Louisiana was in the hospital, and Fulbright of Arkansas and Long of Louisiana, who had opposed civil rights legislation on occasion, "don't really give a shit" one way or the other.

"He told us that left only two able-bodied senators who were ready to oppose civil rights legislation and then said, 'Hell, they're old and we can break them with a good, hard two-week filibuster.'

"That's the kind of killer he was," McCarthy said. "And you had to like him for it."

McCarthy admitted he had said some

harsh things about Johnson.

"I once described what musical instruments were suitable for various politicians to play," McCarthy said. "Humphrey, for instance, I saw as a bass drummer. Johnson, I said, reminded me of an accordion player, and then I asked, 'Did you ever see a serious review of an accordion concert?' It was mean, and I shouldn't have said it."

But then the old twinkle returned to his eye, and he added, "But he did remind me of an accordion player. Someone playing that old squeeze box . . ."

As for Pat and me, we spent the Christmas season preparing for our move to Washington. We never kept the appointment to start adoption proceedings. Several weeks after the convention, we realized we wouldn't need to, and exactly nine months to the day after the turmoil in Chicago, Susan Neville Schieffer made her entrance into the world. Susan was in high school before she made the connection between Chicago and her birth.

"So Mom," she said one day, "I guess there was more than fighting in the streets in Chicago."

The Democrats' return to Chicago in 1996 had its own romantic twist for Susan. She went with us and reconnected with Steven Eichenauer, who had been a friend in graduate school at the University of Texas. They began dating when they returned to Washington, eventually married and are the proud parents of twin girls.

In the Schieffer family, Chicago is a place that holds fond memories.

# Ten

## *Washington*

In January 1969, I set out for Washington and my new job. I was so consumed by the idea of working in Washington in a job that I was sure would lead to the networks that it never occurred to me to think of the load I was putting on Pat. By now she was four months pregnant and just getting over her morning sickness. Not only was I asking her to give up her newspaper column and a wonderful life and friends in a town where she had grown up; I thought nothing of leaving her behind to handle those small details of selling the house and moving. The girl must have loved me. She still says she didn't mind.

I arrived in Washington as most of the Texans were leaving. Lyndon Johnson's term was ending, and in a matter of days Richard Nixon would become president. I reported to my new station, WTTG, the Metromedia outlet in Washington, and learned my first assignment would be to cover the Nixon Inaugural. This was the kind of thing I had always dreamed of, but as the newest reporter on the staff, I didn't get one of the plum assignments. Hundreds of young antiwar protestors had poured into Washington along with Nixon's button-down, middle-age partisans, and my job would be to cover the demonstrators. I've had better jobs. It had rained most of the week, Nixon's people spent most of their time indoors and I spent most of my time outdoors with the protestors. The high point for me, if you can call it that, came on the day the Yippies went to the Washington Monument to hold their own inaugural ceremony. The same group had nominated a pig for president during the Democratic Convention in Chicago and had set off a near riot when they turned the porker loose in a crowd. This time, they intended to swear in the pig as president. So, as the political reporters covered Nixon's swearing-in at the Capitol, I was an eyewitness to a group reading the solemn oath to a pig. By then, the rains had turned the parkland around the monument into a quagmire, and when the pig was let loose, the scene became something out of a Keystone Kops movie. People were slipping and sliding, throwing mud balls, and even those who declined to give chase were soon covered with mud.

I called my mom the next day. None of our Metromedia coverage had been seen in Fort Worth, but she had seen the ceremonies and the Inaugural balls that night on the networks, and she said it must have been thrilling to see it all in person.

She was a little disappointed when I told her I had seen none of it and had not even managed to get indoors. In truth, I had seen a small piece of the Inaugural. Once I was done with the Yippies, I had managed to get over to Pennsylvania Avenue and see a group of protestors boo Nixon's limo as it passed by during the parade.

My new colleagues at Metromedia were a talented group, many of whom would go on to make their own marks on national television. Metromedia's vice president for news, Ed Turner, would eventually join CNN and was a key figure in making it into the formidable news-gathering operation it is today. The station's noon talk show was hosted by Barbara Howar, who had once been an intimate of the Johnson family and would later become a bestselling author, and Maury Povich, son of the legendary *Washington Post* sportswriter Shirley Povich, who went on to host several syndicated talk shows. A recent graduate of the University of Maryland, Connie Chung, had joined the station as a newswriter several weeks before I came there. Some years later, she and Povich would marry. Our immediate boss was a man named Mike Buchanan, who would become a fixture in Washington television and now anchors the local morning news on CBS's

Washington affiliate, WUSA, where Susan Olney, who was Metromedia's star reporter, is now a top producer.

They were all good people, and we had fun together, but I soon realized the job was not at all what I thought it was. Shortly before I arrived, the proposed merger between Metromedia and an insurance company had fallen through and, with it, Metromedia's plan to become the fourth network. What that meant for me was that instead of covering national news, I would be covering local news in a town where I really had no interest in the local scene. In Fort Worth, what the county commissioners were doing was one thing. I had lived there all my life. What the Washington City Council was up to held no more interest for me than if they were local officials in Transylvania. I had come to Washington to cover national news, but I discovered that whenever I tried to check out a national story, I was usually rebuffed. When I called a congressman's office, I was usually asked, "Are you a local or national?" When I was forced to say "local," more often than not I was turned down for an interview. A member of Congress has no interest in being on television unless the broadcast will be seen in his home district. I did find one way around that. Metromedia had stations in New York, Los Angeles and Chicago, and our reports were occasionally seen on stations there, so if it was a congressman from one of those areas I would identify myself as being from the station in his district and I usually got through.

But this was not the job I wanted to be doing. Nor was it nearly as good a job as I'd had back in Fort Worth. As was often the case when I took better jobs in my career, I had taken a pay cut to come to Washington (just as I had taken a pay cut when I left KXOL to go to the *Star-Telegram*). The job itself was not that difficult. I reported to the office around noon each day, and was usually given an assignment covering some protest group that had a beef with one of the local governmental bodies or some obscure bureaucracy in the Maryland or Virginia suburbs. We didn't have beat reporters covering any of these entities. Like most local stations in those days, we generally waited until a story appeared in that day's *Washington Post* and then followed up with our own stories. As the other reporters did, I would sometimes cover several stories and appear that night in two or more segments of our feature newscast, *The Ten O'Clock News*. The newscast was an hour long, and in addition to writing our own stories that we had covered in the field, we were expected to write the anchorman's copy in the segment in which our reports appeared. I had little to complain about, and in a matter of weeks, I was getting most of the choice assignments, but once I realized that Metromedia was not going to become a national network, I lost all interest in it. One night, I returned home from work and told Pat I thought we ought to go back to Fort Worth. She just looked at me. By then she was nearly seven months pregnant, and on her own, with no help from me, had sold our Fort Worth house, moved our furniture to Washington and supervised the renovation of our new home there. "But we just got here," she said, "and now you want to go back? Can we think about this?"

I told her I couldn't stand the job. It wasn't what I thought it was going to be and I saw no reason to keep on with something that wasn't going to get me where I wanted to go.

"Well, we can't move until I have this baby," she told me. "Maybe you can think about it in the meantime."

The next day, I decided to make one last effort to get a job at the networks. CBS had always been my favorite, mainly because Walter Cronkite had always been my favorite broadcaster, so I decided to start at the CBS News Washington bureau. Of all the people who have ever passed through CBS, surely the story of how I got hired is the oddest. After years of applying for a job there, I literally walked in off the street, and in a matter of days was hired. Today, there are consultants who have made a profession out of advising young reporters how to apply for jobs, what to say during job interviews and how to prepare résumés and audition tapes. Most reporters, by the time they have enough experience to be considered for positions at the networks, are already represented by agents who maintain contact with network executives. Many top-flight reporters had agents in those days as well, but all that was unknown to me in 1969. I simply gathered up several tapes of stories I had done and assembled twelve pages of written material about myself. It was not so much a résumé as a short biography that included every journalism prize I had ever won from junior high school on. About the only thing the narrative did not include was that I had been born in a log cabin. (I hadn't, of course, but such an assertion would have fit right in to that self-congratulatory document.) Since I had been turned down in every other attempt I had made to apply for a job at CBS, I didn't call ahead for an appointment. I just barged in the bureau's front door at 2020 M Street and announced I had come to see Bill Small, the bureau chief. These days, of course, I wouldn't have made it past the security guards, but there were no guards in those days, only two telephone switchboard operators who doubled as receptionists. Neither asked if I had an appointment and they directed me to the second floor.

I presented myself to the first person I saw, who turned out to be Marge Geddes, Bill Small's secretary. I gave my name and announced I had come to apply for a job.

"Oh yes," she said, and directed me into Small's office. I was amazed. After all those years of trying to get in to see someone, anyone at CBS, I was being ushered into the office of the chief of CBS News's biggest and most important bureau without even a wait. There was little time to rejoice. To say that Small was tough or that he could be imposing or downright rude when he chose, would be an understatement. He motioned me to sit down and then gave me a withering look and asked, "Well, what do you want?"

It was not the sort of opening gambit to put one at ease, and I all but jumped out of my chair. "Oh," I said, "why, I've come to look for a job. As you may know, I work over at WTTG across town, but I've always wanted to work at CBS News and I've brought some tapes and a biography."

"I don't watch WTTG," Small said.

Boy, I thought, this is not going all that well.

I said, "I used to work in Fort Worth."

Small said he had never been there.

He thumbed through the résumé as I sat silent. Finally, he looked up and said, "Why would anyone want to know any of this?"

Having no ready answer to that, I responded that perhaps he would get a better idea of my work if he watched my tape.

"I doubt we would have an interest in anyone with a regional accent," he said.

Finally, I said, "Mr. Small. I have a job here in Washington, but it's not what I thought it was. I want to go to work at CBS News and I want to apply for any job that might be available. It doesn't have to be on the air. If you don't hire me, I'm going back to Texas." He said fine, and I left convinced that once again I had been turned down. The hardest part was going home to tell Pat. By now, it had sunk in on me that she was in no mood to sell another house, supervise another move and return to Fort Worth.

A week later, as has happened to me so often in my life when things seemed the worst, something totally unexpected happened. Small called me at WTTG and told me he wanted to talk to me. When I asked about what, he said about going to work for CBS. I was so excited, or unnerved or perhaps just stupid, that I went immediately to the WTTG news director, gave two weeks' notice and announced I was resigning. Only after I was in my car and driving to CBS did it dawn on me that perhaps Small had not really offered me a job, and it suddenly occurred to me, What job did he have in mind? I had applied for anything. This time when I arrived at the bureau, I told the telephone operators,

"I'm the new guy. I just got hired to work here," and I made my way to the second floor and Small's office. He took me into the newsroom and began to introduce me as "Bob Gregory's replacement," and said I would be joining the staff in two weeks when Gregory was scheduled to depart. I had heard Gregory on the radio, and because of that, I realized I had been hired as an on-the-air reporter. Small gave me a quick tour of the bureau and showed me where all the big guns sat. "That's Roger Mudd's office, that's where Dan Rather sits and Dan Schorr is over there," he said.

"And where will I sit?" I asked.

"You won't," he said, "if you want to stay."

I chuckled. He didn't. It dawned on me that he was not kidding, and for at least a year, I never sat, but I came to love and admire Bill Small, the best and toughest boss I ever had, and the person who had more to do with my professional success than any other person. It is still difficult for me to believe how lucky I was to get into the bureau that day and introduce myself to Small. As he later told me, he was about to throw out the résumé I had given him when he noticed that my boss in Fort Worth had been Jim Byron, whom he had come to know in Sigma Delta Chi, the professional journalism society. He had called Byron about some long-forgotten Sigma Delta Chi project and mentioned that

I had been in to see him. He said Byron had given me a terrific buildup and he had hired me on that alone. He never looked at my tape, nor had he plowed through the twelve pages of accomplishments that I had given him. Jim Byron was a broadcast news pioneer, but I had underestimated the respect he commanded among other broadcasters. As Small told me later, "If you were okay with Jimmy Byron, that was all I needed to know."

By coincidence, the three men who had the greatest influence on my professional life — Phil Record, who hired me at the *Star-Telegram*; Byron, who was my first TV boss; and Small, who brought me to CBS — all became national presidents of Sigma Delta Chi.

For years, I wondered how I had managed to get in to see Small without an appointment, and only after I began to write this book did I piece together what had happened. As I was leaving Small's office that day in 1969, I recognized another young reporter who was just getting off the elevator and heading toward Small's office. His name was Robert Hager and he worked at the local NBC affiliate. I remember wondering what he was doing at CBS. Hager had joined the NBC network news staff shortly after that and went on to become one of the best aviation reporters in the country, but as I was preparing this book, I called him one day on a

204

hunch. "By any chance," I asked him, "did you go by to see Bill Small and apply for a job at CBS back in the early part of 1969?"

"I sure did," he said. "I got an appointment to see Small, but nothing came of it, and when NBC offered me a network job, I took it."

What apparently happened was that I had arrived unannounced minutes before Hager was scheduled to see Small. Small's secretary, Marge Geddes, apparently got her Bobs confused, mistook me for Hager and directed me into Small's office.

Sometimes it pays to be in the right place at the right time, even if the people in the right place don't know who you are. Hager, I should add, is a person of considerable grace and we had a good laugh about it.

Pat couldn't have been happier when I called with the news. She knew this was what I had wanted all my life, but I suspect she was even happier that we would not be moving.

"And what's the salary?" she wondered.

I had no idea. I had forgotten to ask. I drove back to WTTG and told my colleagues about it. TV newsrooms can be competitive places — everybody is in competition for stories and everyone is usually trying to move up to the next level — but they all seemed happy for me. The first question young Connie Chung asked was, "Do you know if they need anyone else?" By chance, I had an assignment at the Capitol that afternoon and I ran into Roger Mudd, CBS's congressional correspondent and the biggest star in the network's Washington galaxy. I took the opportunity to introduce myself and to tell him I would soon be joining him as a colleague. I told him I loved politics and hoped to be covering some stories at the Capitol. He looked me up and down and finally said, "Really?" I don't recall that he said anything else.

The next two weeks were the longest of my life. Like a child waiting for Christmas, I couldn't wait to start working for CBS. Finally, on the first Monday in May, I reported to the little red brick three-story building at 2020 M Street that is the Washington headquarters for CBS News, and the following Sunday night, May 11, 1969, my first story for CBS News appeared on Harry Reasoner's weekend news broadcast. It was not the kind of story that would have drawn Eric Sevareid's attention. It was a one-minute report on a masked costume ball that Nixon's daughter Tricia had given at the White House for the sons and daughters of the Washington elite. My only instruction from the Reasoner show producer was to "be droll, if possible. Harry likes droll." Droll or not, the broadcast used the piece, which featured one partygoer whose mask was a likeness of Nixon. I also noted that Tricia Nixon's escort for the evening was Barry Goldwater's son Barry, Jr., who had been sworn in as a member of Congress only four days before.

Drawing on my vast Washington experience — one week at CBS and four months at WTTG — I noted that "Washington tongues, easily wagged, are already wagging that this could be the start of a top-level romance."

The wagging was apparently wrong. As far as I know, it was the only date the two ever had, and the story was little noted nor long remembered outside the Schieffer family. But it was big news at our house. Thirty-two years later, my brother Tom remembered he was at the home of a friend, Joe Longley, in Austin. "Mama called from Fort Worth to tell me you were going to be on and we stopped what we were doing to watch the broadcast. We were just as proud as we could be."

Never, in all my years there or at any other time in my life have I worked harder than I did in those first years, though it didn't seem so at the time. Mr. Small, as the entire bureau, including Roger Mudd, referred to him, had a direct and easily understood management style. He expected total commitment and total loyalty from everyone in the bureau. If news happened, he expected us to be there and cover it, no matter the personal inconvenience. He expected the same commitment from the stars as he expected from the little folks. Once, when Robert Pierpoint, one of the White House correspondents, was celebrating his wedding anniversary with a dinner party, the bureau learned that President Nixon had gone to the home of FBI director J. Edgar Hoover for dinner. Dan Rather had broadcast a report that Nixon was considering dumping Hoover, and the bureau assignment editor called Pierpoint and told him to go to Hoover's home and to wait there until Nixon emerged. Pierpoint protested that his guests were just sitting down to dinner and there was no chance Nixon would talk to him anyway. The assignment editor double-checked with Small, who sent word that Pierpoint was to get himself to Hoover's place at once and remain there until the president left. End of appeal. A dejected Pierpoint left his anniversary party and stood for several hours outside Hoover's door.

"As it happened," Pierpoint later recounted, "when John Ehrlichman (Nixon's aide) and the president came out and tried to get in the car, I was standing in a way that made it hard for them to get by without talking to me. I got about a thirty-five-second interview of Nixon saying, 'Edgar is doing a good job and will stay on.'

"So I had a completely ruined dinner party

and a very unhappy wife, but from the standpoint of the company, we got the story and that kind of thing made him the best bureau chief in town." It should also be added that Pierpoint got no congratulations from Small for his little scoop. It was what he'd expected and he didn't thank people for doing what was expected. Small expected our stories to be better than the competition and that may be one of the reasons they often were. The good side of Small was that if you took your assignments with grace and said nothing about the long hours or the endless weeks with no days off, he took care of you. He steered you the choice assignments during the campaign season and at convention time, and made sure the bosses in New York knew you were doing a good job. Pretty soon, you became one of "Small's guys," and that meant you were on your way. He allowed no one in New York to criticize you, nor did he encourage direct praise from New York. All of it had to be funneled through him. He handed out the kudos and the criticism, and God help the correspondent who tried to go around him or over him. New York gave Small the responsibility for the Washington bureau and, something no other Washington bureau chief had ever really had, the authority to back up that responsibility. It should be added that Small was never bashful about demonstrating that authority to the occasional doubters. If a middle manager in New York decided that a Washington news event might not be worthy of coverage, that almost guaranteed that Small would assign a camera crew and correspondent to cover it. It was his way of telling New York that nobody decided what would or would not be covered in his territory and, more times than not, if Small ordered a story covered, it wound up on one of our newscasts, often Walter Cronkite's flagship broadcast. It was not a bad way to run a bureau, I thought at the time (once I became one of Small's guys), and I still feel the same way. The first requirement for being a successful manager is to make sure, first, that you have the authority to carry out your responsibilities and, second, that your people know what's expected of them. Small demanded the first and made sure we understood the second. We knew what Mr. Small wanted, and most of the time we got it done.

Three weeks after joining the bureau, I had a personal lesson in what the bureau expected. Our first daughter, Susan, was born soon after I came to CBS, and on the day she and Pat were to leave the hospital, I went to the assignment desk and asked the assignment editor, a man named Bill Galbraith, if I could have a half day off. When I told him why, he responded, "Jeez, can't she take a cab?" When I screwed up the courage to say no, she really couldn't, he said, "All right, but we'll need you later in the day."

Pierpoint was right to call Small the best bureau chief in town, and the bureau he headed was also the best. With the pairing of Chet Huntley and David Brinkley, NBC News had become the dominant network news operation through most of the 1960s, but by 1969, Walter Cronkite and his team of star reporters had caught up and passed NBC in the ratings and in influence. The downside of Huntley and Brinkley's success was that Brinkley, who was based in Washington, was a brilliant writer and reported nearly all the Washington news himself. Herbert Kaplow, who was NBC's White House correspondent, almost never got on the air unless the president went out of town. When the president was in Washington, Brinkley handled White House news, as well as most of the news from Capitol Hill, and other beats around town. No matter how good a reporter is, when he can't get his stories on television, the people on his beat don't waste time with him. ABC was just beginning to build a Washington staff, and Sam Donaldson, Ted Koppel and Frank Reynolds would later make their marks, but at that point ABC spent so little on news coverage that it was not yet a real player. Washington's big beats — the White House, State Department, Pentagon and Capitol Hill — became CBS territory.

During Edward R. Murrow's day, the CBS News strength had been built overseas, but during the Cronkite era the core of CBS News became its Washington bureau, where all the beat reporters had become household names. Roger Mudd, who had come to national prominence with around-the-clock coverage of the 1964 civil rights debate, covered Congress, and even the print reporters, usually the most influential reporters on any beat, acknowledged that Roger knew more about Congress than anyone else. Dan Rather had already made his reputation for CBS in Vietnam, and his coverage of the Nixon White House would soon make him the most well-known reporter in America. Daniel Schorr, a tweedy pipe smoker who had a way of irritating government officials (and at times his own colleagues), was as good an investigative reporter as Washington had ever seen. Marvin Kalb covered the State Department. An acknowledged Russian scholar, he had been one of the first Westerners in the late 1950s to recognize that the so-called Sino-Soviet bloc was disintegrating, as the Communist governments of the Soviet Union and China drifted apart. George Herman, who covered the courts and financial matters and anchored *Face the Nation* on Sundays, was the office encyclopedia. He seemed to know something about everything. And then there was Eric Sevareid, the acknowledged first among equals, who provided analysis three times a week on the *Evening News.*

"There will never be another bureau like it," Kalb said. "We all competed with each other for airtime, so there was some internal friction. But it was a pleasure, because you knew you were competing with the best. We thought we were the best, and frankly so did our competitors.

"There was such a remarkable diversity, from Sevareid who was high above us all on cloud 3,411, to Dan Schorr, down below, dogged, digging, never giving up until he had a story. One was so ethereal, one so practical, and that's what made it so remarkable."

A successful team is not always a group of friends. There are twenty-five players on a baseball team, and it was said that when the 1975 Boston Red Sox returned from a road trip, they were met at the airport by twenty-five separate cabs. No one on the team liked anyone else enough to share a ride. Yet on the field they melded together and won the pennant that year, one of the most successful ball clubs of that era. It was somewhat the same with the CBS Washington bureau. The correspondents did not necessarily dislike each other and they were usually cordial, but because of the internal rivalries, professional jealousies and competition for the same stories that develop in large news organizations, there was often an edginess to their relationships and they seldom socialized after work. People were already beginning to speculate on who would replace Walter Cronkite once he decided to retire, and most people in Washington expected the job to go to Mudd. But Rather was emerging as a rival, and there was considerable friction between them. There were also territorial disputes between Rather, the White House correspondent, and Kalb, the State Department correspondent, over who would cover Henry Kissinger, the White House national security advisor who was emerging as Washington's best news source. And then there was Schorr. Someone always seemed to have his nose out of joint over something Schorr had done. He had carved out a beat covering the agencies created by Johnson's Great Society programs, but the boundaries of his beat were loosely defined and he had a way of turning up scoops in what others considered their territory, a habit that made for broader news coverage but one that did not always endear him to the correspondent whose beat had produced the scoop. At one point, Mudd said he began to have nightmares about Schorr.

"He was just everywhere," Mudd said. "To the point that one night, I dreamed I got on the Eastern shuttle flight to New York, and there was Schorr sitting in every seat on the airplane. There must have been a hundred of him on that plane. In one seat, he was reading the paper; in another seat, he was looking out the window; in another seat, he was holding a shopping bag. But he was in every seat, everywhere I looked. I woke up in a sweat."

But like the rest of the bureau, Mudd admired Schorr as a great reporter, and when Watergate happened, it was Schorr, under great pressure and constant attack from the White House, who kept CBS competitive on the story.

"We didn't always get along," Kalb said, "but we respected one another because we understood that, together, we were something special. At the end of the day, we would gather in the newsroom to watch the *Evening News* and we were all proud of it."

As the rookie in the bureau, gathering with the bureau stars to watch the *Evening News* was the best part of the day for me. There was considerable backtalk, banter and razzing as Cronkite introduced the various stories (along with any number of Cronkite imitations . . . "Good EVE-ning . . ."), but the room went silent as the Washington pieces rolled by. If Schorr or Rather or Mudd had a real scoop, it would get an "attaboy" or two, but it was a tough crowd. Any note of pomposity or hype or the occasional grammatical error in a story would draw groans or hoots. On occasion, someone would throw an object if a government official said something that was the least bit self-serving. What I quickly learned was that a reporter wasn't really part of the club until his colleagues had poked a little fun at his story, as they did the night I gave the word *tenterhooks* a Texas pronunciation and said "tenderhooks."

The one member of the bureau who didn't join the crowd watching the news was Sevareid, and when Kalb says he stood far above and apart from the rest of us, it was no exaggeration. He was more than a fellow reporter; he was our ideal, what we had all grown up wanting to be. Part of the original Murrow team, he had become the confidant of Walter Lippmann and Supreme Court justices and presidents, and everyone else who seemed important to us — the dashing war correspondent who had been on the last train out of Paris before the Germans came, the adventurer who had escaped from cannibals after parachuting into the jungles of Burma. While the rest of us chased news stories, he sat in his office and thought great thoughts. He agonized about human nature and man's inhumanity to man and other grand themes the rest of us didn't feel worthy to worry about. And oh, how the man could agonize. He would go into a funk for days over a development in the news, and the more he agonized, the quieter he would become, until he would sometimes speak no louder than a whisper. Gary Gates, who worked on the

*Evening News*, told of a colleague who was invited to lunch with Sevareid. Asked how he would prepare for such an occasion, the colleague replied, "Oh, it's easy. All you need is an interested look and an ear trumpet." Once when he seemed in a particularly dour mood, John Merriman, an *Evening News* editor, reassured a colleague, "Don't worry, it's just one of those days when Eric is suffering from an attack of qualms."

He towered so far above the rest of us that I would have found it easier to slap the Queen of England on the back than to approach him and, as it would turn out, he never spoke to me for the first three years I worked in the bureau. I was afraid to approach him, and I am not sure he even knew I was there. We finally exchanged our first words one day in the men's room. He was at the urinal and I was washing my hands, when he began to talk about some weighty issue of the day. I listened as he concluded his business and when he came to the basin to wash his hands, I said I thought he had put it just right. (What a surprise.) After that, he began to speak to me and eventually we became friends.

What I came to understand was that Sevareid was not aloof, but extremely shy, and our encounter in the men's room had come about because I had interrupted his daily ritual. He arrived at ten each morning, read the newspaper and around noon had lunch with a source, usually a current or former government official or another journalist. He returned to the office around two and wrote his commentary. Once done with it, he repaired to the men's room. During the trip, he would try out his commentary on the first person he encountered. Whatever else he might be doing, he would just clear his throat and say something like, "You know I've been thinking . . ." and then he would launch into the gist of what he planned to say that night on television as if the thought had just popped into his head. We never understood it, but it may have been that he just wanted to hear how it sounded as he said it aloud. I can't imagine anyone ever questioned what he said or suggested another way of saying it. I certainly never did, but once the ice was broken that day in the men's room, he always treated me warmly and became one of my biggest boosters. His was a towering intellect and he was the smartest person I ever knew, but when I think of him, the first image that always comes to my mind's eye is that day I saw him standing at the urinal, rehearsing his commentary on some great issue of the day.

Befitting his stature, Sevareid was the only correspondent whose office had a window. The other stars, Kalb, Rather, Schorr, Mudd and Herman, sat in small alcoves that opened onto the south end of a large newsroom and looked more like display cases than offices.

The lesser stars, such as Pierpoint, Bruce Morton, Nelson Benton, David Schoumacher and Pentagon correspondent Steve Rowan, sat in a row of offices directly behind them; third stringers sat in yet another row of offices behind them; and behind them all were those of us who brought up the rear — Marya McLaughlin, Hal Walker, David Dick and me. The others were called correspondents. We four were called reporters. We had no offices, nor did we have desks. For us, there was a metal mail tray behind the third row of offices. To protest that we had no desks, Marya once brought in some doll furniture — a tiny desk and chair and lamp — and placed it in her mail tray, but it made no difference.

Correspondents got desks. Lowly reporters didn't. If we had a story to write, we used a typewriter at the assignment desk. Otherwise, we were not encouraged to hang around the office. Someone on the assignment desk would call us during the evening, usually around eight or nine o'clock, and give us our assignment for the next day. Sometimes it would be out of town, sometimes it would be nothing more than watching a routine congressional hearing. Most of the time our job was simply to watch a hearing for several hours to make sure nothing of significance was said. If it turned out to be something that might warrant coverage on the *Evening News*, we would often be pulled off the story and it would be handed to one of the bureau stars. If we were lucky, we would be allowed to do the radio version of the story or perhaps a new version of it for the *Morning News*. (Except when we worked the same story as Schorr, who preferred to do all versions.)

The correspondents were under contract and worked for a straight salary. In those days, correspondents usually made $40,000 to $60,000 a year, though Roger was rumored to make somewhere in the neighborhood of $100,000. But those of us who were reporters had no contracts and were paid $200 weekly, plus "fees" every time we appeared on television or radio. We were paid $50 for the television pieces and $25 for radio pieces. We were also paid $12.50 for "radio syndication pieces," stories that were not included in our radio newscasts but were fed out to our affiliate stations. In retrospect, it was a great system, in that it allowed the network to hire new people, try them out and get rid of them with no consequences if they didn't work out. The system was abandoned decades ago, and all producers and on-air people who come to the networks are now required to sign contracts. The agents who now represent most television reporters insist on it, but I have always felt the current system precludes the networks from giving more deserving people a tryout.

As had been the case when I left little KXOL Radio for the *Star-Telegram* and when I left local TV in Fort Worth to come to Washington, the move from WTTG- Metromedia appeared to be another cut in pay. But I volunteered for every night assignment, which meant I got a lot of stories on the *Morning News*, and I picked up a valuable habit from the other reporters. If I happened to be assigned to a story at the Capitol, I would get there early enough to grab a couple of stories from the *Washington Post* or *Wall Street Journal* and turn them into syndication pieces for radio. I would broadcast them back to the bureau from the little broadcast booths we maintained at the Capitol. The bureau then fed them out to affiliates. We were limited to two of such pieces a day, but at $12.50 each, I would start the day $25 ahead. On a base salary of $200 a week and adding in those fees for radio and television pieces, I managed to make $33,000 that first year.

After my debut story about Tricia Nixon's costume party I moved on to covering such seminal events as the arrival of a white tiger cub at the National Zoo and the National Miniature Golf Championship at nearby Rockville, Maryland. Shortly after I signed off that piece — "Bob Schieffer, CBS News, at the National Putt-Putt Championship in Rockville, Maryland" — my mother called from Fort Worth to ask, "How long before they let you cover some news?" It wouldn't be that long, and in a matter of weeks I was able to tell her I had been assigned to the White House. Well, sort of, anyway.

President Nixon decided to hold church services each Sunday in the White House East Room, and as the new man in the bureau, the services became my first regular assignment. Only eight years earlier, in the 1960 campaign, John Kennedy had been forced to answer questions about whether a Catholic president could operate independently of the pope, and there had been real concern about keeping the separation between church and state. But the Nixon services took a nondenominational approach and, surprisingly, created little commotion, perhaps because they became such social occasions it was hard to take them seriously as religious events. White House aides used the services as "paybacks" to friends and supporters who had done them favors or invited them to social activities and they became a place for Republicans to see and be seen, perhaps by the Lord and certainly by other Republicans. A visiting minister would be invited in to conduct a sermon and lead the prayers and hymns, and afterward there would be coffee and the Nixons would greet the guests in a receiving line. Reporters were allowed to listen to the sermons from a small roped-off area (all souls may be equal in the eyes of the Lord, but not in the eyes of the Nixon administration), and after the service we were allowed to bring up the rear of the receiving line. We always used the occasion to ask the president a question or two. The redoubtable Helen Thomas of UPI and I spent many Sundays sharing those sermons, and it was during one service that I had my one and only brief, face-to-face interview with Nixon. I had just arrived in Washington and he had been in public life for years, but for all his expertise, what struck me was how awkward and ill at ease he seemed to be. On that particular Sunday, there had been a report that he was about to bring in some new advisors. It wasn't clear if these were to be additions to the White House staff or outside consultants, so when it came my turn to shake hands, I asked if he intended to use "outside help or in-house advisors?"

"Oh, no," he said. "On this one, I want plenty of outhouse advisors." Then, realizing what he had just said, he added, "No . . . not outhouse . . . well, you know . . ."

That was it for my first presidential interview, and he wandered off into the crowd.

# Eleven

## *Nixon's War*

At first, we got along just fine with Richard Nixon. Or at least we thought so.

During his early months in office, most reporters thought relations between the White House and the press were no better or worse than usual. After Johnson's tirades, Dan Rather, for one, thought they were actually a little better.

But when *New York Times* Pentagon correspondent William Beecher broke the story on May 9, 1969, that the United States had been secretly bombing North Vietnamese supply centers in Cambodia for months, Nixon's national security advisor Henry Kissinger went nuts and demanded the news leaks be plugged.

The story of how Watergate did in Nixon has been well told, but I have always believed that Watergate was just the last chapter in Nixon's fall. The spying, the wiretapping and the pattern of deception that would mark Watergate began that summer when Nixon tried to stop the news leaks and rein in the press and let his aides know that he really didn't care how they did it. He just wanted it done. In its own way, it would be Vietnam that would be the root cause of Nixon's destruction, just as it had been Vietnam that took down Lyndon Johnson.

It would be some months before any of us in the Washington bureau would get an inkling of what was going on behind the scenes in the Nixon White House, and years before we would comprehend the full scope of it.

By the summer of 1969, the news from Vietnam was worse and the street demonstrations had become more frequent and more violent. For the junior members of the bureau, and I was the junior of juniors, covering demonstrations became a full-time job. Those who supported the war thought our coverage prolonged it, but we couldn't understand how you could ignore the thousands of people who were pouring into the streets and we covered them as we would have covered any news story. That didn't mean we liked it. It is one thing to be for freedom of speech, and I've never known a reporter who was against it. But having to cover demonstrations, day after day and week after week, is something else. Some of our reporters and camera crews were for the war and some were against it, but the hawks and doves of the Washington bureau whose fate it was to cover the demonstrations shared one belief: We hated the demonstrations and everything connected to them, and there always seemed to be another one to cover. Every day and every night brought a protest of some kind. One day, I would find myself covering college kids who hated the war. Another day, I would be marching down Pennsylvania Avenue with an evangelist who pleaded with bystanders to accept Christ and kill communists. Some of the demonstrations produced news stories, but most didn't. Yet, as news organizations do, we staffed all of them to make sure nothing happened. Public frustration had reached a boiling point, tempers were short and wherever we went there was someone who wanted to take it out on us. Sometimes, young people who opposed the war would pelt us with rocks. At the next rally, war supporters would harangue us, and no matter who was protesting, we were certain to get jostled by the cops. And who could blame them for being in a bad mood? They spent even more time than we did covering the protests. We carried gas masks and crash helmets to every demonstration, but whenever the police resorted to tear gas, we always got a dose. Tear gas is terrible on the sinuses and lungs and, like most of the people in the bureau, I spent most of that fall and winter with a series of colds brought on by tear gas.

On the night Susan was born, I got into my first fistfight since college when a demonstrator on the George Washington University campus threw a coat over the lens of our camera. I grabbed the coat, put it over the demonstrator's head and popped him a good one. I couldn't wait to tell Pat. But when I finally got home, she said her contractions had begun. Unable to find me, she was about to call a cab and go to the hospital. I decided the story of my heroics earlier that evening would have to wait. For the moment, there didn't seem to be much of an audience.

What those of us covering the demonstrations didn't comprehend was that, as much as we hated the demonstrations, those within the Nixon White House had become obsessed with them, and with our coverage as well. At a midwestern governors' conference in July, Vice President Spiro T. Agnew argued, "The Viet Cong remains intransigent because of the slender hope that the voices of dissent at home will force us to alter — perhaps even abdicate — our policy that confrontation with the United States is costly." It was tough language, but it was the kind of talk you always heard when you were covering controversy, so we took it as part of the job and went about our business.

Al Haig, who was then Kissinger's military assistant, told me that by March of that year, Nixon still thought the war could be brought to a conclusion within a year. Haig himself still believes it could have been won in those early months with an all-out bombing campaign on North Vietnam, but by fall Nixon had concluded that was no longer practical and decided the only real option was a negotiated settlement. But he was also convinced that the only way to force negotiations was to convince the North Vietnamese that they faced an all-out attack on their homeland if they refused.

As long as the streets and television screens were filled with antiwar protestors, he felt he could never convince them that the American people would back an all-out war.

As Johnson had wrongly believed that his dramatic announcement that he would not seek reelection would show North Vietnam he was serious about negotiating an end to the war, Nixon believed he could force them to negotiate by threatening an even wider war. To lay the groundwork for that threat, he would first have to smother the dissent back home and bring to heel the television networks that gave the demonstrators their exposure.

No amount of political spin could have convinced the North Vietnamese to negotiate, for the simple reason that they believed they were winning. They had always believed the United States would eventually tire of the war, as had all the others who had come there to conquer them. To convince them that the American people would support a wider war at that point was asking them to believe the impossible: that a country already so torn apart by the war that it had begun to withdraw its forces would somehow reverse course and send troops back in even larger numbers. Yet Nixon believed he could convince North Vietnam of just that if he could quell the dissent back home.

When he was unable to squash the demonstrations being shown each night on television, he declared war on us at the networks.

Though we regarded our White House relations to be all right, Nixon had already decided that he could never bring the press to his side. As he later wrote, he considered it part of the opposition. It was television that he considered most able and likely to influence public opinion, and it was there he would focus his attack.

The plan Nixon endorsed that fall was laid out by Jeb Magruder, a young aide to White House chief of staff H. R. Haldeman. In what became known as the infamous "Rifle vs. Shotgun" memo, Magruder said the shotgun approach of dealing with reporters one-on-one to complain about specific stories was a waste of time. Instead, he suggested a concentrated "rifle approach," aimed far above reporters and directly at the people who controlled and ran the networks. The core of the new approach would be to use the Federal Communications Commission to monitor network news, the Justice Department Anti-Trust Division to investigate possible anti-trust violations and the Internal Revenue Service to launch investigations into "various organizations we are most concerned about." Magruder speculated that "just the threat of an investigation will probably turn their approach." Complaints about bias would go directly from the FCC to the networks. Since the FCC was the agency that licensed the stations, the message would carry an unstated but very real threat.

At CBS, we knew nothing of any of this, and on October 15 all the networks gave extended coverage to a huge antiwar demonstration. A coalition of antiwar groups staged an event called the Moratorium. A quarter of a million people marched on Washington, 20,000 gathered in the New York Financial District, 30,000 in New Haven and more than 100,000 in Boston. Hoping to hold down the size of the crowd, Nixon had said in advance of the demonstration that he would outline his plan to end the war on November 3. But the announcement apparently had no impact. The Moratorium was one of the largest demonstrations ever. It had taken the demonstrators, marching eight abreast, most of the afternoon to walk past the White House.

As he had promised, Nixon outlined his plan to end the war in a prime-time television speech on November 3. At the Washington bureau, as at the other networks, we got advance copies and Henry Kissinger briefed White House reporters in advance. All three networks gave Nixon free time, and at 9 P.M. Eastern time, he addressed the nation. The speech outlined for the first time what Nixon had promised in the campaign, a plan to negotiate an end to the war. Its thrust was that America would continue to fight the North Vietnamese until they agreed to come to the peace table or until South Vietnam's army could be fully trained and equipped to do the job itself. "Whichever came first," as he later wrote in his memoirs.

This was the speech in which Nixon called upon the "Silent Majority" to rise up in support of the war effort. At one point in the speech, he referred to a letter he had received from North Vietnam's leader Ho Chi Minh, a letter Ho had written shortly before his death. Nixon suggested the letter contained nothing new and reflected what he saw as North Vietnam's lack of interest in previous American peace overtures.

When Nixon concluded, all three networks offered summary and analysis, and the reviews were decidedly mixed. On CBS, Marvin Kalb noted that the speech contained no mention of new troop withdrawals, nor did it contain a definite timetable for total withdrawal of U.S. forces. Kalb, the scholar who had first divined the split between the Soviet Union and China, and an acknowledged expert on Communism, also took issue with Nixon's analysis of the Ho Chi Minh letter. Kalb found it some of the "softest, most accommodating language found in a Communist document concerning the war in Vietnam in recent years." On ABC and NBC, analysts said the speech contained nothing new and editorials in the big eastern papers took much the same line the next day.

Nixon always claimed that he never watched television, but said his family had watched the instant analysis that night and was livid. On that particular night, Nixon had apparently watched, too. His son-in-law David Eisenhower later told our correspondent Dan Schorr that he had watched the broadcast with Nixon and that when Kalb had taken issue with Nixon's assessment of the Ho Chi Minh letter, Nixon had said, "Kalb may be right about that."

In any case, the administration put its new plan to intimidate the press into immediate action. In what would become a harrowing night for Haldeman, Nixon began pelting him with phone calls, orders and questions even before the commentators were off the air. Haldeman said he got fifteen or twenty calls from Nixon over the next three hours. "What was being done to counterattack? . . ." "Hit the network chiefs for biased reports

232

. . ." "Get one hundred vicious calls to the *New York Times* and *Washington Post* re their editorials . . ." At that hour, of course, editorials had not yet been written. For the networks, the most ominous event came when — as had been directed in the Magruder memo — the new head of the FCC, Dean Burch, personally called each of the networks and demanded written transcripts of what their commentators had said. Nothing like that had ever been done by any administration.

"It was a new turn in the road," Frank Stanton told me more than thirty years later. Stanton was one of broadcasting's pioneers and was the president of CBS, the network that he and William S. Paley had built.

"I had been dealing with White House people since the Truman administration," Stanton told me. "You knew — if you knew anything about Washington — what this was all about and what they were trying to do."

Usually, when the FCC investigated a complaint, a staffer asked for information in writing during business hours. But the unstated message of Burch's calls was clear. The chairman of the federal agency that had the power to revoke the licenses of television stations was personally calling to review what the networks had said about the president, and it sent shock waves through all three networks.

Corydon B. Dunham, who was executive vice president and general counsel at NBC for many years, said, "I can remember that all the networks were fearful — they realized they were dealing with a different group, people out to achieve their goals in a 'no matter what' attitude."

The irony was that while Nixon and his aides were smarting over press reaction and plotting their press strategy, the public loved the speech. The White House was flooded with telegrams, messages and well-wishes and the first polls showed that nearly eighty percent of the public approved of the speech. With reaction so overwhelmingly positive, one might have thought Nixon would have concluded the press was not worth all the worry and would have seized the moment to mount a serious, new effort to end the war. Instead, he decided to use his new popularity to step up what would become a massive assault on the press. Pat Buchanan, a fiery young speechwriter on Nixon's staff, wrote a speech attacking network commentators and suggested the vice president deliver it. Nixon loved the draft, sharpened some of the rhetoric to an even finer point and, on November 13, Agnew delivered it to a Republican gathering in Des Moines. The networks broadcast it live, even though they had to preempt their own newscasts in many parts of the country.

It was an extraordinary speech by any standard. Agnew ripped into network newsmen as "a small group of men . . . an unelected elite . . . who decide what forty to fifty million Americans will learn of the day's events in the nation and in the world." He noted that ". . . to a man, they all live in Washington, D.C., or New York." (He failed to note that all of them were products of the Middle America that the administration considered the core of its constituency.) "The American people would rightly not tolerate this concentration of power in government. Is it not fair and relevant to question its concentration in the hands of a tiny, enclosed fraternity of privileged men elected by no one and enjoying a monopoly sanction that is licensed by a government? . . . As for the views of the majority of this fraternity, they do not and I repeat, do not, represent the views of America," Agnew charged. "Perhaps it is time the networks were made more responsive to the views of the nation and more responsible to the people they serve."

Network executives were stunned. What did "more responsive to the views of the nation" mean? Was the administration threatening to revoke licenses if the networks refused to adopt some undefined party line? Stanton of CBS called it "an unprecedented attempt by the Vice President of the United States to intimidate a news medium which depends for its existence upon government licenses." But Dean Burch called Agnew's remarks "thoughtful, provocative and deserving careful consideration by the industry."

On November 14, the *New York Times* broke the story of Burch's demands for transcripts of instant analysis, the comments our correspondents usually made after presidential speeches. In the Washington bureau, we learned of it the same way the public had, by reading the *Times*. Stanton told me he had not even revealed the request for transcripts to Richard Salant, the president of the CBS News division.

"I saw myself as the shock absorber on things like that," he said. "I didn't want our reporters to be intimidated and I didn't want that sort of thing to interfere with their duties of covering the news."

Even as the junior of juniors in the Washington bureau, I realized this was something more than the usual friction that existed between news organizations and the institutions and people they cover. And if we needed any more convincing, we got it the following Sunday when Nixon's communications chief, Herb Klein, appeared on the CBS News broadcast *Face the Nation*. He declared that all the news media needed to reexamine themselves. "If you fail to do so," he warned, "you invite the government to come in. I would not like to see that happen."

Dunham, in his 1997 book *Fighting for the First Amendment: Frank Stanton of CBS vs. Congress and the Nixon White House*, chronicles much of the backstage maneuvering during that period, and says Klein later told him he was not making a threat, but merely an observation. But Dunham says there is no question that the networks took it as a threat.

"Looking back," he told me, "what comes through to you is how justified the network apprehensions were. It was all so much more than anyone knew at the time."

Two days after the speech, I was out on the street, one of dozens of reporters and photographers who had been sent out to cover yet another antiwar demonstration. More than a quarter of a million people — perhaps the largest group ever to march on Washington until that point — had converged in and around the Federal City. The crowd was so large, police feared it would take gunfire to stop the demonstrators if they tried to climb the White House fences, and the White House complex was ringed with fifty-seven derelict buses which had been towed in and parked bumper to bumper. It was one of the strangest sights I had ever seen in those months of protests — the home of the president of the United States surrounded by old, worn-out buses. Adding to the weirdness of the day, the White House spokesmen brushed off the hundreds of thousands of demonstrators by pointing out they had not interfered with the president's Saturday-afternoon plans. He had planned to watch the Ohio State–Purdue football game and the White House spokesman said that was exactly what he had done. The buses proved an adequate blockade. Several protestors tried to crawl under them, but were dragged away. But several blocks over, another group tried to storm the Justice Department and fought police hand-to-hand. Those of us on the streets that day caught more tear gas, and by nightfall more than 135 arrests had been made. Yet only NBC broke into regular programming for live coverage and their reports were brief. CBS confined its coverage to several reports on the *Evening News*. The networks had vowed not to be intimidated, but on that Saturday those of us in the field couldn't believe that the biggest demonstrations ever had received only cursory coverage. It was only the beginning of the pressure the White House tried to bring on us and it was working.

Even after demanding the transcripts of network instant analysis, the FCC never brought any formal charges or complaints, but in the weeks after Nixon's speech, our White House correspondent, Dan Rather, discovered the White House had called at least twenty local stations around the country requesting transcripts of what local commentators had said about it. In one instance, an FCC staffer had called the CBS affiliate in Phoenix, inquiring whether CBS commentator Eric Sevareid had said anything about the speech during a visit to the station.

On December 15, Nixon went back on television to announce he was withdrawing another fifty thousand troops from Vietnam. Afterward, the network newsmen summarized the President's remarks.

There was no instant analysis.

As Christmas approached, Nixon's plan to silence the press and stifle the demonstrators seemed to be working. After the October demonstrations, the demonstrators went home, and as the new year began, people were starting to ask, Whatever happened to the peace movement? In early February 1970, I did my first major takeout (a long report) for the *Evening News* and declared the antiwar movement dead. Sam Brown, the dynamic young activist who had organized the huge protests of the previous year, had closed down his Washington offices. "What was supposed to be the protest to bend the will of the administration," I wrote of the October demonstrations, "instead has begun to look like a spectacular last hurrah for the peace movement."

Instead of mass protests, Brown told me, peace activists were refocusing their efforts.

Nixon's appeal to the Silent Majority had not gone unnoticed. Now, Brown said, peace activists had decided to go back to the local communities and try to win over those who had rallied behind the president after his November speech. Instead of concentrating on the casualties the war had generated, they would try to organize rallies around the country on income tax day, April 15, to stress the cost of the war. In my report, I told how peace activists such as Brooklyn priest Dick Neuhaus and Connecticut's Joe Duffey had shifted strategies and were taking more conventional routes, running for public office. A large segment of the peace movement was coming to believe that the best way to end the war was not in the streets, but by winning seats in the House and Senate. Or at least that is what my report concluded. "We have to go after those people that we haven't reached in the past," Brown told me. It would be done, he said, by "a very unexciting but very important process of base-building . . . going back to those towns, putting together those neighborhood meetings, talking to people about the war, distributing literature in the community, providing all the kinds of educational activities that can focus people's legitimate anger about taxes and about inflation at the war."

It was a fine thought, and a fine report, the longest and best story I had ever done for the

*Evening News.* The only problem was that it proved totally wrong. Yes, the demonstrators had left the streets after Nixon's speech, and there seemed little question that the public mood had shifted somewhat. But in reporting the death of the peace movement, I had violated journalism's first rule: Never overlook the obvious. The weather had turned cold as winter approached, and that probably had as much to do with the sudden absence of demonstrators as Nixon's speech. In retrospect, I had probably violated journalism's second rule as well: Be wary of information that seems to confirm what you have been wishing for. By then I had come to believe the war was a lost, misdirected cause that should be ended, but I was exhausted from covering the demonstrations and just wanted them to go away. When I saw signs that what I had wished for might be happening, I gave them more weight than I should have. Seeing only what we want to see and hearing only what we want to hear is the easiest and most destructive habit that a reporter can fall into and has probably caused more stories to be missed than any other single thing. Even after forty years as a reporter, I must constantly remind myself to avoid it. I'm better at it than I once was, but I suspect none of us can ever escape it completely. We all look for signs that confirm our own judgment.

My declaration that the peace movement

was dead to the contrary, when spring came and temperatures rose, the campuses again erupted in protest — this time it was not demonstrations but violent riots. They began when Nixon invaded Cambodia, and took on a new fury when poorly trained National Guardsmen opened fire on protestors at Kent State University in Ohio and killed four of them. Two more students died during riots at Jackson State, in Mississippi. Over the next weeks, the nation's campuses exploded. It took two days to put down a riot at the University of Wisconsin. Many of the country's biggest universities shut down, including all the state universities in California, which Governor Ronald Reagan had vowed never to close. The campuses finally returned to normal, but opposition to the war would not die and the demonstrations against it would go on even after Nixon left office.

# Twelve

## *The Puzzle Palace*

From my earliest days as a reporter, the two
things that always appealed to me were hard
news and covering a beat. The satisfaction of
journalism lay in finding out something I
didn't know and then telling people about it.
Feature stories and cutesy writing held no al-
lure for me. The news was the thing. I've always believed the purpose of television
writing is to tell a story, not to call attention
to the writing, and to me the test of good television writing is when we combine pictures
with clear, declarative sentences to tell the
story in such a way that the story, not the
writing, is remembered. Puns and clever
phrases make me wince, because people
don't talk that way. I always thought Charles
Kuralt and Roger Mudd were the best of all
the television writers, but it was not the
phrases they coined that set them apart. They
were master storytellers and it was the stories
they told that we remember. I never had the
patience to work on features and long takeouts, which is why I never wanted to work at

*60 Minutes*. It's still the best news broadcast on television, but their stories take months to assemble and, frankly, I could never keep a secret that long. When I find out something, my tendency, or maybe it's a fault, is to let people know about it.

I suppose my aversion to feature stories is why I have always been a beat man. Except for those early days at CBS News, I have never been a general assignment reporter, and except for the two years I anchored the *CBS Morning News*, I have never worked from a desk in an office. I have always worked out in the field. The great beauty of staying away from the office is that it keeps you out of office politics, which may be one reason I have managed to stay so long at one network. As it has turned out, I am one of the few Washington reporters — maybe the only one — who has covered all four major beats, the White House, the Congress, the State Department and the Pentagon, for extended periods of time. No one planned it. It just worked out that way, and my friends in the cutthroat world of television never seem to believe me when I tell them most of it was happenstance, that I never asked for any of the assignments.

My first Washington beat was the Pentagon and it came about — literally — because Secretary of Defense Melvin Laird was holding a news conference one spring day in 1970 and there was no one else available to cover it. CBS had recently parted company with its Pentagon correspondent, there was a war going on and because most of the other people in the bureau had other assignments, our assignment editor got in the habit of sending me to the Pentagon for the daily briefings. The plan was to assign a more experienced reporter to the beat eventually, but no one seemed to want the job, and nine months later, Bill Small asked me if I wanted it permanently. It was the easiest sell he ever made. By then, I had become fascinated with the job, but I would have taken it for no other reason than that it meant I no longer had to cover antiwar demonstrations full time.

It would be years, of course, before the demonstrations ended, and as long as they went on, I and the other members of the bureau had to cover them, but at the least, covering the Pentagon meant I was no longer the first to be called when one happened. As it turned out, I didn't have to go far to cover the largest antiwar protest ever in Washington, the May Day Demonstration in 1971. More than ten thousand demonstrators were arrested across Washington, some of them for spilling chicken droppings on the Pentagon steps which, I later reported, caused the military "to step especially smartly" that day.

When I had been sent out to the Pentagon

that first day, I knew nothing of the place, including how to get there. The closest I had come to it was when I had flown over it on the Eastern Airlines shuttle en route to New York. But armed with the room number where the news conference was scheduled, I took a cab there and discovered on arrival that I needed no security pass or identification to get in the building.

The corridors were bustling with people, but I was also surprised to learn that none of them were wearing military uniforms. Only later did I discover that military people assigned to the Pentagon wore uniforms only once a week, part of a long-standing tradition that had been instituted to play down the huge military presence in Washington. What I never understood was why government officials would be defensive or feel they could be criticized for having large numbers of military people stationed at the nation's military headquarters, but civilian clothes were the rule nonetheless, and remained so until Ronald Reagan became president and his secretary of defense, Caspar Weinberger, wondered the same thing I had wondered. Reagan told them to start wearing their uniforms to work, and it proved to be one of the most popular orders he ever issued.

On my first trip to the Pentagon on that day in 1970, the cab let me out at the curb of the Pentagon's Mall Entrance. I walked up the steps as others were doing, and since no one stopped me and there appeared to be no one there to give directions, I asked a passerby if he knew where Room 2E-781 was. I was headed down one of the longest hallways I had ever seen and he told me to just keep going, I couldn't miss it.

After a walk of about a half block, I came to what was obviously a press area. A large open room on my left appeared to be a press room, and across the hall was a briefing room that had been set up for a news conference. Television crews were arranging their cameras across the back of the room and I recognized several reporters. I took a seat marked CBS and saw that the man next to me was Robert Goralski, NBC's Pentagon correspondent.

"Welcome to the Puzzle Palace," he said, when I introduced myself.

Goralski would prove to be a great friend as well as competitor, whose irreverent sense of humor did not always leave him in good stead with his own bosses. Goralski took great pride in his Polish heritage, but Reuven Frank, who was running NBC News at the time, called him in one day and told him he would be a bigger star if he were to change his name. "Fine," said Goralski. "From now on, I'll be *Reuven* Goralski."

He said Frank never mentioned it again, "but when I found myself being assigned to cover a hearing of the House Subcommittee on Hides and Skins (there really was such a committee at one point), I knew I hadn't helped my career."

The joke in the bureau was that, like the lieutenant in the Andy Griffith movie *No Time for Sergeants*, I had been sent to cover the Pentagon because I had had ROTC in college. In the movie, when told his lieutenant "had ROTC," Griffith's character had concluded that ROTC was some sort of disease. In my case, there was just no one else available, and I was sent there by default. The fact that I had had ROTC in college and spent three years in the Air Force didn't hurt.

My trip to the Pentagon that day was the beginning of my first great Washington adventure. To a reporter who had been in Washington less than a year, the Pentagon can be a daunting place. With six and a half million square feet of office space — three times the space in the Empire State Building — it is one of the largest office buildings in the world. Everything about it seems an exaggeration. It has its own fire department, featuring fire trucks made out of converted golf carts that sometimes cruised the miles of hallways with red lights flashing. It also has its own sewage-treatment plant and water systems. Its underground shopping center was one of the first of the suburban malls. A five-sided structure, its hallways and corridors actually formed a series of concentric circles which ringed an interior plaza. The E-Ring, or outer ring, of offices were the prize real estate, because they had windows with an outside view. It was on the E-Ring that the secretary of defense and the chiefs of the various services had their offices. The inner rings of offices with little or no view housed lesser officials and the more sensitive areas where the war planning rooms and the command center were located. The Pentagon was not designed with beauty in mind, but the grassy, tree-shaded interior plaza could be a pleasant place on a day in spring or early fall. At its center was a hamburger stand where the featured sandwich was the Pentaburger. Somehow, it seemed the perfect touch. At ground zero of the number-one military target in America, there was a hamburger stand. Depending on the state of the world, the Pentagon population today ranges from twenty thousand to thirty thousand workers — generals, lower-ranking officers, enlisted men and women and civil servants. It is like a small town, a major part of official Washington that sits apart from the rest of the Federal City on the banks of the Potomac River in Virginia.

For a reporter, it is the best of all beats to learn how Washington works and for all its hugeness, it was an informal, easy place to work and develop sources. A reporter interested in hardware stories could become an expert on military hardware; for those interested in foreign policy, there was no better place than the Pentagon to learn about it; for political reporters or someone interested in the oddities of human nature, and that would be me, there were no more intriguing politics than the maneuverings of the military's joint chiefs of staff and their interaction with Congress and the civilians in the Office of the Secretary of Defense.

As for offbeat, unexpected stories, I never found a beat to match what was served up by the vast bureaucracy of the Pentagon. One day, I walked in and noticed they were taking down the huge oak doors. The doors looked sturdy enough to me, and I asked a carpenter why new ones were needed. "Oh, we're not getting rid of them," he said. "We're going to rehang them at the River Entrance down the hall." Sure enough, I discovered carpenters at the River Entrance taking down the doors there. What no one seemed to know was why doors in one place were being switched for doors at another. What was this particular episode of your-tax-dollars-at-work all about? It took me two days, but I finally got the answer from a three-star general.

"It turns out," he told me, "that the Pentagon has a policy of rotating its doors, the way you rotate the tires on your car. It's supposed to keep them from wearing out."

Did the general believe wooden doors could be worn out?

"I don't know," he said. "I have done all the checking for you on this particular story that I plan to do."

These days, friends are never really sure I'm serious when I tell them that the Pentagon, like most of official Washington, was still open to the public in the 1970s. The Command Center and other sensitive areas were off-limits and guarded by military police. But most of the building was open to anyone who ventured there. No one was required to show identification to enter the building, nor were security passes required. During most of the years I covered the Pentagon, I didn't have a press card. That was not by design; I just never got around to getting one. During the time that Jim Schlesinger was secretary of defense, I would sometimes drop by on a Saturday morning, and if his door was open, I would stick my head in and ask if anything was going on. He would often be at his desk, reading the paper. Sometimes he'd say no and keep reading. Other times, he'd invite me in for a chat.

As it was with every job I ever had at CBS News, I had to figure it out for myself. Maybe it is just the nature of a very competitive industry, but I never had a CBS job where there was someone to show me the ropes. I always seemed to replace someone who had been moved on for one reason or another before I got there.

My three years in the Air Force had given me some idea of how the military worked, and I soon realized that my main job would be to cover the same story I had been covering for years, the Vietnam War. I had seen it in the jungles during my *Star-Telegram* days, I had covered the protests almost nonstop since arriving in Washington and now I would be seeing it from a new place, military headquarters: not the best place to understand a war, but better than a dose of tear gas covering the protests in the streets. It was a great job and I soon settled into a routine. I would arrive around nine each morning, run a phone check on the public-information offices that each of the military services operated, attend the daily briefing by the Pentagon's top civilian spokesman and then make my way around the building, checking with various sources. If I had a story for the *Evening News*, I would call the office for a camera crew around four-thirty and film an on-camera close to the story on the Pentagon steps. In those days, there were no mobile video cameras, and our crews used film cameras. On average, it took about forty minutes to develop the film, so once my close was done, I would drive back to the bureau in Washington, where I would deposit the film at the "drugstore," the name we gave to the film processor in the back of the bureau. While I waited for it to be processed, I would then write a script for the top of the story, the part where my narration would be covered by pictures. Then I would work with a producer to select the "sound bites" that would be included in the report. Usually they came from an interview I had done earlier, or from a news conference that some Defense official had held. Using the script I had written as a guide, a film editor would assemble the edited strips of film on a reel, using Scotch tape to hold them together. My filmed on-camera "close" would be tacked on the end of the reel. The entire package would then be loaded onto film projectors. When Walter Cronkite introduced our stories from New York, a director in Washington set the projectors rolling and we would voice the narration live into a microphone in a nearby announce booth, all the while being careful to keep one eye on a monitor where we could see the pictures rolling by. If we read too fast or too slow, of course, the narration wouldn't match the pictures the viewer was seeing. It was a complicated process and took some practice. But for me, the hardest part was learning to write a story from the bottom up, which is what we had to do, since the close of the stories had to be filmed on-site before we returned to the office to write the top part. It was such a complicated process that I sometimes wonder how we ever got it done, but night after night we would churn out five or six stories for the evening news, and most nights, from a technical standpoint, we did it flawlessly.

I knew virtually nothing about defense policy in those early days, but it soon dawned on me that the Pentagon was one giant courthouse and that was the key to covering the place. The officials at a Texas courthouse are all independently elected officials, all competing for the same tax dollars to run their offices. The best stories about the sheriff usually came from the county commissioners; the best stories about the commissioners usually came from the sheriff. It didn't take me long to figure out that the best stories about the Air Force would probably come from the Army and the best stories about the Army from the Air Force, and that proved to be exactly the case. In fact, one of the best stories I ever got was one which showed that the Army had been dramatically playing down their helicopter losses in Vietnam. Several of my competitors couldn't figure out who had tipped me to the story. But it was no mystery to the Army. They knew it had come from the Air Force, which was always on the alert for flaws in any program that they believed was infringing on their territory, which they considered anything aboveground. As the Air Force saw it, the Army was in charge of vehicles that traveled on the ground. Period. Anything that rose above the earth should belong to them. Because they also believed that the Navy's mission should be confined to boats, the Air Force was also an excellent source for the true cost of Navy aircraft carriers. The Navy, on the other hand, was always a ready, easy source of information about the vulnerability of land-based (read: Air Force) aircraft.

When I'm asked where news comes from, I usually point to those days at the Pentagon. For all the digging by reporters, news usually becomes public because it is in someone's interest for it to come out. The good reporter's job is to decide if it is also in the public interest for the story to be known. If the reporter decides it is, then it is published or broadcast. If the reporter decides that only the news source will benefit if it's published, then the reporter ignores it.

There are times, of course, when a news source triggers a news story by accident, and that's how I got my first good Pentagon story. Our bureau chief Bill Small's pet peeve was the number of people on the public payroll whose sole job seemed to be to lobby the Congress to give their agencies even more tax dollars. He was guest lecturer at a military seminar one day, and was expounding at some length on the Pentagon's "small army of lobbyists," when a colonel who was obviously a stickler for detail berated him for misusing the term *army*. The colonel said the group numbered no more than three hundred, "hardly an army." Small responded that he hadn't realized there were that many, and when he returned to Washington, he called me and told me to find out if the number was right.

"If it is," he said, "it's outrageous and I want you to do a story about it."

It was easy enough to check out. There were more than three hundred of them, many of whom worked in civilian clothes out of offices on Capitol Hill, and their duties ranged from legitimate tasks such as tracing complaints from servicemen and their families who had written to their congressmen, to such things as planning overseas congressional junkets and out-and-out lobbying for bases and military weapons systems. It may have been unfair to call them an army, but there was nothing small-time about their operations. That year, more than 269 special-interest groups which had registered as lobbyists spent a total of $5.1 million on lobbying Congress. The Pentagon, which had registered no lobbyists, had spent some three million dollars on legislative liaison.

Peter Davis, a young filmmaker in the CBS News documentary unit in New York, would later be struck by the same thing. Davis had been groping for a way to do a documentary on government waste. With Small's encouragement, he narrowed his focus to the Pentagon, and in 1971, CBS broadcast the result of his work, a one-hour documentary called *The Selling of the Pentagon*, anchored by Roger Mudd. It was a devastating examination of how the military had spent millions of tax dollars on public-relations campaigns promoting everything from weapons programs to the Vietnam War. It became one of the most controversial broadcasts ever aired on CBS, provoked Congressional hearings, and at one point House Commerce Committee Chairman Harley Staggers, a West Virginia Democrat, tried to hold CBS president Frank Stanton in contempt of Congress because he refused to let congressional investigators rummage through CBS film clips and other materials that Davis had considered for the broadcast but later discarded. Staggers argued that only by going through all the material Davis had amassed, could he determine if Davis had been fair in choosing what appeared in the final broadcast.

At one point in the broadcast, producer Davis had condensed an interview with Pentagon spokesman Dan Henken. The result was that an answer to one question from Mudd appeared to be the answer to another. It was ragged, inexcusable editing, but hadn't changed the thrust of what Henken had said. Nonetheless, critics seized on it and used it to turn attention from the broadcast's conclusions to a controversy over editing techniques. The abuses the broadcast uncovered were never challenged, but the argument over *The Selling of the Pentagon* raged for months. For a network already worried that an increasingly hostile Nixon White House was trying to revoke the licenses of its television stations, it was about as serious as a situation could get. As the controversy wore on, Staggers pleaded privately with Stanton to give in, but Stanton would have none of it. Stanton said that if the government could force a reporter to hand over notes or film that had not been made public, then government could rummage through a reporter's desk. If a reporter couldn't keep notes and sources confidential, then it would be virtually impossible to get sources to tell him anything. Staggers's committee voted to hold Stanton in contempt. But when the matter came to a vote in the House, the leaders of both parties refused to support Staggers, and the House overturned the committee's contempt citation. I had been at CBS News only a few years by then, but when I saw Stanton put his career, and maybe even our network, on the line for a journalistic principle, I knew this was the place I wanted to be. Many years later, when I learned that Stanton's boss and CBS founder Bill Paley had been nervous about defying Congress and had actually made a secret trip to Washington to seek some sort of compromise, I admired Stanton even more.

I always wondered if that colonel who was such a stickler for language ever realized what he had started when he had criticized Bill Small for calling the Pentagon lobbying force an "army."

For all the ways that news becomes public, and for all the efforts of journalists to dig it out, sometimes reporters get news in spite of themselves, and an episode in which I became involved one April day in 1971 is illustrative.

I was whiling away a slow afternoon in the Pentagon pressroom, when our assignment editor, Bill Galbraith, called and told me to get to National Airport as quickly as I could. An antiwar radical named Leslie Bacon, who had been arrested in connection with a Washington bombing, was being transferred from a local jail to Seattle for questioning about a series of bombings there. Galbraith called me because I was the reporter closest to National Airport, where he said federal marshals would be arriving at any moment to take the woman to Seattle.

I raced to the airport, and miraculously found a parking place near the terminal for private planes. As I jumped from the car, I saw one of the cameramen, Ralph Santos, and his crew emerging from a car nearby. At the same instant, I saw two men with a handcuffed woman between them coming toward the terminal entrance. That had to be my quarry. But as I grabbed a microphone from Santos and ran the twenty yards or so to catch up with her, my mind went blank. I remembered she was accused of bombing something, but I couldn't remember what. Was it that Capitol rest room or a Pentagon rest room where a small explosive had been set off earlier? My mind went blank.

Out of breath when I finally caught up with them, I knew I would have only a matter of seconds to shout questions and I didn't want to ruin the film by asking the wrong question, so I shouted perhaps the most generic question ever asked: "Did you do it?"

Unfortunately, she answered, "Do what?"

Stumped again, I responded, "What they said you did?"

"No," she replied.

To my embarrassment, the *Evening News* ran the interview in its entirety, noting that "antiwar activist Leslie Bacon today denied any involvement in the bombing of a Capitol rest room."

The next day, Bill Small called me in and said it wouldn't hurt if I tried to be a little more prepared. "Yes, sir" seemed the only appropriate reply, and I got out of there before Mudd and the other big guns saw me.

My fine piece of journalism would certainly have prompted some choice remarks that I wasn't all that interested in hearing.

It was during those Pentagon days that I came to understand how much time and money large bureaucracies devote to controlling, or at least trying to control, the flow of information.

I discovered one familiar practice immediately. Just as it had been on the other beats I had worked — the Fort Worth police station and Tarrant County courthouse — when the news was good, when it reflected well on the government or some individual in it, it was easy to get. When it was not so good, it was harder to come by. What was new to me was the way the government had found to release news that it wanted made public but didn't want to take credit for. This news came out at so-called "backgrounders." I had covered hundreds of stories back in Fort Worth when a cop or some other official would tell me, "I don't want to be quoted on this, but to help you understand this, let me explain something to you." What might follow would be some extenuating circumstance that would help me comprehend the situation or give me a broader picture of what I was trying to write about. Or maybe it would be information that would put the news source in jeopardy if others knew it had come from him. In such a situation, a reporter quotes "a source" or "an official in a position to know" or uses some other phrase that masks the source's identity. We don't like to do it, but sometimes it's the only way to get information that ought to be made public.

What I discovered at the Pentagon was a variation on the long-standing practice of sometimes keeping a source's name confidential. It was the growing trend to release information at organized "backgrounders." Reporters would be called in and given an extensive briefing on some policy or program by government officials who would refuse to be quoted by name. Usually, we were told it could be attributed only to "a senior official." The advantages to the government in such an arrangement are obvious. The government gets out the information it wants, but if it is wrong or someone takes offense, there is no one who can be blamed or even argued with. Once, in an outburst of exasperation after a briefer told us we could attribute his remarks only to a "senior official," I asked if he would mind if we referred to him as only a "junior official," since it wasn't much of a story. It got a good laugh from the other reporters, but he was not amused.

The other way to hold back information at the Pentagon was to stamp it with a security classification. The government has legitimate reasons to keep many things secret and the list is obvious: war plans, troop movements, the identities of undercover agents, details on how our sophisticated weapons and our defenses are constructed, and the list goes on and on. But I soon learned there was another reason to put a security classification on information: to cover up mistakes and avoid embarrassment. In those days, there were three security classifications — confidential, secret and top secret — and once officials stamped documents with those classifications, they had to be registered and kept in a safe, and the content could not be released to the public until it had been subjected to a declassification review that in most cases took years to complete. In practice, it meant that the government could keep embarrassing information secret but share good news with whomever it chose. As a civilian and a reporter, I had no clearance to read or even see the documents stamped Confidential, the lowest security classification, and any official who shared such a document with me could have been prosecuted. Yet once I had established good working relationships with many of the Pentagon officials I dealt with, I discovered they would often let me read classified documents. Usually, they would let me see documents that supported their point of view, or that demonstrated a shortcoming of some bureaucratic rival. I can't recall anyone ever showing me a document that proved the person showing me the document had made a mistake. I always assumed that other reporters had similar relationships with their sources, and sharing so-called classified information was so common that, as part of my routine, I dropped by each day at the office of one Pentagon official, who allowed me to read the Daily Intelligence Brief put out by the Central Intelligence Agency. It was so widely distributed in the Pentagon that I always assumed that the government wanted the contents known but didn't wish to be known as the source, so I routinely used information from the report in my stories, quoting "intelligence sources" or simply saying, "CBS News has learned . . ." I should also add that the report seldom contained anything startling. Most of what I read there I had usually read in the *New York Times* or the *Washington Post*, which seemed to be major sources. The main question about the classified information I ran across usually was why it had been classified in the first place, which was often the attitude of officials who showed it to me.

Even though officials routinely shared classified information with reporters they trusted, they would occasionally become irritated with something we had written and try to find out where we had gotten our stories, efforts that sometimes bordered on the ridiculous.

Bob Goralski's desk was next to mine in the Pentagon press room, and one morning we arrived to find little cards in our mail trays reading, "Your desk has been checked for violations in the handling of classified information. No violations have been found." Since we were not authorized to have classified documents, we couldn't figure out how we could have violated any regulations. We concluded that security officers had simply searched our desks. Were they trying to intimidate us by leaving calling cards? Maybe. But more likely, we decided, they were just inept and hadn't realized they were in the press room and not some Pentagon office. The reader might ask how we could have possibly believed that government agents could be so clueless, but it was not that difficult in view of some of the security team's counterespionage efforts during that era.

In one legendary investigation, Goralski told me, a probe had been launched to determine how many Pentagon employees might be vulnerable to blackmail by a foreign power. Homosexuals had always been considered prime candidates, but someone advanced the theory that adulterers had as much to hide as homosexuals and could be equally at risk. So agents launched a program to determine how many illicit love affairs were going on after-hours in Pentagon offices. One way to do that, it was decided, was to determine how many condoms had been flushed down Pentagon toilets. I was never able to confirm it, but I was told that some poor soul was dispatched to the Pentagon sewage plant to determine if used condoms could be counted there. Whether it actually happened I was never able to find out, but I always hoped that if it did happen, he never had to confront the question "Daddy, what did you do in the war?"

# Thirteen

## *The Devious Dove*

Melvin Laird was the first defense secretary I covered, and like me, he had arrived at the Pentagon somewhat by accident. A nine-term congressman from Wisconsin and the ranking Republican on the Defense Appropriations Subcommittee, as well as the ranking Republican on a key health subcommittee, he had been a key strategist in Nixon's presidential campaign during the 1968 campaign and was regarded as one of his party's experts on defense and health issues. When Nixon began to assemble his cabinet after the campaign, Laird and Bryce Harlow, another longtime Republican operative, convinced Nixon that he needed a Democrat in his cabinet and that it ought to be Henry (Scoop) Jackson of Washington, a defense hard-liner. They believed he would be a perfect fit as secretary of defense. Some of the people around Nixon were not keen on having a Democrat in the cabinet, but Nixon liked the idea. After all, if the war went badly, it would be harder for Democrats to criticize him if he had a Democrat running the Pentagon. He told Laird to see if Jackson was interested. Laird already knew Jackson was interested and he quickly agreed to take the job. Laird sent word to Nixon that Jackson was ready to come on board. But the next day, Jackson flew to Hawaii for a Democratic retreat, where other Democrats just as quickly talked him out of it.

When Laird and Harlow went back to Nixon and told him that Jackson had reversed course, Laird said Nixon responded, "Well, you sons of bitches got me into it, you'll have to get me out of it" and told Laird he would have to take the job. Laird had already turned down an offer to be secretary of health, education and welfare, and had no interest in leaving Congress, but told Nixon he would think about it. Harlow told him that if he didn't want the job, he should just tell Nixon he would take it only if he could name his own people to all the top civilian and military jobs at the Pentagon. No president had ever given a cabinet officer that kind of leeway, and no one, including Laird and Harlow, thought Nixon would give it to Laird.

"To my surprise, he not only agreed, he actually put it in writing," Laird said. "I was trapped, so I accepted."

Watching Laird operate, I sometimes wondered if Nixon realized what he had gotten when he picked Laird, who was the most accomplished politician I have ever known, with the possible exception of Lyndon Johnson. To the irritation of Nixon's top White House aides, Laird used every ounce of his authority to put his own people in the key slots. No one, from the top military commanders to the "watch officers" who monitored the National Command Post around the clock, got his job until he had been interviewed face-to-face by Laird.

"I wanted to know who the people were that I would be dealing with at three o'clock some morning when there was a crisis," he said.

Laird also established a strict set of guidelines. No one, from the chiefs on down, talked to anyone at the White House unless it was cleared with Laird's office. The civilians notified Laird's civilian assistant, Carl Wallace; the military people checked with Laird's military aide, Robert Persley. In emergencies, they could report the calls later, but there were no exceptions. All contact with the White House had to be reported to Laird.

"I had been around too long to be fooled by these people at the White House, who would tell you, 'The president wants this or that,' " Laird said. "That's how people get into trouble. I made it clear that if the president wanted something, he called me, and I only took calls from two people over at the White House, Nixon and Kissinger."

Laird's rules were a constant source of irritation to Haldeman and Ehrlichman, and at one point Persley's phone was tapped by White House aides, but no Pentagon officials were ever implicated in Watergate.

"I was always proud of that," Laird told me, "and it wasn't because the White House didn't try to draw some of our people into it."

Laird said that at one point, Haldeman and Ehrlichman had called Admiral Noel Guylor, the head of the super-secret National Security Agency, which intercepted electronic transmissions. Guylor went to the White House, where he was told the president wanted his agency to help the plumbers, the group that had been put together to plug news leaks.

"Basically, I just chewed his ass out," Laird said. "In his defense, he had been told the president wanted to see him, but I told him he was never to get involved in any project like that, and he was never to talk to them again, and he understood. He was a good man, and I later promoted him to four stars and named him commander in chief of the Pacific, the biggest job in the Navy, with the exception of chief of naval operations."

If Nixon had not known in the beginning that Laird had an independent streak, he found out several weeks later, when he learned from the newspapers that Laird had selected David Packard, the founder of Hewlett-Packard, to be deputy secretary of defense, one of the most powerful posts in government. When he called Laird and demanded to know why he had learned about Packard's appointment by reading the newspapers, Laird replied that he thought Nixon would have known Packard, since he was from California. Still steaming, Nixon remarked icily that it was a big state.

"I flew Packard down to Nixon's place at Key Biscayne and let them talk for an hour, and Nixon came up to me later and said, 'He's from a big state and he's a big man. He'll be fine.'"

"I knew he would like him," Laird said, with a twinkle.

Laird combined unabashed gall with an encyclopedic knowledge of where the federal government's secret levers of power were located and, like Johnson, did not hesitate to use them. He never lost a battle over a Defense budget and never hesitated to remind his critics of it. He was a master of behind-the-scenes maneuvering, yet he had a straight-ahead style. His great strength was he never lost sight of his goals. As he had done in choosing Packard, he was always pushing the envelope, and seemed to have an uncanny sense of just how much he could get away with. When he wanted to do something, he just did it and worried about the consequences later.

He was also a dove in hawk's clothing, who had decided long before he took the Defense post that the war was a losing proposition. Laird had always been a defense hard-liner, but he came to the Pentagon determined to get American troops out of Vietnam, and he had concluded the quicker the better. He was no cut-and-run liberal, as Nixon liked to say, and he wanted to end the war in an honorable way, but he was determined to end it. This produced endless behind-the-scenes skirmishes with National Security Advisor Kissinger and his then military assistant, Colonel Alexander Haig. To this day, Haig believes that Nixon should have fired Laird for what he saw as Laird's habit of picking and choosing which presidential directives to follow. Haig told me that early on, Nixon also wanted to fire Laird after the North Koreans shot down an American reconnaissance plane flying off its coast in April 1969. The incident was very much like the situation that developed in 2001 when China forced down an American reconnaissance plane that had been flying off its coast. In the Korean incident, however, all thirty-one American crewmen were killed when the plane went down. U.S. planes had been flying similar missions in international airspace off the Korean coast for years, and Nixon was understandably outraged. He saw it, further, as a test of his resolve and concluded "that force must be met with force." Kissinger and Haig agreed. That meant an American air strike on a Korean military base or airfield. According to Haig, Laird and Secretary of State William Rogers argued against a strike. They wanted more information, to determine if it might have been an accident or some sort of isolated incident that had not been ordered by the government. They were also concerned that an attack on North Korea would be seen as a widening of the war in Vietnam, and was all but certain to set off new antiwar demonstrations that would cause the administration to lose more support in Congress. In Nixon's mind, a quick strike would have had just the opposite effect. It would demonstrate to the North Vietnamese that he was not afraid to use force. He believed that that would make them more amenable to negotiating an end to the war.

Laird and Rogers won a temporary victory because there was really nothing Nixon could do at that point — American aircraft carriers were too far away to launch air strikes. He told Laird to start moving the carriers. Once they were off the North Korean coast, he would make the final decision on launching bombing raids. As hours turned into days, Nixon began to wonder if the carriers would ever get there. Not there yet, he kept being told. When Haig questioned Laird's military assistant, he would be told, "I'll have to get back to you on that." After three days, Haig says he determined that Laird had never actually passed on the president's order to move the carriers, and Laird and Rogers eventually won the day. With the element of surprise gone, Nixon decided not to order the strikes on North Korea after all. Instead, he took the less provocative action that had been recommended by his secretaries of state and defense. He ordered armed fighters to escort the intelligence planes on future flights. Only then did Haig and Kissinger realize that Laird had secretly grounded all reconnaissance flights until the crisis could be resolved. In his book *Inner Circles*, published in 1992, Haig says Nixon was so furious with Laird and Rogers that he wanted to fire them both. But he said Nixon realized that firing Laird could not be done without cost. If Laird went, as Haig put it, much of Nixon's congressional support for his war policies would go with him. Further, any secretary of defense who was fired for not wanting to widen the war was bound to become a hero to the antiwar movement. As for Laird, he had no regrets for how he had handled the situation. "We did drag our feet a little on the carriers," he told me in an interview for this book. "But it was a very dangerous time and

274

we later determined that the plane had actually violated North Korean airspace."

Laird has always played down his rivalry with Kissinger, whom he had recruited to help write the defense plank in the platform at the 1954 Republican Convention.

"I was the one who actually introduced him to Nixon," Laird said, "but we never saw eye to eye on Vietnam.

"I was always pushing to withdraw the troops faster, and Henry was always pushing to go slower, because he thought withdrawals would weaken his position at the bargaining table."

Why had Laird given up on the war? "It wasn't that," he told me. "After all my years in Congress, I just knew support for the war was fading. I wanted to get our people out before Congress forced us to remove them. That would have been the worst of all worlds."

When Nixon declared that we would defend Vietnam until we could give the Vietnamese the training and the equipment to do the job for itself, it was Laird who coined the term "Vietnamization," and it was Laird who became the driving force in turning more and more of the war over to Vietnam. Several years after he left the Pentagon and American combat forces had finally been withdrawn, Laird was asked why the war still continued. He responded that the Vietnamization program had not been designed to bring peace; it had been designed to end American involvement in the war. The war had gone on for thirty years; it might go on another twenty. What, then, should the Americans do? Nothing, he said. We had given the South Vietnamese the training and the tools, and if they couldn't do it, there was little we could do.

During his tenure at the Pentagon, Laird had remained a good administration soldier. Publicly, he had defended the war policy and Nixon's decisions, so most of us covering the Pentagon did not really understand at the time just how strongly he was pushing troop withdrawals within the inner circles. But Michael Getler, one of the reporters who covered the Defense beat for the *Washington Post*, says there is no question in retrospect that Laird was a driving force in winding down the war.

"I came to see Laird and Kissinger as the two poles of Nixon's war policy," Getler said. "Kissinger was the grand strategist determined to remain focused on the big, long-range picture. He brought a sort of European view, he worried about power relationships between nations. Laird was the guy from the grass roots, the former congressman who counted body bags coming home. He understood the effect the war was having back home and especially the effect it was having on the young people.

"People forget that Nixon ended the draft, and Laird was a driving force in getting that done, just as he was a driving force in pushing to turn more of the war effort over to the South Vietnamese Army and getting the American prisoners of war back home."

In September of 1971, the big news at our house was the arrival of our second daughter, Sharon. Unlike Susan, who had arrived somewhat unexpectedly, Sharon seemed reluctant to join the world. Seventeen days past her due date, an exasperated Pat was convinced the baby was never coming and resorted to an old Texas solution. We went for dinner at a Mexican restaurant in Virginia and she ordered the El Grande Combo Plate and ate it all. That did the trick. Sharon was born later that evening.

Our life soon settled into a pleasant routine. At home, our activities revolved around our two daughters, and at work I was beginning to get a handle on the Pentagon. The Nixon White House, meanwhile, continued its war on the press. Much of it was unknown to us at the time, but what we did know about were the broadsides coming almost daily from Vice President Agnew. And there no question the attacks were having an impact. Agnew struck a chord with a certain segment of a public already frustrated with a war that was going badly and a rebellion by young people they couldn't understand. Our reporting was constantly questioned, and occasionally our patriotism, as well. CBS enjoyed an especially good relationship with its affiliate stations, but we were beginning to hear criticism from many of them about how we were covering the war and the administration. Some of the criticism was legitimate; there were two sides to whether we should have been in Vietnam. But as we have since learned from tapes in the National Archives, much of it was generated by the White House as a result of programs developed by Chuck Colson, the lawyer who had become Nixon's chief network intimidator.

As part of his strategy to bring the networks to heel, he visited all the network chiefs in New York and then wrote Nixon and Haldeman long, glowing accounts of how he had frightened and intimidated them. Whether the network chiefs were as frightened and intimidated as Colson reported is doubtful, but to their credit, neither Bill Paley nor Frank Stanton ever told any of us covering the administration about the visits. Because, Stanton told us later, he did not want the threats to color our coverage or intimidate us in trying to gather news. We knew the administration was putting pressure on us; we just didn't understand how much.

Despite Nixon's claims that he paid no attention to press coverage, documents that have been made public from that era show a lot of television was being watched within the Nixon White House. Staffers apparently spent large blocks of time watching news programs and writing each other long memoranda about it. There are so many memos, it raises questions about how they found time to do other work. No transgression by television seemed too small to set off a round of memos. A memo unearthed by my colleague Eric Engberg told of how the White House high command (presumably Nixon) had become so upset about routine coverage we had given to a state dinner for the president of Mexico that presidential aide Jeb Magruder (later to gain Watergate fame) put two of his men on the case. It took them a week, but they reported back that a review of tapes showed White House correspondent Dan Rather's story "showed clips of guests John Wayne and former President Johnson" and told of a scare set off by firecrackers, but had no favorable description of the event. He recommended that Press Secretary Ron Ziegler call in Rather for a "discussion." To foster the impression that the public was upset, the aides ordered the mailing of letters to CBS under Mexican-American names "to decry the absence of coverage."

It was our White House team that caught the brunt of the attacks, but it was not just CBS that came into the White House cross-hairs. At one point, Mort Alin, who monitored network broadcasts for the White House, warned his superiors that NBC was becoming increasingly negative toward Nixon and was making a broad appeal to the "new culture." The evidence? The network's "cinéma verité" editing techniques and correspondent Frank McGee's switch from horn-rim to granny glasses.

The organized phony letter-writing campaign would become a cornerstone of the White House strategy for dealing with what it saw as unfavorable press coverage.

On January 2, 1972, Nixon granted a prime-time, one-hour interview to Dan Rather, and at the bureau we thought it had gone well and figured the administration would have thought so, too. It had produced banner headlines in the next day's papers — first, that Nixon linked any pullout of remaining forces in Vietnam to the release of American prisoners of war, a story that one would assume the White House wanted, and second, that Agnew would again be the president's running mate, an announcement that conservatives had been pressing the White House to make. Nevertheless, newly discovered tapes of phone calls that Nixon made after the interview suggest he was as interested in reaction to Rather as in the answers he had given to Rather's questions.

In one telephone call that was recorded a

little over an hour after the interview, Haldeman assured Nixon that the first public soundings had been good, and various Washington officials and Nixon friends believed Nixon had made his points well. Nixon's first question, however, was, "Any of them get across the point that Rather was very antagonistic?"

Haldeman assured him they had.

Later, Nixon told him, "We ought to really do a job on Rather on this. I really think that if you can get ahold of Colson and tell him to really get a raft of letters and wires and other — really raising hell about saying, 'He got antagonistic.' Don't you think this is a good idea?"

Haldeman assured him Colson was already on the case.

On another tape recorded at 11:36 P.M., Colson could be heard telling the president, "I have the wheels in motion."

Nixon told him exactly what kind of letters he wanted and what kind of comment he wanted to generate.

"Rack him up pretty good," the president instructed, "with — more in sorrow than in anger, you know. That we hate the son of a bitch, but he dropped the ball, and all that sort of thing."

Colson noted that Rather had an unlisted phone, so there was little that could be done that night, "but the minute he arises . . ."

Nixon suggested telegrams be sent, and that some be directed to Paley and Stanton. Colson closed the conversation by promising to "have some fun" with Rather. "Yeah," the president said. "Keep the heat on him."

By then, generating phony letter-writing campaigns had become so routine, White House aides used it for more than just trying to exaggerate complaints about slanted coverage. A month before the Rather interview, NBC had aired a documentary on a day in the life of the presidency that was overwhelmingly positive (embarrassingly positive, said an NBC staffer some years later). But Colson wasn't satisfied. He issued orders to get the White House letter-writing operation going to NBC about the show. He directed that some letters should go to anchorman John Chancellor, and some to NBC. He said the letters should appear to be coming from young people, not partisan Republicans.

"They should appear to be from people saying, 'Gee whiz, wasn't it wonderful to get that intimate look at the presidency,' " he wrote, ". . . or 'We really learned something from this.' "

Why would a top government official engage in such a trivial pursuit, and tell staffers in writing to make up such lies?

"If we do," Colson wrote, "I think there is a very good prospect that NBC might rerun the show."

★ ★ ★

By mid-1971, the relations between journalists and the White House were growing worse, and they were exacerbated when first the *New York Times* and then the *Washington Post* began to print the Pentagon Papers, a long multivolume history of the Vietnam War. Although it had been given a high security classification, which meant it could not be released to the public, the history contained no information that would appear to put the nation in danger if released. What was new was that it showed how, over and over, officials in the Kennedy and Johnson administrations had given out optimistic reports about the war, even though the information they were receiving privately showed just the opposite — that the war was going poorly. As is well known, the publication created an uproar and the Nixon administration went to court to stop publication. When the Supreme Court ruled that the government couldn't block publication of anything in advance, except in the rarest circumstances of national security, it became a landmark case for press freedom. For me, however, it was one of the most embarrassing lapses of my career. By coincidence, Secretary of Defense Laird was our guest on *Face the Nation* on the Sunday that the *Times* printed the first installment of the Pentagon Papers. As Pentagon correspondent, I was invited to be one of the guest questioners that Sunday, but neither I nor anyone else on the panel thought to ask him about it. To us, he hadn't been there in the period covered by the Pentagon Papers, so it didn't occur to us to ask him about it. What we didn't know was that Laird had been prepared to tell us the administration was going into court to try to stop the rest of the papers from being published. As he left that day, he wanted to know why we hadn't asked about it, and no one had a ready answer. From the first day, Laird put his own spin on the story, referring to the documents as the "McNamara Papers." To the end, he never referred to them as the Pentagon Papers.

I had always felt stupid for missing the significance of the story, but I later learned that in the beginning, Nixon had not been all that concerned about it himself. As Haldeman later revealed in his memoirs, Nixon at first dismissed the whole thing as something that had nothing to do with him. It was Kissinger, Haldeman said, who convinced Nixon that the wholesale release of classified information was an attack on him, and that it would be seen as a sign of weakness if he didn't retaliate. Whatever the case, I should have asked Laird about it, a point that my colleagues in the Pentagon press corps did not let me forget.

Still, in the weeks to come, the Pentagon Papers resulted in one of my favorite Pentagon stories. Once the Court ruled that the *New York Times* and *Washington Post* could print the papers, those of us covering the story began hounding the Defense Department to release the entire set. Defense officials refused, saying they were "classified." Some days later, I wandered into the Pentagon's underground shopping mall bookstore and discovered that a commercial publisher had printed the entire four volumes of the Pentagon Papers and had put them on sale. There they were, on sale to the public in the basement of the building where government copies were being kept upstairs in a safe, classified top secret! To me, it was the perfect illustration of the absurdity of the government's security classification system. I raced to a phone and called the office for a camera crew. By the time they arrived, word had spread that the books were on sale, and lines of military people, some in uniform, had cued up to buy them. Pictures of the lines, combined with several interviews with those waiting to purchase the books and comments from Pentagon officials stating that the books were still officially classified and couldn't be released, made a fine story for the *Evening News* that night, and even produced a call from Walter Cronkite, who told me, "If you hadn't had those pictures of people standing in line, I would have been convinced you made that up."

Unnecessary secrecy became my pet peeve, and when Pentagon security agents again searched my desk after I had broadcast some long-forgotten piece of "sensitive information" I got a Top Security Cover Sheet — the kind that was required to be placed on classified documents when they were stored in safes — and stapled it on my notebook. When Pentagon officials would call news conferences, I would show up with my "Top Secret" notebook. The chairman of the joint chiefs of staff, Admiral Thomas Moorer, looked like he was going to blow his cork when he spied me lifting my "Top Secret" cover and writing in my notebook during one of his news conferences, and minutes later I got a call from the assistant secretary of defense, Jerry Friedheim.

"Please just don't do that anymore," he pleaded with me. "I know you're joking, but the chairman doesn't, and every time you do it, I get chewed out." Friedheim was perhaps the best public-affairs officer I ever dealt with, and a trusted friend, so I promised not to do it again. But I told him it would be nice if he could stop the security people from going through my desk. I don't know if it was because of him, but there was never another sign of my desk being searched.

As happens on any beat, the news moved away from the Pentagon in the early months of 1972. Nixon had continued to draw down the American force in Vietnam, but peace negotiations seemed to be going nowhere. Nixon made his historic trip to China, there was a breakthrough on arms control during his trip to Moscow, but those were stories to be covered by our White House correspondent, Dan Rather, and our State Department man, Marvin Kalb. It was also an election year, but Roger Mudd, Dan Schorr, Bruce Morton, and David Schoumacher had that story well in hand. The *CBS Evening News with Walter Cronkite* was becoming the *CBS Evening News* without *Bob Schieffer*. So, I was relieved when Bill Small called me in early in June and told me to plan on spending the rest of the summer in Miami. Both political conventions would be held there, and CBS News needed someone on the scene to do the advance pieces. It meant I would be getting a piece of the political story.

On June 17, the weekend before I had planned to fly to Miami, a peculiar story appeared on the front page of the *Washington Post*. It said that five men had been arrested trying to break into the headquarters of the Democratic National Committee at the Watergate Hotel. The story said the break-in was apparently part of an elaborate plot to bug the telephones there, and one of the burglars was apparently a former employee of the CIA. My first thought was: Why would someone want to bug the phones in a political headquarters? The story said four of the men were Cubans from Miami with anti-Castro connections. Whatever they'd had in mind, it seemed to have no connection to politics or anything I would be covering. I remember someone saying, "It's just some crazy Cubans doing crazy things." That sounded about right to me, and when I left for Miami, it was not to look for people connected to the break-in; it was to cover what I thought would be the big news that year, the Democratic and Republican conventions.

# Fourteen

## *1972: Control and Chaos*

The political conventions don't amount to
much anymore. Once the parties began se-
lecting their nominees in state primaries,
there was no longer any real reason to hold
conventions, and in recent years, they have
become little more than marketing devices,
more akin to auto shows than places where
political business is conducted. Purged of
controversy, the arenas where great ideas
were once debated have become showplaces
where the parties roll out the new candidates
in much the same way auto dealers roll out
the new models. Stripped of even mild suspense, they have also become deadly dull. It
is hardly surprising that, year after year, convention television ratings have continued to
sink. The low ratings are often cited as evidence that Americans are losing interest in
politics, a conclusion I have always thought
to be dead wrong. It's not a lack of interest in
politics, it's because the conventions have become so incredibly boring. Given the choice,
who would watch an infomercial, which is

what the conventions have become. Today, television executives look on the conventions as a burden. They wouldn't say it out loud, but when they plan convention coverage, the thought foremost in their minds is simply this: How little time and resources can we devote to it without being criticized?

When I was sent to Miami to cover the conventions that summer, there was a far different mind-set. Television executives saw the conventions as the arena where the networks could engage in hand-to-hand combat, a place to show off their news organizations and enhance their corporate images. Television people planned their year around the conventions. Some had been known to postpone weddings to be available for convention assignments. For correspondents and producers, conventions were the places where careers were made and broken. For the networks, the stakes were even higher; if a news organization's convention ratings were good, that usually ensured good ratings for our evening news broadcasts in the years to come.

When I arrived in Miami that summer, hundreds of CBS technicians were already on the scene, building the elaborate anchor booths inside the convention hall, and our executives were already ensconced in rented oceanfront villas. In those days, our philosophy at CBS was if NBC sent one crew to cover a story, we sent two. If they sent two, we sent three. As a key producer, Sandy Socolow, said one day, "At CBS, nobody ever got fired for spending too much." In those days, it was a true statement.

I was thrilled to be part of it, little knowing that the conventions I would see unfold that summer would bring out the worst in the convention system. Both parties held their conventions in Miami that summer. The Democrats met in July, in what would be the last truly open convention, and it would be a disaster. The Republican gathering in late August would be tightly controlled and devoid of news, and would become the model for all conventions of the future.

There was no suspense about who the Republican nominee would be, and by August, Richard Nixon was so far ahead in the polls there was little doubt he would be reelected in November. Nixon's top aide, H. R. Haldeman, had decreed there would be no dissent of any kind at the convention that summer, and with Nixon forces in complete control, the convention was totally scripted, purged of all controversy and spontaneity. It was also deadly dull, so dull I can remember only three things about it. The first image that sticks in my memory is the night that entertainer Sammy Davis, Jr., gave President Nixon a big hug during an outdoor concert. Presidents are not used to being touched, and

Nixon was so ill at ease that he would sometimes flinch when people got close to him. When Davis grabbed him that night, Nixon appeared so stunned by the contact that his face took on the expression of a man having a stroke.

My second memory is from the night that our reporter Daniel Schorr somehow obtained a copy of the convention's master script, which allowed him to predict in advance when "spontaneous" demonstrations would break out. The script was so detailed that it even included various speakers' rehearsed "ad libs," including an aside from John Wayne, who seemed to look away from his script, and in his best John Wayne voice, drawled, "Don't get settled down for a speech from me, 'cause speech-makin' isn't my business." At today's carefully planned conventions, the networks are given detailed scripts well in advance. But in 1972, we still thought of them as spontaneous events, and watching Schorr with his secret script predict coming events such as balloon drops and floor demonstrations made for some hilarious moments.

My third memory is one of the worst moments of my life. Since I had been traveling most of the summer, Pat decided to join me in Miami for the Republican convention. She flew to Texas and dropped off our daughters at my mother's in Fort Worth, and arrived in

Miami on the night before the convention was to begin. By then, Susan was just over two years old, Sharon, eleven months. It was the first time both of us had ever gone out of town without them, and it would prove to be a short separation. Pat had been in Miami no more than two hours when my brother called from Fort Worth. Sharon had developed a high fever and they had taken her to the hospital. Fearing meningitis, doctors had given her a spinal tap. They thought she was all right, but wouldn't know until the analysis was completed and her fever broke.

We were terrified. Pat took the next plane back to Fort Worth; I was to follow on the next one if Sharon hadn't improved. It was the worst night of our lives, but by the time Pat arrived at the hospital, Sharon's fever had subsided as rapidly as it had risen a few hours earlier, and she was jumping up and down in her hospital bed when Pat walked in. It had been tonsillitis, not meningitis. Even so, Pat decided to sit out the convention in Fort Worth, and it would be many years before both of us ever left the girls at the same time, and only once until they graduated from high school did Pat and I ever fly on the same airplane without them.

The Democratic convention, which had come first that summer, was everything the Republican convention was not. Not only was it unscripted; it was unorganized, out of control, and soon plunged into complete chaos. Democrats shouldn't have been surprised. In 1972, a disastrous convention was just one more stop in a year when nothing had gone as they hoped or expected. Nixon would eventually be reelected in a record landslide, but in January of that year he had been running virtually dead even in the polls with Maine senator Edmund Muskie, who had actually led Nixon in several polls the previous year. Muskie had been the overwhelming favorite to win the Democratic nomination, but he had run a campaign that depended heavily on the endorsements of top Democrats around the country, while George McGovern, a little-known South Dakota senator, had run as an antiwar candidate and worked the other side of the street — the young and disenfranchised, those who had been barred from participating in the bloody Chicago convention in 1968. As Muskie had found out, endorsements from the establishment didn't buy you much in 1972. He won the first primary in New Hampshire, but only by half as much as expected after an episode in which he seemed to cry while defending his wife from attacks in a local newspaper. His supporters issued frantic press releases, pointing out that "Jesus wept," but voters were not impressed, and when Muskie ran fourth to George Wallace in the Florida primary, his campaign was all but over, and McGovern, arguably the weakest candidate in the field, wound up the Democratic candidate.

Wallace had been the wild card that year and he had a potent new issue — busing. Playing on white fears of the growing political power of blacks in 1968, he had carried five southern states while running as an independent presidential candidate. But he had returned to the Democratic Party in 1972, when a federal judge had ruled that children could be bused out of their neighborhoods to achieve racial balance in the schools. If ever there was an issue made for George Wallace, it was "busin' of little chil'ren," and he rode it hard and successfully, ranting against the "pointy-headed intellectuals, and the hypocrites in the media and the federal government" who sent their kids to private schools and put other people's children on buses. With Muskie and Nixon polling around 42 percent in the polls, Wallace consistently scored 12 to 17. But even after he won the Florida primary, no one really thought he could win the Democratic nomination. Instead, it was generally believed that once he was formally denied the nomination in Miami, he would mount another independent run and that the election would turn on that. It was, in fact, what many Democrats had hoped for, and with good reason. As long as

Wallace, with his great popularity in the South, remained in the race, Nixon never rose higher than 43 percent in the polls, the percentage of votes he had captured when he had beaten Hubert Humphrey in 1968.

Then Wallace was shot.

On May 19, while campaigning in Maryland, he was inexplicably wounded by a deranged gunman named Arthur Bremer. The shooting left Wallace paralyzed from the waist down. The next day, he won both the Maryland and Michigan primaries, but the wound that would leave him in intense pain for the rest of his life forced him to drop out of the race.

In the beginning, old-line party regulars had not taken McGovern's candidacy seriously. He was a one-issue, end-the-war candidate, and one-issue candidates never won. But as Muskie's campaign crumbled and other candidates fell during the primaries, it was McGovern's guerrilla army that had all but sewed up the nomination by the time we got to Miami that summer. Even then, no one was quite sure how he had done it, nor did they give him much chance come fall. He was anathema to Democratic leaders in the South, who saw him as the leader of long-haired antiestablishment radicals. Early in his Senate career, he had alienated organized labor, and he was never able to win over the big-city bosses, blue-collar workers or the ethnic groups that had always been the core of Democratic support in the Northeast. Not only would McGovern never have the support of those groups; he had rewritten party rules to exclude most of them from the Miami convention. After the convention riot in Chicago, young activists had vowed never again to allow party bosses to dictate who came to conventions and who would pick nominees. McGovern had seized the moment and become chairman of a commission to overhaul party rules. The rules were rewritten. No longer would just the voices of old white men be heard. The doors of the Democratic Party were being opened to women and blacks and Hispanics. The reforms were long overdue, and by the time party regulars realized McGovern's rewritten rules made it easier for an outsider to capture the nomination, outsider McGovern had done just that. But there was a downside. To ensure that all the various groups were represented, a system of quotas was introduced. Half of every state delegation had to be women, a certain percentage, black or brown. A confusing maze of formulas that no one really understood was put in place. Yet for all the quotas, there was no requirement for Jews, Poles and Italians, the ethnic groups that had been the very core of the Democratic Party in the Northeast. Nor was there any place for the ward captains and precinct leaders who, year after year, had gotten out the big-city vote. Not only were they not invited; they were made to feel unwelcome. They were the Old Crowd and it was a new day.

What the newcomers somehow forgot was that winning politics is usually the politics of inclusion, not exclusion. The candidate who wins finds ways to bring people into the tent, not keep them out. What I saw that year was something I would see many times over the years: When campaign rules and laws are to be overhauled, no one comes to the task with total objectivity. They are always rewritten to give someone an advantage. The changes wrought by McGovern corrected many wrongs, but they were designed to take power from the establishment, and that year McGovern was the antiestablishment candidate.

The crowd that gathered in Miami was not the crowd that had come to Chicago, and you could sense it the moment you walked onto the convention floor. Martin Plissner, our CBS News political director, had surveyed all the delegates that summer, and his research told it all. Twenty-three percent of the Miami delegates were under thirty; fewer than 3 percent had been under thirty in Chicago. Blacks had risen from 5.5 percent in Chicago to 15 percent, women from 13 to 38 percent. Perhaps as significant as who was in the hall were those who were absent. There were 255

Democratic members of Congress that year, but only 50 had made the cut as delegates. And as Theodore White noted in *The Making of the President 1972*, neither were Democratic mayors such as Dick Daley of Chicago, Joe Alioto of San Francisco, Frank Rizzo of Philadelphia and Sam Yorty of Los Angeles. The Miami delegates could claim they had been chosen by a process that had been more open and fair. What they couldn't claim was expertise in the job at hand: winning an election.

As the newest member of the campaign team, my convention assignments were not the choicest. During the afternoons, I was usually on protest patrol and spent a lot of time with various demonstrators, some of whom enjoyed running naked. I never understood why, since most of them weren't much to look at, but aren't the uglies always the ones that want to show their wares?

During the evening sessions, I roamed the convention-hall perimeters, and one night I interviewed a man who was upset because health officials wouldn't let him take his donkey into the hall. His complaint was that he had obtained a ticket for the donkey, and anyone with a ticket, man or beast, had a right to go in. I can't remember much about the interview expect the poor man kept shaking his head and saying, "I just think it's unfair after I brought him all this way."

★ ★ ★

We soon learned that the new voices who had come to Miami had not come to remain silent. As more and more of them insisted on talking, party officials lost all control over the proceedings. The opening session on Monday night did not conclude until 4:30 Tuesday morning. The Tuesday session was even worse. It ran until 6:30 Wednesday morning. As the sessions went longer and longer, I was allowed onto the convention floor to spell Mike Wallace, Dan Rather, Roger Mudd and our regular floor reporters, and one evening I found myself on the floor, literally. I had located Allen Ginsberg, the famous Beat Generation poet, sitting cross-legged on the floor doing meditations. I would ask him a question and he would respond, "Ah Oooom . . . Ah Oooom." I notified the anchor booth, and in short order Walter Cronkite switched to me in some puzzlement. It took a minute to explain what was going on to Walter, but once he understood, he said, "Put your earphones on him, so he can hear me. I want to talk to him." I held the microphone and stood there as Walter and Ginsberg discussed the fine art of meditating. At one point, Wal ter apparently said a couple of "Ah Ooooms," too, but since Ginsberg was wearing my earphones, I couldn't hear. I was too junior to complain and just happy to be there, but Walter's habit of telling the floor reporters to put their earphones on the person they were interviewing, so he could chat with them, royally annoyed some of the senior correspondents. Hughes Rudd, one of the more acerbic CBS reporters, once became so infuriated that he told me, "If the old son of a bitch does that to me one more time, I'm going right up to the anchor booth and put the earphones on him and tell him to interview himself!"

The long sessions that had given us junior reporters a chance to get some practice were as bad for McGovern as they were good for us. He had chosen Missouri senator Tom Eagleton as his running mate, but on the night McGovern was to make his acceptance speech — the most important speech at any convention — various groups had insisted on nominating their own symbolic choices for vice president. The process dragged on well past midnight, as everyone from Dr. Benjamin Spock to CBS's own floor reporter Roger Mudd had received votes. (Roger got two votes and deadpanned to Walter that he considered it "a base to build on.") By the time McGovern finally got to the podium, it was 2:30 in the morning and the television audience had shrunk from more than 17 million homes to 3,600,000. Only on Guam was McGovern seen in prime time.

Frank Mankiewicz had been McGovern's

senior strategist that year, and three decades later, he spoke candidly about what a disaster the convention had been.

"But we didn't know it then," Mankiewicz said. "We had no understanding of television and how it worked. We knew it was a mistake that McGovern didn't get on in prime time. But we left Miami thinking it had been a good convention, democracy at work, open give-and-take, everything our campaign stood for.

"It was not until a week or so later that people told us how it had all looked on television, and on television it didn't look like democracy at work. It looked like people out of control. It looked like total chaos."

In that week after the convention, Mankiewicz would also discover it was only going to get worse. Tom Eagleton, the man McGovern had chosen as his running mate, had forgotten something. He had forgotten to tell McGovern he suffered from mental illness.

# Fifteen

## *The Last Serious Campaign*

Bruce Morton had been the CBS correspondent assigned to McGovern, but the networks always beefed up their campaign teams after the conventions and I got the good news that I would be joining him on McGovern's campaign plane. In one way or another, I've covered every campaign since, but '72 was my first national campaign, and first campaigns are like first loves — no matter what comes later, you never forget them — and the McGovern campaign was like no other.

It would be a week before we got any inkling of the "Eagleton problem," and I spent the week after the convention crisscrossing the South to see if McGovern had any support there. He didn't. Man-on-the-street interviews are notoriously inaccurate gauges of public sentiment, but I remember spending several hours on an Atlanta street one afternoon and being unable to find a single person who intended to support him. Georgia's moderate young governor, Jimmy Carter, told me he intended to meet McGovern at

303

the airport if he came to Georgia, but had no intention of campaigning for him. It was clear Carter didn't see McGovern as the kind of candidate Georgia was looking for.

"I'm a businessman," Carter told me, "and I don't feel like a scoundrel. I've worked with my hands all my life. I'm a farmer and I believe there's a feeling that McGovern has not adequately expressed willingness to, and appreciation for, hard and honest work."

The state's Democratic National committeewoman, Mary Hitt, was even less flattering. She said some of McGovern's ideas seemed "communistic." On a one-hour special the following Sunday, I reported that McGovern's chances in Dixie were not looking all that good.

By then, McGovern knew he had even worse problems. The campaign headquarters in Washington had received anonymous calls telling of rumors that Eagleton had been hospitalized for mental illness on several occasions, and in a breakfast with Mankiewicz and Gary Hart, McGovern's top aides, Eagleton finally confirmed it all. He had been hospitalized three times during the 1960s for depression (he called it melancholy), had been given electroshock treatments twice and was still on medication. He had not revealed any of it to McGovern because he believed he had long since been cured. It was like a long-ago broken leg that had healed, he told them. After the convention, McGovern had gone to a lodge in the Black Hills of South Dakota to rest, and when Mankiewicz told him what Eagleton had said, he invited Eagleton and his wife to join him there and discuss it. *Time* magazine and the Knight newspapers had also picked up the reports and had asked McGovern for comment, but had not yet printed the stories, and the reporters covering McGovern had no idea it was about to break. When McGovern and Eagleton called a joint news conference the following Tuesday, Adam Clymer, who was covering McGovern for the *Baltimore Sun*, expected so little he brought along a fish he had caught that morning to show it off to the other reporters.

"It was a fine fish," Clymer remembered, "an eighteen-inch trout, but when I got there, everybody was talking about rumors of a big problem with Eagleton. No one knew what it was, but I realized I needed to take the fish back to the car and get to work."

The news conference was a stunner. McGovern introduced Eagleton, who laid out his medical history. McGovern followed with an unqualified endorsement and said he had no qualms about Eagleton remaining on the ticket. And for twenty-four hours, he stuck with him. The next day, he said he not only wanted to keep Eagleton, but supported him "one thousand percent." It was a statement that would dog him the rest of the campaign, but that night, McGovern placed a late-evening call to Karl Menninger, at that time perhaps the most well-known psychiatrist in the country and one of the founders of the Menninger Clinic.

"I found him in Saratoga Springs, New York. It was midnight," McGovern told me. "He said he was sick at heart, because he wanted me to be elected and that he just hated Nixon. I asked him what to do, and he said he couldn't diagnose Eagleton on the phone, but he said half the people in the country were scared to death of mental illness.

"Menninger said that group of people wouldn't support me if I kept Eagleton on the ticket. Then he said the other fifty percent of the people had relatives with mental illness, and they would never forgive me if I kicked him off.

"I said, 'Well, it sounds like I'm damned if I do and damned if I don't, so what should I do?' And he said, 'For the security of the country, it's probably best to ask him to step down.'

"I don't think he would give that advice today. Eagleton was a manic-depressive with suicidal tendencies. You could have stabilized that today with lithium, but lithium was just coming into use then. They didn't know much about it.

"After saying I was behind him a thousand percent, it made me look like a damn fool, but I decided we had to ask him to leave."

McGovern spent the rest of the week sending back-channel hints to Eagleton that he should step down. The signals seemed clear to everyone but Eagleton. He campaigned furiously, drew large and friendly crowds, and returned to Washington on Sunday to appear on CBS's *Face the Nation*. What followed was one of the most extraordinary spectacles ever. As Eagleton was telling the *Face the Nation* interviewers that he intended to stay on the ticket, and that as far as he knew he still had McGovern's support, Jean Westwood, McGovern's handpicked chair of the Democratic National Committee, was on the NBC program *Meet the Press*, saying it would be in the party's best interest if Eagleton stepped down.

As first reported by Teddy White, that night, Eagleton and McGovern met secretly at the home of a mutual friend. "He congratulated me on my *Face the Nation* appearance and I congratulated him on Jean Westwood's hatchet job on *Meet the Press*," Eagleton's notes of the session later showed.

"He said he had nothing to do with it, and I said, 'George, don't shit me.'"

They made it official the next day. Eagleton was stepping down and the search for a new running mate would begin.

McGovern had made no real background check on Eagleton. He had been selected at the convention by McGovern and his aides during a harried meeting when all of them were operating on only a few hours' sleep. Their first choice had been Boston mayor Kevin White, but Ted Kennedy hadn't wanted him, so they had settled on Eagleton.

In an interview for this book, McGovern told me, "Eagleton was a midwesterner, he was Catholic, he was strong with labor and I needed that, and he was strong with the Muskie people and I needed them. I checked with Mike Mansfield, who was the Democratic leader in the Senate and he gave him a big endorsement and that was good enough for me, so I decided to go with Eagleton."

In truth, McGovern's chances of being elected were so remote that few Democrats were interested in being on the ticket with him that year. Polls showed that only Ted Kennedy's presence on the ticket would improve McGovern's chances, but Kennedy had turned him down repeatedly. At various times that year, seven Democrats — Kennedy, Connecticut senator Abe Ribicoff, Minnesota senators Walter Mondale and Hubert Humphrey, Wisconsin senator Gaylord Nelson, Maine senator Edmund Muskie and Florida governor Rubin Askew — had told McGovern they had no interest in running. He had tried to sound out Sargent

Shriver, former head of the Peace Corps and former ambassador to France, but he was in Moscow and unreachable.

With Eagleton gone, the search had to be restarted. McGovern went back to Kennedy three times, only to be turned down three times. He canvassed the others one by one; some said no privately, Humphrey turned him down publicly and Muskie drew the decision out over several days before finally saying no.

This time around, Shriver was easier to locate, said yes, and the choice was approved by the Democratic National Committee, which had been called into special session in Washington. Many years later, I asked Shriver if he had been surprised that McGovern called. "Not really," he said. "I was watching it play out and he was getting to the bottom of the barrel and someone said, 'He may have to call you,' and then he did."

Why did Shriver say yes when so many others said no?

"Nixon," he said. "I just didn't think much of him."

The night Shriver was formally picked, I interviewed McGovern and asked if he felt he was somehow starting over.

"I think you can say that," he responded, "but I'm not discouraged."

But of course he was. He told me later he knew the campaign was lost when the

Eagleton affair blew up. In May, with Wallace still in the race, McGovern had pulled to within five points of Nixon in the polls. But after Wallace was shot, Nixon began to climb, and after the Eagleton debacle he kept climbing. As the Republican convention opened in late August, Nixon had climbed to 57 percent in the polls and led McGovern by an astonishing 23 points. The lead would grow even wider after the Republican convention. Theodore White said being assigned to the McGovern campaign that year was like being assigned to cover a wake.

To me, it was more like a football game that was sixty to nothing in the first quarter. You knew who was going to win, but you had to wait awhile for it to be official. I couldn't have cared less about the lack of suspense. It was my first campaign and, like the football fan who stays to the very end, no matter how lopsided the score, I wanted to be there for every play.

I spent the first few weeks traveling with Shriver, and as McGovern had predicted, he proved a tireless campaigner. He knew in his heart of hearts the campaign was going nowhere, but went out day after day and did his duty. Shriver was an affable man, but what I remember most about those weeks was his wife, Eunice — JFK's sister. She had one of the best political minds I have ever encountered and was one of the most intense women

I have ever known. As she was driving home some point to me one day on the campaign plane, I looked down and she had actually grabbed the lapels on my coat to make sure I was paying close attention. It was also on Shriver's campaign plane that I first came to know his daughter, Maria. She was sixteen. In today's carefully controlled campaigns, where consultants monitor every movement of a candidate's family, it would be unthinkable to allow a candidate's daughter to roam freely in the press section of the campaign plane, but Maria spent more time with us than with her family.

"I kept telling Mummy and Daddy that being back there with you guys was where the action was. I didn't want to be in the front of the plane with all those campaign people who were up there being serious," Maria said.

It was during that trip that she decided that she wanted to be a reporter. Ten years later, she would be working in the CBS News Los Angeles bureau, and when I suggested to one of our bosses at the time that I thought she had anchor potential, she was brought to New York, and we anchored the *CBS Morning News* on several occasions. Howard Stringer, who was then running the news department, wanted to pair us as the permanent anchor team on the morning show, but I turned it down. I had already had one unhappy experience as *Morning News* anchor several years earlier and had moved back to Washington. I had no interest in moving to New York and getting up at 4 A.M. each day, but Maria and I have remained friends since. CBS paired her with Forrest Sawyer and they anchored the morning broadcast for a year. When control of the program was temporarily taken from the news department and given over to the entertainment division, she departed to NBC, where she became one of their major anchors of prime-time specials. Sarge Shriver hadn't had much luck as a political candidate, but to me he was always something much more impressive: He was a good father. As Maria was making her way up the television ladder and facing career decisions, he would sometimes call me for advice on what she should do. "Here's what I think," he would say, "but what do you think?" If I agreed with him, he would say, "Well, I wouldn't ask you to tell her something you don't believe, but if that's what you believe, is there some way you could tell her that? She won't take it seriously if I tell her."

Maria was never fooled, of course. When I would pass on the advice, she would invariably ask, "Have you been talking to Daddy?"

After two weeks with Shriver, I joined the CBS entourage on McGovern's campaign planes. And it was an entourage. On most days during the fall campaign, we usually had twelve to fifteen CBS people traveling with McGovern. Bruce Morton and I were the television correspondents, and Connie Chung, who had just joined CBS, was the radio correspondent and did occasional pieces for the weekend and morning news. There were also two television producers, one radio producer and two camera crews, which included a cameraman, sound technician and an "electrician" who held lights and acted as an assistant to the cameraman. Roger Mudd, Walter Cronkite and other major correspondents whom we called "bigfoots" would also join us from time to time to do features and major takeouts.

As costs have gone up in recent years and network news divisions have come under increasing budget pressures, network producers and reporters find themselves constantly having to justify the expense of every move. But we spared no expense in 1972. Our assignment was to do whatever was necessary to cover the campaign, and we did. It was an enormously complicated process. Videotape minicams were still years in the future and we covered the campaign with film cameras, which meant that the reporter covering the story on any given day had to break away from the campaign in midafternoon to get his film developed, a process that could usually be done only at a local television station. The campaign would go on to another town, and

313

the reporter and producer who had put together the story for the *Evening News* would stay behind and transmit their story to New York from the local affiliate, then catch up with the campaign by flying commercially to the town where the campaign was overnighting or, if that wasn't possible, reconnect the next day. This meant that all three networks assigned two reporters to every campaign, and we would alternate on who did the daily story. If I stayed behind to do the story on Monday, Bruce Morton would take care of the *Morning News* story for Tuesday, and then he would break off from the campaign and do the Tuesday-evening story. By then, I would have rejoined the campaign and I would do the Wednesday-evening story.

The reporters on Shriver's plane had been a small, fairly orderly group, but the boisterous crowd traveling with McGovern was much larger and required two commercial jetliners. McGovern and his staff rode in the front section of the first plane, *The Dakota Queen*; the correspondents for the major newspapers and one correspondent from the major networks took up the rest of the plane. Reporters from the smaller papers, reporters who were on the campaign temporarily, radio reporters and the television technicians rode on the second aircraft, which was known as the Zoo Plane, a name that evolved out of the

314

newspaper reporters' habit of referring to the TV technicians as animals. *The Dakota Queen* was the prestigious place to be, of course, and when a reporter committed some perceived transgression, McGovern's people would threaten him with banishment to the Zoo Plane. Once, after Robert Novak had written a scathing piece in which he said some Democrats referred to McGovern as the candidate of the "three A's — acid, amnesty and abortion," McGovern banished him to the Zoo Plane. "Fine," said Novak. "But there'll be no more Mr. Nice Guy from me." McGovern soon relented, however, and Novak got his seat back. What the Zoo Plane lacked in cachet, it more than made up for in good times, and it was not the worst place to be if you had no work to do. Unlike the writers who used their time aboard the plane to write their copy, the TV technicians had nothing to do once they were in the air, and they took full advantage of it. The networks were footing the bills, the whiskey and food were free, and on long flights, the Zoo Plane sometimes looked like an airborne version of the toga party in *Animal House*.

Back on *The Dakota Queen*, we spent long hours debating among ourselves whether McGovern really had a chance, and if there was anything he could do to turn the campaign around. Most thought the answer was no, but some still believed it could be done, and on a campaign plane, I came to understand that fall, you can come to believe anything. I came to call it "aluminum tube syndrome." You spend most of your day inside an aluminum aircraft, sealed off from the rest of the world. Your needs are cared for, food is brought to your seat, and you talk to no one except other reporters and campaign aides. There are brief intervals when you are actually on the ground, but you have no real freedom. You are herded from place to place by Secret Service agents and observe the candidate from areas that have been carefully roped off to separate you from the public. Humans are creatures who roam the ground, not the skies, but after a while on a campaign, a reporter finds his senses reversing. He becomes more comfortable aloft. It is there he is fed, there he is among his friends. He is no longer a stranger confined to a pen of ropes that separate him from strangers. You won't find better or more interesting companions, and campaign planes are places where life-long friendships and not a few divorces have been made, but they are probably the worst of all places to cover or really understand a campaign, because you never have a chance to talk to the most important people in the process, the people who vote. You can never judge how a campaign is going to go when your only contact is with the candidate and his aides.

Bob Schrum, who has been one of the shrewdest of the Democratic campaign consultants over the years, was a young speechwriter for McGovern. One morning during a swing through Texas, I had taken him to one of the few restaurants that served Mexican food for breakfast and I told him McGovern was going to lose Texas and lose it badly. He thought there was an outside chance McGovern could still eke out a victory there and wanted to know how I could be so certain.

I gave him some kind of answer, but I didn't tell him my real evidence, which was the kind of thing you didn't pick up on a campaign plane. What convinced me that McGovern was going nowhere in Texas were the actions of my brother Tom, who was in graduate school at the University of Texas and had decided to run in the Democratic primary for a seat in the state legislature. McGovern was going to make a campaign swing through Texas and had planned several stops, including our hometown of Fort Worth, where Tom was campaigning. I hadn't seen Tom in a while, and I told him to meet me at the rally and we could visit. He called back the next day and said it would probably be better if he drove to Austin and met me there, that it wouldn't be good for him to be seen at the McGovern rally, and as it turned out, the only Democratic elected official I remember seeing at McGovern's Fort Worth rally was Sheriff Lon Evans, who explained he had come there in a law-enforcement capacity. Tom and I had a good visit in Austin. He won his race handily, and for a time was one of the youngest members of the legislature. McGovern lost the state mightily. I may not have seen a lot that year, but I saw that one coming. If a young, idealistic graduate student making his first foray into elective politics was uneasy about being seen with the Democratic presidential candidate, I couldn't see how that candidate was going to have much of a chance.

By late fall, more and more details about Watergate were coming out, and McGovern tried to make it an issue, but it never caught on.

"Bob Woodward and Carl Bernstein of the *Washington Post* were so far ahead on the story that the other papers just didn't want to follow up," said McGovern's top advisor, Frank Mankiewicz. "The other guys just didn't want to say 'as the *Washington Post* reported . . .' "

Perhaps more of a factor was that the story just seemed so preposterous. It was hard to believe that anyone, especially a campaign that was as far ahead as Nixon's was, would be involved in something like Watergate. It was a crime that simply made no sense. As the campaign moved into its final weeks, it became just one more issue that did not resonate for George McGovern. Nixon had opened a new relationship with China, engineered a new arms agreement with the Soviet Union, brought the economy around with wage and price controls, and when Kissinger announced in the closing days of the campaign that "peace is at hand," there didn't seem to be much left for McGovern to say.

Well, there was one thing.

And whether they liked him or not, what McGovern said late one afternoon in the last week of the campaign will forever endear him to the reporters who traveled across America on that hapless quest. It had been a particularly bad day in a particularly bad week, and McGovern was working the airport-fence line at the last stop of the day in Battle Creek, Michigan. He had bloodied one hand as he reached across a chain-link fence to shake hands with several hundred supporters. A heckler had somehow gotten behind them and was moving down the line with McGovern, shouting obscenities and calling him a Communist and other names. Finally, McGovern stopped, reached across a young man in front of him, put his hand behind the heckler's head, pulled him close and whispered something in his ear. The man's face went blank and his mouth dropped open, speechless. Bruce Morton of CBS was the pool reporter walking near McGovern, and as McGovern moved on, he asked the heckler what McGovern had said.

"Why, he told me to kiss his ass," said the heckler, who seemed truly stunned and hurt by the remark.

As pool reporter, Bruce was obligated to report the remark to the rest of the traveling press corps. It set off an uproar. Trying to maintain a straight face, Frank Mankiewicz told reporters, "He's a Democrat. Did you think he was going to tell him to kiss his elephant?" The reporters loved it, but it had created a journalistic dilemma. The word *ass* was considered an obscenity. It had never been used on television and was seldom printed in newspapers. At CBS News headquarters back in New York, high-level meetings were convened. The debate went on for most of the afternoon. Finally, it was decided that Bruce would report that McGovern told the man to "kiss a certain part of his anatomy." The *New York Times* also declined to use the word "ass," but the *Times* reporters covering McGovern, Jim Naughton and Doug Kneeland, were two of the most mischievous men in all of journalism and they were not about to let it go. The next day, they filed a follow-up report with this lead: "Democratic presidential candidate George McGovern, who yesterday told a heckler to 'kiss his ass,' today turned the other cheek to President Nixon." The lead never made it into the good gray *Times*, of course, but Naughton and Kneeland never expected it would.

Twenty-nine years later, at age seventy-nine, McGovern told me, "Sometimes you regret things like that. But I always felt good about that one." Some months later, he was on the Senate floor when he was asked by Mississippi's conservative senator, James O. Eastland, if he had really told the heckler to "kiss his ass." When McGovern said yes, Eastland grinned and said, "Good, that's the one thing you said in that campaign I agree with."

On election day, Nixon crushed McGovern as expected, carrying every state except Massachusetts and the District of Columbia. It was virtually a noncampaign. Four years earlier, Nixon had said that anyone who refused to debate his opponent should not be president, but he'd refused to debate McGovern, and all but denied there was a contest. His spokesman, Ron Ziegler, would bristle during his daily press briefings when reporters asked, "How's the campaign going?" Dan Rather began signing off his reports, "Dan Rather, CBS News, with the Nixon campaign at the White House." It made for a laugh, but had little impact. In 1972, Nixon didn't have to campaign, and he knew it. As Eric Sevareid had so often said, "Given the choice, people will always choose order over chaos." Americans were tired of the war and they wanted it to be over. But they wanted it done in an orderly way and they did not trust the disheveled radicals that McGovern seemed to represent. They wanted, and would eventually adopt, many of the reforms that McGovern championed, but the loud voices and demands for instant change that McGovern represented frightened them. In time, they would change, but McGovern's people wanted them to go faster than they were prepared to go.

In retrospect, McGovern believes that whatever chance he had to actually beat Nixon evaporated the day Wallace was shot.

"Nixon could never get above forty-three percent in the polls as long as Wallace was around. If Wallace had stayed around and run another independent campaign that fall, we might have had a chance. But once Wallace was out of it, Nixon got virtually all of those votes. They would have never gone to me."

McGovern told me he went to see Wallace in the hospital several days after the incident, and Wallace told him he was convinced that someone in Nixon's camp or some Nixon supporter had been responsible for shooting him.

He said Wallace told him, "Those boys are more worried about me than they are about you. It was just too slick. They had to have had something to do with it." There has always been speculation that the Wallace shooting was the ultimate Nixon campaign "dirty trick," but there has never been evidence to support the theory. But there is no question that Nixon knew the importance of the Wallace voters. Billy Joe Camp, who was Wallace's press secretary, told me in an interview for this book that after the Republican convention in 1972, Nixon's postmaster general, Winton Blount, brought Wallace a copy of that year's Republican party platform. He quoted Blount as walking into Wallace's hospital room and saying, "Here's your platform, George. We just passed it."

McGovern, at seventy-nine, seemed at peace with himself and his life when I spoke with him one winter day in 2001. He lives now in Montana with his wife of fifty-eight years, Eleanor. He had served during the Clinton administration as ambassador to several international organizations dealing with hunger, and he had just accepted a nonpaying post to act as an ambassador working on hunger issues for the United Nations.

After the campaign of 1972, he had returned to the Senate, was reelected for another term and joined with Republican Senator Bob Dole on a variety of issues dealing with hunger. Together they took the lead on legislation expanding the school lunch programs and other initiatives to feed the poor.

What I had always wanted to ask him was whether anyone ever gets over the rejection that comes with the kind of overwhelming defeat he suffered in 1972, and his candor surprised me.

"No, I never did," he said. "I went on with my life and I tried not to brood, but every four years I would think, well, maybe I ought to give it another try. I only succumbed to the urge once in eighty-four." (He had run a low-budget campaign, traveling without staff, and vowed to drop out if he did not finish first or second in the first four primaries. His campaign proved a refreshing novelty and he managed two third-place finishes and then dropped out as promised.)

But did he play '72 over in his mind, wondering what he might have done differently?

"Oh yes," he said. "Many times I have wondered what would have happened if any of the seven people I had sounded out about being on the ticket had accepted before I took Eagleton. That's what I have always wondered."

Did he really think he might have beaten Nixon?

"Not really," he told me. "But I might have done better. I think there were some states I would have carried, and if I had done that, I would have been the odds-on favorite to get the nomination in '76 when it went to Jimmy Carter."

Mark Shields, the columnist and political commentator, had been a strategist on the McGovern campaign and had argued that McGovern needed to put more emphasis on his war record. As a bomber pilot in World War II, McGovern had been a true war hero, and Shields wanted to stress it in a campaign commercial, but other aides had nixed the plan, fearing it would offend McGovern's antiwar constituency.

In retrospect, did McGovern feel that was a mistake?

"Well, I thought it was a good story," he said. "I didn't think it was appropriate for me to bring it up. I just kept waiting for the press to bring it up, but no one ever really did. I just didn't know much then about how to get a story like that out."

Did he then feel Eagleton had double-crossed him?

"Well, he should have told me," McGovern said. "If he had told me, we might have had time to plan a strategy. But it made me look like a damn fool. We know so much more about mental illness and depression than we used to. I know so much more . . ."

McGovern's voice trailed off. His own daughter, Terry Jane, had fought a lifelong battle with deep depression and alcoholism. Despite repeated attempts to treat the diseases, in 1996 she was found frozen to death after she had wandered into a snowbank during an alcoholic stupor. McGovern wrote a touching book about the hurt of losing a child and speaks often to groups fighting alcoholism, but it is still difficult for him to talk of Terry's death without losing his composure.

The book about his daughter was also a factor in finally healing the breach that had separated the men for so long. When McGovern came to a book signing at a St. Louis bookstore, he asked Eagleton to introduce him. Eagleton did, and McGovern has since been a guest in Eagleton's home. Both are Cardinals fans and they went to a ball game together. Eagleton has lost most of his hearing, still takes medication for his depression and no longer gives interviews about 1972. But in a gracious letter, he told me that when McGovern came to visit, they had touched on 1972 only in an oblique way.

"Somehow I mentioned that Lincoln, Churchill, Lyndon Johnson and other public figures had experienced serious depression," Eagleton wrote.

For all the mistakes and human hurt it produced, McGovern says he will always be proud of the campaign, because it was the last campaign where the issues were so real and so clearly drawn.

"It was about ideas," he said. "Ours were rejected, but we put them out there and people had an opportunity to think about them."

"It really was the last one like that," Mankiewicz added. "Today, serious reporters write stories about whether candidates are staying on message. But they don't pay much attention to the message itself."

Ninth-grader Bobby Schieffer in his bow tie, having just won his first journalism prize. (SCHIEFFER FAMILY)

## The Fort Worth Press

### HIGH SCHOOL NEWSPAPER CONTESTS

# Certificate of Award

*This Certifies That*

Bobby Schieffer

is winner of....first........place in the.....column........division of
The Fort Worth Press high school newspaper contests, conducted in co-operation with the Fort Worth High School Press Association.

THE FORT WORTH PRESS

May 14, 1952

Editor

The prize certificate.

The young Ed Murrow — a publicity shot from KXOL. Note the cigarette. (KXOL)

Twenty-year-old Schieffer interviewing cop and kids at the site of a drowning, for KXOL. (FORT WORTH STAR-TELEGRAM)

The Johnson City Windmill during LBJ's 1948 Senate campaign. The second white hat from the right is my father. Down in the shadows somewhere is me. (LBJ LIBRARY)

Young Air Force Second Lieutenant Schieffer at Travis Air Force Base with LBJ. I autographed a print of this picture, "To Bob, a fine officer and a good friend, LBJ," and put it on my desk. Came in handy. (SCHIEFFER FAMILY)

At Dallas police headquarters the day John F. Kennedy was shot. (KXAS/NBC5)

With my mother, sister Sharon and brother Tom the night before I left for Vietnam to report for the *Star-Telegram*. (FORT WORTH STAR-TELEGRAM)

A *Star-Telegram* ad.

Our man in Vietnam: with Captain Gail Anderson, with whom I flew dive-bomber missions. (FORT WORTH STAR-TELEGRAM)

332

With South Vietnamese soldiers, holding a rifle just taken off a sniper; on a rest break in the Mekong Delta. (FORT WORTH STAR-TELEGRAM)

The news anchor at WBAP-TV (now KXAS), examining a long roll of wire copy. (KXAS/NBC5)

A WBAP ad. (THE DALLAS MORNING NEWS)

The Pentagon public affairs office gave the network guys — Robert Goralski, Roger Peterson and me — gag T-shirts. The next thing we knew, this photo was hanging in public information offices all over the Pentagon. They did it as a joke — I think. (PENTAGON)

With Secretary of Defense Melvin Laird. (PENTA-GON)

The four floor men at the 1976 Democratic National Convention — Dan Rather, me, Morton Dean and Roger Mudd. (CBS NEWS)

The White House beat was a mixed bag. Covering Gerald Ford in Vail was a bit different from covering Jimmy Carter in Plains. (SCHIEFFER FAMILY)

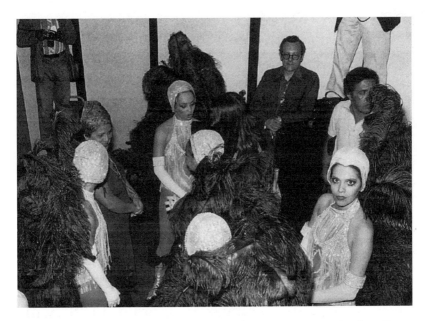

It's a tough job, but somebody's got to do it. Our hero reporter investigating the chorus line while on President Carter's trip to Rio, 1978. (WALLY MCNAMEE)

At *Face the Nation*. (KARIN COOPER/GAMMA FOR CBS NEWS)

Four presidents. Talking to Gerald Ford, with Walter Cronkite and Eric Sevareid; Jimmy Carter; Ronald Reagan (and White House chief of staff Don Regan), with Tom Brokaw and Dan Rather; Bill Clinton. (WHITE HOUSE)

With CBS chairman Bill Paley, 1980. He always dropped by on election night. I liked Paley, but he made me furious when I was doing the *CBS Morning News* — and I saw him being interviewed by Brokaw on *Today*. (CBS NEWS)

Election night, 1996. Rather apparently thinks I did it. I point to Andrew Heyward, president of CBS News. Whatever the problem was, this photo shows the traditional way to handle it in our business. (CBS NEWS)

The day the Starr Report was issued. Producers Dick Meyer and Mary Hager ran in bootleg copies from a congressman's office, edited it on the floor, then crawled over and handed it to me on the air. (BILL YATES)

Three important women in my professional life (left to right): Carin Pratt, producer of *Face the Nation*; Janet Leissner, CBS Washington bureau chief; Gloria Borger, my partner on *Face the Nation*. (PAT SCHIEFFER)

And the three most important women in my personal life: my wife, Pat . . . (CBS NEWS)

. . . and my daughters Susan and Sharon. Above (Susan on the left), with their two favorite newsmen, at the 1988 Democratic National Convention. (CBS NEWS; KARIN COOPER/GAMMA FOR CBS NEWS)

Sharon on the left and Susan. All grown up.
(CBS NEWS; KARIN COOPER/GAMMA FOR
CBS NEWS)

My brother Tom and I have always loved baseball, but he got a little further in it than I did. Above, fourteen-year-old Bob, catcher for the River Oaks Lions, and four-year-old Tom. Below, with Tom at the Ball Park in Arlington, the stadium he built as president of the Texas Rangers. (SCHIEFFER FAMILY; LINDA KAYE)

# Sixteen

## *The Nixon Endgame*

When Richard Nixon was sworn in on January 20, 1973, he enjoyed the greatest mandate of any president since George Washington.

He had beaten McGovern by eighteen million votes, the greatest numerical margin ever. He had swept every region of the country, he had carried the blue-collar vote and business groups and every ethnic group except blacks.

Yet by the end of the year, it had all slipped away, slowly at first and then with a great rush, like air escaping a punctured balloon. People had paid no attention when McGovern had tried to tell the Watergate story, but when the burglars began to tell their story, people listened.

As promised, Nixon had brought home the last of the American troops in Vietnam, but even that had not been enough to draw attention from Watergate, and then, in October, a separate scandal would surface involving his vice president. Spiro Agnew would be forced from office after it was discovered that he had taken bribes while serving as governor of Maryland.

As it was with most of the Washington press, at the CBS Washington bureau we hadn't paid much attention to the Watergate break-in during those first days after it happened. After the election, I had returned to the Pentagon beat, and with the coming of the new year, I had a new secretary of defense to cover. Once the plans were in place to bring the troops home from Vietnam, Mel Laird was anxious to wind up his tenure as secretary of defense, and Nixon named Health, Education and Welfare Secretary Elliot Richardson to replace him. I was looking forward to seeing how Richardson, a Boston Brahmin who was such a contrast to Mel Laird, would run the place. As it turned out, I never saw much of him. He stayed at the Pentagon just over three months as Nixon, trying to save himself from Watergate, kept reshuffling the government. From the Pentagon, Richardson would become attorney general and eventually be fired during the infamous Saturday-night massacre, when he refused Nixon's order to fire Watergate special prosecutor Archibald Cox. James Schlesinger, a Defense intellectual and strategist who had formerly headed the Atomic Energy Commission and the CIA, was named to replace Richardson at the Pentagon. He would prove an able Defense chief and an interesting contrast to Laird, but as the Watergate story grew, it took priority over everything. My title was still Pentagon correspondent but, like everyone else in the bureau, my main job was to cover Watergate.

Dan Rather remembers that our bureau chief, Bill Small, recognized there was "just something smelly" about Watergate in those first hours after the story broke, and insisted that it be reported on that night's *Evening News*. But it was not until after the summer political conventions in Miami that the rest of us really began to understand just how big this story was going to be or how much Nixon and his people had come to despise us.

At one point, Rather had been startled to read in the paper that Nixon aide John Ehrlichman had told our boss, Dick Salant, that Rather ought to be taken off the White House beat and reassigned to Austin, Texas. Salant later admitted that the incident had been his fault and that Ehrlichman's suggestion had come only after Salant had asked what he thought of the CBS White House coverage, but the episode was a precursor to what was ahead.

We were well aware, of course, that we were not the administration's favorites, and dealing with the White House had always been fairly frosty. There was also Agnew's ranting, which was so constant it became part of the background noise. For the CBS reporters, the first serious sign of just how determined Nixon's people were to control what we said about them had come in the closing weeks of the campaign, when the first installment of a two-part series on Watergate ran on the *Evening News*. We hadn't come up with much on Watergate at that point, and the report contained little that was new. It was basically a summary of what the *Washington Post* had reported. But it was the first long television report on Watergate and brought the entire nation up-to-date on many details that had been known only to *Post* readers. The story ran on a Friday night, and it sent Colson and his White House associates into a rage. Only after the second installment had been inexplicably postponed and a truncated version eventually run later in the week, did we find out that Paley himself — after calls from the White House — had intervened and ordered the report rewritten. Even then, most of what we learned about the White House role was just guessing. Our bosses kept most of it to themselves.

What had upset the White House, Dan Rather remembers, was that the story had finally moved from the printed page to television.

"Their strategy was to isolate the *Washington Post* and contain the story there and keep it off television," he said. "In public, they would just deny everything. In private, they would tell reporters, 'You're headed for trouble if you go down the road the *Washington Post* is on.' CBS broke the pattern."

The public hadn't noticed by then, Rather said, but from the moment the Watergate story broke, the Nixon White House attitude toward the press hardened.

As Nixon turned more and more to trying to untangle himself from Watergate, Colson reopened his behind-the-scenes attacks on CBS. As Frank Stanton, the CBS network chief, remembered it, Colson again raised the possibility that licenses for the television stations CBS owned might be revoked, unless CBS gave the White House more favorable coverage.

"It was very unpleasant," Stanton remembered. "Unlike anything I had experienced."

In public, Clay Whitehead, another White House aide, warned network affiliates that the government held the power to revoke their licenses if they carried network programming that the government considered biased. The White House backed up the threats by generating letters from the public to local stations, complaining about CBS network coverage. The strategy was to drive a wedge between us at the network and the local stations that carried our coverage. And, it was working to some extent. During some network news analysis, some of our affiliates began running disclaimers saying that the "views being expressed do not reflect the views of this station."

For CBS, 1973 was a watershed year. Frank Stanton had reached the mandatory retirement age of sixty-five and was scheduled to leave the network. It was Stanton, along with founder Bill Paley, who had built CBS, and for all practical purposes had invented broadcast news. Stanton was the man who had run the store for Paley, the impresario. He was the detail man who had set the rules for everything, from the look of office stationery to a management structure that insulated the news department from corporate and commercial pressure.

Throughout their long careers, Paley and Stanton had a love-hate relationship and never socialized, but their combined skills had built a broadcasting empire and a news department that had no equal. They were legends in an industry too young to have many, and that spring, Paley planned a huge retirement party for his longtime associate at Washington's Corcoran Gallery of Art.

All of official Washington had been invited to say good-bye to Stanton. It would also be the place for Arthur Taylor, the thirty-seven-year-old investment banker who had replaced Stanton, to do some serious schmoozing with the people who counted in the capital.

Taylor had actually been named network president the year before, when Stanton had been elevated to the new office of "Vice Chairman," a position that had been created to provide some overlap between Stanton's departure and his successor's arrival. (Taylor had been picked for the job after Paley's first choice, Charles Ireland, had dropped dead.)

The Corcoran is a half block from the White House, and John Ehrlichman invited Taylor to drop by his office for a chat before the party. Ehrlichman came right to the point. The White House wanted friendlier coverage, and what was Taylor planning to do about it? Taylor remembers telling Ehrlichman there was nothing he could do about it, because he had no control over the news department. He said Ehrlichman asked if he would just try.

"I told him no, and the reason why, which was if I did, the news people would report it on the news," Taylor said. "He more or less dismissed me after that and I left.

"On the way out, I told him what Stanton had told me to tell him, that the White House would get the coverage it deserved, good when it did well, bad when it did badly.

"It was a good exit line, but it got me onto the enemies' list, and for the first time, the IRS audited my taxes that spring."

In a matter of months, it would be Ehrlichman, along with Haldeman, who would be forced out, but the White House pressure continued through the year. (Taylor would soon lose his job as well, not because of White House pressure, but because of an unrelated dispute with Paley.)

When Taylor had reported his White House conversation with Ehrlichman to Paley, the CBS chairman had warned him to be "careful of those people," according to Taylor. But to those around him, Paley seemed increasingly uncomfortable with the White House complaints and those from our affiliates, and one day without warning, he surprised all of us by ruling that from then on, CBS was canceling its policy of offering "instant analysis" after presidential speeches.

Since his prime-time interview with Nixon in 1971, various White House officials had tried to get key CBS affiliate owners to demand that Rather be taken off the White House beat, and eventually he would be removed, but that summer he got a promotion. Walter Cronkite had just negotiated a new contract that gave him an unprecedented two months of vacation. Under the new arrangement, Roger Mudd would fill in for Walter during July and August. Roger had anchored the Saturday *News* for seven years and wanted his weekends back. He said two months of filling in for Walter during the summer was all the anchoring he needed, so he gave up the Saturday job. In addition to covering the White House, Dan had been flying to New York on Sundays to anchor a fifteen-minute newscast that CBS broadcast at 11 P.M. He was the in-house favorite to get the Saturday job, but to my surprise, Bill Small told me a tryout would be held, and along with Dan, Barry Serafin and Charles Osgood, I was one of those who would be considered. Over the next weeks, each of us anchored the Saturday *News* several times and, as predicted, Dan got the Saturday job. The good news for me was that I was chosen to replace Dan on the Sunday night broadcast. Thus, I began twenty-three years of traveling to New York from Washington on the weekends to anchor news broadcasts. In 1976, when Dan moved to *60 Minutes*, I would replace him on the Saturday *News*, a job I would hold for the next twenty years.

The new lineup meant that every CBS news broadcast would be anchored by a Texan. Walter Cronkite was actually from Kansas, but claimed Texas as his home because he had grown up there, attended the University of Texas and begun his career as a wire-service reporter in Austin. Hughes Rudd, a crusty, sardonic feature writer who would be taking the *Morning News* anchor job, was a proud graduate of Waco High

School, who received his higher education flying a glider into France during the Normandy invasion. (Gordon Manning, the CBS executive who selected Rudd for the job, said he had picked him because Rudd looked the way most people felt early in the morning. Rudd related that he was glad to take the job because a man his age had to get up early anyway to go to the bathroom.) Rather, who was taking over the Saturday *News*, was a native of Wharton, Texas, and a graduate of Sam Houston State Teachers College, while I had been born in Austin, had grown up in Fort Worth and got my degree (barely) from Texas Christian University. There was no small irony in all this. Vice President Agnew had spent most of his term berating the effete Ivy Leaguers who controlled the media. None of us had noticed much Ivy on the walls of TCU and Sam Houston State, or at the University of Texas for that matter.

As accustomed as we had become to Agnew's attacks, we had been convinced that he was out to get us, so we shed few tears when he was forced from office in October of 1973. I have few memories of Agnew's ouster, nor do many reporters. Watergate was raging, a new crisis had broken out in the Middle East and then, without warning, the story of Agnew and his troubles erupted. One day he was vice president, and then one day he was gone, forced from office after a federal prosecutor in Baltimore discovered he had taken bribes for years while governor of Maryland, and that even after he had become vice president, he had taken one $5,000 payment from a Maryland man. That payment was given to Agnew, said a friend, with the explanation that it had been raised for his re-election campaign for governor and ". . . since you never ran, it's yours."

I never knew much about Agnew and can't recall ever interviewing him. But he had taken such relish in his role as Nixon's attack dog that I always assumed he had been a Nixon admirer. So I was surprised in 1980 when he wrote a book in which he said that Nixon had thrown him to the wolves to draw attention from Watergate and claimed that Nixon's chief of staff, H. R. Haldeman, had made vague threats on his life if he did not go quietly. No such assertions were ever proven nor were they taken seriously, but only after I began research for this book did I understand just how deep Agnew's animosity for Nixon ran. A friend who remained loyal to Agnew throughout his life said Agnew went to his grave believing Nixon had set him up. The friend said Agnew believed not only that Nixon had used the federal investigation in Maryland as an excuse to get rid of him, but also that Nixon had actually encouraged investigators to look into his dealings.

John Damgard, a Washington lawyer who worked for Agnew as vice president and maintained contact with him after his fall, wouldn't comment directly on that assertion, but he said Agnew was always suspicious about why the government decided to begin the investigation that led to his downfall.

Agnew dropped from sight after leaving Washington. Virtually penniless, he paid the $10,000 fine that was part of his penalty with money that had been sent to him by his friend Frank Sinatra, and when the government billed him for $160,000 in back taxes, Sinatra loaned him the money to pay those costs as well.

Agnew had moved to Palm Springs after the scandal, but I had always wondered how he supported himself. I had heard there was some mysterious Middle Eastern connection, so I asked Damgard about it.

"Oh yes," he said. "He and King Faisal of Saudi Arabia had struck up a friendship of sorts when they met during a huge celebration of the anniversary of the Persian Empire.

"All the dignitaries had tents and there were many hours when they had nothing to do between receptions and ceremonies. Agnew liked to shoot pool and we had shipped in a pool table for him. It turned out the king had a fondness for pool, too. He heard the balls clicking in Agnew's tent and asked if he could join him.

"He didn't speak English, and Agnew didn't speak Arabic, but they whiled away several afternoons shooting eight-ball.

"The king never forgot, and Agnew was able to do a lot of business out there," Damgard said.

Nor did Agnew ever forget what he thought Nixon had done to him. Damgard said Agnew told him that Nixon had tried to call him several times over the years, but he always refused to take the calls. When the Nixon family invited him to Nixon's funeral, he at first declined, asking Damgard, 'Why would I want to do that?'

"I reminded him that, for all the slights, Nixon had twice chosen him as his running mate," Damgard said. "So he went and I think he was probably glad he did."

The fall of Richard Nixon has been well told and there is no real need to replow those fields here, but for me, those twenty-six months were a blur of events that still seem unbelievable.

In the end, it would be the tapes of his own conversations that would do him in, and to Al Haig, who had been brought in to replace Haldeman as chief of staff, that was the great irony.

"Half the stuff on the tapes wasn't true. It was just the false bravado of Nixon. He wanted to be one of the boys, a tough guy. A

357

lot on the tapes was just that — bravado."

Haig went on to become Ronald Reagan's secretary of state and earned a lot of bad publicity when, after Reagan was shot, he declared that he was "in charge." But I have always felt he deserved considerable credit for holding the presidency together during the final days of the Nixon White House, and he may have come to know Nixon better than any of those around him.

"Nixon feigned courage and bravado enough in his life that he finally developed it," he told me one day.

In the Washington bureau, we worked that year as we had never worked, and we sometimes wondered if it would ever end. Dan Rather at the White House and Dan Schorr, who had taken over most of the investigative responsibilities, carried most of the load, but they got help from our Supreme Court reporter Fred Graham and two new additions to the bureau, Lesley Stahl and Connie Chung, who did a lot of the thankless "grunt work," the endless stakeouts at doorways, courtroom corridors and other key locations where we thought we might get a picture or at least a scrap of information from someone involved in the story. Connie had been a bright young newswriter at Metromedia when I had worked there during my first months in Washington, and I was the talent scout who had brought her to the attention of Bill Small, who was looking for every bit of help he could get because of the increased workload that Watergate had put on the bureau. Connie, who had a quick wit, and Lesley, who was one of the most doggedly determined reporters I have ever known, proved tireless workers and soon earned their stripes in a bureau that, until then, had few women in professional positions and had never had more than one female correspondent at a time. Once asked the secret of her quick rise to a network job, Connie quipped that since she was Chinese, Bill Small had actually hired her to iron his shirts.

For me, many days would start at 6 A.M. when I would trudge into the bureau to do a live report on the *Morning News*. I would then put in my regular shift at the Pentagon, only to have assignment editor Bill Galbraith call late in the afternoon to say I would be needed that night to stake out some administration official who was thought to be appearing at some function or other and who might or might not have something to add to the Watergate story.

Galbraith's favorite line always was "Probably nothing will happen, but I'd feel naked if I didn't have someone out there." After about three or four of these late-night assignments, I suggested he get himself a nice coat if he felt naked. He didn't laugh. Assignment editors never do.

★ ★ ★

Television tells a story best when it has pictures to illustrate it, and Watergate was not always a picture story but we found ingenious ways to report it. Once the existence of the tapes became known, investigators pressed to have them released and, to counter the pressure, the White House at first released several dozen leather-bound volumes of edited transcripts. Even in their edited form, the transcripts provided a trove of information, but we didn't know what to do with them. Newspapers could print long excerpts, but that wouldn't work on television. Nor did picking out a few key phrases and putting them on the screen with graphics.

It was bureau chief Small who devised the plan that we eventually used to tell the story. He got network clearance for a one-hour special and selected several correspondents to read the transcripts aloud. Barry Serafin was chosen to read Nixon's lines, I was chosen to read John Dean's lines, and various other correspondents were assigned the roles of Haldeman, Ehrlichman and the others. We all protested that we weren't actors and that we would look silly trying to act out the parts, but Small told us, "Don't act, just read them."

We did it under protest at first, but as we rehearsed, we realized it might work. I got so carried away that I went home and put on a tan suit and striped tie, so I'd be dressed just as Dean was during his appearance before the Ervin committee. That night, we stood at small podiums and read the transcripts in flat monotones. We had no pictures. But to hear the sentences read aloud gave them an even more sinister flavor. The White House had edited out all curse words, substituting "expletive deleted," and to hear that phrase several times in one sentence just added to the bizarre nature of the the proceedings. The readings proved such an effective way to tell the story that the network cleared more time for similar specials in the future, and we were all awarded Emmys. Small certainly deserved one for coming up with the idea, but I'm not sure his troupe of budding thespians did.

Even those of us who covered it tend to forget how long Watergate went on. It had begun in June of 1972, and it was not until almost twenty-six months later, August of 1974, that it finally played itself out. Like London during the blitz, for those of us in Washington, Watergate had become part of our lives. And then one day it was over. After all the long hours, all the adrenaline and pressure, the Nixon presidency collapsed. I was at the Pentagon in the office of Air Force general Daniel (Chappie) James when he took a phone call.

"That was the White House," he told me.

"They said to prepare for the transfer of power."

That was it. Nixon was leaving. Gerald Ford, who had been selected by Nixon and confirmed by Congress to replace Agnew, would become the nation's first unelected president.

I called the CBS News desk and was told to get to the White House as fast as I could, and to do whatever Dan Rather told me to do when I got there.

There had still been no official announcement to confirm that Nixon was leaving, but so many people were crowding into the White House press room that Dan suggested the most helpful thing I could do would be to go across the street to Lafayette Park where CBS was setting up a camera. We had broken into programming by then and I was soon talking to Walter Cronkite on television, describing the scene around the White House. Hundreds of people had begun to gather there: tourists, kids out on a lark and the kinds of rough characters who stop at car wrecks hoping to see some blood. It was like being in the middle of a crowd that you somehow felt might charge you at any moment for no real reason. I wasn't really scared, but as night fell, I was on my guard. There was one moment of comic relief when a Mayflower moving van pulled up to the White House curb and stopped. Walter Cronkite had just switched to me for an update on the latest activity outside the White House, and when I saw the big van I told him, "Well, Walter, I don't know if this means they've decided to leave tonight or what, but you can see that moving van has pulled up and stopped." It seemed like a scoop to me, but the words were hardly out of my mouth when the traffic thinned and the van lurched on. I said something to the effect that apparently the Nixons weren't leaving just then, after all. Walter thanked me and switched to someone else.

From my perch in Lafayette Park, I watched on a TV monitor as Nixon made it official at 9 P.M. Eastern time. He would resign the presidency at noon the following day. By now, it was clear that many in the crowd around the White House had availed themselves of liquid refreshment, and they cheered long and lustily. You never know what several hundred drunks might do, but to my relief, they made a few catcalls but otherwise left me alone.

The next day, I was dispatched to Andrews Air Force base to watch Nixon board *Air Force One* for the last time as president. It was a scene that would be carried live on television, and I was part of a crowd of hundreds of television technicians, reporters and onlookers, but it was a scene I had seen unfold dozens of times. We had a rule in those days that when the president was outdoors, we always sent a camera crew to cover him, just in case something untoward happened, and as one of the more junior members of the bureau, I had often drawn the assignment of going to Andrews to watch presidential departures. What struck me that day was how normal it all looked. Nixon walked briskly up the stairs to the aircraft door, as he always did, and once there, turned as he always did and waved. He smiled as he always did. It was a smile of no mirth but then it never was.

It was so normal, it was eerie. Later, Defense Secretary Jim Schlesinger told me I had missed one detail that Nixon's people had not.

"The Air Force always sent one of its generals out to see Nixon off," Schlesinger told me. "But that day, they sent a colonel, and I got a call from the White House complaining that I hadn't sent a general. I hadn't even realized it until they called."

Schlesinger's relations with some at the White House had been strained during that period, and remain so today because in those final weeks he had taken extraordinary precautions to prevent a military coup, safeguards that rankled several White House aides.

Among other things he had ordered General George Brown, the chairman of the joint chiefs of staff, to notify him immediately if Nixon tried to give direct military orders to any of the military's theater commanders around the world.

Haig thought (and still believes) that Schlesinger was grandstanding. Schlesinger had always liked Nixon, and remains an admirer of his achievements in arms control, but he decided to take no chances in those final weeks. Nixon's low tolerance for alcohol was well known to those around him. He sometimes slurred his words after one martini and his behavior had been more and more erratic toward the end, but that was not what worried Schlesinger. He had just been witness to too many odd occurrences during his years in government. On his second day as head of the CIA in the years before he came to the Pentagon, White House counsel John Dean had asked him to remove CIA files regarding Watergate from the Justice Department and to leave a letter in the files saying the papers had been taken to the CIA for "national security reasons." He had refused. Later, friends said he had been perplexed when Haig had once asked him to use the facilities of the super-secret National Security Agency to duplicate the White House tapes. No reason was given, but Schlesinger again refused unless a member of the Independent Counsel's Office approved it.

When I asked him more than two decades later if he really thought Nixon might have tried to use military force to stay in office, he did not answer directly.

"In the oath I took to become secretary of defense, I swore to defend the constitution against enemies, foreign and domestic," he said. "I did what I thought was necessary."

At Andrews Air Force Base, I watched *Air Force One* with Nixon on board make a routine takeoff and then I drove back to the White House, where Gerald Ford was to be sworn in as the new president at noon, Eastern time. By then, Nixon would be somewhere over Missouri, his beloved Middle America. Once Ford was sworn in, Nixon's plane would lose its designation as *Air Force One*, because only the aircraft the president is aboard carries that designation.

As we watched Nixon leave, we had speculated that he would still be president for several hours and would still have the power to launch nuclear war and all the other majestic powers of the presidency right up until the time Ford was sworn in. Until the moment Ford was sworn in, it was Nixon who would have access to the codes necessary to launch the nuclear forces. We were worried, but apparently those closest to Nixon were not.

"We weren't worried, because we knew Nixon had no idea how to do it," one of them told me later. "He had the codes, but he didn't know what to do with them. He didn't know how to do anything like that. He would have had to call Kissinger. He left all the me-

366

chanics for things like that to him."

Of all the public figures I have encountered, Nixon remains the most perplexing. He was the oddest person I ever met, the antipolitician who somehow rose to the top in politics, the insecure loner in the world of huge egos and extroverts, a man of extraordinary pettiness, yet a person of broad vision, whose views on arms control and international relations were far ahead of many of his contemporaries and most in his own party. He could be shallow and mean, yet he had some kind of deep inner strength that enabled him to remake himself again and again. If he could not rise above the disgrace of his presidency, he was, at the least, able to move beyond it, and toward the end led a useful life in which his advice was sought by the leading figures of his time.

"He was full of politics, but he wasn't really a politician," his longtime friend and former White House counsel Leonard Garment said. "I can remember flying with him when he was a private citizen, and he would tell me, 'Now, you take the aisle seat, I don't want people coming up and touching me.' It was an odd thing for a man who had spent all his life in politics, but for him the politics was part of the strategy to ward off loneliness."

For me, the great lesson of the Nixon administration is that it underlines what a trap the White House can become, even for a politician as devious and as knowledgeable as Nixon. The White House complex at 1600 Pennsylvania Avenue is the center of the most sophisticated communications network in the world. Yet, it can also be the most difficult spot on earth to get accurate, objective information. Once inside the White House, the president can cut himself off from the world. Every person who comes there does so at his invitation. All who work there, work for him. For many of those who serve him, it is the high point of their lives. They have fought hard and served tirelessly to get to the White House and they become territorial about their responsibilities and are always on alert for anyone — journalist, opinion-maker, member of Congress, old friends from the outside world — who might come between them and their access to the president. In such an atmosphere, it is easy for even the most well-meaning aide or the closest friend to tell a president only what he wants to hear rather than what he needs to know. In the Nixon White House, where the paranoia began at the top, it was the easiest of all.

"The White House, above all, is a great incubator of paranoia," Haig told me.

Nixon did not want to hear bad news and shut himself off from those who brought it. Encouraged by sycophants whose only aim was to gain his favor, his frustration at news leaks became an obsession aimed at punishing, if not destroying, the press. It was a ridiculous, time-wasting, if not hopeless, quest. But behind the White House gates, with the awesome power of the federal government at their disposal, talking to no one but each other, even the most outrageous things seemed possible to Nixon and his men. When Nixon would become angry and he wanted to find out how many Jews worked in the bureaucracy, or demanded that the IRS be set upon some perceived enemy, there was always someone at his side willing to carry out the orders. I once asked Nixon's old friend Mel Laird if he thought Nixon had somehow lost his mind somewhere along the road to the Watergate cover-up. "No," Laird told me, "I think he just thought he could get away with it." Henry Cashen, who worked as a young aide to Chuck Colson, said he finally learned that "real loyalty meant saying enough is enough" and that his old boss, Colson, had run at only one speed: "full throttle." In the closed world behind the White House gates, there was no one to tell him to slow down.

The greatest danger that any president faces is being cut off from the accurate information he needs to make decisions. As Nixon became more and more frustrated with his inability to control the press, he cut himself off from all sources of outside information, even

369

newspapers, preferring instead to get his news from summaries keyed to his own biases, which had been prepared by his staff. He may have found it a more pleasant way to get the news, but not always the most accurate. When Nixon and his people cut themselves off from the press, what they really did was cut themselves off from reality. For all its faults, it is the press — the interaction with reporters in interviews and at press conferences — that gives a president the best feel for what is on the public mind. The press may have its own biases, but reporters are often the only people the president sees who are not on his payroll or have nothing to sell him, and there is always some value in that.

As I look back on the Nixon White House more than two decades later, what I find striking is that for all the efforts of Nixon and his people to manipulate the press, it really didn't matter. His opening to China and his overture to the Soviet Union remain significant achievements that remain untarnished even by the skullduggery of Nixon's political team. Good policy, if it is good policy, rises above whatever is said about it at the time. Good policy always trumps a bad press. Had Nixon and his people remembered that, rather than devoting so much time to getting even with their critics, they might have saved their presidency.

# Seventeen

## *The Pardon*

Every schoolchild knows that Neil Armstrong was the first man on the moon. But who was the second? I have no idea, nor do most Americans, but I know how he felt. I replaced Dan Rather at the White House.

Dan's turbulent years covering the rise and fall of Richard Nixon had made him the most famous reporter in America. To aspiring young journalists out to right the world's wrongs and take on the establishment, he was their idol. To Nixon and his aides and even to some of the conservative owners of our affiliate stations, he was the devil incarnate. But love him or hate him, he had become one of the most recognized people in America. I, on the other hand, was becoming well known in the journalistic community and within CBS, but I was hardly a household name when Bill Small called me one week after Nixon's resignation and told me I had been selected to replace Rather as the network's White House correspondent.

For the first time in my life when I had been

offered a job, I blurted out, "Why?" Small, never one for casual talk, said, "Because we want you to."

By then, Small had left his job as Washington bureau chief and been promoted to senior vice president for news in New York. Rather, he told me, was being promoted to a new job in New York, where he would become anchor for all CBS News documentaries, a post last held by Edward R. Murrow. Dan was convinced at the time, and remains convinced today, that he was pushed out of the White House because of pressure from a group of affiliate owners who were unhappy with his coverage. There is no question that a group of affiliate owners, many of them in the South, had been upset with Dan, and White House officials had done whatever they could to stir the pot. It had all come to a head earlier that year when Nixon had held what was billed as a "news conference" at the National Association of Broadcasters convention in Houston, where Rather had worked before coming to the network. Station owners and managers were given a rare opportunity to ask the president questions, but to give it all a veneer of authenticity, Rather and the White House correspondents from ABC and NBC were also allowed to question Nixon.

As Rather rose to ask his question, the hometown crowd cheered (there were some scattered boos as well) and it led to the now-famous confrontation in which Nixon asked, "Well, Mr. Rather, are you running for something?" To which Rather said, "No, sir, Mr. President, are you?"

Nixon had no use for Rather, and my guess is that by then the feeling was mutual, but all of us can recall moments of anger or surprise when we blurt out something we wish we hadn't said, and as I watched the exchange on television, I saw the remark in that context. I winced, but it didn't seem all that big a deal and I remember wondering if, for once in his life, Nixon had tried to make a joke. Apparently, he had not. He saw no humor in the episode. As I was doing the research for this book, I got some new insight into just how furious he was. Arthur Taylor, who had replaced Frank Stanton as head of the CBS television network, was also at the convention, and told me about an illuminating and previously undisclosed incident. As he was leaving the press conference, he said a Secret Service agent approached and asked him to come to Nixon's hotel suite.

"When I got there, Nixon was absolutely livid. He began shouting, 'How dare your reporter dishonor the president in that way?'" Taylor said. "He went on and on, and when I said I didn't believe Dan had dishonored the president, he actually put his right hand on my shoulder and shoved me. It was remarkable."

Taylor continued to support Rather when he returned to New York, and he was somewhat surprised to discover that his boss, Bill Paley, the CBS board chairman, had also taken offense at Nixon's behavior. That surprised Taylor, because Paley had became increasingly uncomfortable with affiliate criticism of our coverage of the White House, but on this one he took Dan's side.

"I remember him telling me that Nixon was trying to embarrass our man in front of his colleagues, and he didn't like it," Taylor said.

I have always tended to believe what Rather believed — that he was taken off the White House beat because of affiliate pressure — but Paley's reaction to the Houston incident is telling. In those days, nothing happened at CBS without Paley's approval, and if he was taking Dan's side, it was unlikely that anyone within the company would have challenged him.

Even so, I still have my doubts that CBS executives just suddenly decided to wipe the slate clean for no other reason than that a new president was coming to the White House. But whatever the reasons, the change was ordered. I was sent to replace Dan and handle day-to-day coverage. Phil Jones, who had covered Ford as vice president, was added to the team to develop overview stories that went beyond the daily happenings, and Bob

Pierpoint, who had covered Nixon with Rather, would stay on to handle investigative pieces and radio.

Dan had developed a national following by then, and many of his fans were working reporters and the newspaper columnists around the country who covered television. To them, there was no question about what had happened. Dan hadn't been pushed; he had been shoved off the White House beat.

The CBS public-relations people kept emphasizing that Dan was getting a promotion, that in being named to head up the documentary unit he would be filling the chair that had been vacant since Edward R. Murrow had left CBS. But several TV critics noted that it was in that chair that Murrow had had the problems with Paley and the CBS brass that had caused him to leave CBS.

In a biting Sunday strip, cartoonist Garry Trudeau had me standing in front of the White House, reporting as follows:

"White House sources told newsmen today that the president said . . . uh . . . um . . .

"All right, all right, all right, I know what you're all thinking. Where's Dan Rather? Right?

"You're wondering why he got the axe, right?

"Well, I don't know really . . . I mean . . . I wasn't in on the decision at all!

"It was the affiliates — they just couldn't take him.

"I mean let's face it, Dan wasn't exactly MR. TACT!

"Sigh, I dunno . . . Maybe it's just as well in the long run, I mean, you know?

"Anyway, this is Robert Schieffer at the White House.

"Look, don't get me wrong! Personally I liked the guy, a lot!

"But . . . but . . . that's the way it is."

The strip was right on except for one thing. My real name is Bob, not Robert.

I didn't quite know what to think. It was pretty funny, but still . . .

Pat put it all into perspective.

"Who would have thought you'd be the star of television and the funny papers," she said.

Well, there was that.

So I called Trudeau and asked for an autographed copy of the original. He sent one along. I framed it and went to work covering the White House. That comic strip became my favorite souvenir, still hangs in my bathroom, and after all these years, I can't help but grin when it catches my eye.

The first thing to say about the reporters who covered the Ford White House was this: We fell in love with Jerry Ford.

If you were a Washington reporter who had

been working in the Watergate pressure cooker for two years, there was just no other way to put it, and it was the worst kind of school crush. The kind that always breaks your heart.

It began that first afternoon of Ford's first day in office. Since I had been sent out to Andrews Air Force Base in the Maryland suburbs to watch Nixon's departure, I didn't get back to Washington in time to see Ford take the presidential oath in the White House East Room. But I did get there in time to see him introduce his new press secretary, Gerald terHorst, in the White House Press Room. TerHorst was the Washington correspondent for the *Detroit News* and had covered Michigan congressman Jerry Ford for years. He was a well-known, well-liked member of the White House press corps.

"One of your own," Ford had called him that afternoon.

He was also a slight, little fellow, and when Ford introduced him, Peter Lisagor of the *Chicago Daily News* shouted, "Lift him up so we can all see him, Mr. President!"

The room erupted in laughter, the good-natured laughter of friends who were paying terHorst the highest compliment — the well-sharpened needle.

It was the first time in two years that anyone had laughed in that room that had been the scene of so many tense briefings, and as the laughter rolled across the room and turned into chuckles, it was as if a hard rain had stopped, the clouds had parted and everything looked and smelled different. No one could remember the last time Nixon had come to the press room, but suddenly there was the new president, not really holding a news conference but chatting, bantering with reporters as he had done so many times over the years with the reporters who had covered him on Capitol Hill.

Jack Kennedy had counted many reporters as friends, and they moved freely in his social circle. Ford had never had that kind of relationship, but he had had a good professional relationship with dozens of journalists who covered him at the Capitol. Unlike Nixon, who was never comfortable with them and considered them part of the opposition, Ford had an easy, relaxed way with reporters, treated them with respect, and they had always responded in kind. To the reporters on Capitol Hill, he had never been a camera hog, nor was he the one reporters went to for "source stories," but he was usually accessible and was known to be a "straight shooter." Jerry Ford was never one to air his party's dirty laundry, but he had a reputation for telling the truth.

And he was so normal. He liked a good locker room story, a drink before dinner and golf on the weekends, and like the rest of us he sometimes seemed to have a hard time remembering he was the president.

He once told me that when he had been the leader of the House Republicans and had come to the White House for conferences, he always picked up a handful of White House matchbooks and took them back to his congressional office. He said he gave them to visiting constituents, who thought they were wonderful souvenirs. One day after he became president, he said he was going through the White House and realized he was still unconsciously stuffing White House matchbooks in his coat pocket. He said he had to laugh at himself when he realized he now had all the White House matches he would ever need.

Only a person as at ease with himself as Jerry Ford was would have told such a story, and after the weirdness of the Nixon years, those of us in the White House press corps couldn't get enough of it. Press coverage is like a pendulum. It never stops in the middle. Invariably, it goes too far one way or the other, and we went overboard on Ford. We chronicled his every move and he let us behind the scenes to get the pictures we needed to do it — Jerry Ford puffing on his pipe as he conducted a staff meeting, Jerry Ford stripping down to his trunks and allowing us to film him swimming laps at his Alexandria, Virginia, pool on his first Sunday as president. (He spent the first week of his presidency commuting from Virginia while the Nixons' furniture was moved out of the White House.) When he told us he read the sports page before he read the front page, we made a story out of that, and when we heard he made his own breakfast, we asked to watch. And to our surprise, the request was granted. Ford's photographer David Kennerly arranged for several wire-service photographers to snap away as the PRESIDENT OF THE UNITED STATES TOASTED HIS OWN MUFFINS!

What a scoop!

And then one Sunday morning — one month to the day after Nixon announced he was resigning — Gerald R. Ford called us all to the White House and broke our hearts. He announced he had decided to pardon Richard Nixon.

We couldn't believe it. I remember being called at home and being told the president would have "an important announcement," but I had no idea what.

Ford had gone to church that morning, not with his family, as was usually the case, but alone, and when he emerged, reporters asked his plans for the rest of the day.

"You'll find out shortly," he told them, but he gave no other hint.

When I got to the White House, my friend from the McGovern campaign, Adam

Clymer of the *Baltimore Sun*, was already there, and said he had been on the first tee at a golf course when he got the call and there were rumors the announcement had something to do with Nixon. Surely to God, he's not going to pardon him, we mused, but surely to God that is exactly what he did. Ford told the nation that, after careful consideration, he had concluded it would be years before Nixon could get a fair trial and that he did not intend to allow Nixon or the country to be put through such an ordeal, and he said only he could bring an end "to the bad dreams that continue to reopen a chapter that is closed." Therefore, he said he had decided to grant Nixon "a full, free and absolute pardon." Whatever he had done, Nixon had beaten the rap. Some of his associates had already gone to jail and others would soon go, but Nixon never would.

I was stunned, and my feelings reflected that of many Americans. Over the next week, Ford's public-approval rating, which had been well above 70 percent, plunged below 50 percent, a deficit he was never able to recoup. (Among reporters, writer Richard Reeves wryly noted, it had gone from 100 percent to 0.) The extraordinary honeymoon with the press ended as quickly as it had begun, and terHorst, who had been press secretary for less than a month, resigned in protest. Ford would eventually reestablish friendly relations with the press, because it was impossible not to like him. But once he pardoned Nixon, we never looked on him in quite the same way. For the rest of his term, there would be questions about a deal: Had Nixon agreed to resign and make Ford president in return for a pardon?

I had never really worked out in my own mind what I thought should be done with Nixon, but I did not believe that he should have been pardoned before charges were brought against him, and as for the politics of it, I thought it was a blunder of gargantuan proportions.

Because it happened without warning on a Sunday morning, we broadcast Ford's announcement in its entirety in a CBS News special that evening. We also included reaction from elected officials, and it was clear that the pardon was going to set off a firestorm on Capitol Hill. Some Republicans praised it, but much of the praise was guarded. Most of the Democrats took an unforgiving line. Maine senator Edmund Muskie said Ford had set an undesirable precedent, a double standard. Texas senator Lloyd Bentsen noted the obvious, that Nixon had been pardoned by the man whom he had appointed to the presidency, a man who had not been elected by the people.

Even so, there was some disagreement that night among our correspondents about the long-term political ramifications. During a round table at the end of our CBS broadcast, Bruce Morton, who was our main political correspondent, thought it would hurt Ford in the short term, but would not have a lasting effect. By the time the 1976 elections rolled around, he said people would be worrying about other things.

I disagreed. I recalled that during his confirmation hearings for vice president, Ford had been asked, if Nixon should be forced from office, would the new president have the right to pardon him, and Ford had replied that the new president would have that authority, but that "the country will not stand for it." I said I not only thought the pardon would be one of the issues if Ford ran, I thought it would be the main one: "People are going to say, 'This man said he would not do this, and now he's done it.' How will we know that he's going to keep his word from now on?"

Over the next weeks, the furor over the pardon came to a boil. Ford was met with angry pickets during his first road trips as president. On Capitol Hill, they demanded to know if Ford had worked out some kind of deal in advance with Nixon. Finally, Ford had to go to Capitol Hill personally and do what presidents almost never did, appear before a congressional committee, where he swore, "There was no deal, period. Under no circumstances." That calmed the situation somewhat, but Ford had paid a heavy price, and his relations with the press and the public were never quite the same.

Campaigning for congressional candidates had been a part of Ford's life for as long as he had been in politics, and as the furor over the pardon began to calm, he did what he had always done in campaign years. He hit the road.

He logged more than 26,000 miles that fall, campaigning for his Republican colleagues, but the elections were a disaster for his party.

The economy was in the Dumpster, the pardon was fresh on the minds of many, and the Republicans lost forty seats in the House and four seats in the Senate. Not one House candidate that Ford had campaigned for won, and when the new Congress assembled, Democrats would hold a two-to-one majority.

In 1976, Ford did run for the presidency, of course, and most analysts thought the pardon had been the decisive issue in his defeat. Ford, himself, in his book about his White House years, began the final chapter with a list of "what ifs." Listed first was the question "What if I hadn't pardoned Richard Nixon?" Still, Ford believed he had done the right thing.

In his book, Ford wrote that he had "failed

to anticipate the vehement reaction and thought there would be greater understanding and forgiveness."

But in private conversations with friends on the day he issued the pardon, he seemed to understand exactly what the consequences would be. He and Mel Laird were playing in a golf tournament at the Burning Tree Club that weekend, and he had gone directly to the golf course after making the announcement. Lyle Mercer, who was playing in Ford's foursome, told me that the president had seemed distracted; toward the end of the round, Mercer said to him, "Mr. President, that was a courageous thing you did."

Ford thanked him and said, "It's really going to hurt me politically, Lyle, but it is just something I had to do for the country and for Nixon."

In those days, I didn't buy the Ford argument that the pardon was good for the country. I thought it was a terrible thing to do, but as the years have passed, I have concluded that Ford was right and I was wrong. Whatever doubts I had about the wisdom of his decision were removed as the Clinton impeachment unfolded. As I watched the ordeal that Clinton and his pursuers put the country through, I thought back to that Sunday when Ford pardoned Nixon, and tried to construct in my own mind what it would have been like if Richard Nixon had been brought to trial. How would it have affected the country to see a former president being questioned in the dock or led away to prison? We can be sure it would have taken years for the drama to play out, and as Ford had said on the day he pardoned Nixon, "During this long period of delay and potential litigation, ugly passions would again be aroused, and our people would again be polarized in their opinions."

As I watched and reported on the relentless partisan pounding that took place during the Clinton impeachment, when no one on either side could look at the situation in an objective way, I was able to comprehend more easily what Ford had been talking about. No solution is ever perfect, but I have come to believe that Ford did choose the best course of action available. By pardoning Nixon, he gave the country a chance to cool down and move beyond a scandal that had hung over it for almost two years, a scandal that had come hard after the country's longest and most divisive war and the assassination of a president. It was a break the country sorely needed, and I now believe that Ford did it knowing full well what it would cost him. In that sense, it was an act of real political courage. Ford's presidency did not last long, and if one looks at his legislative accomplishments, they didn't amount to much. But if we judge presidents by the impact they had on their time, it is hard to overlook what Gerald Ford did. He settled the country down and allowed it to return to normality, and did so at the cost of his own political future. In the turbulent period that stretched from Johnson to Clinton, it may well be the impact of Gerald Ford that is remembered as most significant.

Covering the White House is the most glamorous job in all of journalism and, in television, the most prestigious. It is the place where the networks assign reporters who have been put on the fast track, the testing ground for future stars, and it is the White House correspondent who generally gets more air time on the *Evening News* programs than all the other reporters, but I soon learned what other White House reporters knew: It was not always as exciting as it seemed from the outside and could sometimes be downright boring, a place where real reporting was sometimes all but impossible and where you had contact with the president and his staff only when they chose to see you.

White House reporters have security passes that allow them inside the White House, but only in the walled-off section known as the press area. This includes the briefing room familiar to television viewers, where the White House press secretary holds his daily session with reporters. Newspaper wire-service and magazine reporters who cover the president on a regular basis have desks off the main briefing room, and the television companies have small, closet-sized booths toward the rear. A hallway leads to a series of offices occupied by the president's press staff, but entrances to the rest of the White House are blocked off by Secret Service agents. Reporters can generally talk to members of the press staff and are free to call other White House officials on the phone, but if the calls are not returned, there is little a reporter can do about it.

As the White House has gone from one administration to the next in recent years, succeeding presidents have put tighter and tighter controls on information, with the result that most news from the White House is "spoon-fed," that is, reporters assemble at the White House and wait for officials to give them handouts. It was not as bad in those days as it is today, and the reporters make a valiant effort and try to develop sources, but without White House cooperation, it is all but impossible. In the George W. Bush White House, for example, officials who return reporters' phone calls must report the contact to the press office, all interviews must be arranged through press contacts, and all television appearances by administration officials throughout the bureaucracy must be arranged and approved by the White House Press Office. When the White House throws walls up around the press, it is hard to get beyond them. It's not that the news that is handed out is unimportant. On the contrary, almost everything the president says or does is important to someone and must be reported, but to a reporter it's not the most interesting kind of work.

Eleanor Randolph, then of the *Chicago Tribune*, who covered the last months of the Ford White House and the beginning of the Carter White House with me, said she never got accustomed to it.

"That press room could get pretty small and really close in on you, when you had to stand around for hours just waiting for some scrap of news.

"When I left the White House beat to cover Congress, it was like taking off a girdle."

The saving grace was travel. When the president went on the road, reporters and White House officials couldn't help but be thrown together, and there is no experience quite like traveling with a president of the United States. News organizations pay each reporter's travel costs, but the White House does the rest. The White House Travel Office issues each reporter spiffy luggage tags that read "White House Press," charters the airplanes the press rides on (and pays for), makes the hotel reservations, delivers the reporters' baggage to their hotel room doors and hires buses to deliver the reporters from the airport where their chartered plane lands to wherever the president is appearing (or at least to roped-off, heavily guarded areas in the vicinity).

It was during my early travels with Ford that I realized what an advantage the traveling White House can be for presidents who are campaigning. When a president and his enormous entourage of handlers, Secret Service agents and the trailing press arrive, it's like the circus coming to town. When Ford began to campaign for the presidency, I remember stopping in one town where local officials had been handing out flyers announcing, "Come See *Air Force One!*" In smaller type, it gave the time and date and noted that President Ford would be aboard.

The good news for Ford's White House press corps was that he was constantly on the road, which gave us plenty to write and report. The bad news was that we were never home.

After barnstorming around the country for Republican congressional candidates that fall, Ford left for Japan, South Korea and Vladivostok, in the Soviet Union. There was serious arms control business to discuss with Leonid Brezhnev, and his first meeting with the Soviet leader went well. The rest of the trip was mostly ceremonial, and it was becoming clear to me that much of a White House correspondent's duties amounted to standing outside historic palaces or government houses, waiting to get a picture of the president when he emerged after meetings with whoever the leaders of that country happened to be. Whiling away the hours outside an ancient pagoda in Kyoto, Japan, as Ford and Kissinger were being shown the inside, we noticed that all who had entered the temple had removed their shoes, which were carefully arranged outside the door. When a soft rain began to fall, aides opened umbrellas and held them over the shoes. When the rainfall increased, each pair of shoes was moved to a covered area. Since we had nothing else to do, we speculated about who determined which official got to carry the president's shoes. And what about the Kissinger wing tips?

"Oh, they just walked over there by themselves," quipped NBC's John Chancellor.

For all the tediousness of waiting for the president to do this or that, traveling with the president would be a great way to see the world if you didn't have to work. I went to China twice as part of press entourages and never saw the Great Wall, but a few reporters actually signed on the trips for the sightseeing. Naomi Nover, a grandmotherly woman of indeterminate age, whose late husband had long before operated a regional news service for small newspapers in the Midwest and Rocky Mountain areas, would go on White

House trips long after her husband's death and his news service had ceased to have any clients. She took copious notes and wrote page after page of copy, which she sometimes offered to share with other reporters, but everyone knew the reports went nowhere. But because she was a kind soul who had once bought a refrigerator for the White House Press Room and dedicated it to the memory of her dead husband (President Ford graciously declined an invitation to participate in a dedication ceremony), we treated her with courtesy and she became something of a mascot for the press corps. And because she bore a striking resemblance to George Washington, with her prominent nose and tight white curls, she also became an attraction in our traveling road show.

During those inevitable hours when we were standing in the roped-off press pens waiting for the president to emerge, we would amuse ourselves by calling over locals and telling them she was the great-great-great-great-granddaughter of the Father of our Country. The locals would ooh and aah, and in minutes, everyone in the crowd would be staring at Naomi and nodding sagely. Bill Plante, who covered the Reagan White House, remembered that on a trip to China in 1984, Naomi had been trying to get into the press area, where reporters were watching the president and Mrs. Reagan pose for photos among the Chinese artifacts. When the Chinese guards refused to let Naomi through, Gary Shuster, then of the *Detroit News*, whipped out a dollar bill, directed the guard's attention to Washington's picture there and then pointed to Naomi. Naomi got in.

In retrospect, it may be that we didn't work as hard in those days as it seemed at the time.

# Eighteen

## *Stumbling Along*

Here's the difference between covering the White House and the other Washington beats. When you're the Pentagon correspondent, for example, and the secretary of defense takes his vacation, you can take your own vacation. Or just go home.

When you're the White House correspondent and the president goes on vacation, you have to go with him. If that president was Jimmy Carter and he was taking a few days off in Plains, Georgia, and he didn't want you along anyway, that could be fairly tedious, especially if it was over a holiday. If the president was Jerry Ford, it wasn't a bad deal at all. Ford owned a condo in the resort of Vail, Colorado, and for years, he and his family had been going there over the Christmas holidays to ski. When the White House announced that Ford intended to continue the traditional trip as president, and that the press corps who traveled with him would be allowed to take our families along on the press plane (we had to pay their way, of

394

course), it seemed a great way to celebrate Christmas and ring in the New Year. Pat, and Susan, who had just turned five, and her sister Sharon, who was three, joined me on the press plane, with families of the other reporters. We rented a house on one of the Vail ski slopes from a man who had made his fortune as Vail's first garbage hauler, and invited my mother and brother and sister to come out from Fort Worth and join us. It turned out to be a great vacation for them — and for Ford, who went skiing every day.

But there is a difference between going on vacation and watching someone *else* take a vacation, and even though Ford was doing little of consequence, the holiday season is always a slow news period and the *Evening News* broadcasts at all three networks wanted stories from us almost every night, which meant we had to do a certain amount of work.

Gathering the news — and there wasn't much of it — wasn't the problem. Ford's new press secretary, Ron Nessen, a former NBC reporter, would hold a briefing, and then Ford would head to the ski slopes. We would trudge after him and get some pictures as he came skiing by with his family and Secret Service agents.

Everyone who has ever skied knows that even the most adept skier occasionally takes a fall, but when the president of the United States takes a fall, that's news, and in a slow holiday news period, it was big news, and Ford took several tumbles.

The coverage provoked considerable criticism, especially from some of Ford's aides, but as John Chancellor of NBC said, "When the president of the United States takes a header, what are you gonna do? Keep it a secret?" And at first, Ford himself didn't seem to mind.

Putting together a story of the president falling on the ski slopes is not the hardest kind of journalistic task. It boils down to saying "Watch this!" and showing the pictures. The hard part was getting the story on the air. To do that, the three networks chartered a huge Alouette helicopter, which flew out from Denver each day and picked up one correspondent and one producer from each network and then flew us back over the Rocky Mountains to Denver, where we could develop our film at the local affiliate station and transmit our stories over leased telephone lines back to CBS News headquarters in New York. It was not an inexpensive proposition. In those days, it cost about a dollar a mile to lease the line to transmit the story back to New York, and when you added in the cost of the helicopter and other incidentals, such as lodging and transportation costs for correspondents and producers, the reports on Ford's ski accidents probably cost in the neighborhood of $25,000 each.

It took something over an hour to get to Denver from Vail, and on clear days, the helicopter ride was breathtaking. One minute, the ground would be only a hundred feet below the chopper, then it would pass over a mountain peak and the ground would suddenly be thousands of feet below.

It was not the view that took my breath away on the first flight. It was when the pilot told us that the air was so thin at those altitudes that the helicopter did not have enough power to get over the highest peaks.

Not to worry, he told us; the standard procedure was simply to wait until there was an updraft, which would easily lift us as high as we needed to go. It seemed to work. As we headed toward the highest peaks, he would simply fly the helicopter in lazy circles as he waited for a draft to give us the lift we needed and, sure enough, we would then be on our way.

There was one other breathtaker. The weather was not always clear. On one flight, we got caught in a white-out caused by blinding snow. I had been shot at on the Ole Miss campus and flown dive-bombing missions in Vietnam, but flying around in the mountains in a helicopter when the visibility was zero was not my idea of fun.

"This is great," I remember telling producer Mark Harrington, who was with me that day. "We're going to be killed trying to get a news story on the air about the president falling down on his skis."

When we landed in Denver that day, I was fairly shaken, and when Harrington and I called the *Evening News* in New York to tell the executive producer, Paul Greenberg, what we had in mind for a story that night, I was soon babbling about the harrowing flight.

"I understand," he said, "but I've got big problems here. I can't be dealing with all that."

Such is the world of television on deadline.

Filing a story from Vail, in the Rocky Mountain time zone, meant that we were up against an early deadline. The *News* aired at 6:30 P.M. back on the East Coast, 4:30 in Denver, which meant we had to have the film developed and the story edited and ready for transmission to New York by around 4 P.M. Denver time. That meant that once we flew there from Vail, drove to the local television station and got the film developed, we had about forty-five minutes, never more than an hour, to get our story done.

Since the networks didn't want to pay for another helicopter to take us back to Vail, we rented cars for the return trip, and since the mountain road between Denver and Vail was only two lanes in those days, the trip usually took four hours. That meant we were lucky to get back to Vail by 9 P.M. Except for a couple of exceptions, we repeated the process daily for two weeks.

Even with the daily travel, the Vail encampment was not without its pleasures. Once we got into the routine, we were up early and took ski lessons before we began the day's news-gathering. On Christmas Eve, Ford put on a "news lid" for the evening and the next day, promising no announcements of any kind unless some emergency arose.

My mother had brought out a big batch of tamales from Texas, and Tom Brokaw, then the NBC White House correspondent, and I threw a party one night for the press corps. Ford dropped by and, being the perfect hostess, Mom prepared the president a plate of tamales, carefully removing the tamales' corn-husk wrappings.

It was a move she would always regret. The next year when Ford had begun to campaign for president, he went to Texas and, during a stop at the Alamo in San Antonio, someone gave him a tamale. Ford took a big bite — corn husk and all — and of course had to spit out the husk, to the delight of photographers.

"The poor man didn't know tamales had a husk," Mom lamented. "If I'd just showed him how to unwrap them instead of removing those husks, he would have known."

For a man in his sixties, Ford was in remarkably good health and shape. He swam laps every morning, played golf on the weekends and was a good skier. The falls he took on the ski slopes that winter had provoked some laughs (Ford himself laughed about it) and had it stopped there, it would have amounted to nothing. But television is a powerful medium that burns images into the viewers' memory, and when Ford went to Europe in the spring, and his heel slipped on a wet step as he was coming down the ramp on *Air Force One* and he fell headlong down the stairs, his stumbles became a staple of late-night television comics. A young comic named Chevy Chase became famous for imitating Ford's pratfalls on *Saturday Night Live*. Overnight, Ford's image as a well-conditioned, good-natured former athlete changed into Ford, the clumsy oaf. He became the butt of jokes, including one that had Vice President Rockefeller "a banana peel away from the presidency."

It had been no laughing matter in the first minutes after Ford fell down the aircraft stairs. We had been in Salzburg, Austria, and the press plane had landed ahead of *Air Force One*. With our camera crews, the American press had been taken to the roof of the airport terminal so that we could get pictures of Ford's arrival, and when we saw him fall, we at first thought he had been shot.

Ford was on his feet quickly, and remarkably he was unhurt. The fall had been a nasty one. But it was the fall that Americans remembered when they saw it on television, not Ford's meeting there with Egyptian president Anwar Sadat. As John Chancellor had said in Vail, "If the president takes a header . . ."

To say Ford was clumsy was not only unfair; it was inaccurate. Ford, a onetime college football player, did have a bad knee, but he was anything but clumsy. Yet after the fall in Salzburg, he became self-conscious about it, and the more self-conscious he became, the more he began to run into things: doors, walls, whatever was there. Like a child who vows not to step on the crack in the sidewalk and then finds it impossible to walk without stepping on the cracks, Ford seemed to find it impossible to go through a door without bumping something. He began to bump his head with such frequency on helicopter doors that Press Secretary Nessen tried to block us from watching Ford board helicopters.

One day, when the press was herded into the Rose Garden to watch Ford leave the South Lawn of the White House by helicopter, we were told to stand in a roped-off area behind a tree, which we discovered allowed us to see the helicopter but blocked our view of the door. We protested, but a Secret Service agent said, "Sorry, that's where they told us to put you."

The incidents continued on into the fall and plagued Ford throughout the campaign.

When, on two successive trips to California, two crazed women tried in separate incidents to take shots at him, events that in no way could be blamed on Ford, it just added to the impression that bad luck and odd mishaps seemed to follow him.

Being somewhat clumsy myself from time to time, I always had some sympathy for Ford. Nevertheless, I continued to report the bumping stories, and late in the campaign, in Kalamazoo, Michigan, there had been another one. Ford had been whistle-stopping across the state in a train and, after speaking to the crowd from a balcony on the last car, he had turned to reenter the train and, bang, the train lurched and he bumped his head on the doorway.

As the train had gone on to the next stop, I had stayed behind in Kalamazoo to file my story, and once that was done I went to the airport, where I booked a flight to catch up with the campaign.

It was on that plane that the gods got even with me for all those stories I had done about Ford running into doors. As I was taking my carry-on bag off my shoulder and preparing to sit down, someone at the back of the plane shouted, "Hey, Schieffer!" I was startled and turned to see who it was. It was Hal Fischer, one of the producers from our Chicago bureau. I turned and, happy to see him, said, "Hey, Hal." Unfortunately, I had not stopped walking and ran head-on into the overhead luggage compartment. I hit my head hard enough to see stars and fell to my knees. Except for a good headache, I wasn't hurt, but the next time I saw the president, I felt duty-bound to tell him.

"By God," he said, "I wish I could have seen it!"

Because it was so short, Ford's tenure in the White House was mostly about campaigning, and nine months after he had come to office, Ford decided he would seek the nomination after all. For one thing, he saw little competition. What he had not counted on was Ronald Reagan. Despite what his own people had been telling him, Ford couldn't believe that the author of the Eleventh Republican Commandment, "Thou shalt not speak ill of another Republican," would actually challenge a sitting president. What Ford didn't understand was that Reagan thought he was the rightful heir to the Republican legacy, and that Ford was just a place-holder, a place-holder who had enraged Reagan's people by choosing Nelson Rockefeller, anathema to the conservatives of his party, as his vice president. Nor did Ford know that John Sears, a young Republican lawyer who would go on to run Reagan's campaign, had felt that Reagan was just getting too old to sit out another election cycle.

When Ronald Reagan finally got to the White House four years later, he became known for his ability to use "visuals" to make his point on television, but in 1976, Ford's people had already recognized that image, how the president looked on television, would be a major factor in the campaign. They were never as successful at using television as Reagan would be, but they tried, sometimes with comic results. Ford's polls showed that voters hadn't liked all his travel for congressional candidates in 1972, so the advisors tried to link Ford to the White House whenever possible. One of his advisors, Bob Mead, who had been Dan Rather's producer before joining the Ford team, suggested more colorful settings for the president's news conferences. Like other presidents before him, Ford generally met with reporters in the White House East Room, but Mead suggested using the White House itself as a backdrop. So Ford began to meet with reporters in the White House Rose Garden.

Taking it one more step, the advisors scheduled another news conference on the South Lawn, several hundred yards from the White House. The idea was the president would stand with his back to the White House, and it was a beautiful backdrop. What said that the president was staying home, tending the nation's business, better than seeing the White House there behind him? The problem was that in order to get the president far enough away from the White House that it could be used as a backdrop, the news conference had to be held close to the busy street that ran past the White House grounds, which meant that many of the president's answers and the reporters' questions were drowned out by traffic noise and airplanes landing at nearby National Airport. And because there had been a heavy rain the night before, steam had begun rising from the lawn. Before it was over, the whole scene looked like something from *Brigadoon*.

As the year progressed, Ford began to understand that it would take more than pretty pictures of the White House to stop the Reagan challenge. As a sop to the Right, Ford unceremoniously dropped Rockefeller as his running mate. At the convention in Kansas City, he picked Bob Dole to run with him and barely defeated Reagan for the nomination. But conservatives remained lukewarm about him, and carrying the burden of the Nixon pardon, the polls showed him far behind his surprising Democratic challenger, Jimmy Carter, as the fall campaign began. Then, he misspoke during one presidential debate and said Poland was not under the domination of the Soviet Union. His advisor Jim Cannon later wrote that Ford had meant to say the

United States did not accept Soviet domination over Eastern Europe, but by the time Ford had straightened it out, it was too late. He lost the election in a cliff-hanger. Carter got 49.9 percent of the popular vote; Ford, 47.9.

Covering Ford that fall, I never really felt that he was going to win. Toward the end, the polls suggested he was gaining strength, but somehow, after the years of Nixon, I always had the feeling that the electorate just wanted a change, and I never believed there was really much that Ford could have done about it. Jimmy Carter's campaign pledge had been "I will never lie to you," which in different times would have been the least that we expected from our public officials. But in those days after Vietnam and Watergate, it was a message that resonated with millions of Americans.

Whatever his chances, for reporters Ford was a great candidate to cover. He liked campaigning and was usually accessible, and perhaps because we were all still getting over the dreariness of the Nixon days, there was almost a giddiness among the reporters covering Ford. It was a rare campaign swing that did not include at least one elaborate practical joke. Jim Naughton of the *New York Times*, another of the reporters with whom I had become friends on the McGovern campaign, had a nonstop streak of mischief, and during a stop in Peoria, Illinois, had actually convinced the Secret Service to help smuggle a live sheep into the room of *Newsweek* reporter Tom DeFrank. DeFrank was a graduate of Texas A&M, an agricultural school where students were said to have a special fondness for farm animals.

During a West Coast swing, Naughton convinced the man who played the San Diego Chicken at sports events to sell him a spare chicken costume, or at least the head. At an airport news conference in Oregon, Naughton donned the chicken head, walked into a gaggle of reporters and asked Ford about egg prices. Ford laughed and answered.

As it had been on the McGovern campaign, when I had met many of the young staffers who would go on to become people of power in succeeding Democratic administrations, it was during the Ford days that I came to know many of the Republicans I would deal with over a lifetime of Washington reporting. Jim Baker, who would one day be Ronald Reagan's chief of staff and later George Bush's campaign manager and secretary of state, had gotten into national politics during the Ford campaign. He began as the campaign liaison with the League of Women Voters and eventually wound up running it. Donald Rumsfeld, later to be the second

George Bush's secretary of defense, had been Ford's White House chief of staff until Ford sent him to the Pentagon to replace Jim Schlesinger as secretary of defense.

When Rumsfeld left for the Pentagon, it was his thirty-two-year-old deputy, Dick Cheney, who became the youngest-ever White House chief of staff.

When the second George Bush named Cheney as his running mate, some may have winced, but I didn't — nor, I suspect, did many reporters who had covered the Ford White House. For us, he had been the go-to guy on matters large and small.

And in my case, he had done me the kind of favor no reporter ever forgets.

During a campaign stop in New York, Ford had taped an interview with Barbara Walters, which was to be aired the following morning on the *Today* show.

She had also apparently threatened Ford's press secretary, Ron Nessen, with death if anyone else interviewed Ford before hers aired. So I wasn't surprised when Nessen just laughed when I requested an interview, too.

To make matters worse, Walter Cronkite had called and told me he planned to join the campaign for a few hours when Ford stopped in Yonkers, and asked if I could set up an interview with Ford for him. Nessen again said exactly what I had expected: "Of course not." This time, he said it with a smirk.

That's when I went to Cheney. Would it be possible, I wondered, for Walter to pay a brief courtesy call on Ford?

Cheney said maybe. . . .

And would it be possible for Walter to bring along a camera crew?

Cheney just looked at me.

Please, Dick, I remember begging. Just for a minute. He's my boss.

Well, maybe for a minute, I remember Cheney saying. And when I saw just a hint of that wry, crooked smile that sometimes crosses Cheney's face, I knew I had won.

Sure enough, by the time Walter arrived, Cheney had sent word that the president would see Walter for just a minute. We sent the camera crew to the room where Ford was resting, and Walter, mike in hand and with the crew trailing and the camera rolling, was ushered in. Like most Americans, Ford liked Walter and was genuinely glad to see him, and Walter wasted no time.

"Hello, Mr. President," he said, as he shook hands, "Are you going to take your flu shot?"

Flu shots have long since proved their worth, but many Americans were having doubts about them and some had experienced bad reactions, and whatever Ford said in response to Walter's question would be news.

When Ford said yes, and that he thought

everyone should take one, it was more than just news; it was big news for us and terrifying news to Ron Nessen, who would have to explain to Barbara Walters why her interview was no longer exclusive. Nessen grabbed the sound man and tried to drag him out of the room.

Walter just smiled, "thanked" Nessen and said good-bye to Ford, who seemed to find the whole thing fairly humorous.

Nobody loved a scoop more than Walter (and especially if it was his scoop) and a few hours later, when he began the *Evening News*, his scoop was the lead story. "Good evening," he said. "President Ford told me on the campaign trail today that he would take his flu shot . . ." Then he replayed the entire interview, all twelve seconds or so of it. He didn't mention that the brief clip viewers had seen was the entire interview.

Adding to the sweetness of the moment, Dick Growald, an old friend of mine from Fort Worth who was a reporter for United Press International, was traveling with us that day, and I told him how Walter had managed to scoop Barbara Walters.

My fingerprints were nowhere on the story, but Growald's account made Walter out to be a combination of Walter Winchell, Walter Lippmann and Superman, and it was picked up by hundreds of papers across the country, including the *Washington Post*. That irritated

410

Nessen even more, but Walter was happy, and when he was happy, I was really happy.

The next day, he called and said, "I don't suppose you're going to mention that Growald was a buddy of yours?"

"No, Walter," I told him. "That kind of detail just clutters up a story."

Ford and his wife, Betty, were living in Rancho Mirage, the golf resort community in the Southern California desert, when I called him one January morning of 2002.

He still plays golf twice a week. After two knee operations, he confines himself to nine holes at a stretch, but he told me, "At the age of eighty-eight, I have no complaints."

Like me, polls show many Americans now believe he did the right thing in pardoning Nixon, but I asked if he had ever had any regrets.

"No," he told me. "If anything, I have become more certain that I did the right thing."

Had it cost him the election?

"It had to be a factor, with the election as close as it was," he said. "There were people who hated Nixon so much they would never forgive me for granting the pardon. The Nixon-haters — you were there, you know how vehement they were — there just had to be some carryover. The election was so close, if I had won Ohio, which I lost by thirteen thousand out of four million votes, and had

411

carried one small state, Delaware or Hawaii, I would have won the election.

"You can't help but feel the pardon had an impact. Whether it was the critical one or not, you can't be certain."

When I said I thought it had been the critical issue, he said, "Well, I would agree that it was the one with the most devastating impact."

We exchanged some pleasantries, and as I was about to conclude the interview and say good-bye, another thought popped into my head. Did Nixon ever thank him for the pardon?

"No," Ford said, "not to me directly."

I wondered in my own mind — after all the turmoil it had caused Ford — if he believed Nixon owed him thanks. I asked him if he felt Nixon should have thanked him.

"Well, it would have helped," he said.

Ford said he and Nixon had never discussed the matter. Nixon had never raised it, nor had he.

"But it does seem he would have said thank you, doesn't it?" I said.

Ford just chuckled.

"That's Nixon," he said.

# Nineteen

## *Jimmy*

Ed Bradley had covered Jimmy Carter during the campaign, but since I was the White House correspondent, I was sent to Plains, Georgia, after the election to cover the man who would be our next president.

From the week after the election in November until late January, when Carter was inaugurated, I lived with the rest of the press corps at the Best Western Motel in Americus, Georgia, Monday through Friday and then headed to New York on Saturday to anchor my weekend news broadcast. By then, Dan Rather had moved to *60 Minutes* and I had replaced him as anchor of the Saturday *News*. I would take an early flight to New York, spend the day there and then fly to Washington on Saturday night to see Pat and the girls. On Sunday, I would fly back to Atlanta, an easy hour-and-a-half flight from Washington.

It was the trip from Atlanta to Plains that was always an adventure. During the early stages of his campaign, Carter had often flown in a small propeller plane owned by

413

Tom Peterson, a local pilot from Plains, and after the election, CBS hired Peterson to shuttle our people from Plains to Atlanta. Plains had no airport to speak of, but Peterson used a grass field as his headquarters. He was a terrific pilot, and except for the occasional deer that sometimes became frightened at the sound of the airplane and darted in front of our plane on takeoffs and landings, it was not the worst landing strip I had ever landed on during daylight.

Nighttime was another story. My flight from Washington was delayed one Sunday, and when Peterson met me at the Atlanta terminal I remember asking if we could still get to Plains before dark. He said it would be no problem. For him, it wasn't. It was pitch-dark when we approached Plains, and since the airstrip had no lights, I tried to sound casual when I asked what he intended to do. He said he intended to call his wife, which is what he did. She drove the family car to the end of the runway and turned on the car's headlights.

"Nothing to it," he said. "I know those lights are where the airstrip ends and I just line up on 'em." He did, and it was a fine landing, but after that I always made sure I got to Atlanta when there was plenty of daylight left to get to Plains.

It didn't take long to figure out that Plains, Georgia, was a long way from Jerry Ford and the White House I had been covering. This would be a different deal, and when Ford went back to Vail that Christmas, the back-to-back stories that Phil Jones and I did on the *Morning News* one day couldn't have illustrated the difference more clearly. Phil had been my partner covering Jerry Ford, and when I had switched over to Carter he had stayed behind to cover the lame-duck president. In Phil's report from Vail that morning, he was standing on a ski slope, resplendent in a handsome new ski jacket, with the snow-capped Rocky Mountains behind him. Then, the camera switched to me. It had been another rainy day in Georgia and there I was, standing in red Georgia mud with the Plains water tower behind me.

Reporters who had covered Ford genuinely liked him, and he liked them. That was not the case with Carter. Many of the reporters who covered him during the campaign were turned off by his blunt manner. They believed Carter tolerated them as people who had to be dealt with in order to be elected, but few thought he had any feeling for them, one way or the other. Sam Donaldson of ABC, who had covered Carter longer than any other reporter that year, remembered how, late one Friday evening in Keene, New Hampshire, Carter had canceled a plane that had been chartered to take him and a small group of reporters to Boston. Carter was furious that the plane was late, and decided to drive. Donaldson couldn't blame him, but when he asked, "Do you have an extra seat, Governor?" Carter said one word, "No," and walked away, leaving his staffers and the reporters stranded. Donaldson finally found a rental car and gave Carter's staffers a ride back to Boston.

I heard many such tales when I arrived in Plains, and there was no question that Jimmy Carter and Jerry Ford were different ducks, but for some reason I always got along with Carter, and if he did not treat me as a personal friend (which I wasn't), he always treated me with courtesy and professional respect, and one evening he invited me to have dinner with him at Faye's Barbeque Villa, a local restaurant housed in a double-wide mobile home. It was operated by Faye Wells, the wife of a Georgia highway patrolman, who did the cooking once his patrolling was done each day. It served enormous steaks and was really the only place in tiny Plains to get a decent meal, and we generally ate there every night.

Carter had obviously asked me to dinner to get acquainted with the new reporter who would be covering him. I appreciated that and came away impressed with his lack of pretension, and I was also impressed with his wife, Rosalynn. It became clear that Mrs. Carter was going to be a major advisor in the next administration and we all had an enjoyable conversation. The only problem involved the Carters' soon-to-be-famous eight-year-old daughter, Amy. She was a quiet child who read a book throughout the meal. Unfortunately, toward the end of the meal she went to the rest room. For some reason, she did not want to or could not figure out how to get out of the rest room. The Secret Service agents were preparing to take the door off its hinges, when one of them finally talked her through the procedure to unlock the door. She emerged and went back to her book. Girls will be girls. As a father of two of them, I knew that much.

As president, Carter would draw some derisive giggles when he revealed that he and Amy had discussed nuclear weapons policy over the dinner table, but the stories were apparently true. Even so, Carter's interest in the subject may have exceeded that of his daughter.

Ambassador Edward L. Rowny, a three-star Air Force general who spent much of his career negotiating arms control with the Soviets, told me that Carter introduced him to Amy in 1978 at a reception in Geneva, where the Carters had come to visit the U.S. Arms negotiating team. He said Carter told him Amy had some questions about arms control and nuclear weapons and left the general with the child. Rowny — ever the loyal military man — said he asked her, "Do you really want to talk about nuclear weapons?" He said she murmured no, and asked to be excused.

Life in Plains was unlike anything I had ever experienced. Being from Texas, I love "characters," and although Texans do not consider themselves southerners (we consider ourselves Texans, which is a whole different story), I have an appreciation of small towns and southern ways. Having said that, the cast of characters I found in Plains was the most unusual group of people I have ever encountered. No man, politician or otherwise, should be held accountable for his relatives, but the Carter clan had a little of everything. One of Carter's sisters had been a born-again Christian evangelist, his other sister rode a motorcycle and his brother, Billy, owned a run-down gas station that resembled something out of the *Li'l Abner* comic strip. His mother, Miz Lillian, a lovely white-haired woman who had joined the Peace Corps at age sixty-eight, became the campaign reporters' favorite interviewee. Miz Lillian had a view on almost everything and everybody and was delighted to tell us about it on camera. Not far behind the main characters was a group of cousins and nephews and nieces with names ranging from "Cousin Beedie" to "Snaggum" and "Turk." Carter himself was called "Cousin Hot" by the relatives, Hot being short for Hot Shot. Cousin Beedie was the only person I have ever known who was both an antique dealer and worm farmer, and he was something of a success as both. He did a profitable business at his Plains antique shop and shipped worms to fishermen all over the United States.

When Brother Billy's daughter was married, I was invited to the reception. Billy wore a yellow tuxedo and greeted guests on the terrace of his backyard swimming pool. In the center of the pool was a rowboat filled with ice and hundreds of cans of Billy Beer, one of Billy's early efforts to capitalize on his new-found celebrity.

Carter's staff was also one of the most informal I had ever known. We didn't see much of Hamilton Jordan, the young aide who had run the campaign and who would later serve as Carter's White House chief of staff, but we were in daily contact with Jody Powell, Carter's thirty-two-year-old press secretary, who had started with Carter as his driver and who knew him and had served him longer than any other aide. Powell lived with us that fall at the Best Western, which could best be described as a cheap motel built around an old swimming pool. When Powell had an announcement, he would signal us by hanging a bedsheet on the balcony railing outside his room.

In recent years, presidential press secretaries have sometimes been lower-level clerks who are given a set of talking points and sent out to read them to reporters. But Powell was a true advisor to Carter, and because he knew Carter so well and was usually part of the decision-making process, we knew that what he told us reflected the president's thinking. I don't know of a press secretary since who had the access Powell had.

Until 9-11, the press was pretty rough on George W. Bush, and I always thought one reason for it was that the advisors who had real access to him had delegated direct contact with reporters to lower-echelon officials whose knowledge of Bush was sometimes limited to what they were told by more senior aides who sometimes didn't tell them much. A press secretary best serves a president when he can not only articulate the president's message but also give the president an accurate sense of how it is playing with reporters. Powell always knew what we were up to, because he was with us so much.

After our nightly trek to Faye's for our big steak, we would all wind up at the Best Western bar, a dark, dank beer joint called the Pirate's Den, which featured country music on the jukebox and friendly waitresses who, Ed Bradley once said, were "mostly widows of men killed in knife fights."

Garrett Morris, an old friend from Texas, once said that the time between 11 P.M. and midnight should have been called the "smart hour," because it was during that hour in beer joints everywhere that solutions to every world problem suddenly emerged, and we spent many "smart hours" in the Pirate's Den that fall, debating the problems that would await Carter and how he would solve them.

Such heavy discussion does not come without cost. When I arrived in Washington to cover Carter's inauguration, I had gained an even twenty pounds.

Carter arrived in Washington with all the right ideas. After the long years of Vietnam and Watergate, we did need to open up government and restore confidence in our institutions and we did need to make human rights, if not a cornerstone, at least one pillar of our foreign policy. There was just one problem for Carter. He was exactly what he had advertised himself to be, an outsider with no Washington experience, and he got off to a rough start. Being president, as every president learns, is a lot harder than it looks. It never ceases to amaze me when I hear people who have made a success in business say a good businessman could straighten out the government in no time, an opinion that is totally wrong. No business executive has to work with a board of directors that has 535 members, but that is exactly how many members of the House and Senate look over a president's shoulder and in varying degrees must be catered to, listened to or, in some cases, just made to feel important. As former governors from Ronald Reagan to Bill Clinton and George Bush have discovered, working with members of Congress who come from a diverse country spread over a huge continent is very different from working with members of a state legislature.

There is really no training ground for becoming president, and for all his good ideas, by the time Carter's team figured out how to make the government work, it was too late. With the benefit of hindsight, Carter himself does not argue with that assessment.

"Bob Strauss used to say we had used up all our luck just getting to Washington," Hamilton Jordan would remember years later. "And we made a lot of mistakes. But part of it was that we took on some very tough issues early on. Pushing through the Panama Canal Treaty so early in the administration really hurt us. It was the kind of thing that most presidents would have put off until the second term, but President Carter jumped right on it and it really cost us."

In an interview for this book, Carter told me that convincing two-thirds of the Senate to approve the treaty, which set out a timetable for Panama to take control of the canal, was the single hardest thing he had ever done in politics, including getting himself elected president.

"It was so patently unpopular, that of the twenty senators who voted for it who were up for reelection, only seven returned to the Senate," he told me in the winter of 2002. "It was the most courageous vote that the Senate — in my opinion — ever cast."

Carter still believes he had no other choice. Had the treaty not been ratified, there would have been a revolution in Panama, he said. With it would have come attempts to sabotage the canal, and he would have been forced to send in U.S. military forces to protect it.

The political capital Carter was forced to spend in those months would never be recovered, and he would eventually be overwhelmed by a bureaucracy and a Congress that he did not understand or trust in the beginning, and a Congress that never really trusted or understood him to the end.

Carter had huge majorities in both houses when he arrived in Washington, but as he later wrote in his memoir *Keeping Faith*, "Most of the members had never served with a president of their own political party, and their attitude was one of competition rather than cooperation with the White House."

The years have not softened that view.

In the interview for this book, he told me,

"Fairly early in my administration, [Ted] Kennedy and the very liberal wing of the Democratic Party decided I shouldn't be there."

Carter found himself to the right of Kennedy and the liberals in his own party on fiscal affairs, balancing the budget and dealing with the military, and as a result, he said, "I had to turn to the Republican leaders, Howard Baker and the others, for my allies. I had to go to the minority more than to the Democratic majority leader, Bob Byrd."

Congress had no more understanding of Carter than Carter had an understanding of Congress. He had campaigned as an outsider and Congress appreciated that. All of them understood campaign rhetoric. But once he got to town, they expected him to work with them and to understand their problems, but he continued to work from the outside. When one of his aides had suggested that he would have to deal with Washington state's powerful senator, Scoop Jackson, Carter had reportedly said, "Why? I beat him in the primary." No one around Carter now remembers the remark, but Congress believed he had said it and it soured relations instantly. When the White House flooded Congress with proposed legislation early in his term, Congress never understood what he really wanted and what he didn't. To Congress, the Carter White House seemed to say that every program was of equal priority.

I always thought Carter's early inability to get anything done on Capitol Hill had something to do with his religious background. He was a sincere, devout Christian and his approach to Congress seemed to be that if you were right and you cast your bread upon the waters, then it would take care of itself. But not in Washington, where even the Lord's work requires returning congressional phone calls.

Every president travels, but no one ever took the kind of trips Carter took. There never seemed to be any real theme to his travels. Zbigniew Brzezinski, his national security advisor, wanted him to go everywhere, and sometimes that seemed to be the purpose of his travels. Every time he left the country, the plan seemed to be to touch down in as many widely separated capitals as possible. On one trip, we started in Brazil and took a swing through Africa before we headed home. Lane Venardos, the CBS News producer who traveled many miles with me in those years, said that trip summed up the problem with the Carter White House. "We spent one night in Rio de Janeiro, one of the nicest spots on earth, and three nights in Lagos, Nigeria." In those days, Lagos was one of the less appealing spots in all of Africa. The military controlled the country, and the capital city still had some dirt roads, and during our stay a body washed up on the beach of the hotel where the press was housed. One day, as we returned to the hotel, we saw a commotion near the entrance and discovered the police, armed with long sticks, beating a hapless thief who had stolen a piece of our television equipment from the hotel lobby. In those days, Lagos was that kind of place.

The longest trip I ever took with a president was Carter's first extended foray. We started in Poland, touched down next in Tehran, then pressed on to New Delhi, worked in a side trip to Aswan to visit Egyptian president Sadat, flew from there to Paris, took a train to the coast to see the Normandy beaches, made one more stop in Brussels and then headed home. The trip got off to a terrible start. In Warsaw, the new president said he was anxious to get to know the Polish people, only to have his speech mangled by a State Department translator who told the crowd the president wished to know them in the biblical sense. It was not until later that we understood the astonished looks on the faces of the airport crowd.

That trip also produced the only scoop I ever got by dancing. Walter Cronkite had been scheduled to go on the trip, but canceled at the last minute, so when we got to Tehran, I was invited in Walter's place to attend a New Year's Eve dinner given by the

Shah of Iran. Only a few reporters had been invited and I thought it would be a great place to observe Carter and the Shah. It was also one of the last opportunities, since the Shah would soon be overthrown, but that night he presided over the most lavish dinner I had ever attended. Vintage wine flowed, there seemed to be barrels of caviar, and after dinner, the crowd moved into another area that had been set up as a discothèque. King Hussein of Jordan was also in town and joined the bejeweled crowd, and soon all the guests, including President and Mrs. Carter, were on the dance floor. Barbara Walters of ABC was also on the trip and the two of us were taking in the scene from the sidelines, when I said, "Barbara, let's dance over and wish the Carters a Happy New Year." She said sure and we made our way through the crowd to the Carters. There had been rumors that Carter might make a surprise visit to Sadat, who had just made his historic trip to Jerusalem, so once the pleasantries were out of the way, I asked the president if he was going to Egypt.

"I am," he said. "I haven't told all the staff yet, but Sadat wants to see me and we're going to work out the details." Barbara and I all but broke each others' legs as we split and raced to the phones. We reported our scoop on our respective radio networks and I began my television report that evening by saying,

"President Carter told me in an interview today that he would go to Egypt this week . . ." I have done some fancy footwork in my time, but I didn't put in the dancing part. Nor did Barbara, as far as I know.

If there is one thing to know about Barbara, it is that she is indefatigable. She never gives up, she never lets up, she finds no question that is beyond asking and she is probably the toughest competition I ever went up against. During the 1980 Republican convention, she literally beat on the door of our convention anchor booth and demanded to be let in while Walter Cronkite was interviewing Gerald Ford. I always wondered what she had intended to do if we had let her in. Would she have tried to sit down and join Walter in questioning the former president, or would she have jerked Ford away and taken him to the ABC booth? Whatever the case, when you scooped Barbara, you knew you had done something, and she scooped us all when we got to New Delhi. The Indian prime minister, Moraji Desai, was eighty years old and we heard that he attributed his long life to drinking a glass of his own urine each morning. One reporter from each network was given the opportunity for a one-on-one interview with Desai, but when her turn came, only Barbara had the gumption to ask the prime minister the question we all wanted to ask, "Was it really true, the story about the urine?"

"Why, yes," he said. He told how he refrigerated it each night and spoke at some length about its medicinal qualities. I should also add that he lived well into his nineties.

There was another memorable moment on that trip. Desai had taken Carter to see a village that was being heated by fuel created from cow dung. Part of the process involved boiling the stuff in an open pit. As Carter and Desai were looking at the pit, Sam Donaldson shouted, "Mr. President, if I fell into that, would you dive in and save me?"

Carter didn't miss a beat.

"After an appropriate interval," he said.

For all its meandering and false starts, Carter's presidency was not without its accomplishments. There is little question that the Panama Canal Treaty had a stabilizing effect on the region at a time when the Soviet Union was trying to stir up trouble there, but it remains as controversial today as when the Senate ratified it. When the timetable for turning the canal over to Panama finally reached its final stages during the Clinton administration, Carter noted that neither Clinton, his vice president nor his secretary of state attended the ceremonies.

Carter also completed the SALT II treaty that had been started by Ford and Kissinger and aimed at reducing the nuclear arsenals of the United States and the Soviet Union, and he brought Egypt's Anwar Sadat and Menachem Begin to Camp David for thirteen days. The framework for peace they worked out did not bring peace, but at the very least, it bought some time and cooled the violence for a while. It was on the framework of Camp David that Israel and Egypt later concluded the treaty under which they established diplomatic relations, exchanged ambassadors, and Israel was given unrestricted access to the Suez Canal.

"What we sometimes also forget," Hamilton Jordan told me, in an interview for this book, "is that for all practical purposes it removed Egypt as a combatant in the region. That has not changed, and in that sense, Camp David enhanced Israel's security."

While those were significant accomplishments, most of Carter's presidency was engulfed in turmoil he could never control. Overwhelmed by what he saw as an increasingly unfriendly Congress, and unable to forge the kinds of working relationships he needed within his own party, he tried to rescue his presidency by revamping his cabinet. Gerald Rafshoon, an Atlanta ad man who'd handled his campaign advertising, was brought in to help him hone his message, but there was too much to make over and it would only get worse. When an energy crisis led to long gas lines, and Iranian militants took over the U.S. Embassy in Tehran and held American diplomats hostage for more than a year, Americans wanted a change. And they chose Ronald Reagan. In 1976, Reagan's own campaign manager, John Sears, had believed Reagan would be too old if he waited until 1980 to run, but the Old Actor fooled all of them and won decisively.

In his own way, Jimmy Carter has fooled all of them, too. Today, he presides over a staff of 150 people at the Carter Center, the institution he established in Atlanta to work for human rights and eradicate disease in some of the most remote regions of the world. It has been so hugely successful that when I talked with him in January 2002, I told him he might well be the only person who had won the presidency, but did not consider it the highlight of his life. The assertion brought a chuckle, but he did not challenge it.

Whatever the case, what happened after he left the White House was not something he had planned. He told me he had faced two awesome tasks when he left the White House. He had placed his holdings in a blind trust during his presidency, only to discover he was a million dollars in debt when he left Washington. He was forced to sell his peanut farm and equipment to pay off his debt, and he turned to writing books to support himself. (He has written fifteen to date, all of which have sold well.)

The second task he faced was to build a presidential library, which, he said, "was an onerous thing for me as a defeated Democrat, but I finally did that."

It was while he was raising funds for the library, he said, that he got the idea of establishing a place like Camp David had been, where he could study the conflicts of the world and see which ones might be conducive to his involvement as a mediator. It was from there that the concept of the Carter Center, a place for international conflict resolution, took shape. In the beginning, Carter and a small group of experts worked on election supervision and acted as mediators, but they have since expanded into supervising large-scale agriculture and medical programs. Today, Carter raises money for an institution that has a $35 million budget and receives an even larger amount of free medicines and other contributions, which Carter's people distribute around the world.

Carter and his people have presided over more than thirty elections to protect existing democracies or in countries where there has never been one, and Carter has shown himself to be a remarkably efficient mediator.

"I capitalize on a principle of politics, which is self-delusion," Carter told me. He said every candidate who has ever run for anything believes "that if the election is honest and the people know me and know the jokers running against me, they will surely vote for me.

"So I tell them, let the Carter Center in and there will be a fair election in your country, even though you've never had one, and we will ensure the best candidate will win."

More remarkable than his work in conflict resolution has been the Carter Center's accomplishments in eradicating disease, especially in the poorest regions of Africa. Carter has worked out arrangements to receive free medicines and vaccines from large American drug manufacturers such as Merck, and last year Carter's people delivered the drug Mectizan, which prevents the disease of elephantiasis, to more than seven million Africans.

In 1986, the Carter Center began a program to eradicate Guinea worm disease, an insidious malady that comes from drinking infested water and produces two- and three-foot-long parasites within the human body. The disease was once rampant in many remote African nations, but since the Carter program began, it has been virtually wiped out in Ethiopia, Uganda and ten northern states of Sudan; and the number of cases reported overall has been reduced 97 percent.

Carter is also involved in a new program with Microsoft founder Bill Gates to help the

South African government treat AIDS.

"I was grieved when I didn't get reelected," Carter told me. "But it didn't take us long to see that we had a different and, I think, a more expansive and exciting life.

"To me, it is not a sacrifice. It's a challenge and an adventure and a very gratifying life."

Jimmy Carter had left the White House broke, in debt and with no real plan of what to do next. It was a time of life when most people would have looked for ways to do less. Somehow, he found a way to do more.

"One thing that sticks in my mind," he told me, "is a cartoon I saw in the *New Yorker*. A little boy looks up at his daddy and says, 'Daddy, when I grow up I want to be a former President.'"

When he is not traveling, Carter splits his time between Atlanta and the house he still keeps in Plains. He and Rosalynn have been married more than fifty-five years, he is a grandfather eleven times over, and when he is in Plains on Sundays, he still teaches Sunday school.

Plains itself remains much as it always was. Tom Peterson, who used to fly me from Atlanta to Plains in the old days, still flies the occasional charter passenger, but he never did pave the grass airstrip.

Like other private plane dealers and charter pilots, he is feeling the economic pinch brought on by the attacks of September 11, and he wonders if the restrictions put on private aviation will ever go back to the way they once were.

One day in January 2002, he said Air Force fighter planes forced down a small private plane at the Plains landing strip because the pilot had flown too close to where Vice President Cheney was quail-hunting. "It was the biggest mess you ever saw," Peterson said. "It took all afternoon to straighten it out."

# Twenty

## *The* Morning Show: *A Time out of Time*

By the summer of 1979, Jimmy Carter was having his problems, but I was riding high. I had developed some good sources in key places, managed a couple of minor scoops and, in my own mind, anyway, believed I had finally stepped out of the long shadow that Dan Rather had cast as the nation's most famous White House correspondent.

Anchoring the Saturday *News* was also going well. The broadcast's executive producer was Joan Richman, one of the first women to rise to management rank in network television, and she favored the same no-frills approach to news that I did. We had two rules: Nothing went on the broadcast unless both of us thought it belonged there, and if late news broke, we tore the broadcast apart to get the late information on. When the choice boiled down to whether to run a feature story or news, it was no contest. We went for the news. Joan used to say there was nothing like

436

a little news to pep up a newscast. I agreed. So, apparently, did our viewers. We had strong ratings, and with the broadcast going well, I was occasionally given the ultimate compliment. I was asked to substitute for Walter Cronkite on the weekday broadcast.

I'll never forget the first time I filled in for Walter. Even though I had been at CBS for some years by then, filling in for the most trusted man in America was a big deal. I was plenty nervous, and told one of the producers on the broadcast, Bill Moran.

"What should I say at the beginning?" I asked him.

Moran stared at his typewriter for a moment, wrote out something and handed it to me.

"How about this?" he asked.

He had written the following: "Good Evening, Walter Cronkite is on assignment, Roger Mudd is sick, Dan Rather is in Alaska, and H. V. Kaltenborn is dead . . . so here I am."

I didn't say that, of course, but it broke the tension and helped to relax me enough to get through the broadcast.

For years, I've used the story as the opening line of speeches and lectures, and it always gets a big laugh, but I have noticed lately that its usefulness may be coming to an end. When I talk to younger audiences, they don't know who H. V. Kaltenborn is.

Richard Salant, who had run CBS News for sixteen years, had retired in 1979, and most of us in Washington had been hoping our former bureau chief Bill Small would get the job. Unfortunately for Small, he had fallen out with Eric Sevareid, who had told Paley that Small was the wrong man for the job. Instead, the job went to Bill Leonard, a longtime news executive who in recent years had been serving in Washington as the company's corporate lobbyist. (Eventually, Small would leave CBS to head up NBC News.)

It was Leonard who conceived the idea of a new kind of laid-back broadcast that became *Sunday Morning*. He hired a brilliant, onetime NBC producer named Robert (Shad) Northshield, to develop the program, and installed Charles Kuralt as its host. It was the perfect vehicle for the mellow voice and graceful writing that had become Kuralt's trademark, and Northshield designed the perfect program for watching on a lazy Sunday. Modeled on Sunday newspapers, it included long, thoughtful features on wildlife and the arts, and survives today, still one of the most popular news broadcasts on CBS. The more he thought about it, the more Leonard became convinced that the same format would work during the week, and he called me out of the blue one day and asked if I would be interested in anchoring it. I was a little surprised. Small had always been my patron and I had always been a hard-news guy involved in the day-to-day coverage. Leonard had spent most of his executive years presiding over documentaries and special projects, what we called the soft news. But, he said he liked my work.

I flew to New York to talk about it, and he told me that hosting the *Morning Show* would be unlike anything that I had done and would mean moving to New York, but that it was the kind of career move I probably ought to make. He told me Cronkite would be retiring in a few years, and while I wasn't the leading candidate to replace him, I was certainly among those who would be considered, and anchoring the morning news would be a good place to show what I could do. One should never inhale such talk too deeply, but of course I did. And after surprisingly little disagreement, I worked out an arrangement under which I would be paid more than triple what I was making as a White House correspondent. Leonard also agreed to let me continue as anchor of the Saturday broadcast. That meant I would be working six days a week, but I saw it as insurance. If the *Morning Show* didn't click, and if you judged success by the ratings, nothing CBS had ever done in the mornings ever had, I would still have the Saturday broadcast.

If the *Morning Show* was a success, I could always give up the Saturday broadcast in a year or so. And I was certain it would be a success. I had never failed at anything I had ever set out to do.

It was the week before Thanksgiving, and I was euphoric, if for no other reason than I would now be making some real money for the first time in my life, and when I got home and told Pat, I was almost giddy. It was the biggest thing that had ever happened to me professionally.

"I'll not only be heading up a new show," I remember telling her. "I get to *keep* the Saturday news."

I was stunned by her reaction. She was not happy. She was crestfallen.

"But we'll have to move to New York," she said.

"Sure, but this is a really big promotion for me, what I have been working for," I said.

"But what about us? Did you give any thought to that?" she asked.

Looking back, I am not sure that I had.

The girls were doing well in school, and while I had been on the road so much covering Carter and Ford, Pat and her friend Beth Gibbens had started their own business, a toy store. Using a new marketing concept that stressed personal service and toys that had been taken from their boxes and set out so children could actually play with them, their business was thriving. Until that moment, I hadn't given the toy store much thought. We

440

talked about it over the next few days, and as I knew she would, Pat said she would sell the store and work it out, and by Thanksgiving Day she was beginning to feel better about it and even said at one point that it would be fun to live in New York.

The girls didn't agree. We had just begun to eat our Thanksgiving turkey when I told them about Dad's big promotion and that we would be moving to New York. Susan let out a blood-curdling scream, jumped up from the table, ran into the front yard and began rolling around on the wet grass.

"Why would you tell us on Thanksgiving?" she shouted. "This is nothing to be thankful for."

I had never felt worse. For the first time, it dawned on me that what had looked like a big break from my point of view was anything but for the rest of the family. I was headed off to a new job, but I would be working with people I knew. I was moving up in the world. But *they* weren't getting a promotion. They were being taken away — and taken by surprise — from everything they knew: their friends, their school, their home. The more I thought about it, the more I realized how right Susan had been. For the family, this was nothing to be thankful for. I had just been too wrapped up in myself to understand or even notice.

My career was taking off, but my family was drifting away from me, and I hadn't even noticed. I had been gone so much their lives no longer really included me. Pat had the store and the girls had their friends.

It had always hurt me when I would come home, ready to spend time with them, only to have them seem uninterested and complain that if they did something with me, they would have to change the plans they had made to be with their friends.

What I had not understood was that children (and wives) learn to adapt to any situation, and they were learning to get along without me. At work, I was on the fast track, but I had not understood what it was costing me at home.

I started the new assignment in mid-January, and since the girls were still in school and the place we had purchased in New York wouldn't be ready to live in for a few months, I found a small apartment and lived there until school was out and Pat and the girls joined me that summer.

It was one of the most difficult periods of my life. The morning news hours were awful under the best of circumstances. I got up at 3:30 A.M. and arrived at CBS by 4. The broadcast was an hour long, but the editorial staff consisted of one copy editor, Mike Whitney, and a writer named Frank Telch. Frank and I wrote all the copy, a stack of scripts that would sometimes stand three to six inches high by the time 7 A.M. rolled around and the show went on the air. By then, I was exhausted, not to mention completely wired from all the coffee I had drunk to stay awake, and still ahead was the job I had been hired to do: anchor the broadcast.

Still, it was a schedule to which I could have adjusted had I not been determined to hang on to the Saturday *News* and fly back and forth to Washington to have some semblance of a family life. To do all that, I would spend Sundays in Washington and take the last shuttle to New York at 9 P.M. I would arise at 3:30 A.M. and go to the studio, spend Monday and Tuesday nights in New York, and fly to Washington after the broadcast on Wednesday mornings. I would spend the day in Washington, have dinner with the family and fly back to New York Wednesday night on the 9 P.M. shuttle flight. I would be up again at 3:30 A.M. for the Thursday broadcast, spend Thursday night in New York, but after the broadcast on Friday I would fly back to Washington.

Then came Saturday. I would take the 10 A.M. shuttle back to New York, spend the day there, anchor the Saturday *News* and fly back to Washington on the 9 P.M. shuttle. It was a ridiculous schedule, but I somehow managed it for nearly four months. By the time Pat and the girls moved to New York that summer, I was on the verge of collapse, brought on by what I now know was sleep deprivation. I was drinking so much coffee to stay awake that the caffeine was making it impossible for me to sleep when I wanted to. I would sometimes go twenty-four hours without sleeping, and as I now understand, the sleep deprivation was beginning to affect my judgment. Sleep deprivation is a cause of many aircraft accidents, and I have been told that airline pilots who have been deprived of sleep sometimes look at instrument gauges but fail to understand what the gauges show, and in those days I would sometimes look at the clocks, but would not know what time it was. I would see the clock, but what I saw just didn't register.

I had done my fair share of drinking over the years, but I had never felt a need for alcohol. I drank to have fun. Now, I was finding that the only way I could go to sleep was to take a drink, and the more tired I became, the more alcohol I seemed to need.

Once Pat and the girls got to New York and we were all in one place, it got a little easier, but not much, and at the office the new show was not going all that great.

The Sunday version with Kuralt was getting a lot of attention, and producer Northshield was spending most of his time on that. He had never been all that keen on producing the Monday-through-Friday version anyway. He thought he had been brought in to do the

444

Sunday show, which was more than enough work for one man, and he was never happy about being told he would have to do the weekday version as well.

I was never comfortable with the laid-back format. To me, the long features that worked so well on Sunday just didn't seem to me to be what people who were getting up to go to work were looking for on a weekday.

With my addiction to straight hard news and Northshield's love of features, we were not destined to see eye to eye on much, and we didn't. The show got off to a slow start. The ratings jumped a little, but not nearly enough to make us competitive with the *Today* show and a new broadcast called *Good Morning America* that ABC had begun.

CBS had been the traditional also-ran of morning television, and our broadcast seemed likely to continue the tradition, and I had no idea what to do about it. I stayed at the office later and later each day, trying to micromanage every detail when what I should have done was go home, get some rest and let others worry about it, but that was not my way.

As a beat reporter all my life, I had never spent much time working inside the office, and that in itself was a new, and to me, unpleasant business, made even worse by the hours. Getting up at 3 A.M. meant getting up when most heart attacks occurred, and none

445

of us ever really got used to it. Sally Quinn, who had left the *Washington Post* to anchor the *Morning News* in a previous, unsuccessful attempt to overhaul it, said it was the only place she had ever worked where people talked more about sleep than sex. Diane Sawyer, who took her turn on the *Morning Show* several years after me, said it was like being on Moscow time when everyone else was on New York time.

One of the hardest parts for me was that I was always used to being in the middle of things, and in 1979, the *Morning News* was definitely part of the CBS sideshow. The *Evening News* was in the center ring, the main attraction and what everybody on the payroll wanted to be part of. The correspondents were polite about it, but we got the leavings, the leftovers. Sometimes I wondered if people just forgot we were there. I had always been told that the company founder, Bill Paley, liked to watch the *Morning News* while having his breakfast in bed, but I had to wonder one morning when I looked up at one of our studio monitors and discovered him sitting beside Tom Brokaw on the *Today* show set.

It turned out he had written a new book and he had gone on *Today* to promote it. We hadn't even been aware that he had a book to promote. What was worse, our executives had been too timid to ask about it afterward. I was a little irritated, but going to battle with the chairman and founder of CBS didn't seem all that appetizing, especially if I was going to have to do it alone, so I tried to put it out of my mind. Tom Brokaw and I became friends during our days covering the White House, and I chalked it up as a scoop for him and tried to forget it. Brokaw was not about to let that happen. Several days later, I received a large envelope containing a picture of Paley sitting beside Brokaw, and on the bottom Brokaw had written, "I told Bill you're doing a great job. You owe me a chicken-fried steak! All the best, Tom."

I laughed, but I'm not one to let a debt go unpaid, so I called my brother in Texas and told him to send Tom a chicken-fried steak. But a raw one, and I sent it regular mail. It must have smelled terrific by the time it reached Tom's New York apartment. Tom never admitted that he got it, but he had to admit I got him a few weeks later.

An item in a gossip column gave me the opening I needed. The item quoted rumors that Brokaw might be replaced on the *Today* show by Alan Alda, the star of the hit series *M*A*S*H*. I turned it around and wrote a phony fan letter to Tom, telling him I had seen in the paper that he was going to replace Alda on *M*A*S*H*. I told him how much I had admired his acting skills and thought it was a much better place for him than on the

*Today* show. I signed a fake name and sent the letter on its way. Tom apparently thought the letter was for real, and several days later, I was startled when he read it on the air, with a few tut-tuts and an assurance to his fans that he was not going anywhere.

I wrote him another letter on CBS stationery, and thanked him for clearing up the situation. This time, I didn't have to sign the letter. He knew who had written it.

To his credit, he put another fairly sharp needle to me the next day, when he told his viewers that the first fan letter had been a fake. "I'd tell you who wrote it," he deadpanned. "But you wouldn't recognize the name."

In any case, when 1980 rolled around, I couldn't wait to get back to politics, and when the year's first political event, the Iowa caucuses, occurred, we anchored the broadcast from Des Moines and I had a big scoop. George Bush won, and the morning after, I interviewed him live on the set and he told me he had "the Big Mo."

I had never heard the phrase and said, "The big what?"

He explained he meant momentum. My response was something like, "Oh, okay," but except for "voodoo" economics, it was the phrase candidate Bush would be most remembered for that year.

The "Mo" soon evaporated and Ronald

Reagan would eventually get the nomination and, with Bush as his running mate, win the election, of course, but in the weeks after the Iowa caucuses we took the show to New Hampshire for the primary there and it was there that I realized hosting a morning show was not what I was cut out for.

We had set up studios at the Manchester Inn, a historic hotel where reporters covering the primary generally headquartered. As I was making my way, bleary-eyed, to the studio one morning, I ran into all my newspaper buddies — equally bleary-eyed for different reasons — heading down a hallway. They were closing down the bar and heading to bed. I, on the other hand, was going to work. They seemed to have the better schedule.

What I discovered about working in New York, as opposed to Washington, was that in Washington we seemed to spend most of our time talking about the government. At the worldwide headquarters of CBS News in New York, the talk was mostly about CBS, and the talk of CBS News that spring was about who was going to replace Walter Cronkite. Walter had reached the mandatory retirement age of sixty-five and would be stepping down after the inauguration of the new president in January. Among the correspondents and producers, a real split had developed over who should get the job. Some wanted Roger Mudd, who had been talked about as the heir apparent for years, but many thought Dan Rather would be picked, and the trade press printed a rumor a day that Roone Arledge of ABC was trying to lure Rather away and that NBC was also bidding for his services. Charles Kuralt had his backers, as well, and one or two people even thought I was a long shot.

I didn't think so, but the tiny little voice of ambition kept whispering, "Well, maybe," so I didn't totally dismiss the possibility.

As one who had replaced a famous reporter at the White House, I knew it wouldn't be easy for whoever got the job. Walter wasn't just the most trusted man in America; he had come to represent something beyond that. The faith that people had come to place in Walter had increased the credibility of television itself.

I would be remiss at this point if I didn't say a little something about Walter.

In all the years I have worked at CBS News, the question I am still most often asked is, "What is Walter really like?" and I always say that the first thing to know about him is that he is the most curious person I have ever known. Curiosity is the one trait shared by all great reporters, and Walter has enough curiosity for an entire newsroom.

When he was anchoring the *Evening News*, he seemed to want to know about everything.

If he passed a car wreck after work, it was as if it were the first car wreck he had ever seen, and he would stop and check it out.

Everything was a story to Walter. Once, during my White House days, Walter had come with us to Europe on one of Jimmy Carter's trips, and after a long day in London, we were sharing a cab back to our hotel when an ambulance with sirens blaring passed us.

On a day that had begun eighteen hours earlier, this was of no interest to me. But to Walter, it was as if World War III had begun.

"Follow that car," he barked to the cabbie. I had never known of anyone but Dick Tracy to issue such a command, and off we went.

"With the IRA so active, you never know what this could be," he said. As it turned out, the IRA was busy elsewhere and it was nothing more than a car wreck, but to be on the safe side, Walter thought it best that I leave the cab and check it out. I did.

When Walter ran the *Evening News*, we dreaded the WWs that came in torrents from the anchor desk. WW stood for "Walter wants" or "Walter wants to know," and it was our signal to get hopping, and there was usually plenty of hopping to do because Walter wanted to know everything. Especially around 6 or 6:15 P.M., when we were hard against the deadline for the *Evening News*. Gary Gates and Hugh Heckman, who worked on the broadcast, kept a file of Walter's queries.

Among the choice questions that Walter posed to them:

"How long is Greenland?"

"How much oil is there in the world?"

"In Poland, is he called Father Christmas or Santa Claus?"

The word *unflappable* was invented for Walter. The studio could burn down around him, but he could sit before a television camera for hours and guide us through the calamity of the moment, no matter how complicated, and never lose his place or his composure.

Only once did he admit to losing his focus. It was during the 1970s, when the *Evening News* launched a series on the environment called "Can the Earth Be Saved?" Each time we ran a story in the series, a graphic would appear behind Walter's shoulder showing a huge hand holding Planet Earth.

To the technicians and producers, the graphic became known as "the hand job," and when an environmental story was slated for the *Evening News*, the director, Ritchie Mutchler, would often shout to his assistant, "We'll need the hand job tonight!" To the crew it was as routine as saying "Quiet on the set!" but one day, Walter called the director aside and said, "Uhmm, could we call that thing something else? Every time I hear you call it that, my mind sort of wanders."

Walter dominated television as no other correspondent before or since, and I have always believed a big part of his success grew out of his curiosity and, second, out of the fact that he couldn't hide his love for the news. He never left the impression that he thought he was smarter than the viewers, only that he had done his homework and was working hard to get the story for them. Walter loved his job and his viewers knew it. He had been my hero before I came to CBS and what made me admire him even more was that he was that rare individual who was exactly the same on camera and off.

He called me with a question once while I was working the White House beat, and for once I had an answer.

"Well, thank you, Bob," he said in that famous cadence. "This old gray head just had a question mark above it."

He really talked that way.

Walter's replacement was about ninety percent of what we talked about that spring, so I suppose I was thinking about it as I walked up West Fifty-seventh Street on my way home from the office one day.

It must have been around two or two-thirty that afternoon, and as I passed a neighborhood restaurant, a man who had once been a top correspondent at CBS came lunging out the door. He was obviously drunk, and as he staggered into the street, he was almost run down.

He had been one of the most talented men in broadcasting, but from the day that Walter was chosen to anchor the *Evening News* he became a bitter man, and he grew more bitter as the years passed. As those years went by, the boozy lunches became longer and more frequent, his marriage fell apart and whenever I would see him, he seemed to have an aura of unhappiness about him. He had thought that he, not Walter, should have had that job, and his friends said he never really got over it.

As I watched him stagger into the street that day, I said to myself, Whoever gets Walter's job, I will never let that happen to me.

I walked on to our apartment, and about an hour later the phone rang. It was my friend Lane Venardos, the producer who traveled with me on White House trips.

"Have you heard the news?" he asked. "They just announced that Rather got the job. Dan Rather's going to replace Walter Cronkite!"

I decided that night that what I needed to do was go back to Washington and do something I knew how to do — be a reporter.

The *Morning News* hadn't worked because the format had been wrong and because I hadn't gotten along with Northshield, which was probably more my fault than his, but mainly it hadn't worked because I didn't know how to be a host. As with most things, it wasn't as easy as it looked. I had gone to New York on the outside chance that I might be named to anchor the *Evening News*, but it hadn't worked. The contest was over. Dan had won, I had lost, and it was time to move on. What I had hoped for, the job I had wanted from the day I walked in the CBS door, was not going to be mine. Dan and I were too close in age for me to ever be considered his replacement down the line.

I had come to New York believing I could make our broadcast competitive with the other networks, and in my own mind I had failed miserably: the first professional failure of my career. I didn't exactly know how I was going to overcome it, but I knew one thing: No one would ever see me stumbling drunk out of a restaurant in the middle of the day. I was sure of that much.

When I approached Bill Leonard about returning to Washington, he was neither interested nor really able to focus on it. Roger Mudd had walked out the door the day that Rather had been chosen to replace Walter, and he never returned. He later went to NBC and finished out his career in public television. Leonard had his hands full dealing with that, but as the *Morning News* ratings continued to sag, I was convinced that I would be thrown overboard if I didn't get off that sinking ship, and Mudd's departure gave me the opening I needed.

"Send me back to Washington to replace Mudd," I kept telling Leonard, and as fall approached, I had the feeling that the executives at Black Rock, our corporate headquarters, were watching those low ratings and were also telling him to send me somewhere. Finally, he agreed. Twenty-one months after I had come to New York to anchor the new show, I would be going back to Washington.

By then, Pat and the girls had settled in and were really enjoying New York. Susan, who had been terrified of leaving Washington, had been elected a class officer six weeks after enrolling at Chapin, her new school in New York, and Sharon, who had been such a shy little person that she would not participate in show-and-tell at her school in Washington, had come out of her shyness so completely that she had a role in the school play.

I got a lot of "Oh nos" when I told them we were moving back to Washington. But this time, they knew what they were returning to and it went down a lot easier.

It was not so easy for me. I left New York believing it had defeated me. For the first time in my life, I had failed, but as is so often the case in life, what sometimes seems the worst to us at the time turns out to be the best, the experiences from which we learn the most and which we later come to understand were the important turning points in our lives. It would take me many years to understand that, but I would come to realize that anchoring the *Morning News* had given me the opportunity to hone my television skills. I had always considered myself primarily a writer at that point, and I had never worked much without a script. On the *Morning News*, I had my first real chance to practice doing live interviews and I had learned to ad-lib since, many times, I had had to work without a script.

It would take me years to realize it, but those twenty-one months on the *Morning News* had been like a graduate course in learning how to handle the on-the-air emergencies — the film that breaks, the guest who fails to show — all the situations that require an anchor to make snap judgments while millions of people are watching.

People sometimes ask me if I get nervous during a television broadcast, and the honest answer is no. I once did, but in those twenty-one months on the *Morning Show*, I had the chance to make every possible mistake and figure out a way to recover from it. Once you realize there is life after mistakes, you gain a self-confidence that never goes away, and after that I was never nervous.

Learning to relax on television does not come naturally; it is an acquired skill and can only be acquired by doing it over and over. It is like riding a bicycle; it requires no brain-power but lots of practice.

Nor have I ever forgotten that spring day when I had been walking home and had seen a once-talented man stagger into the street drunk because he had not been picked for the one job in the world that he judged would make him a success.

No one job is the key to happiness. Nor, usually, is it the job that makes the man or woman. It was not the anchor chair that made Walter Cronkite. It was Walter Cronkite who made the anchor chair what it came to be. It took me a long time to understand that, and it is a hard lesson for all of us. Real satisfaction does not come from getting a particular job. It comes from how well we do whatever job we have.

New York would be a turning point for me professionally, and it would be a turning point for our family. My years of travel and the long, sleep-deprived days and nights in New York had put an enormous strain on our marriage and on my relationship with the girls. It had taken a long time for me to understand that being a good husband and a good father required as much work and practice as being a good journalist. For the first time in my life, I worked at it, and with practice, I got better at it.

I had understood none of this at the time, of course. That would take years. As we left New York, I could see only one ray of sunshine through the clouds on my horizon. The stock market had gone up, and with it, New York real estate prices. We sold that apartment we had bought twenty-one months earlier for nearly four times what we had paid for it.

# Twenty-one

## *It Was All Foreign to Me*

My interest in foreign policy came late. It just didn't cross my radar screen until I went to Vietnam. Even then, I was thinking more about war and battles than grand strategy. I got to know a little more about it during the years I covered the Pentagon, and when I traveled the world with Ford and Carter I visited somewhere in the neighborhood of three dozen countries. Even then, it was interesting, but never my passion. I was a political reporter and it was always the politics of whatever beat I covered that got my attention.

That attention would change abruptly in the spring of 1982, when an improbable war broke out between Great Britain and Argentina. For hundreds of years, the two countries had argued over who owned some barren islands off the coast of Argentina, three hundred miles due east of the Straits of Magellan. The British called them the Falklands, the Argentines called them the Malvinas, and on April 2, Argentine forces surprised British intelligence and the rest of the world by landing troops and taking the islands in a blaze of gunfire. A small contingent of British Marines, a group that numbered no more than eighty men, had been ordered by London not to surrender, and they put up a valiant fight, but were easily overcome by the huge force of Argentines.

It was a victory that would not stand, said the Iron Lady of Great Britain, Margaret Thatcher. That afternoon she ordered the first vessels in what would be an enormous armada of warships to sail for Argentina. Eventually, more than one hundred naval and commercial ships, even the mighty tourist liner, the *Queen Elizabeth 2*, which was converted into a troop carrier, would make the voyage across the eight thousand miles of Atlantic Ocean that separated London and Buenos Aires.

It would mark the first time since 1945 that Western nations had gone to war over territory, one reason that Argentina's action had been such a surprise. It seemed so ludicrous, it was beyond the realm of possibility. Or at least that was what even experts on the subject thought.

The rising tensions between the two countries had received little pickup in the U.S. press, and what little there was escaped my attention. The invasion came on a Monday, and the weekend before, Pat and the girls and

I had returned from our best vacation trip ever — two weeks in Egypt and a trip down the Nile. We landed in New York on a Friday night, and the plan had been to rest there so I would be fresh to anchor the Saturday *News* the next day. It was not to be. On the last day of our vacation, we had all contracted food poisoning, and we spent Friday and Saturday in a New York hotel room taking turns doing what people with food poisoning do.

To me, it is a mark of professionalism to be able to handle a news broadcast under any conditions, sick, on no sleep, when the equipment breaks and when everything around you somehow doesn't work. Anchoring a news broadcast is a little like flying an airplane — long periods of boredom interrupted by the occasional moment of terror. The test of a great pilot is how he handles the plane when a wing falls off. The same is expected of a professional broadcaster. We are paid for holding the broadcast together during those times when everything else has gone wrong. A broadcaster may be feeling like hell, but we're not hired to work only when we feel like it. We're paid to put our problems aside until we get the broadcast on the air. I had always been able to do that and was proud of it, but not that Saturday. For the first time in my life, the bell rang and I couldn't answer. I was just too sick.

By Monday, we were all well enough to

take the shuttle flight to Washington and, Monday morning, I dragged myself into the office, dehydrated, but according to my appointment book, I felt well enough to make some phone calls to news sources.

That was at the top of the page. At the bottom, I had scribbled a quick note: "Gone to Argentina." In the hours after the invasion, Ed Fouhy, one of the CBS executives, had called from New York to say "they" want you to cover the war. It was always those "they" people who wanted you to do something when the task might not meet with your approval.

Actually, I was fairly ambivalent about the whole thing. It sounded interesting, but it wouldn't have bothered me if someone else had been chosen for the assignment. The only problem for me was that I was still a little queasy.

Nevertheless, late that afternoon I took a flight to Miami and changed planes for the eight-hour flight to Buenos Aires. Buoyed by my first solid food in three days, I arrived in time to file a story for the Tuesday *Evening News*.

That first story must have been an analysis. I had been on the ground only a matter of hours, and we always used to joke that when you hit a story blind, the easiest thing to do is an analytical piece. You needed to be there a couple of days and gather some facts before you could write a decent straight news story.

There would be plenty of those. Over the next three months I would file more than forty *Evening News* reports from Argentina, more than eighty pieces for the *Morning News*, and I anchored several Saturday *Evening News* broadcasts from there, one from the balcony of the Casa Rosada, the Argentine presidential palace.

If ever there was a war to go to that spring, it was the war in Argentina. Lebanon also blew that summer and it was a dangerous place to be, the kind of war where reporters risked their lives to get the story.

In Argentina, we were not burdened with such a problem. Western reporters were confined to Buenos Aires and the shooting, when it came, was a thousand miles south of us. CBS moved in a huge contingent of reporters, cameramen and producers over the next weeks, but none of us ever got close to the Falklands. In fact, only one American reporter ever got there from Argentina. Robin Lloyd, an NBC correspondent, finagled his way there on an Argentine plane one Friday afternoon shortly after the invasion. He was there only several hours, but that was long enough to take pictures of the troops and tape a stand-up, and we felt properly scooped, but no other reporters ever got there. After considerable cajoling, I almost got there toward the end of April.

The army flew me to Comodoro Rivadavia, far to the south of Buenos Aires, and a camera crew and I were scheduled to fly to the islands on a supply plane at first light the next morning.

I was one day too late. I had just gone to sleep in my hotel room in Comodoro Rivadavia, when the phone rang and the army officer who had arranged the trip told me the the next day's flight had been canceled. He said he did not know the reason. With news from the outside world being censored, I would not know the reason either, until I returned to Buenos Aires and learned that the British had landed on South Georgia Island, which was eight hundred miles from the Falklands and from where the British would finally launch the operation to recapture the Falklands. (Britain maintained a small Antarctic survey group on the island, but a group of Argentine Marines had raised their own flag there when they had accompanied a scrap-metal dealer there in March to salvage an abandoned ship.)

After the British landed on South Georgia, the only reporters who got to the battlefield were those who had crossed the Atlantic aboard the British ships.

For the press corps in Buenos Aires, it was a series of long days hanging around Argentina's Foreign Ministry and the U.S. Embassy to pick up what scraps of information

465

we could as we waited for the enormous British fleet to arrive. To be frank, it was very easy duty. The U.S. ambassador, Harry Schlaudemann, was an expert on South America, and told his staff to help us when they could, and they often did. They let me read some of the cables they were sending back to the State Department and I even developed a source or two among the Argentine foreign service officers. (The information was always self-serving, but it helped me to understand their side of it.) Charles Krouse, who had been a foreign correspondent for the *Washington Post*, had recently gone to work for CBS and he had good contacts at several of the other embassies and we made a good team.

We had set up a small studio in a Buenos Aires hotel and I would begin the day there. Buenos Aires is thousands of miles from the United States, but it is only an hour ahead of Eastern time, which makes it one of the easiest foreign spots to report from. A translator would prepare a summary of the war news in the local newspapers and would assemble whatever tape we had gathered from government sources, stringers and our own crews, and the producers and I would fashion it into a series of reports for the *Morning News*.

Once the *Morning News* was done, I would make the rounds of government offices and call on various people at the embassy. Toward early afternoon, I would return to our little studio and compare notes with Eric Engberg, Krouse and our other reporters. If they had information that warranted separate stories, they did them. Otherwise, I melded what they had gathered into my report. Our senior foreign correspondent, Tom Fenton, was covering London's side of the story, and our reports would often be placed back-to-back on the *Evening News*. For thirty straight nights, one or the other of us was the lead story and the other was second, a string I have not matched since.

The best part of the assignment was the food. Argentines love to eat, they eat meat at every meal and they follow the Spanish custom of taking dinner very late, never earlier than 8 P.M., sometimes as late as 10, and Buenos Aires is a city of great restaurants.

A restaurant called La Mosca Blanca (The White Fly) became our hangout, and despite the unappetizing name, it remains one of my all-time favorites. The specialty was a steak called *bife de lomo,* a huge cut of meat that filled a platter large enough to hold the average American family's Thanksgiving turkey. Atop the steak, the cooks would place an enormous mound of French fries. Atop the fries would be two over-easy eggs. Atop all this — and by now the stack of food seemed about a foot high — would be strips of grilled peppers. That was the main course. We usually ordered some kind of meat appetizer, barbecued ribs, perhaps, to start. La Mosca Blanca was not the place to cut back on cholesterol, and why the entire nation had not already died of heart attacks (they also smoked incessantly) I never understood. But that spring and summer in Argentina, I followed the same rule as on political campaigns when we never knew what the hectic schedule would bring. That rule was, if there is food, eat it. If there's a chair, sit in it. If there is a bathroom, use it.

In Argentina, we ate as if there were no tomorrow. After all, we told ourselves, there was a war going on and we could all die. Actually, none of us believed that. The food was just too delicious to resist.

It took weeks for the British fleet to make its way across the Atlantic, and as it did, the war took on the aspects of something out of the eighteenth century. To an American public that still remembered Vietnam and watched one clash after another in the Middle East, where action was always followed by immediate reaction, it seemed the British ships would never get there. To many Americans, the whole thing became an *HMS Pinafore* kind of comic exercise. In this one, the Brits had the ships and the Argentine officers strutted around in the fancy uniforms.

It was anything but an operetta.

Before it was over, more than a thousand people would die. There had been senseless casualties when the Argentines had invaded, and when the well-trained British forces finally struck back, it was a slaughter. To me, Argentina's army was more akin to a metropolitan police force than the military units I was accustomed to seeing. Its primary purpose was to keep Argentina's military rulers in power. It protected them from Argentina's people. Defending the country against foreign enemies was a secondary mission.

Casualties on both sides were heavy, but in the end Argentina's army was no match for the British troops.

We know in retrospect that Argentina's military junta had decided to seize the Falklands to divert attention from the country's sagging economy, but I always believed many lives could have been saved, and the islands returned to British control, if Margaret Thatcher had been willing to negotiate an end to the war, as Ronald Reagan had urged. Instead, she was determined to teach the Argentines a lesson, and she did. The junta fell apart in the weeks after the Argentine forces in the Falklands surrendered, and Argentina returned to democratic rule. For Mrs. Thatcher, whose popularity had been sliding before the invasion, the "Falklands factor" would prove a boon. Her popularity soared with the victory and never again would she be taken lightly, at home or on the world stage.

In some ways, the swiftness of the British victory was almost as surprising to the Americans in Buenos Aires as it had been to the Argentines, which we attributed to how much we had been subconsciously influenced by the daily barrage of Argentine propaganda.

We had access to our American wire services, and even though we were unable to see American television, we were able to hear our *Evening News* broadcasts by telephone, but what we saw daily were what the residents of Buenos Aires saw, newspapers published by the country's three armed forces, the army, navy and air corps. They were published in Spanish and English and gave us a daily dose of good news about how invincible Argentina's forces were and how well they were doing. It was the only news the residents of Buenos Aires got. Often it bore no resemblance to what we got from our Western sources. We didn't trust it, but it did cause us to question the news coming from home.

Another thing I came to understand in Argentina was the value of the exchange programs operated by the State Department, programs that allow foreign opinion-makers and students to come to America in exchange for Americans studying in other countries. I realized this one night shortly after my arrival, when one of our translators had arranged a dinner with a group of Argentines, one of whom was the hard-line editor of the navy's newspaper. The conversation had turned to whether I thought the Americans would side with Argentina in the war. After all, they said, we shared the same continent and had a mutual-defense pact. Unlike the rest of South America, they said, the people of Argentina shared a common European heritage with the people of the United States. "We are white people like you, not Indians," I remember one of them saying. What I found surprising was that that they equated Argentina's taking of the Falkland Islands with the Americans' declaration of independence from King George back in 1776, and their assumption was that most Americans shared that view and would come to their aid if war with Britain actually came.

I was truly the skunk at that garden party when I told them that in truth, most Americans had given virtually no thought to the Falklands, nor did they think much about Argentina, let alone its dispute with the British.

My statement drew gasps of disbelief and one boo, the first and last time that has ever happened to me at a dinner party. My next statement was no more well received than my first had been. No, I told them, I could envision no circumstances in which the United States would oppose Great Britain in any war. Only the editor of the navy newspaper sided with me. I was glad for an ally, but more interesting to me was why it was the military hard-liner, of all people, who took my side. He said it was because he had gone to the United States some years earlier to study jazz on a State Department grant. He didn't like my view, but he understood I was right, he said, because he had come in contact with many Americans.

Over the years, as I have watched a series of congressional demigods denounce such programs as wastes of money, I always remember that night in Buenos Aires. If more people in Argentina had understood what he had known, perhaps one thousand lives would not have been lost in a ridiculous war over the piece of barren real estate that Charles Darwin once called "one of the ugliest places on earth."

I returned home with a plan to set up a group of stringer correspondents across South America which would ensure that never again would we be caught so off guard if another story like the Falklands happened.

I was so enthusiastic about my plan that I flew to New York to outline it to the new CBS News president, Van Gordon Sauter.

I told him how we could put together a network of stringers throughout Central and South America for practically nothing. I told him we could hire them for fifty to one hundred dollars a month each, and pay them only when they performed some minor task, such as writing a monthly news summary of developments in their areas. Most of their information would be of no interest to us, but they would comprise an early warning system, and if something did happen, they would be valuable resources. It was a contact developed through one such local source that had enabled NBC to get its correspondent onto the Falkland Islands, if only for a few hours.

I thought the idea would appeal to Sauter, who favored unconventional approaches, and he gave me a fair hearing. But he had doubts there would be many more such stories from that region that would create the interest the Falkland invasion had, and I left convinced he would do nothing about it. If so, he would be following in a great American journalistic tradition. James Reston, the longtime columnist for the *New York Times*, had once said people would do anything about South America but read about it.

I thought no more about it until some weeks later, when Sauter called and said he didn't think we needed a network of stringers in South America, but he had another proposition: How would I like to become the State Department correspondent? I would be replacing Marvin Kalb, whose work had set the standard for diplomatic coverage. Kalb had left CBS in a contract dispute, and Sauter thought I would be an able replacement. I had no problem with that. Kalb was a great reporter, but I had replaced Dan Rather at the White House. It wouldn't be the first time I would be replacing a famous reporter. I had another concern. What about covering politics? Sauter assured me I would still have a major role covering campaigns, but between election years I would cover diplomatic affairs. I suggested it might look odd for the diplomatic correspondent to be covering politics, and we came up with a compromise. I would cover the State Department except during election years, but my title would not be diplomatic correspondent. Instead I would be chief Washington correspondent.

That had a nice ring to it and I took the job.

I took it, first, because the foreign policy I had learned in Argentina, and covering Henry Kissinger during the years I had traveled the world with Presidents Ford and Carter, had been interesting work.

And I had never been in the State Department. Had I known what awaited me there, I might have declined.

Of all the bureaucracies I have covered in four decades as a Washington reporter, the State Department bureaucracy was the one I found hardest to penetrate, and in fact I never did. It was like a university in which the chemistry department seemed to have no connection with the history department. Each little fiefdom seemed totally wrapped up in its own area of the world, and saw no connection between it and any other part of the world.

The Foreign Service officers I had encountered in the field were helpful, intelligent people, but gathering them in one place, their headquarters, made them all but impossible to deal with. As Harry Truman had once said about economists, there was always too much "on the one hand, but on the other hand." The Pentagon bureaucracy was an action bureaucracy. Left to its own devices (and it never should be), the Pentagon will find a way to take some action. It may be the wrong act, but the Pentagon will act. Left to its own devices, the State Department can be counted on to do nothing. That may be the way of diplomacy, but to a reporter (or at least to me), it is maddening. I could never seem to get a straight answer from anyone.

A story that I found as I went through one of my notebooks from that period gives the flavor. The story I wrote was about a memo issued by a department official after the building had been overrun with rats. Normally, a business overrun with rats notifies the employees and calls in an exterminator or buys a cat. Not the State Department, where every official document is crafted to ensure that no one in a position of authority can possibly be at fault, whatever the problem. Not the State Department, which feels it must go to any length to ensure that, whatever the problem of the day, it is not as bad as it could be.

Thus, the State Department memo began: "The problem of rodent control in office buildings was recently highlighted by reported observations of rats."

On examination, that is not gobbledygook, but a masterpiece of double-talk. It does not admit there *are* rats, only "reported sightings," and it conveys that rats are a problem everywhere, not just the State Department. The memo went on to suggest that rats were not the problem we might think they are. "The appearance of rodents in a building is an unpleasant and disquieting experience," the document stated, "but there is no documented evidence of health implications."

It was a matter of little consequence, but it was the same bureaucratic mind-set that would cause a spokesman to make the statement below when a group of us had asked if the United States would retaliate for the bombing of the Marine headquarters in Beirut.

The spokesman said, "The Israelis did what they did, and the French did what they did, and we are doing what we are doing. If we do something, that's what we will do."

I'm sure it was a personal failing, but I never got used to answers like that.

★ ★ ★

Covering Henry Kissinger had been one of the great delights of covering the White House. What reporters understand and what many outside of journalism don't is that ideology is not what draws reporters to one government official and causes them to run for the door when they see another.

Of course, reporters have opinions, feelings, biases, if you will. Only a person in a coma does not. Reporters are human and are there to gather news, and there is no question that some officials get better coverage than others. But it's usually because that official is a good news source, not because of his or her ideology. Protecting a source is perhaps the main sin of Washington reporters. We could all do better at correcting the problem, and there has been more emphasis on that in recent years, but the reasons are not what many critics believe they are.

Kissinger was perhaps the most influential of all of Nixon's advisors and remained a key figure as Ford's secretary of state, and for that reason alone, he made news, but he also cultivated the press and was able to play it like a fine violin. Even when they knew they were being used, Kissinger was such a good source that reporters cooperated, knowing they would get a story out of it.

Kissinger turned the "background" briefing into such an exercise of high art that when he took a vacation, I wrote a story in which I reported that not Kissinger, but "Senior American Official, the fellow who shows up wherever Kissinger happens to be, was the one taking a few days off."

I noted that Senior Official had first come on the scene when Nixon had refused to allow Kissinger to be seen and heard on camera because he feared Kissinger's German accent would remind people of Dr. Strangelove. Senior Official had done a splendid job in Kissinger's stead, and even after Kissinger had been allowed to speak on his own, I reported, he had still called on Senior Official to help him brief from time to time.

I wished Senior Official a happy vacation and hoped he wouldn't be recognized.

The *Washington Post* picked up the story and ran it on the Op-Ed page, and apparently even Kissinger got a chuckle, which was not always the case. He kept up with every word written about him and would sometimes go into a rage when he felt the press had slighted him, and I tangled with him on several occasions.

Even so, reporters delighted in needling him. On a trip to China, he had taken reporters on a tour of the countryside, and when the reporters saw an aging Chinese woman at the side of the road, Kissinger asked if the reporters wished to question her.

"Yeah," said UPI's Helen Thomas. "Ask

her if she knows who you are."

No one could put the needle to Henry better than Helen. Once, when he had been brought into the White House press room, he said he didn't know if he could do an adequate job because Ford's press secretary, Ron Nessen, had limited him to twenty minutes, and as a college professor his lectures usually ran to forty-five minutes.

"Then start at the end," said Ms. Thomas.

Unfortunately for me, Henry Kissinger had long since left the State Department when I arrived. As had Al Haig, who had been Reagan's first secretary of state.

The office was occupied by one George Shultz, a loyal, patriotic American. But after the flamboyance of Kissinger and the volatility of Haig, a very bland pudding.

He was, in fact, a good secretary of state. That was the important thing for the country and his boss, Ronald Reagan, who was not the keenest student of foreign policy. The bad part for reporters was that George Shultz couldn't make news if his life depended on it. Nor did he seem to mind. He had the goofy idea that he had been hired to run American foreign policy. He didn't pay much attention to press coverage, and as far as I could tell, didn't watch television. I followed Shultz around the world. I was with him in Beirut when an enemy rocket passed over the house where he was sleeping, shuttled with him across the Middle East, and waited outside conference room doors from Beijing to Cairo and Madrid as he negotiated with world leaders. If there was good news, he generally held it until the president could be given credit for it, and if there was bad news, he tried to make the best of it. Those were admirable qualities, but not necessarily traits that ensured a place for him (and me) on the *Evening News*.

During his second term, Reagan became embroiled in the Iran-Contra controversy, and it would be Shultz and his in-house rival, Defense Secretary Caspar Weinberger, who would emerge as voices of reason. When zealous White House aides had proposed the secret arms-for-hostages deal, it was Shultz who had argued that what could not be done directly could not be done indirectly, and it was Shultz who had told the president to his face that he might risk impeachment if he tried some of the things being proposed by his White House team.

It was also Shultz who had finally gotten Reagan back on track after the scandal, and Shultz who testified before Iran-Contra investigators in televised Capitol Hill hearings, with no lawyers and no notes, because it was the taciturn secretary of state who had nothing to hide.

It was not until those days that I came to appreciate Shultz for what he was, a moderate, mainstream Republican of impeccable integrity who had served the country well.

But in the years when I had covered him on a daily basis, all I knew was that he was a difficult man to do a television story about, and for a reporter learning the State Department beat, that made for hard duty.

The State Department probably deserved better coverage than I had the ability to give it in those years, but I suppose we both survived. Whatever the case, when 1984 rolled around, I was ready for a break.

I couldn't wait to get to New Hampshire and the year's first presidential primary.

# Twenty-two

## *The New World Order: CBS in the 1980s*

When I had come home to Washington after my *Morning News* adventure in New York, I plunged right into covering politics, so it wasn't until we got past Ronald Reagan's inauguration in January 1981 that I realized my world had been turned upside down. CBS was always in some kind of turmoil. We were always in some kind of well-publicized row with the government, and the correspondents were usually in some argument with each other. That was part of the charm of working for the biggest and most influential news organization. We thought we were the best, and the attention just validated that. But the decade of the '80s would bring something altogether different from what we had known before.

The whole network landscape was changing. In corporate America, takeovers were the new rage. NBC and ABC would be swallowed up by larger companies and CBS would come under the control of New York financier Lawrence (call me Larry) Tisch.

The coming of cable and VCRs meant viewers had more choices, and with the clicker they no longer had to leave the sofa to change channels. With more choices, the audiences of all the networks had begun to shrink, and as audiences shrank, it became harder to sell commercials.

At CBS News, the people who had hired me and had run the place for years had moved on.

My old bureau chief and patron, Bill Small, had moved on to NBC. Dan Rather had replaced Walter Cronkite in the anchor chair, and Richard S. Salant, the man who had run CBS News and set its standards for sixteen years, had retired. For most of the 1980s, the fate of the news division would be in the hands of Van Gordon Sauter, who would introduce us to a new concept of what constituted news.

Even Bill Paley, the man who had founded the company and remained its largest stockholder, would be eased aside. He was still a major presence in the company, but had been stripped of most of his real power. After Frank Stanton, Paley's longtime number two, had retired in 1973, Paley had groomed a series of bright, younger outsiders to replace him. Or at least that had been the plan. Once the newcomers arrived and settled in,

Paley would become jealous and fire them. Arthur Taylor was an early example. Paley named him to succeed Stanton as president of the company in 1972, and at first he seemed to be exactly the kind of person to run what even then was called the Tiffany Network. He was only thirty-seven and had already developed a reputation at International Paper as a sharp businessman, but he was also a student of Renaissance history whose interests ran far beyond business. At *News*, we liked him because he seemed in the mold of Stanton. He understood the importance of news and, more important, he recognized that news should be insulated from commercial pressures both inside and outside the company.

Unfortunately, Taylor began to attract the kind of favorable attention that made Paley nervous.

"Mr. Paley was very attentive to what his friends said," Taylor told me. "One of them said to him, 'That Arthur Taylor certainly seems to be doing quite well,' and that was the death sentence for me."

Others who found too much of the spotlight falling on thcm would suffer similar fates, but Paley met his match in Tom Wyman, who had come to CBS from the Pillsbury food conglomerate. The other directors had become concerned with Paley's maneuvering and, with their help, Wyman had eased Paley aside in 1985 and installed himself as chairman and chief executive officer of the company, and he had not been all that subtle about it. As Larry Tisch, who was on the CBS board, told me later, Wyman had literally frozen Paley out, barring him from programming meetings and other gatherings, a move that Tisch thought unnecessarily cruel to a man who had founded the company.

Once he had consolidated his own power, Wyman's main task was to keep an eye on corporate raiders. It was the era of mergers and hostile takeovers: General Electric would eventually acquire NBC, and ABC would be gobbled up, first by media giant Cap Cities and later by Disney, an even larger entertainment conglomerate. It was known that corporate raiders, including Martin Davis and Ivan Boesky, had designs on CBS, but it was the cable guy, Ted Turner, who finally went after CBS.

Wyman was able to rebuff the challenge, but at a high price. CBS borrowed a billion dollars to buy back a big chunk of its own stock. Saddled with a billion-dollar debt, CBS was no longer an attractive takeover target, and the Turner threat evaporated. The problem for Wyman was to pay down the debt, and to do it he ordered across-the-board cutbacks throughout the company, including the news division. We were blindsided. News had been under the protective wings of Paley and Stanton for so long that we couldn't imagine this kind of thing happening to us. These were things that affected the other parts of the company — the divisions that were supposed to make the money. But it was happening to us. Wyman sent down orders to eliminate ten percent of the news jobs. Paley no longer had the power to stop it (and he may not have wanted to). Stanton had retired and Salant had gone to NBC.

Layoffs were ordered for the news division, and the most charitable way to characterize their handling is to say that our people had had no experience with such actions, but whatever the reason, they could not have handled them in a more inhumane way.

Show producers and other supervisors were told to rank the people who worked for them in order of how valuable they were. The lists went to management, and the top executives reviewed the names and ordered those on the bottom rungs of each list fired. Seventy-four CBS News employees were declared expendable, and fifty more were sent into early retirement. Those discharged were given a list of benefits, and severance pay, and told to be out of the building the following day. I was in New York the day the notices went out, and I had never seen anything like it. People ran into the halls screaming

486

and crying. Some of them had worked at CBS News for years and now they were being told — ordered — to leave. Those who tried to appeal to upper management were unable to find anyone from upper management. There was no one to whom they could appeal. Some of them would find work elsewhere. Others never did, and one producer who had worked with me on the weekend news eventually committed suicide.

It was the first day in a new world for CBS News. From that day forward, we would be expected to pay our own way and eventually to earn a profit, and what was happening to us would soon spread across the industry. Perhaps we had lived in a world that was no longer realistic and perhaps what management was now asking was not unreasonable, but of all the good and bad days I would experience as a CBS News correspondent, that day was the worst. Even so, the turmoil was only beginning.

Dan Rather replaced Walter Cronkite as anchor of the *Evening News* in the months after Reagan's inaugural in 1981.

He had been chosen the year before by Bill Leonard, the old CBS News hand who had succeeded Dick Salant as president of the news division. (Leonard had been nearing retirement age when he was picked and was an interim president, but he made two important decisions: he picked Dan and he created the new *Sunday Morning* program.) It was well known that Salant wanted Roger Mudd to succeed Cronkite, and at one point, Leonard tried to pair Mudd and Rather as co-anchors. Rather actually agreed, but Mudd refused, and when Leonard picked Dan, Mudd walked out the door of the Washington bureau and never returned. For years, the news division had been split between Mudd and Rather factions, but I had always thought of myself as a friend of both. I was happy for Dan (I would have been happier had I been chosen), but I was also sorry to see Roger leave. He went on to a second career at NBC and PBS, but I felt his departure was a great loss to CBS.

In any case, Dan had gotten off to a slow start. Replacing Walter, the most trusted man in America, would not have been easy for anyone. He had come to dominate television as no one ever had, and it would not be easy for the American people to forget him; and Dan's early efforts to show he was his own man, that he was not Walter, fell flat.

To bring new energy to the broadcast, he decided to deliver the news standing rather than sitting, and when others tried to talk him out of it, he compromised by leaning against the counter behind the anchor chair where Walter had delivered the news. Instead of lending the informality he had hoped for, it looked awkward. As he leaned forward and faced the camera in front of him, Dan appeared to be in some sort of crouch. I knew Dan well enough to know that while he was always willing to experiment and try new approaches, he was never afraid to abandon them when they didn't work. I was as certain that he would soon be back in the chair as I was of my own name.

Nevertheless, the power of the *Evening News* anchor is such that when I arrived in New York to anchor the weekend broadcast the following Saturday, there was no chair. Since we did the broadcast directly from the newsroom where we wrote and edited it, I sat in that chair to do my writing. I told one of the crew to find my chair because I needed to get to work. He patiently explained that we no longer used a chair, that I would be sitting on the shelf behind the anchor desk. But how could I type from there? I wanted to know. He had no answer, but said he would have to get permission from the executive producer before he could get a chair.

"Look," I remember telling him. "I know Dan. He'll be back in a chair next week. Just get the chair, and if you get in trouble, I'll take care of it."

He did, and the following Monday, Dan was back to sitting in the chair and when I arrived the next weekend, the chair was behind the desk.

Dan would become more comfortable in the months ahead, but the *Evening News* ratings had begun to slide, as they usually do when there is an anchor change. It was the ratings slip that opened the door for Sauter to become news president. Because of his age, Leonard had been expected to serve only a short time, but when the ratings dropped, Gene Jankowski, the president of the CBS Broadcast Group, decided to make immediate changes. Jankowski hadn't been impressed by the people Leonard had been grooming to replace him. He saw them as "yesterday people" and Rather saw them as "Cronkite people," so Jankowski decided to bring in an outsider to fix things.

The outsider was Van Gordon Sauter, a longtime CBS executive but one who had spent little time in the network news division. He had done a variety of things over the years, from serving as the network censor to a successful stint running the sports division. But he was best known for turning around the flagging station that CBS owned in Los Angeles. He was equally known for his eccentricities.

When he had run the station in Los Angeles, he had lived on a boat, kept a parrot in his office and strolled the hallways in deck shoes. This was no Salant or Murrow or Cronkite. Nor was his idea of what constituted news anything like theirs.

He wanted us to go after stories that hit viewers in the gut, stories that gave viewers an emotional jolt. It was that special "moment" in a story — a tear running down a child's cheek, the look of fear on the face of a soldier — that stayed with viewers and made a story memorable. Or at least as Sauter saw it. We had always thought of CBS News as the *New York Times* of the air. Sauter wanted us to aim at a much broader, truly national audience. To be successful, he envisioned a national electronic tabloid.

Sauter came on board in 1981 and was given the title of executive vice president under Leonard, but it was well known that he had been given the authority to do whatever he needed to do to fix the *Evening News* broadcast, and shortly before I left to cover the war in Argentina in the spring of 1982, Leonard retired and Sauter added the title of news division president to the authority he already enjoyed. Another former station manager, Ed Joyce, was brought in as his deputy. As we understood it, Sauter was the visionary and Joyce was there to hold down costs.

For a while, it worked, the *Evening News* ratings went back up, and for most of the early years of Sauter's reign I stayed under his radar. He set about changing the way we told stories. Finding those "moments" that made the story memorable became the objective. But there wasn't much way to juice up the story of the war in the Falklands, even though war doesn't lack for emotional moments. And for sure, when I returned and went to the State Department, there were not many "moments" to be found in George Shultz's activities. If my stories from there were not always crowd-pleasers in Sauter's view, they were tolerated as stories that needed to be covered. When I left the State Department to cover the presidential campaign of 1984, I covered it the same way I had always covered politics. In truth, I didn't disagree with Sauter's storytelling techniques. Television is about pictures, and when you can tell a story by showing the people who are affected by government programs, it is bound to have more impact than when you show a politician in Washington just talking about that program.

I agreed with Sauter that, too many times, we had been satisfied to tell the story the easy way, from Washington. Where I differed with Sauter was that I believed that you also had to cover the stories that didn't lend themselves to pictures. I didn't believe a story had to be entertaining to earn a place on the *Evening News*. In any case, Sauter never ordered me to do a story I didn't want to do, and when I had a problem he always gave me a fair hearing, even when we disagreed.

Bruce Morton and I split most of the campaign coverage in 1984. While other CBS reporters rode the planes with the candidates, Ronald Reagan and Walter Mondale, we leapfrogged from one primary to the next, doing the overview stories about the local campaign, organizations and what was going on in the key states. He spent the weeks leading up to the Iowa caucuses in Iowa, while I headquartered in New Hampshire to report what was happening in the days before the primary there.

Reagan was trying to become the first president since Eisenhower to be elected to a second term, and the only real question in voters' minds was whether he was getting a little dotty with age. When he quipped during his first debate with Mondale that he would not "hold Mondale's youth and inexperience against him," it brought down the house, and most of the reporters covering the campaign decided it was over at that point. The old feller might be a little hazy on detail, but he still had it, he hadn't lost his marbles, and that was about all voters wanted to know that year, a point validated on election day when Reagan won in a landslide.

I figured I would go back to the State Department after the election, but to my good fortune, technology would soon intervene and save me. Satellites and other advances in electronics were making it possible for all the

*Evening News* anchors to travel more, and when Dan went on the road, I would go to New York and share anchor duties with him, doing the part of the broadcast he couldn't do from wherever he might be. Or filling in if the technology failed or if he didn't arrive at the remote site in time to do the broadcast.

Sauter and his deputy, Joyce, had ordered yet another overhaul of the *Morning News*, and I would also find myself filling in there from time to time. I continued to anchor the Saturday *News* on weekends, and had I been on a baseball team, I would have been what they call a role player — a guy who can come off the bench and play two or three positions. In the world of television, where egos range from large to extra-large, colleagues would sometimes ask in all seriousness if I didn't find it demeaning to be waiting around just in case Dan wasn't available. That part didn't bother me at all; I was being well paid, and while it was not exactly the career track I had dreamed of, it was indoor work that saved me from having to go back to covering the State Department. I also took some pride in being able to do whatever I was called on to do.

The *Morning News* was a bigger mess than ever. After my unsuccessful stint there, it had been expanded to a two-hour broadcast with a *Today* show format and it was anchored by Kuralt and Diane Sawyer. We had all been wary when Diane was hired. Her only journalistic credentials had been as a weather reporter at a Kentucky station and she had worked as a press aide at the Nixon White House. But she was not long in making believers of us. She had been assigned as the backup reporter at the State Department and she'd proved to be a relentless reporter and competitor, and she was a terrific broadcaster. In no time, the bosses were looking for a way to showcase her, and the *Morning News* was the perfect spot. New producers were brought in, and she and Charles made a good team, but the ratings continued to sag, and when Sauter and Joyce arrived they did what new management always did — they tried to remake the *Morning News*.

Their plan was to dump Kuralt, Sawyer and everyone connected with the show, but after a lunch with Diane, Sauter began to see star qualities and decided to pair her with Bill Kurtis, the deep-voiced anchor of the CBS station in Chicago.

The move stunned us and reverberated throughout the broadcasting community. Kuralt was one of the most distinguished correspondents at CBS. Not only was he unceremoniously dumped; his salary was cut in half, according to leaks in the trade press.

It was shoddy treatment for one of the most respected and well-liked reporters in all of CBS, and the fact that he was being replaced by a "local anchor" made it all the worse. Kurtis had nothing to do with any of it except to take a job that he saw as a promotion, but replacing Kuralt in such circumstances ruined whatever chance he might have had to enjoy cordial relations with his new colleagues.

What surprised all of us was that, over time, the broadcast did seem to be finding an audience, and at one point in 1983 actually beat the *Today* show. But it was clear to anyone who knew Diane that she was becoming restless. For all her glamour, she is a serious person, and she found no joy doing live interviews with yo-yo champions, so in 1984, she stunned Sauter and Joyce by announcing that she was joining *60 Minutes*. On the organization charts, Sauter and Joyce were in charge of *60 Minutes*, and its producer, Don Hewitt, reported to them. That was not the reality. *60 Minutes* had begun to make so much money that no one was about to cross Hewitt. He had offered the spot to Diane, and she was allowed to take it, and there was nothing Sauter or Joyce could do. Joyce did insist that he would not allow CBS funds to be used to pay for a *Morning News* farewell party for Diane.

Diane's departure led to one of the worst disasters ever for the news division. On orders from Broadcast Group President Gene Jankowski, Sauter replaced her with Phyllis George, the former Miss America who had become a popular personality on CBS Sports. Phyllis was many things, but she was not a journalist, and she arrived at the *Morning News* with a thud. Because she was from Texas, we had become friends, and I thought her to be a friendly, good-natured person. But for a person who had spent considerable time in show business, first as Miss America and then as someone who had been a part of the Hollywood scene, I found her remarkably naive. Her first husband had been the Hollywood producer Robert Evans and at the time she came to CBS she was married to John Y. Brown, the multimillionaire governor of Kentucky, yet she had the childlike innocence of someone who had been protected from the mundane workings of everyday life. I found it somewhat refreshing, but some others did not. After she had been seen asking a cabdriver if you paid the fare before or after the trip, her new colleagues giggled that she didn't even know how to take a taxi.

Phyllis had a sunny-side-up smile and assumed that everyone liked her, and she was crestfallen to find many at the *Morning News* resented her "star status," her million-dollar salary, her limos, and even her mink coat. It left her nervous and insecure, and it showed on the air.

She had never done serious interviews and needed help in preparing for them, but she got very little assistance. Soon, her co-anchor

Kurtis was complaining, and leaks about her incompetence began showing up in the TV columns. As it got worse, she became more insecure, and malapropisms became a staple of her on-air delivery. The worst incident came when an Illinois woman named Cathy Webb, who claimed to have been raped by a man named Gary Dotson, had a religious conversion and recanted her accusation. Dotson had been sent to prison, but was soon released, and the two made the rounds of the morning shows.

Phyllis's interview was no worse than those on the other broadcasts, but at the end she smiled and asked, "How about a hug?"

The two declined the invitation to embrace, and it became one of the most embarrassing episodes in CBS News history. The CBS switchboard lit up with outrage and some of the broadcast's own producers were calling TV columnists to make sure they knew about it.

By that time, Sauter had been promoted to a job at Black Rock, the corporate headquarters across town, and Joyce had been named president of CBS News. But he still reported to Sauter and both knew something had to be done. To further complicate matters, Kurtis and Joyce had fallen out over what Kurtis saw as a lack of support for the program, and to settle that, he was let out of his contract and allowed to rejoin his old station in Chicago.

That set off another chain of problems. When Kurtis returned, he was given the anchor slot that had been assigned to an African-American reporter in his absence, and when that man was pushed aside to make room for Kurtis, it set off such a furor in the black community that Jesse Jackson led a boycott against the station. Not until CBS agreed to name an African-American, Jonathan Rogers, to become general manger of the station, did the turmoil die down. It had been a disaster for CBS, but a windfall for Kurtis. He resumed anchoring at the station, but formed his own production company as a sideline and went on to become one of the leading independent producers and anchors of documentaries. It's a rare night when there is not a Bill Kurtis production on at least one cable channel.

Meanwhile, back at the *Morning News* in New York, the problems had multiplied. There was no one to replace Kurtis and they didn't know what to do with Phyllis. That's when I got a call from Joyce's ebullient deputy, Howard Stringer.

Howard had grown up in Wales and had worked his way through the CBS ranks after coming to America as a young man. He was a friend, and we had worked closely together on several projects including a five-part series of documentaries called *The Defense of the*

*United States,* which I always felt was some of my best work.

But Howard is more than a friend whose work I respect. He is also witty, smart and one of the most charming people in America, and he was in fine form that morning.

"Mate," he said, "I need a favor and I'm going to make it worth your while. I'm going to double your pay if you'll come up here and do the *Morning News.*"

I remember exactly my first thought. Oh shit, not the *Morning News* again.

People weren't lining up to double my pay, so I had to listen, but I had no interest in doing the *Morning News.* I had truly been there and done that, and it had been the single worst experience of my life, so I managed to say, "Howard, I'm flattered but I don't think so."

Howard is as persuasive as he is charming, and we agreed that I would do it for a week, just to give him some breathing room while he and Joyce tried to figure out what to do.

When I got to New York, I realized they wanted more than an anchor. They were looking for a coach to teach Phyllis how to be on television, someone who could help her settle down and feel comfortable. And, someone who could stop all the backbiting.

"If you can just find a way to stop all these leaks," Joyce told me, "you'll have done a great service and earned your pay."

The way we left it was that I would fill in until a permanent replacement could be found. But I made sure they understood that I had no intention of moving the family back to New York. I had done that once, and by now the girls were in high school and I just wasn't going to put them through another move.

Whether or not I had anything to do with it, Phyllis did relax after that. That summer, the same thing happened to her that had happened to me during my earlier stint on the *Morning News*. She got better with practice. But by then, it was too late. The executives had given up on her, and believed viewers would never forgive her early gaffes, and we all knew it would be only a matter of time until changes would be made.

When Phyllis took an occasional day off, my friend Maria Shriver filled in, and one day Howard wondered aloud if I would be interested in doing the show permanently with Maria. I took his remark to be idle musing and told him that I thought Maria had great potential and she was a friend, but it just wasn't my thing.

It turned out to be a pleasant summer. Because I didn't want the job, I was completely relaxed, and my attitude was entirely different than it had been in the days when I had seen the *Morning News* as a possible stepping-stone to the *Evening News*. Since the newscasts at the top of the hour amounted to no more than headlines, I let others write them and concentrated on the live interviews. Rather than come to work at 4 A.M., as I had done in my previous tour, I came in around 5 or 6 A.M. Instead of trying to produce the broadcast and micromanage every detail, I left that to others. In my previous turn at anchoring the show, I had believed that if I let others make all the decisions, I would be little more than a performer and no longer be a journalist. That summer with Phyllis, I found another solution: If the producers wanted me to do something that I found embarrassing or that I just didn't want to do, I simply said no. Otherwise, I saw my job as making the broadcast as good as I could between seven and nine each morning, and I let others worry about it the rest of the time. And I found a way to resolve my old problem of sleep deprivation. Instead of trying to set a schedule for sleeping, I just slept when I got sleepy. If that was at ten in the morning, then I went to sleep at ten. If it was later that night, I went to sleep then.

As summer wore on, I told Howard that he didn't seem to be having much luck finding a replacement. He assured me the search was on, but that I could still have the job if I wanted. I thanked him again and told him I really would like to return to Washington by September. He promised to do what he could, and that Labor Day weekend, Joyce told Phyllis that she was being replaced. Yet another anchor team — Maria Shriver and Forrest Sawyer — was named for the *Morning News.*

Pat took the extra money I had earned that summer and redid the kitchen. We always called it the *Morning News* kitchen.

Joyce lasted only a few months longer than Phyllis. He caught a lot of the blame for the *Morning News* fiasco, though Phyllis had been hired by Jankowski and Sauter. The layoffs had left the news division reeling and he fell out with Rather over what Dan saw as his lack of support for the *Evening News.* By late fall, the news division was in open revolt.

How I managed to make my way through the office politics of those months still amazes me. I was thought of as a junior member of the old guard, but Joyce needed me to hold the *Morning News* together that summer, and I managed to stay on good terms with him and, looking back on it, under different circumstances he might have been a good CBS News president. He would be forever linked to Sauter, but as I came to know him that summer, I thought his news values were much closer to those of Salant. His problem was that he had handled the budget cuts poorly, had alienated most of the key people who worked for him, and as fall approached, Jankowski knew that something had to be done to put down what was by then an open rebellion in the news division. Joyce went off to a temporary job at Black Rock and Sauter was sent back for a second try at running the news department.

The following July, there was another round of layoffs, and news people became even more contemptuous about it. In his newspaper column, Andy Rooney wrote that "CBS, which used to stand for the Columbia Broadcasting System, no longer stands for anything."

The trade press was even more critical and talked of Sauter as being the man who was destroying CBS News.

In the board room at Black Rock, the corporate headquarters across town, the top echelon of the company was immersed in an even nastier, though less publicized, fight. Tom Wyman, the corporate chief who had pushed Paley aside and fended off the takeover attempt by Ted Turner, had run into serious trouble with his own directors, one of whom was Larry Tisch, a billionaire financier who had come to the board the old-fashioned way. No junk bond financing and fancy tender offers for him. He just began buying CBS stock on the open market. When he'd acquired a sizable chunk, Wyman had invited him to join the CBS board. By the fall of

1986, he had acquired 25 percent of the company's stock. When Wyman infuriated the directors by failing to tell some of them that he had been trying to sell the company to Coca-Cola, they ousted him. Tisch took over running the company and, over the objections of some of the directors, reinstalled Paley as chairman of the board. "The others were fed up with Paley," Tisch told me in an interview for this book. "But I felt he was the glue that held the whole thing together."

It also left Tisch firmly in control.

In the news department, we saw it as great news. Tisch had several friends at CBS News, among them Mike Wallace, and word spread quickly that Tisch liked news and was our kind of guy, the kind who would restore the news division to what it had once been under Paley and Stanton. When word filtered out that one of Tisch's first acts had been to fire Sauter, a producer ran through the newsroom shouting, "Ding dong, the witch is dead!"

In those first weeks, I liked everything about Larry Tisch. I liked his rough edges, the way he could cut to the chase and get to the nub of things. I liked that he made it a point to come to Washington and have dinner with the correspondents and producers in the Washington bureau. He seemed to know

505

everybody who counted in politics — my beat — and he had an opinion on everything, and I liked that, too.

He told us he didn't spend money foolishly, but he intended to spend it where it counted — on the stuff that went on the screen. He told us he would cut expenses, but that he would do it by cutting needless layers of management, not by cutting the things we needed to cover the news. For all the cuts he would later order — and eventually he ordered the deepest cuts of all — I still believe he meant it. He just had no idea how a news organization went about covering the news, or how much redundancy was required to ensure that you didn't miss a big story, and we were partly to blame for that. Nor did he know anything about broadcasting and the complex relationship that exists between the networks and their affiliates, and by then he was too rich to need advice.

I have a theory that, at a certain point, people can become so wealthy that those around them are afraid to give them honest advice. I call it the "too-rich-to-get-the-truth syndrome."

Here's an example: Men like Ross Perot and Bill Gates were brilliant enough to amass great fortunes, but how long do you suppose it has been since they proposed something and an underling replied, "That's total bullshit, boss. Only a moron would come up with something like that." It's the kind of remark that keeps the rest of us connected to reality, but when you're rich enough, it just docsn't happen. Tisch was a great businessman, but as he now candidly admits, his lack of knowledge about broadcasting hurt him badly in the beginning.

For all of Tisch's business acumen, network broadcasting was different from anything he had ever dealt with. It is different, because the networks don't sell their programming; they pay local stations around the country to carry it. It works this way: The network sells commercials — that's where the network gets its revenue. But in order for the programming and the commercials to be seen by a vast national audience, the network pays the local station to run the programming in the station's area. No other business does it like that.

Tisch would order massive budget cuts and Wall Street would love it. But what pleases Wall Street in the short run is not necessarily what is best for a news department's image in the long run. Why? Ask yourself this: You're sitting in front of your TV. The network newscasts you get come into your home free; they don't cost you a thing. Which one are you going to choose? The one that is delivered by a news department that has let it be known that it spares no expense to gather the news or one that brags it has covered the story on the cheap? People watch the news channel they believe is the most trustworthy. They make that judgment based on the credibility of the anchor and the organization behind him (or her). When viewers believe a news organization's first goal is to cover the news as cheaply as possible, it does not build trust or credibility, and viewers will turn away. People watch television for different reasons, but the overwhelming reason they pick one news broadcast over another is because they believe it is the most credible.

Tisch believed he had no choice but to cut expenses, and it didn't bother him at all to have the reputation as one who frowned on wasting money. In truth, he was proud of it. I was the featured speaker one night at a dinner for our affiliate station managers, which was being held in a hotel Tisch owned. I brought down the house when I told the crowd, "You could always tell when you were in a Tisch hotel because they kept the Gideon Bibles on chains so they couldn't be stolen."

I was told Tisch enjoyed it, but good-humored about it or not, we could never convince him why we needed "all those people."

When Tisch got rid of Sauter, he picked Howard Stringer to run the news department. Howard was a popular choice, and early on he took Tisch on a tour of the overseas bureaus. It seemed like a good idea at the time.

When the two arrived in London, everyone there made it a point to be in the bureau. People who work in overseas bureaus always feel neglected, and when anyone from the home office — especially a new boss — comes calling, they line up to see him.

Tisch's first question was why were so many people in the bureau instead of out looking for news. It was a proper question. The proper answer was that normally they *were* out looking for news, but today they had come in to suck up to the new boss.

At a dinner for the correspondents and producers that night, it got worse. As always happens when the visiting brass comes to call, the people of the bureau made the case that they had all kinds of stories that ought to be broadcast, but those idiots back in New York just wouldn't put them on the air. It was the complaint that New York executives always heard when they visited overseas bureaus. Telling the boss that they were getting screwed by the people in New York was a tradition as old as foreign correspondents wearing trench coats.

Being new to the business, Tisch came away with an entirely different impression. If the people in New York weren't using the material that was being offered by the London bureau, he wanted to know, then why did they need so many people in the London bureau?

"The worst was Rome," Tisch said. "They must have had fifteen or twenty people sitting around, and when I kept asking why, the only rationale they could come up with was 'Well, what if the pope dies?' "

He may have had a point there. We could have gotten along with fewer people, but Rome was Rome and people fought to be assigned there. When Tisch got to Moscow (not a sought-after assignment) and discovered only a four-person bureau, he was convinced the overseas force could be reduced.

Tisch continued to ask his executives, "Why do you need all those people?" and in the spring of 1987, reports that more layoffs were coming were confirmed. CBS announced the third cutback in sixteen months, and the new layoffs dwarfed the previous two. The news staff was cut 15 percent; 215 news people, including fourteen on-air reporters, were let go; the budget — now in the neighborhood of 300 million dollars — was cut 33 million.

The newsrooms in Washington and New York were in shock. Rather went at Tisch head-on. In a *Times* Op-Ed piece headlined "From Murrow to Mediocrity," he wrote: "Our new chief executive officer, Lawrence Tisch, told us when he arrived that he wanted us to be the best. We want nothing more than to fulfill that mandate. Ironically, he has now made the task seem something between difficult and impossible." By then, Walter Cronkite had joined the CBS corporate board and he, too, was in a rage. He was given an hour to protest the cuts, and board members listened politely, but the cuts stood.

Tisch still believes he had no alternative.

"Everybody knew we had to cut costs. The network audiences were declining and that meant revenues were declining," he told me one winter day in February 2002.

What no one understood at the time, Tisch argued, was that the networks could simply no longer afford the enormous news departments they had once supported, a conclusion CBS management had recognized before he took over. He said it was Wyman who had actually directed the cuts.

"The stock was depressed, and he was the one who ordered the cuts, and when he had presented them to the board, the board approved them, but when I took over nothing had been done," Tisch said. "He ordered the cuts, but he hadn't executed them. I was the one who took the heat for it, but it had to be done."

Tisch has no apologies, but feels he got more of the blame than he deserved.

"The press takes the side of the press," he told me, "so they always took the side of the news department. My public relations were terrible. Everyone knew what had to be done, but no one would stand up and share the responsibility with me."

Tisch now believes that had he been a broadcaster, he could have headed off some of his problems. Unlike most businesses, the press is constantly looking over the broadcaster's shoulder.

"I wasn't used to that," Tisch told me. "If I had spent more time in broadcasting, I would have had a better idea of how to handle it."

Tisch had picked Howard Stringer to run *News* and later selected him to run the network, where he enjoyed considerable success, but it was clear that he now believes Stringer should have taken some of the heat for the news cutbacks.

"Howard was the Teflon man," he told me. "One of the best politicians in America. He picked the people to be fired, but his fingerprints were never on any of it."

For all of us in the News department, the new economics meant we had to ask a new question about covering the news: How much would the story cost? Producer Sandy Socolow's old adage, that "no one ever got fired for spending too much to cover the news," was no longer operative. On the contrary, spending too much was held against you.

The new way would save money, but there would be other costs. When the United States launched the Gulf War, we had shut down so much of our overseas news-gathering operation that we literally had to rebuild it before we could cover the war. When the fire broke out, we had to rebuild the fire department before we could send a fire truck.

Once we were up and running, we covered the war as well as any other news organization, but the night the air campaign on Baghdad began was a sad night at CBS News headquarters in New York. We watched on studio monitors as CNN correspondents reported from the scene and sent back photos of the first explosions in the Baghdad night. As Tom Bettag, then the producer of the *Evening News*, would later say, "It was a tough night for all of us at CBS. We covered the bombing from our New York studio with graphics."

Tisch would finally sell CBS to Westinghouse in the 1990s and the company would be sold again to Viacom, the present owner. In a funny way, we have come full circle. Viacom had begun as a small syndication company that had been spun off from the original CBS in the 1970s.

With more and more channels, audiences would continue to shrink and there would be more contraction at all the networks.

Network news had changed forever.

I asked Tisch why he had decided to sell the company, and he said it was because he never really felt like a free agent, as he had at Loews, the company he had owned for many years.

"I made up my mind I would either buy the whole thing, if the directors invited me to, or I would sell it," he said. "But in the end, I just thought it was in the stockholders' interest to sell.

"We got a nice price and everyone was very pleased."

# Twenty-three

## *Capitol Hill*

When Larry Tisch moved Howard Stringer to Black Rock to run the network, he hired David Burke, a longtime ABC executive, to run CBS News. Burke had run ABC *News* on a day-to-day basis for Roone Arledge and he was a fine choice. He had solid news judgment and I found him to be a serious, straightforward boss, but I was surprised when he called me to his office one day in January 1989 and asked if I would be interested in covering Congress.

Phil Jones, one of my closest friends at CBS, had covered Congress for twelve years (since the Carter administration), but Burke said Jones was moving to a slot on *48 Hours*, our prime-time news broadcast, and he needed to find a replacement.

I accepted on the spot. I had spent most of 1987 and 1988 covering the presidential campaign, and on election day I had more or less worked myself out of a job. I had returned to the Washington bureau and had no real beat. After two years mostly on the road covering the campaign, working the Capitol beat would give me more time at home, and Congress had always been my favorite part of Washington.

Most people saw the White House as the glamour beat, but to me the Capitol had always been the most interesting part of town and the easiest place to find news. There are 535 members of Congress, 435 House members and 100 senators, and they have thousands of staffers, many of whom are experts on foreign, domestic or defense policy. No matter how arcane the question or subject matter, there is usually a staffer in some corner of the Capitol who has the answer. Best of all for reporters who cover the place, the elected officials are independent contractors. They don't work for someone else, nor do they have to check with someone else before they comment on anything, and they see reporters as a way to communicate with the voters who sent them to Washington. A president can command television and press attention anytime he wants, but members of Congress must compete with each other for attention, and for reporters that's a recipe for news. Better still, a reporter can usually find them, even when they don't want to be found.

A reporter who covers the White House or one of the federal agencies usually must go through the public-affairs or press office to speak to officials there. Most of the members of Congress have staffers to deal with the press, but when senators and members of Congress come to their chambers to vote, a reporter who waits at the door can usually buttonhole them for comment. The Capitol is the last place in Washington where that is possible — where you can be in daily, direct contact with the newsmaker rather than an aide, and it is the reason that Congress remains, in my mind anyway, the most interesting beat and the one that is still the most fun to cover.

Congress is also the place where people from all over America come together, and it is the greatest collection of characters ever assembled under one roof. The first time I ever sat in the press gallery overlooking the House floor, I remember thinking that down there was the real National Zoo, because down there were the examples of all the different kinds of people who made up America. On special occasions, such as the evening when the president delivers his State of the Union message to a joint session of the House and Senate, it is still breathtaking to me to look down on them, each so different from the others, some of them so smart, some of them so ordinary, yet each so representative of the corner of America from which they had come. It is in the Capitol that America's differences are sorted out and common ground is sought and eventually, though never easily, found. It is not always pretty, but as Newt Gingrich once said to me, "It's rough, but this is what we do instead of having military coups; this is how it's supposed to be." To see all of them from all over America — the wise old lions, Robert Byrd of West Virginia and Pete Domenici of New Mexico; the fresh-faced comers, Harold Ford of Tennessee and Rob Portman of Ohio; and so many women now, from tough, street-smart Barbara Mikulski and Brooklyn-born Barbara Boxer of California to Texas's hard-charging Kay Bailey Hutchinson — to see them all in one room, at one time, is for me a grand and awesome sight.

I had been on the congressional beat only a matter of weeks when I became involved in one of the biggest stories I would ever cover there, the nomination of John Tower to be secretary of defense.

It was a story that would pit the senator I had known the longest, Tower of Texas, against the senator I knew best, Nunn of Georgia.

Tower and I were never close, but we had a good working relationship and I liked him. I had first come to know him during my days at the *Star-Telegram*. He always came to Fort Worth to participate in the Gridiron show put on by local journalists. He was a good sport about the spoofs, seemed to genuinely enjoy himself, and he was good company at the show and the dinner afterward with Gridiron members. I had stayed in contact with him when I came to Washington, and since he was a longtime member of the Armed Services Committee, I had interviewed him from time to time during the days when I covered the Pentagon.

Nunn and I had been personal friends for years. We had been introduced by a mutual friend, Bill Stuckey, a former Georgia congressman, who operates the famous Stuckey's stores along the interstate highways. Our wives were all friends and we played a lot of cards and golf together. Sam and Bill introduced me to Sea Island, Georgia, the resort on the Georgia coast where our families have vacationed together over the years and where we eventually built a vacation home.

When George Bush nominated Tower to the Pentagon post, he seemed a likely choice. It was well known that he had always wanted the job, and since he had served as chairman of the Armed Services Committee during the years when Republicans held the majority in the Senate, he was thought to be well qualified and a sure bet to be easily confirmed. But Republicans no longer controlled the Senate, Nunn had ascended to the Armed Services chairmanship, and in the weeks after Tower was nominated, I began to hear reports that

519

Nunn was having second thoughts about Tower's qualifications.

It soon broke into the open that Nunn's second thoughts were based on FBI reports. During the first round of FBI checks, Nunn had told investigators he knew of no problems with Tower. But as the investigation progressed, he became convinced that Tower had a serious problem with alcohol.

Although we were friends, Nunn never shared such information with me, and when I asked him about it, he refused to discuss it. But in an interview for this book, he told me that he had been surprised when the first reports from the FBI had come back to him.

"There was no question that Tower had a serious problem with alcohol," he told me. "Whether or not he was an alcoholic, he had a problem that he refused to acknowledge, and this was at a time when the military was going through serious problems with drugs and alcohol."

During the presidential campaign, Nunn and Virginia senator John Warner, the ranking Republican on the Armed Services Committee, had notified both Republican and Democratic presidential candidates that they had developed a set of guidelines they intended to use to evaluate nominees for all top Defense Department posts who would be coming before their committee for confirmation. One of the things they told the parties they intended to consider was whether nominees had alcohol or drug problems.

"We had talked with numerous Defense officials, including [former Defense Secretary] Jim Schlesinger, who told us they were concerned that too many nominees were winding up in Pentagon jobs that shouldn't be there," he said.

"I was not against Tower being in the government. I thought he could have made a valuable contribution, and I suggested to them at one point that Tower would be a first-rate national security advisor.

"I just didn't believe he ought to be the guy at the top at the Pentagon. It wasn't the example we needed to be set . . . when they were having all these problems with alcohol and drug abuse."

The fight over Tower's confirmation would become one of the nastiest partisan disputes ever. Tower claimed he had no drinking problem, but in an effort to win Senate confirmation, took a pledge to drink no hard spirits if confirmed.

Tower partisans said Nunn's problem was very simple: he was just jealous, that he wanted to be secretary of defense himself. If Nunn couldn't have the job, Tower's people said, then Nunn wanted to run the Pentagon from his post as chairman of the Armed Services Committee. He did not want a strong person like Tower in the Defense post.

When Nunn finally announced that he would oppose Tower's nomination, Tower got it in his mind that because Nunn and I were friends, I was part of some kind of plot to do him in. I had covered the story from the start, but Tower's suspicions were incorrect. Sam and I were close friends, but he was one of the worst sources I ever had. He was one of those rare politicians·who seldom shared secrets with anyone, even his own staff, and if he ever leaked a story, it wasn't to me. It just wasn't his style. To the chagrin of most of the reporters who covered him, when Nunn had a story, he usually went to the Senate floor and announced it. One of the reasons that we had remained such close friends over the years was that I realized early on that he wasn't going to give me any exclusive leaks, so I just stopped trying to get them.

Tower never believed it.

In his memoir *Consequences*, he said Dan Rather had always given him fair coverage, but he couldn't say the same for me. He pointed to a Sunday when I had confronted him on *Face the Nation*. Lesley Stahl was the moderator of *Face the Nation* in those days, and when Tower agreed to be the featured guest, she invited me to join in the questioning.

In his account of the session, Tower referred to me as Nunn's golfing buddy and said I had given "a convincing performance as a surrogate prosecutor for the Georgia senator."

For sure, it was one of the most acrimonious interviews I have ever participated in. I had tried to nail down some allegations about Tower's drinking and, frustrated that I was getting nowhere, I said in exasperation, "Senator, let's switch from whiskey to money!" I went on to ask him about an incident that had occurred after he had left the Senate and become a private lobbyist and consultant. The questions were legitimate, but I'd prefaced them with such a smart-aleck remark, and my irritation was so apparent, that I clearly came off as someone who was more interested in nailing Tower than in seeking information. Looking back on it, neither Tower nor I came off very well that Sunday. The interview was a good lesson for me, but it took me some years to recognize that. An interview is most successful when the questioner asks questions, not when the questioner tries to argue. And the interviewer who tries to put down the person being questioned never comes off well.

The investigation ran on for weeks, and as the raw data from the FBI background checks became available to more and more senators (it was never made public), both sides began to leak selected excerpts. At one point, Nunn is convinced, Tower partisans leaked allegations they knew to be false in order to knock them down and raise questions about the credibility of the investigation. At another point, someone unearthed a story about how Nunn had driven his car into a roadside ditch after a night of drinking in college.

In the end, Tower was not confirmed, in a vote that fell mostly along party lines, and the hearings would be remembered as some of the bitterest ever.

Nunn is very conservative and had always been the favorite Democrat of many Republicans, but after the Tower hearings, many of the relationships that he had enjoyed with Republicans would be forever changed.

Nunn has never really discussed publicly what happened behind the scenes during the turmoil, and when I talked to him in early 2002 during an interview for this book, I told him I had always had the feeling that neither he nor the president had really expected the situation to go as far as it did. I had always believed that neither of them wanted a head-on confrontation and that both of them had believed the other would eventually back down.

"I don't know about that," he told me. "The president was under tremendous pressure from within his own party to back his nominees.

"I never had any problems with the president himself; it never got personal with us. But one of the problems was that during the campaign some of the more conservative people in his party had accused him of being a wimp. George Will had written a column about it, and to them, backing cabinet nominees became a test of manhood. He was under extremely heavy pressure not to back off Tower, and he didn't."

Nunn had some sympathy for Bush's predicament. Bush had nominated Tower before any of the FBI checks and, like Nunn, had been unaware of any problems then.

I asked Nunn if he had ever tried to head off the confrontation before it became public. Had he warned Bush that he had problems with Tower's nomination?

"Yes," he said. "John Warner and I went to the White House and laid out the problems in a private meeting with Bush. He listened. But he was noncommittal."

I asked him directly if, in fact, he'd opposed Tower because he wanted to be secretary of defense himself, as Tower's people had charged.

His answer startled me. He said he had actually been offered the job before it was offered to Tower.

"That was the most awkward part for me," he said. "In the days after Bush's election, Jim Baker called me and offered me the position of secretary of defense . . . I didn't want the job. If I had wanted it, I would have told Jim Baker that when it was offered.

"I had gone to California for a conference that Red Fay (the old JFK intimate) used to put on. Baker called me there. I told him I would think about it, and two days later I declined. I appreciated it, but I wanted to stay where I was."

He said he had never revealed the offer, because it had been made in confidence.

Baker later confirmed to me that he had called Nunn.

"Obviously, the president doesn't offer a cabinet post to anyone until he knows if that person is interested in serving," Baker told me in an interview for this book. "But we wanted to know if Sam was interested before we got too far along in the search. George Bush thought highly of him."

Although he took a heavy pounding from Tower partisans, some Republicans did support Nunn privately.

Nunn said Mike Deaver, who had been one of Ronald Reagan's closest advisors, sent him a note when Republican tempers were at their hottest. Deaver had his own problems with alcohol and he told Nunn, "You were trying to do what was right, and you did."

"I appreciated that," Nunn said. "He understood what we had been dealing with."

Nunn also remembers being at a veterans' organization gathering at a Washington hotel two days before the final vote on Tower's nomination.

He said Wyoming congressman Dick Cheney, already one of the most influential members of the House, was also there, and pulled him aside. He said Cheney told him, "Sam, I want you to know there are a number of us on the Republican side in the House who believe you are doing the right thing."

Little did Cheney know that the Senate's rejection of Tower would be a turning point in his own life. In the days after Tower's nomination was voted down, it was Cheney that Bush would nominate to become secretary of defense. It would be Cheney who would come to be seen as one of the most effective Defense chiefs of modern times and Cheney who would preside over the Pentagon during George Bush's most successful endeavor, Desert Storm.

"I'll tell you this," Jim Baker said later. "With Cheney there, we had one of the best national security teams ever assembled. We had all worked together in previous administrations — myself, Cheney, Powell, Scowcroft. There are always tensions, it's built into those jobs, but there was less backbiting, more cooperation, among that group than any national security team before or since."

In his memoir, Tower said he supported the selection of Cheney, but noted archly that Cheney had not been subjected to the kind of scrutiny he had endured. In fact, Cheney was confirmed quickly, and it would be the reputation that Cheney established as Defense chief that would eventually cause George W. Bush to select him as his running mate.

Tower died on April 5, 1991, when a small commuter plane he was aboard crashed. His memoir had just been released and the trip had been part of a series of appearances he had been making around the country to promote the book. One of his daughters had accompanied him on the flight. She, too, died in the crash.

They had been en route that day to a book signing on Sea Island, Georgia, where Sam and I and our families had spent so much time over the years.

I would cover other bitter congressional showdowns over the years, and the confirmation of Clarence Thomas to the Supreme Court was nastier, literally. When witnesses came forward to accuse Thomas of sexual harassment, testimony turned to pubic hairs on Coke cans and porno flicks and the kind of subjects seldom uttered on Capitol Hill. When the Judiciary Committee called a special session one Saturday, Dan Rather and I co-anchored live coverage and Dan began the broadcast by warning parents that they might want to keep children away from the television because some of the testimony was expected to be graphic.

At one point, Dan asked me what set the Thomas hearings apart from other confirmation battles.

I told him I couldn't ever remember when we had begun a confirmation hearing by warning viewers to keep the kids away from the TV set.

He agreed. But as sensational as the Thomas hearings became, to me they never reached the level of personal bitterness that marked the Tower hearings. What set the Tower hearings apart was the personal acrimony that developed among the Senators themselves. During the Thomas hearings, and the even more acrimonious hearings when Robert Bork was rejected for a Supreme Court seat, it was outside interest groups that were responsible for many of the wild allegations and destructive comments, and there had been some of that, to be sure, during the Tower episode, but mostly it was an internal battle fought among the Senators themselves, and there is no more bitter fight than a fight that goes on within a family.

In that sense, the Tower hearings were atypical. But raw, hard-edged partisanship has become the rule, rather than the exception, in the modern Congress.

When people ask me how Congress has changed over the years, I tell them it has changed enormously. Washington was designed to be a partisan place, but what has changed is the sour spirit and the hard edge that marks the partisanship of recent years. The win-at-any-cost tactics that once stopped when the election campaigns ended has slopped over into the legislative process. Ask the most liberal of the liberals or the most conservative of the conservatives and you will get the same answer: Congress, and Washington in general, has become more partisan.

Oddly, those who are seen by the public as the most partisan are often those who are seen within the institution as the ones most willing to reach across the aisle to search for common ground. Massachusetts senator Edward Kennedy and former Senate Republican leader Bob Dole are examples. No one has ever questioned Kennedy's partisan, liberal credentials, nor was Dole ever mistaken for anything but a partisan Republican during his long career in elective office.

Yet, through the years, Dole found common ground on hunger issues with George McGovern, and together they authored landmark legislation. Dole also worked with Kennedy on measures to help the disabled, and again meaningful legislation resulted.

Kennedy, the last of the old-line liberals, has worked successfully on children's issues with Orrin Hatch, one of the most conservative of all the senators, and in 2002 found himself being praised during the State of the

Union message by President Bush because of the work they had done together on education legislation.

But they are the exceptions, and one day I asked Kennedy why he thought Republicans and Democrats seemed to have such a hard time working together anymore.

Like most members of Congress, he believes there is a more partisan atmosphere, but he believes that part of it is the natural outgrowth of very difficult times. The country has finally emerged from the Vietnam era, but the distrust of government that began in those years remains. The country is going through cultural changes, and Congress has been forced to confront a series of emotional issues — civil rights, race, gender, disability, sexual orientation — topics with raw nerve endings.

"We are dealing with monumental issues," Kennedy told me. "There are always going to be some issues that are just very difficult to find common ground. But we have to try."

The problem, Kennedy says, is that it is much harder to forge bipartisan alliances, because the friendships that once crossed party lines are much rarer than they used to be. Members of Congress no longer know each other personally, as they once did.

On that point, there is little disagreement among insiders in both parties, and there are several reasons for it.

With the coming of jet aircraft, constituents expected their congressional representative to spend more and more time in the home district. Living in Washington became politically incorrect, and even members from the West Coast now commute back to their home states on most weekends. Many never move their families to Washington. They argue that this keeps them in closer contact with the folks back home, but it leaves them in a perpetual state of jet lag. During the hours they are in Washington, they are seldom in contact with each other, except during formal dealings on the House or Senate floor or in committees. The personal relationships that used to develop between Republicans and Democrats almost never happen anymore. With so much pressure to spend more time in their home districts, Congress and the Senate generally meet only Tuesday through Thursday, and to get a week's work done in three days, the sessions run long into the night. The dinners and other activities that used to bring members together informally no longer happen. There is just no time. When members do have a free evening, it is usually devoted to fund-raising activities.

The growth of the lobby and the spiraling cost of campaigning is also a major factor in the growing partisan divide. Lobbyists once divided on party lines; some firms worked for

Democrats, others for Republicans. But in recent times, the big lobbying firms have discovered there is money to be made working both sides of the street. Most large firms now employ Republicans to lobby Republicans, Democrats to lobby Democrats. Since former members of Congress are allowed access to the House and Senate floors, the most sought-after lobbyists are almost always former members. Congress has become the stepping-stone to the more lucrative job of lobbying. With the same firms lobbying both sides of an issue, keeping the two sides apart rather than bringing them together has become good for the lobbyist's bottom line.

The back-slapping, hard-drinking, cigar-smoking lobbyist of the old cartoons has been replaced by the former member of Congress whose main job is to tell his lobbying firm which of his old colleagues to give money to in order to get results on a given issue.

Campaigns have become so expensive, and the politicians must spend so much of their time raising money, that neither the candidate nor the lobbyists have time for the old-fashioned schmoozing that was once the hallmark of the lobbying trade. It's all very businesslike now for both sides. For the politicians, the challenge is how to raise the most money in the least amount of time. For the lobbyists, the challenge is to know which politicians to shower with money in order to get maximum results.

Moderate politics, a willingness to study issues and seek workable compromise, is no longer cost-effective. The politicians who send out fund-raising letters promising to give each issue careful study won't raise a dime.

But if that politician targets those who are known to favor a certain issue and he lets that group know he will champion their cause no matter who opposes it, the money rolls in. The amount he can raise depends on how sharply he can draw a contrast between those who favor an issue and those who oppose it.

There are sincere people on every side of every issue, but one reason that Congress continues to debate and vote on so many of the same issues over and over — like gun control and abortion — is that such issues bring in money to both sides. Liberals who favor gun control rail at the antics of the well-financed gun lobby, but in truth they welcome the endless debate over guns because it is a proven way to raise money from their supporters, just as the pro-gun lobby is a ready source of campaign cash for pro-gun forces. The debates over the perennials, as insiders call them, have little impact on the country, since they usually bring little or no change in the laws. But they are not really about the country's business; they are about the business of the members themselves and their own survival.

What is remarkable about the process is that when members have to do it, they can put the partisan games aside and do what is necessary. In the weeks before the September 11 attack, the Senate had been in a nasty partisan fight over "who lost the big surpluses" that had been projected earlier in the year.

Yet, in the week after the attack, the House and Senate authorized forty billion dollars in disaster relief and passed the legislation by a unanimous vote.

Afterward, I asked the Senate Democratic leader Tom Daschle how the country could afford to spend so much in light of all the earlier concern about who had lost the surplus.

"Well," he said, "I think the question is, Can we afford not to?"

Daschle and the other top congressional leaders, Senate Republican leader Trent Lott, Republican House speaker Dennis Hastert and House Democratic minority leader Richard Gephardt, had been evacuated by helicopter during the attacks, after reports spread that another plane piloted by terrorists was headed toward the Capitol. (Most officials believed at the time that the plane that ultimately went down in Pennsylvania was on its way there.) The leaders were taken to a secret location, and for the first time in years, found themselves alone together. As Hastert later told me, it had a profound effect.

"We looked at each other," he told me, "and we decided if we're gonna get through this thing, we need to stand together to do it."

They decided that the most important thing at that point was to show the world that the terrorists had not brought the government to a halt, so they agreed to get Congress back into session the following day. Then they laid plans to appropriate whatever money was needed to see the country through the emergency. That night, they all stood together on the Capitol steps in a show of unity and several hundred of their colleagues joined them. Spontaneously, the group began to sing "God Bless America."

Hastert said it sent chills down his spine, and some members of Congress cried openly.

For me, it was one of the most moving scenes that I can remember in all my years in Washington, and it was a reassuring moment, one in which I realized that Congress — for all its partisanship — was capable of coming together when there were serious matters to handle. When the leaders had been forced to shut themselves off from the advisors, fund-raisers and handlers, they were still able to work together on the nation's business.

But such moments are rare. As long as so many people have a financial interest in keeping the partisan lines so sharply drawn, the partisan divide will grow even wider.

# Twenty-four

## *Sunday Services*

The Sunday talk shows hold a unique place in Washington. NBC's *Meet the Press* and CBS's *Face the Nation* are the longest-running broadcasts on network television.

*Meet the Press*'s inaugural broadcast was on November 6, 1947, and *Face the Nation* came along seven years later, on November 7, 1954. A program with a similar format called *Capitol Cloakroom*, hosted by Walter Cronkite, had been aired several years earlier on CBS — a fact that was not taken lightly by Lawrence Spivak, who had created the NBC broadcast. He called Cronkite, accused him of stealing his format, and at one point threatened to sue him personally. Walter told Spivak it was a little unrealistic to believe there could be only one place on television where government officials could be interviewed, but the call unnerved him.

"It was the first time anyone had ever threatened to sue me," Walter told me. "Our guest the following Sunday was Oklahoma senator Robert Kerr, and I was so upset by the whole thing that I ended the broadcast by saying, 'Senator Kerr, thanks for joining us on *Meet the Press.*' "

Walter said his pal Bill Downs, one of the CBS News correspondents who had covered the war in Europe with him, called that afternoon and said, "Walter, you may set a record for the shortest tenure of anyone who ever hosted a CBS program."

It is no news to report that Walter survived that early gaffe nicely. The program was eventually renamed *Face the Nation,* and it has been on the air ever since.

By prime-time standards, neither program has ever attracted large audiences, but it's who watches, not the size of their audiences, that makes them important.

The Sunday shows have become the place where trial balloons are launched and where positions are staked out. The talk on Sunday becomes the subject that Washington debates throughout the week.

In a way, the Sunday shows have become what the super-columnists once were in the 1950s and early sixties. In those days, when an official had an idea to float or a solution to propose, or an opponent to undermine, his thoughts often appeared — usually anonymously — in the columns of Scotty Reston, the Alsop brothers, Drew Pearson or even Walter Lippmann.

In the age of the twenty-four-hour news cycle, officials no longer have the time to float ideas and positions anonymously. With so many outlets for news, they know anonymous ideas are likely to be lost in the great information maw or, worse, grabbed up by someone else who will claim credit for them.

Columnists such as Tom Friedman of the *New York Times* and Bob Novak still get their share of scoops, but these days, when officials have something to say they often come on one of the Sunday shows and say it. The Sunday shows offer them the chance to discuss their ideas at some length, and there is a bonus: the major newspapers and wire services monitor the shows, and if news is made, it will be picked up and written about in the Monday-morning papers.

It was not always so. In the beginning, the networks kept the shows on the air as a way to fulfill their FCC-mandated public-service requirements, and as the years passed they were seen as prestigious but low-priority broadcasts.

That changed in 1981, when Roone Arledge junked the ABC Show *Issues and Answers* and developed a new broadcast modeled after *Nightline*, the 11:30 P.M. show he had created to carry news about the American hostages being held in Iran.

He expanded it to an hour, put a young producer named Dorrance Smith in charge and installed David Brinkley as moderator.

Brinkley had left NBC that year after a run-in with NBC *News* president Bill Small, my old mentor who had gone to NBC after his own run-in with CBS brass.

Arledge believed that the way to develop a strong news department was to build it around strong correspondents and producers. When he heard that Brinkley was upset, he snapped up the NBC star before he really had a place for him, and devised the Sunday broadcast as a showcase for his new star. *This Week with David Brinkley* changed the Sunday morning landscape. Brinkley was a good questioner who did his homework. His strength, however, was not in his interviewing but in his writing and the terse, wry observations he brought to the news. After several weeks of experimentation, Arledge sat two tough, but very different, questioners beside him, columnist George Will, who became the house conservative intellectual, and Sam Donaldson, who soon developed into the broadcast's district attorney (Sam's characterization, not mine, but right on). At the end of the show, Brinkley would moderate a round table in which Donaldson, Will and a guest reporter, often Tom Wicker of the *New York Times*, and later Cokie Roberts of National Public Radio, would chew over the events of the week. It was the kind of free-wheeling discussion in which Ed Murrow and his team of reporters had once engaged during their end-of-the-year broadcasts on CBS, but it had not been done on a regular basis for years. Donaldson and Will would square off just as Dandy Don Meredith and Howard Cosell had squared off on *Monday Night Football*, another Arledge creation during the days when he had run ABC Sports. It was fresh, informative and entertaining, and *This Week* zoomed to the top in the Sunday-morning ratings. Soon it was one of the most successful shows on ABC.

Even with the success of the Brinkley show (as it is still called in the industry even though Brinkley has long since retired), working on a Sunday talk show during the 1980s was not considered a front-line assignment by correspondents at NBC or CBS.

When Lesley Stahl was offered the job of moderating *Face the Nation* in 1983, she first turned it down, and eventually accepted the job as something of a consolation prize. She had wanted instead to anchor a weekend *Evening News* broadcast. She had been covering the White House in those days, and when she had threatened to take a job at another network, CBS executives had promised in writing to name her anchor of one of the weekend news programs within eighteen months. At CBS, the *Saturday News* had always been seen as a showcase for up-and-coming reporters. Roger Mudd had been the first anchor of the broadcast, Dan Rather had anchored it toward the end of his tenure as White House correspondent, as I had during my White House days. Lesley wanted her turn.

As the deadline in her contract approached, she reminded CBS News president Van Gordon Sauter that he had not fulfilled his promise. Sauter told her he had no intention of giving her a weekend show, even though the promise had been written into her contract. But he wondered aloud: Was there a chance she might be interested in *Face the Nation*?

"He locked the door and told me he wouldn't let me out until we came to an agreement," she told me. "I finally told him I would think about it."

Stahl wrote about the encounter in her memoir *Reporting Live*, and eventually took the job. She would go on to anchor *Face the Nation* for eight years, became one of television's toughest interrogators and kept the show competitive with Brinkley's.

But to me, there is no better example of how the role of the Sunday shows has changed and how their influence has grown than Lesley's initial reluctance to become the moderator of *Face the Nation*.

My guess is there would be few reporters today who would choose a weekend anchor job if given the choice between that and moderating *This Week* or *Meet the Press* or *Face the Nation*.

When Lesley moved on to become a correspondent on *60 Minutes* in 1991, I had none of her reservations about moderating *Face the Nation*. When Eric Ober, at that point the president of CBS News, offered me the job, I had only one question: When do I start?

It didn't take me long to realize that of all the jobs I had had over the years, this was the best. I got to interview everyone who was anyone, and I didn't even have to go to them; they came to me. I also realized something else: Elected officials and Capitol Hill staffers who had paid little attention to me before were suddenly my new best friends. They all wanted to be on *Face the Nation*. That helped me get stories for the *Evening News* as I covered Congress during the week. And being on Capitol Hill every day helped me in booking guests for Sunday. It was a perfect fit, and since Congress usually didn't convene on Fridays, that became my day off.

People often say to me, "Covering so many topics, you must have a good-sized research staff," but the truth is we have no research staff as such. As I like to remind my many bosses, we have the smallest staff in network television.

The executive producer of *Face the Nation*, my longtime friend Carin Pratt, had been at the broadcast seven years when I arrived there in 1991, and she has a full-time staff of exactly one — producer Denise Li, who has been with the broadcast for thirteen years. Two days a week, they get help from Arlene Weisskoff, who splits her week between *Face the Nation* and the Washington bureau assignment desk. Carin is the driving force, and the three of them work with me in deciding whom to book as guests. Together, they take care of everything from arranging satellite time and providing transportation for our guests to overseeing all the technical requirements needed to get a network broadcast on the air. In between all that, they clip newspapers and stay in constant touch with press secretaries, news sources and the other contacts necessary to put together a show. If Carin or Denise or Arlene left, it would take at least two people to replace each of them — three, in Carin's case. I have never tried to surround myself with a large staff. I have found over the years that I am most productive when I have more work than I can possibly do. The core of my management philosophy is that one smart, energetic person is better than two or three of average energy and talent. And with me, energy trumps talent every time.

The secret is in finding the right person for a job and then staying out of the way while he or she does it. In television, especially, where egos become so ridiculously inflated, it is also important that those who work with you know that you want them to tell you the truth. Carin and I are best friends, but one of the most important functions that she performs is that when I come up with an idea that she doesn't like, she has no trouble saying, "Oh, bullshit, you don't want to do that."

In TV land, that kind of advice is not always easy to get.

Because our staff is so small, *Face the Nation*'s costs are the lowest of any broadcast on television. But because so many of those who watch our show tend to be opinion-makers and government officials, the CBS sales department sells our commercials for premium rates. That's what you call a good business and, journalism aside, it's why the bosses like us.

When I began the broadcast in 1991, we continued Lesley's occasional practice of having a guest reporter join in the questioning but in 1997, we asked Gloria Borger, a columnist at *U.S. News & World Report* and former *Newsweek* reporter, to join me at the *Face the Nation* table. Gloria is one of the most informed reporters in Washington and her value goes far beyond the questions she asks. She has contacts throughout the government because of her many years covering the Capitol, and she helps plan the broadcast each week, keeps us up to speed on the latest Washington buzz and provides a great backup for me on Sunday mornings. No matter how focused a reporter may be during an interview, a second reporter at the table is always a backstop and apt to pick up something the first reporter missed. It's Gloria's follow-ups that often make the news on *Face the Nation*.

She's also a fearless questioner.

When Bill Clinton's accuser Paula Jones said she could prove Clinton had made unwanted sexual advances because she could describe certain "distinguishing characteristics" in his genital area, it was Gloria's question that provoked Clinton's lawyer Bob Bennett to declare, "The President is normal, in size, shape and direction."

Bennett told me after the broadcast that he wasn't speaking from personal observation, but had gotten the assessment from Clinton's doctor. I asked if he thought Clinton would be upset that he had commented on such a delicate subject.

"Oh, he might be upset that I didn't say he had one of the biggest ones ever," Bennett said, laughing.

Gloria said she just hoped her mom hadn't been watching.

Several months after I took over *Face the Nation*, Tim Russert, NBC's Washington bureau chief, became moderator of *Meet the Press*. Rumors spread that the show would be expanded to an hour. I may have been wrong about a few things in my life, but I wasn't wrong in my assessment of that one. I knew it meant big trouble.

In a long memo, I outlined my concerns to CBS News executives in New York. I told them that unless *Face* was also expanded to an hour, I didn't believe we could compete with broadcasts that were trying to get the same guests that we were and had twice as long to question them. There was another disadvantage for us. All the Sunday shows are careful not to book guests and then cancel them at the last minute. High-ranking officials and politicians often rearrange their schedules to be on a Sunday show. If a show gets a reputation for booking people and then canceling them at the last minute, the guests are wary about committing to that show the next time. With an hour show, guests can be booked weeks in advance, then if the news changes suddenly, those guests can be moved to the second half-hour, and experts and officials connected to the late-breaking news can be put at the top of the broadcast.

I sent the memo to New York, but never heard back. As I had predicted, Russert proved to be an excellent questioner, and with twice the time to interrogate his guests, *Meet the Press* soon passed us in the ratings. Since then we have battled *This Week* for second.

Competition for guests is a fierce, never-ending battle that has become even fiercer as Fox and CNN developed their own Sunday shows, and we constantly maneuver in an effort to get the right guests at the right time. If we're lucky, we usually have our key guests nailed down late Thursday or early Friday morning, but more often, it's sometime Friday before we can be sure, and occasionally we're still making calls on Saturday. During the Florida vote recount in November 2000, we spent one hectic Saturday night trying to locate Jim Baker, who was heading Bush's effort there, and it was nearly 11 P.M. before we finally locked him in. That made for a short turnaround, since I usually get up at 5:30 on Sunday morning in order to read the papers and do last-minute research for the broadcast, which we broadcast live at 10:30. The competition for guests has become so fierce that recent administrations have tended to rotate top officials among the three shows, which spares them from weekly fights over who goes on which Sunday show.

As ferocious as the competition sometimes becomes, Tim, as well as Sam Donaldson and Cokie Roberts of *This Week*, and I have all maintained friendships over the years. When Sam and Cokie left the broadcast in 2002 and were replaced by George Stephanopoulos, I was sorry to see them go. I don't really know George, but he seems to be a serious person. I also count Wolf Blitzer of CNN and Brit Hume and Tony Snow of Fox as friends. Part of it is that, like the politicians we cover, we can compete during the day and laugh about it over a drink. But there is also something else. All of us are proud to be part of Sunday mornings. It has become the last time period on television when serious people can have serious discussions about serious things. All of us feel a responsibility to keep it that way.

In Washington, *Face the Nation* airs at the same time as *Meet the Press*, and someone once asked Russert what he watched on the rare occasion that *Meet the Press* was preempted by some special event. "Why, *Face the Nation*," he answered.

If *Face the Nation* were preempted and I were asked the same question, I would answer, "*Meet the Press*."

There is no better way to study the human ego than to book guests for the Sunday talk shows. Some senators keep detailed lists of not only how many times they have been on each show, but how many times their colleagues have appeared. Some politicians have asked us not to book members of another party when they appear, a request we have never granted. Some insist on appearing only if they are the sole person being questioned in that segment. Others demand to be given the last word, another nonstarter. Nor do we ever give those being interviewed the questions in advance.

Walter Cronkite recalls that he invited then Senator Lyndon Johnson to appear on one of the shows that preceded *Face the Nation*, and when Johnson arrived, he presented Cronkite with a list of questions he wanted to be asked. When Cronkite explained that guests were not allowed to know what questions would be asked and certainly could not dictate questions, Johnson got up and headed for the door.

"I finally got him stopped in the hallway," Walter said. "I told him that if he would just come back, we would be asking him questions in the general areas he wanted to cover, but we couldn't ask him those specific questions, and finally he said, 'Well, okay.'

"But when the broadcast began, Bill Downs, who was one of the questioners, asked a question that wasn't within a hundred miles of what Johnson wanted to talk about, and he just froze. From then on, he never said much of anything beyond 'yep' and 'nope.' It was the longest half hour I ever spent on television."

Some guests can be shameless in their demands. When we first came to know about Monica Lewinsky, her lawyer William Ginsburg was one of the most sought-after men in America. Every journalist wanted to talk to him, and Ginsburg reveled in the attention. One Sunday, he agreed to appear on all five Sunday talk shows, a stunt that has since been dubbed "a full Ginsburg."

Racing from one studio to the next meant he would have only minutes to spare between appearances, and our producer Carin Pratt thought we would have more control if we furnished Ginsburg a car to deliver him on his rounds. When she reached him on his cell phone, however, he said Russert had already volunteered to furnish him a car and driver on Sunday.

"But could you furnish me one to use today?" he asked. He apparently had some errands to run. We agreed, of course. We didn't want to take a chance on offending him and being the one show where he didn't appear that weekend.

At times, when all the shows are competing for the same people, nailing down a guest can be as complicated as working out a nuclear arms agreement. A person — usually a press secretary — will ask how much time we are willing to give his boss. If we say five minutes, the press secretary may reply, *This Week* has offered seven minutes in a segment by himself. Can you make us a better offer?" Most times we don't, but sometimes we do, if we think it's likely the person will make some news.

Most of the time, we can take a guest at his or her word when he or she agrees to be on our show — but not always. We've never booked a guest who didn't show, but we've come close. We once booked a Hollywood director for a segment on movie violence. He was to be interviewed by satellite from our studios in Los Angeles, but still had not shown up twenty minutes before the broadcast. Carin got through by phone to a limo driver we had sent to his home, the driver beat on the door and it turned out the man had overslept. He dressed en route and made it to the studio with literally seconds to spare. His on-time arrival proved the highlight of the interview. He didn't have much to say.

On the Sunday after independent counsel Kenneth Starr's report on Bill Clinton was made public, we thought we had lost our lead guest, Senate Judiciary Committee chairman Orrin Hatch, one of the most decent and reliable people in Washington. Jean Lapata, one of his aides, had arrived about a half hour before the broadcast and said he was on the way, but ten minutes before we were to go on the air, he still hadn't arrived and I became worried that he might have taken ill, so I walked outside the bureau to look for him. I saw his SUV in our parking lot and he seemed to be slumped over the wheel. "My God," I thought. "He's had a stroke."

As I got closer, I saw he was talking on a cell phone. I rapped on the car window and said, "Senator, get out of there and come in. We're about to go on the air."

Hatch looked up, clearly startled, and

glanced at his watch. Then I could hear him concluding the conversation.

"It was President Clinton," he told me sheepishly. "He called me just as I pulled in the driveway. He was asking me what I thought he ought to do. I told him he needed to stop all this legal hairsplitting and just be contrite and ask forgiveness."

"Just hold it until we can get inside and get on the air," I told him. It was the first time I had ever stopped anyone who was trying to tell me what a president had told him. We raced in, our makeup artist Marge Hubbard powdered his nose as he clipped on his mike, and his chat with the president made a fine little news nugget for that morning's broadcast.

When we promise a guest that he or she will be interviewed on our broadcast, we don't break that promise unless there is some catastrophe in the news. But we've learned that in rare instances our guests don't take their promises to us as seriously as we take our promises to them. Once, Carin booked a professional ethicist to be on the broadcast. She had talked to him at length and he agreed to be interviewed by satellite from his office.

On the Friday before the show, she called him back to give him the time and logistical details, only to be told he wouldn't be appearing on the broadcast after all. Instead, he would be appearing on another show.

"But why?" she asked. "You gave your word."

"Well," he said, "they are giving me more time."

"But you gave us your word," Carin said. "And you're an ethicist."

"I'm sorry," he said. "I just got a better deal."

The weekend after Richard Nixon died, I closed off the broadcast with a round table of people who had served in the Nixon White House. It had been an unusual broadcast. We made no headlines that Sunday, but looking back on Nixon's life had been thought provoking and interesting. The tenor of the program was such that I thought it deserved some sort of "button," as we call it in broadcasting — a short, concluding essay that summed up what we had heard in the preceding half hour, so I closed with some personal observations that ended with the lines "Richard Nixon had left the White House in disgrace, but he left this life with dignity."

The reaction stunned me. It was greater than the reaction to anything or anyone who had ever appeared on the broadcast. Some of it came from Nixon admirers, some from those who didn't like him, but what struck me was that all of them seemed to want a little food for thought on Sunday morning. The comment had provoked viewers to offer their own thoughts and assessments of Nixon, and we were flooded with letters.

Maybe they wouldn't have had the same appetite on a weekday evening or on a weekday morning, but it seemed to strike them right on a Sunday. So, several weeks later, I tried it again. Again, the comment was favorable, so Carin and I decided to make the closing commentary a regular feature of the broadcast, at first when we had time for it. Later, we made time for it. Except for Andy Rooney, who had done personal essays for years on *60 Minutes*, no one since Eric Sevareid had done commentary on CBS. In fact, when I began them, I wasn't sure CBS News standards allowed it, which is why I never asked permission. I should have done so, but I figured that if I was doing something wrong, somebody would tell me, so I just pressed on, and one day Andrew Heyward, who has been the president of CBS News in recent years, called to say, "By the way, we like those commentaries. Keep it up." It turned out commentary was well within the CBS News standards; it was just that Andy Rooney had been the only one to avail himself of the opportunity.

I have been fortunate to win several awards for the commentaries over the years, but that's not what brings the real satisfaction in doing them. Sitting down each week to write them forces me to sort out how I feel about an issue. It's a great exercise to keep the old brain sharp. The columnist Bill Safire once said he thought every president ought to write his own speeches occasionally because it forces the writer to decide what he believes. The same is true for reporters. It's all well and good to be objective in reporting the news, but we shouldn't use that as an excuse to take a pass on what we believe, or at least to understand the arguments on both sides, which for me is the great benefit that comes from writing commentary.

Since I began writing the essays, I've commented on matters large and small. Some weeks I'll know on Monday what I intend to write about; sometimes the idea doesn't come until Saturday night. Sometimes, when the well has run dry, I'll say to Pat, "I'm at a dead end. Got any ideas?" and more than once she has saved me — usually by saying, Well, you've been ranting about such-and-such all week, why don't you write about that?

Response to the commentaries has not always been predictable, but here are some that have drawn the most intense reactions:

When Clinton's man James Carville took a swipe at Paula Jones and said, "You never know what you'll catch when you drag a hundred-dollar bill through a trailer park," I responded: "I've known some nice people who lived in trailers and some real trash that lived in big houses." Viewers loved that one, even some who claimed to be Clinton fans.

When President Bush proposed voluntary national service in the wake of 9-11, I proposed one year of mandatory service for everyone at the age of eighteen, and told how those of my generation had had no choice. I told how I had enrolled in ROTC and spent three years in the Air Force, not for noble reasons but because I thought it was better than being drafted and spending two years as an Army enlisted man. I concluded that I didn't know how much my small service had helped my country, but it had sure helped me.

I figured I would get mostly critical mail for wanting to draft someone's son or daughter. Instead, the comment drew the most overwhelmingly favorable response of anything I have ever said on television.

That was not the case during the 2002 Winter Olympics, when I compared curling to miniature golf, and said I thought it was something people did as an excuse to have a drink afterward.

Most of the mail that week was overwhelmingly critical. I was called everything from an ignorant fool to unpatriotic, and several viewers suggested that if CBS didn't fire me, I ought to resign.

People feel strongly about their sports.

The next morning, I was on Don Imus's radio show and he was kidding me about it. I told him my real worry was that my critics might discover that I didn't like basketball, either.

During the first six years I moderated *Face the Nation*, I continued to fly to New York on weekends to anchor the Saturday edition of the *Evening News*. Covering Congress during the week was a full-time job, but I tried to take Fridays off, since I was working both Saturday and Sunday. At first, that worked just fine, but when Newt Gingrich led the Republican takeover in Congress in 1994, it became harder and harder to do.

Democrats had controlled the House for more than forty years, but Gingrich had devised an ingenious strategy to end their control, and it worked. He found a way to nationalize the House races by drawing up a list of things Republicans promised to do if they became a majority. The list included everything from balancing the budget to term limits for elected officials. Gingrich called it the Contract with America, and in late September more than three hundred Republican House members and candidates went to the Capitol steps and pledged to support it.

Clinton had been in office two years, and by that time he was flailing. His administration seemed such a jumble of confusion at that point that a reporter asked him if he considered himself relevant. He took umbrage, as might be expected, but Gingrich had recognized he was vulnerable. Candidates for House seats didn't just run against their opponents; they ran against Clinton. They used the Contract with America to say what they were for, and they found a devastating way to illustrate what they were against — Clinton. They ran television commercials in key districts in which the face of the Democratic candidate would appear on the TV screen and an off-camera voice would say, "If you like Bill Clinton, you'll love Joe Schmo," then Schmo's face would slowly turn into Clinton's.

The strategy worked, and when the new Republicans came to Washington in January, it represented a sea change in American politics. As Dan Baltz and Ronald Brownstein would write in their book *Storming the Gates*, power had shifted to those who "loved their country, but hated the government."

The impact it was having on me was that I suddenly had more work than I could really handle. Almost every day produced a story of some kind, and if you were covering Congress as I was, you didn't want to miss any of it. During one stretch, I realized I had worked forty straight days without a day off; during another stretch, I worked twenty-five straight.

The year 1995 was one of the busiest I ever had at CBS News, and 1996, a presidential year, was even busier. As I was preparing to fly to New York one Saturday for the weekend news, Pat said, "You know, you really don't have to do all this. Come summer, you'll have done the Saturday *News* for twenty years and you did the Sunday *News* for three years before that. Why don't you see if they can find someone else to do it? You might enjoy a day off now and then."

Find someone else to do it? It was as if someone had suggested that I cut off an arm or a leg. I had been doing that broadcast so long, it had become a part of me. I couldn't imagine not doing it and besides, I told her, I liked it. But the next night, the flight from New York back to Washington was canceled because of bad weather, as it often was during the winter months, and I found myself on the train. That meant it would be well after 1 A.M. when I got home. Since I needed to be in the Washington office no later than 6 A.M. on Sunday morning in order to read the papers and do my last-minute preparation for *Face the Nation*, it meant a short turnaround on only a few hours' sleep. The more I thought about it, the more sense it made. I realized how tired I had become. I decided I didn't need to keep doing it. Until Pat had brought it up, I had just gotten into such a rut that I hadn't even considered it.

I decided she was right and we agreed that my last Saturday *News* ought to be in August, when we would be broadcasting from the anchor booth of the Democratic convention in Chicago. It was to the Democratic convention in Chicago back in 1968 that Pat and I had taken our first real vacation together, and it was nine months after that convention that our first daughter, Susan, had arrived. Since it had been a place for beginnings, it seemed a fine spot for an ending. My last Saturday broadcast was from the anchor booth of the Chicago convention hall, and I admit my voice choked as I said good night on the broadcast that evening, but Pat was standing next to the anchor desk just off-camera, and when I signed off she gave me a hug. For the first time in a long time, I was available for dinner on Saturday night. Except for vacation breaks, it would be our first Saturday night out in twenty-three years, and the first one was on the house. Missie Rennie, the longtime producer of the weekend news and one of our closest friends, arranged a good-bye dinner for Pat and me and all the CBS crew at a Chicago restaurant. There were many toasts and a few tears, too. We had all worked together for a long time and we decided there were a lot of good things about the Saturday *News*, the main one being that the bosses weren't around the office on Saturdays so you could do it the way you wanted to with minimum interference.

The only thing wrong with it, we concluded, was that it was always held on Saturdays, which really put a crimp in your weekend.

The end of my tenure on the Saturday *News* closed off something that had been a part of my life for so long that I went through a sort of withdrawal. It was different, but not altogether unpleasant. I never want to leave the impression that I was put-upon during those years. Many people must work much harder than I ever did in those days, and I was amply rewarded. But except for vacations, it had been twenty-three years since I had enjoyed two days off in a row — Friday and Saturday — and at first I didn't know what to do with myself. Two days in a row seemed like two weeks, but it was not long until I discovered I had more energy and I felt better than I had in years.

I missed my weekend news friends in New York but I did not miss riding the airline shuttle between New York and Washington. Before 9-11, New Yorkers and Washingtonians rode the shuttle between the two cities as regularly as commuters in many towns ride the bus or take taxis.

When I began riding the shuttle in the 1970s, it was operated by Eastern Airlines, who used the old Electra prop planes for the forty-minute trip. Fares in those days ran about thirty-seven dollars, round trip, and no ticket was required to board the aircraft. When the gates were opened, passengers just piled on. Eastern guaranteed every passenger a seat. When one plane was filled, another was rolled to the gate. No drinks or snacks were served, but once aloft, the flight attendants came down the aisle with cash registers mounted on service carts. As they passed your seat, you paid with cash or credit card.

On Saturdays, I would drive to National Airport, park and take the 10:30 A.M. shuttle to New York, arrive at CBS before noon and spend the day preparing that evening's newscast, which was broadcast at 6:30 P.M. As the show's final credits rolled at 7 P.M., I would rush outside, where a car would be waiting to take me back to La Guardia airport. If I was lucky, I could make the 7:30 flight back to Washington and be home by 9 P.M. If not, I would take the 8:30 or, if the weather was bad, return on the train.

For all the hassle, the shuttle provided many hours of entertainment, and over the years I struck up numerous shuttle friendships, not just with the flight crews but with various and sundry Washington luminaries. During the years before he became chairman of the Federal Reserve, Alan Greenspan would take the shuttle each Saturday to visit his mother in New York. We would often chat and he even taught me a little about economics. New Jersey's then senator Bill

563

Bradley and New York's affable longtime senator Daniel Patrick Moynihan were also frequent shuttle fliers, as was Tom Downey, at one point the youngest member of Congress. For me, the shuttle became yet another place to gather news, develop sources and trade gossip.

Riding the shuttle could also be a humbling experience on occasion. Those of us in television news are a lot like the supporting characters in those old Western movies. People often know our faces, but can't quite connect them with our names.

On shuttle flights over the years, I was mistaken for Morley Safer, Dan Rather, Richard Threlkeld, and once for Ed Bradley. On another occasion, a woman mistook me for her mailman (she knew I delivered something to her home). I used to correct people, but these days I just answer to whoever it is people believe me to be. If someone calls me Morley and asks for an autograph, I just sign "All the best, Morley Safer." Why ruin somebody's day? My favorite mix-up was the time I was seated next to a woman who was certain she knew me. "I know you, I know you, you're . . . you're . . ."

She was obviously struggling and I tried to help.

"I'm Bob Schieffer," I told her. "You see me on the news."

"No," she responded. "That's not right,

564

but I'll get it in a minute."

I saw no reason to get in an argument about who I was, so I focused on the newspaper for the rest of the flight.

Over the years, Eastern Airlines finally gave way to other carriers, and during the time I flew up and down the northeast corridor, the shuttle was operated by a series of companies — Trump Air, New York Air, Pan Am, and currently Delta and National Airways.

I happened to be on one of the last Pan Am flights before that line shut down, and as we were on final approach to Washington that Saturday night, a Pan Am steward I had known over the years approached my seat with a stack of cocktail napkins stamped Pan Am Shuttle.

"You're with us so much, I thought you might like these as a souvenir," he said.

It was a thoughtful gesture. I thanked him and asked what the future held for him since Pan Am was closing down. He told me not to worry, that he had already secured a job with Delta, which was taking over the shuttle route.

Several weeks later, I spotted him aboard the new Delta shuttle, shook hands and offered my congratulations. He looked a little sheepish and said, "I owe you an apology. I had seen you on the shuttle so much that I thought you were a Pan Am executive. It wasn't until last week, when I saw you on television, that I realized you work for CBS."

I decided right then that I had been right to give up the Saturday *News*. When you are riding airplanes so much that the flight crews believe you work for the airline, it's probably time for a break.

That's one more reason I like *Face the Nation*. We do it in Washington. I can be home ten minutes after the broadcast.

# Twenty-five

## *The Charmer*

I met Bill Clinton on the morning after the worst speech of his life, and I wasn't really looking forward to it. I figured he would be in a foul mood, and asking someone why he had become a national joke overnight wasn't my idea of a terrific assignment.

It was at the 1988 Democratic convention in Atlanta, and the night before, Clinton had made the now-infamous speech nominating Michael Dukakis to be the party's presidential standard-bearer. What was to have been the bright young governor's moment in the spotlight had been a total disaster. He had droned on so long that he got the loudest applause when he said, "And in conclusion ...," and it wasn't just applause. The relieved delegates broke into thunderous cheers, and for a moment, there was an almost delirious pandemonium. I had gone to the VIP area to watch the speech with Congressman Dick Gephardt and his wife, Jane. Gephardt had been one of eight Democrats who had sought the nomination that year, and I had planned

567

to ask him some perfunctory questions after the Clinton speech about whether the party would unify behind Dukakis in the coming campaign. But as Clinton droned on, the voice of *60 Minutes* producer Don Hewitt was in my earphone shouting, "Forget that stuff about the fall campaign. Just ask Gephardt why Clinton wouldn't shut up!" I assured him that would be no problem. Gephardt had already turned to me and said, "My God, this is never going to end." I should have known, of course, that Gephardt was too much the politician to say such a thing on camera, and sure enough, when Dan Rather switched to me after the speech, Gephardt just grinned and began talking about the importance of winning in November.

Dukakis and his strategists had picked Clinton to make the nomination speech because they wanted Dukakis to be introduced to the nation by one of the party's brightest and most articulate young spokesmen. Instead, the postspeech comment hardly mentioned Dukakis. All anyone talked about after the speech was how Clinton had blown his moment in the national spotlight. More than one political career has been wrecked on the shoals of a bad speech, and there was talk that night that if Bill Clinton had not ended his career, he had brought it to a full stop. It was one of the best sidebar stories of the entire convention, but still I was not happy about being rousted out of bed the following morning and told to go to Clinton's hotel and get his reaction. To me, Clinton had made a total mess of what had been a golden opportunity, but asking how he felt about it was sort of like asking a survivor at a car wreck how he felt about losing a relative in the crash. I have never found piling on when someone is down the most rewarding kind of work, but I headed off to Clinton's hotel, linked up with a camera crew, and was surprised to discover Clinton, fresh and dapper, chatting with a group of people in the hotel lobby. I asked if he had a moment for an interview. Surprisingly, he said, "Sure."

What I saw and heard that morning would be instructive in understanding the man who would later become president. Bill Clinton, as we would come to know, was nothing if not indefatigable.

No, he told me, he did not believe it had been a bad speech. It was just not the right speech for that particular hall. He had warned the Dukakis people that it might run long if the crowd interrupted with cheers. What happened, he said, was that Dukakis staffers on the convention floor had instructed delegates to cheer every time Dukakis's name was mentioned. They had instructed him, on the other hand, to finish the speech, even if it ran long, because they saw it as their best chance to tell viewers watching on television who Dukakis was. The speech was not for the people in the hall; it was for the people watching on television.

I asked if he could see the people on the podium signaling him to cut it short.

"The problem is, nobody from the campaign did that," he told me, emphasizing that his orders from the campaign strategists had been to press on and tell the nation about Dukakis.

When I mentioned that he had gotten some bad reviews, he said, "I wasn't doing it for me. The alternative was, I knew I could get better reviews if I just got off there.

"But I was afraid that they would say then, that Clinton had this chance on national television to promote Michael Dukakis and he didn't do it. Instead, he played to the crowd and made them happy and sacrificed an opportunity to make a case for Michael Dukakis on television. It was kind of a no-win deal, I think."

In another part of the interview, Clinton said he was "up there as a soldier trying to do my duty, and I hope I did that."

So there it was. Clinton had not been at fault. The good soldier who had been trying to do his duty for Dukakis had been the victim of a bad strategy. It would be the first time we would see Clinton portray himself as a victim, but it would not be the last.

Bill Clinton could see opportunity where

others saw only embarrassment. Maybe he had become a national joke, but he was finally on the national radar screen, and no one knew how to take advantage of that better than Bill Clinton. He maneuvered an invitation to appear on the *Tonight* show with Johnny Carson. When Carson set an egg timer on his desk as Clinton sat down, the audience went wild. Clinton poked a little fun at himself, and not for the last time in his career, he refurbished his image and turned an embarrassing situation into an asset. From that night on, we should have realized that Bill Clinton was a politician to watch.

I should have paid attention, but I didn't. Clinton campaigned for Dukakis in 1988, but I paid him little notice over the next three years. We heard reports from time to time that he wanted to run for the Democratic nomination in 1992, but most of us who reported on politics didn't take him to be a serious candidate, mainly because we kept hearing he had a "zipper problem." There were just too many rumors and innuendos about his weakness for female flesh ever to believe he could stand the scrutiny of a national campaign. It was the "zipper problem," the talk went, that had kept him from running in 1988, and Clinton had reportedly said as much to some of his supporters.

That all changed in early 1991. When U.S. forces drove Saddam Hussein back into Iraq, the popularity of President George Bush soared and he seemed a certainty for reelection two years hence. The major figures in the Democratic party who had been making noises about challenging Bush — New York governor Mario Cuomo, foremost among them — suddenly wanted no part of a presidential race.

But Clinton was not a major figure in the party and had nothing to lose. He seized the moment, thus becoming the first politician of modern times to get the presidential nomination of a major political party because no one of national stature really wanted it.

By December 1991, he appeared to be not only a serious candidate but also the Democratic front-runner, and we invited him to be on *Face the Nation*. It was a brilliant performance. There were sensitive arms-control negotiations going on with Soviet leader Gorbachev, and President Bush was involved in delicate budget negotiations with Congress, and I came to the interview armed with tough, detailed questions — the kind of questions that could trip up someone who didn't deal with arms control on a regular basis. To my surprise, Clinton handled all of them with ease. As a small-state governor, he had little experience in foreign policy, but that morning he came off as someone who had been dealing with arms-control issues and foreign affairs all his life. He was no less impressive when I turned to domestic issues. After the broadcast, I remember telling Carin Pratt, "I don't know how much this guy really knows, but I never touched him."

It was the last time Clinton would appear on *Face the Nation* until well into his second term as president. He made appearances on the NBC and ABC Sunday shows the next month, but then Gennifer Flowers revealed her long affair with Clinton and he stayed clear of the Sunday broadcasts until after the election. For a while, it appeared Ms. Flowers had brought his campaign to an early halt, but when Mrs. Clinton stood by her man during the dramatic *60 Minutes* interview, Clinton portrayed himself as something of the victim — this time of unfair attacks by political enemies back home — and he cruised to the nomination.

Clinton had begun calling himself "the comeback kid" after he'd finished second in the New Hampshire primary, but I believed then, and still believe, his comeback had more to do with the weak field he was running against than anything he did. Had any Democrats of national stature — Cuomo, Georgia senator Sam Nunn, New Jersey senator Bill Bradley or Tennessee senator Al Gore — been in the race at that point, Clinton's campaign might well have ended there. But his main competition came from Paul Tsongas, a Massachusetts senator with a long history of cancer; Bob Kerrey, then a little-known senator from Nebraska; and Jerry Brown, the eccentric California politician who had been known as Governor Moonbeam during his time as California's chief executive.

Still, you had to give Clinton credit; he had been willing to run when others wouldn't, and his luck continued into the fall campaign. The Democrats who had declined to run against Bush when he was at the height of his popularity after the Desert Storm victory had not anticipated that he would later break his "Read My Lips — No New Taxes!" promise. To me, he'd had little choice. It was the only practical way out of a deadlock that had developed with Congress over how to get the economy moving again. But the "Read My Lips" declaration had been the one memorable phrase of Bush's campaign, and when he'd backed off, the conservatives in his own party deserted him. He would later apologize, but the conservatives never forgave him.

That wounded Bush badly, but what sealed his fate was another development that neither he nor the Democrats had anticipated — the decision of Ross Perot to make it a three-way race.

It is conjecture, of course, but I have always wondered what would have happened had Bush not apologized for raising taxes. The action had made a budget agreement possible with the Democrats and had been a major factor in getting the economy back on track. But what if Bush had just said, "I know it means breaking my word, and I know it will hurt me politically. But this is so important I have to put the good of the country ahead of my political future. When it's a choice between my political future and the good of the country, I'll do what's right for the country every time."

Perhaps it would have changed nothing, but when a politician can convince voters he is sacrificing his own political future for the good of the country, it is usually good politics.

Whatever the case, Bush chose a different strategy, and with Perot siphoning off enough votes from those who were disgusted with both parties, Clinton won, and with the victory came a fine gift from Bush. The budget agreement that had probably been the main factor in Bush's defeat had been just the tonic the economy needed. It went virtually unnoticed, but when Clinton took the oath as president, there were signs that the economic recovery had already begun.

Clinton may have been lucky and ambitious to the point of shamelessness, but he remains one of the most charming, persuasive people I ever met. He was also one of the most skilled politicians I have ever dealt with.

In the end, he was also the most disappointing.

In the weeks before his inauguration, Pamela Harriman, the Democratic fundraiser, held a party at her Georgetown home to introduce the Clintons to Washington. Everybody who was anybody in the Democratic Party was there, as well as key members of both parties from the House and Senate. Pat and I were among a smattering of journalists and their spouses. It was a crowd that has seen presidents come and go, but Clinton wowed them. Pat had never met him, but she sized him up immediately.

"He's got it," she said. "When he shook my hand, he held it just an instant longer than a person normally would, and he held eye contact just a second longer than someone you meet usually does — not long enough to consider it flirting, but just long enough to make you feel that at that moment, you're the most important person in the room."

I hadn't really thought of it in that way, but I realized that when I had shaken his hand it had been much the same. He had called me by name, and for a moment there had treated me like an old friend. In a way, he reminded me of our legendary hostess that evening, the still glamorous Pamela Harriman. She had been married to Winston Churchill's son Randolph during World War II, and was later the wife of Averill Harriman, the hugely rich longtime power in Democratic politics. Throughout her life, she had been known for her many romantic conquests, including CBS's own Edward R. Murrow during the days of the London Blitz. Well into her seventies she was still considered alluring by men half her age, and when she looked at you, adoringly, it took a strong man not to succumb.

Clinton seemed to have the same mesmerizing impact on everyone he met that night.

Early in the administration, we would meet the Clintons again, when we were among several dozen people invited to a small dinner at the White House. It was an eclectic group that ranged from a former Arkansas basketball coach to historian Michael Beschloss and his Iranian-born wife, Afsaneh. She was seated between the president and me, and as we waited for her to come to the table, the president leaned over to me and said, "I put her here because I wanted to ask her about some of this stuff that is going on right now in Iran." It had been so long since I had run into any politician who seemed interested in the opinion of anyone that I was taken aback. Even more stunning, the president himself had obviously arranged who sat where.

Over the years, I had been a guest in the White House many times, but never in the way we were entertained that evening. Before the dinner, Clinton took us on a tour of the living quarters and the Lincoln Bedroom and he conducted the tour himself. He seemed to know the history of every room and every piece of furniture. I have been in Washington long enough to know that we don't get such treatment because politicians consider us cute and clever. We get invited because I am the moderator of an influential talk show. Still, it is hard not to be flattered by such attention, and it was a great evening. Clinton talked candidly about a variety of issues, drew everyone into the conversation and seemed genuinely interested in the opinions of his guests.

I should have known better, but I left the White House feeling as if I was one of a special few. Some weeks later, I would learn that our invitation had been part of a carefully organized charm offensive. During those first months, the Clintons had invited practically every reporter who had a press card to similar gatherings. The "special few" were those who hadn't been invited. I was reminiscing about it several years later with my brother Tom, after the stories broke about campaign contributors who were awarded sleepovers in the Lincoln Bedroom. He laughed and said, "At least you got invited before they started charging for it."

Even so, I thought it was a smart move, and I gave Clinton credit for his adroitness in working the press. I saw it as just another example of his political skills. I confess a prejudice. Because I come from Texas, I do not subscribe to the notion prevalent in the northeastern part of the country that all wisdom somehow originates there. I come from a long line of conservative Texas Democrats, but I claim no political party. I vote the person, not the party. I'm a registered political Independent, but I always pull for folks from our part of the country who can show the people from the Northeast they don't know everything. The more I saw of Clinton, the more impressed I was.

It was not so much his politics — though I did agree with him in general on a variety of issues — but his political skills that I admired. The tragedy of Clinton's presidency was not the way it turned out, but what it might have been.

In retrospect, he managed some rather remarkable feats. He made it tougher for those on welfare to qualify for welfare allotments, yet managed to retain their overwhelming political support. At the same time, his expansion of the Earned Income Tax Credit meant more money for the working poor. He joined with Republicans to pass a major trade agreement over the strong opposition of his core supporters, labor and urban blacks. And, he was able to rein in federal spending and balance the budget at a time when the economy had begun to boom.

What might this person of such remarkable political skills have accomplished had it not been for Monica Lewinsky?

To cover Clinton was to cover chaos. Whether it was something small — loading the wrong speech into the TelePrompTer for an important speech to Congress — or more substantive matters — the collapse of Hillary Clinton's ill-fated plan to reform health care or the budget stand-off with Republicans that led to the shutdown of the government — events always seemed on the brink of spinning out of control. Some kind of turmoil, some weird, unexpected development always seemed to lurk just around the corner, and all of it fed the increasingly bitter mood that had settled over the Capitol.

Newt Gingrich and the Republicans had chafed for forty years under Democratic control of the House, and when they finally won majorities in both houses two years into Clinton's first term, they did so largely by running against Clinton and the government itself. The battles had been rough and Congress turned as partisan as I had ever seen it. The administration responded in kind, and the Clinton White House became one of the most partisan I had ever dealt with, and the bitter divide extended throughout Clinton's first term and into his second.

Clinton's reelection had come easily when

Perot mounted another third-party run and Republicans nominated Bob Dole. Most of us who covered Dole liked and respected him, but his popularity never really traveled beyond the Beltway. Dole was the counterargument to the old saying "No man is a hero to his valet." The insiders who knew Dole best liked him the most, and that included Democrats as well as Republicans. But survey after survey showed that that feeling never took hold outside Washington. Dole had been running for years for one office or another, and out in the country he was seen as the ultimate insider, a trait that can make for a good officeholder but never plays well with voters. Dole was a true hero, whose withered arm was the result of being wounded in World War II, but when he talked during the campaign about building a bridge to the generation that had fought the Nazis in World War II, Clinton seized on it and talked of building bridges to the future. If there had ever been a real contest, there was no contest after that.

The future beats the past every time.

The first years of Clinton's second term were even more turbulent than we had become accustomed to during the first four years. As the midterm election year of 1998 began, I was really hoping for a breather, and I started the year with a warm and fuzzy little scoop. I reported that seventy-seven-year-old John Glenn was going back into space. Glenn and his wife, Annie, are two of the nicest people in politics, and Pat and I had come to know them over the years. Even so, ex-Marine Glenn was too much the straight-arrow Boy Scout respecter of the rules to be much of a leaker, so I had never gotten much news out of him. This time it was different. He was so proud to be going back into space he couldn't keep it a secret and told me about it himself.

In a commentary the next Sunday, I kidded him and declared the mission to be a good thing, because even people my age needed older role models.

I remember telling Pat that afternoon that it was sort of fun to have some good news to report for a change. It had been so long since we had any, I was a little out of practice.

As it turned out, I could have put my good-news skills back in the toolbox right then. It would be years before I would need them again.

In the coming months, we would learn about Monica Lewinsky, we would receive the Starr Report — the first X-rated government document I had ever had to decipher — and I would spend the rest of the year reporting on such topics as presidential phone sex, Oval Office trysts and that "stain on the blue dress." I had a scoop or two along the way.

Among other things, I was among the first to report that the president of the United States had given the independent counsel a DNA sample to determine if, in fact, he was responsible for the stain on the blue dress. I'd never had a scoop quite like that one, but in the spirit of full disclosure, I must also report that NBC's Lisa Myers scooped me on the story of the games Clinton and Monica played with the cigar. Sometimes you're just going to get beat on a story and there's nothing you can do but tip your hat to the competition. (Lisa and I have been friends since the days when we covered Jimmy Carter together. She was as uncomfortable with all this as we all were. Linda Douglas, who covers Congress for ABC and is the mother of a teenage daughter, said, "This wasn't a story we took home to talk about over dinner.")

I also got stuck with one bad story. After grand jurors took testimony from Clinton under oath at the White House, I was among several who reported that, at one point, Clinton had lost his composure, cursed and stomped out of the room. Grand jury proceedings are secret, but I had begun to pick up reports about Clinton's outburst within hours after his session with the jurors. White House officials insisted there was no way they could know what had taken place and refused to comment, and the president's lawyers weren't talking. Finally, I asked one of my best sources on Capitol Hill, a Democrat I had known for years with strong ties to the White House, to check it out. Several hours later, I got a call back. Yes, my source said, the story was true. White House aides were telling their allies at the Capitol to brace themselves, that it wouldn't be a pretty picture when that tape was finally released. The president, the source was told, had become so irritated with the prosecutor's badgering that he really lost it at one point. Since I had total confidence in my source, who had never steered me wrong, I reported the story and repeated it in several other reports over the following months. Since the White House never denied it, it never occurred to me that the story might be inaccurate.

I couldn't have been more wrong. When the tape was finally released, it showed the president sparring with the prosecutors, and there was a lot of legal hairsplitting, including the president's now-famous declaration that "it depends on what the meaning of 'is' is." But at no time did the president lose his temper, or even his composure. Nor did he curse and stomp out of the room. My source had been used (unwittingly I still believe) to feed me information that was false. I believe the false information was put out deliberately by someone who wanted to make the story sound worse than it actually was, so that when the tape was finally released, the public would say, "Why that's not nearly as bad as the press said it was going to be." I don't believe the White House circulated the original rumor, but once it was out there, my guess is someone of the president's staff decided to let it stand, believing it would cast the president in a more sympathetic light when the tape was made public and reports that he had lost his composure were shown to be false.

I could be wrong, maybe they didn't mislead me on purpose, but Clinton's key aides and his lawyers knew the story was wrong, and over the ensuing months, they never tried to contact me about it and they made no attempt to knock it down.

Once the story of Monica broke, we reported on little else. Scott Pelley, Bill Plante and Mark Knoller handled the story from the White House and I covered the developments on Capitol Hill. It was a hectic time of long days and nights, but the day I shall never forget is the day that independent counsel Kenneth Starr released his report on the investigation.

Democrats had hoped to block the public from seeing it, at least temporarily. But the day it was delivered to the Capitol, Republican leaders in the House forced an early vote and, shortly after, the House voted overwhelmingly to release the five-hundred-page document. Only the supporting documents, and there were box upon box of them, were to be kept confidential.

The report arrived during the afternoon, but all three networks had already been on the air with special reports for most of the morning. There had been a prayer breakfast at the White House, the president had attended and we had covered it live.

The president had been one of the speakers, and when Vice President Gore had introduced him, he had called it "an unusual and unusually important day for the country."

To be sure, it was unusual. The president began by telling the gathering that he agreed with those who said he had not been contrite enough in talking about the Lewinsky affair. He went on to say that he now realized he had sinned and he promised to repent.

In the meantime, however, he said he had instructed his lawyers to mount a vigorous defense.

Even at that late date, we had no real idea of what the report contained. After all, Starr was releasing the results of an investigation that had begun as a probe of a real estate transaction called Whitewater in which the Clintons had been involved during his time as Arkansas governor. The investigation had expanded when Paula Jones had filed her sexual harassment suit against Clinton, claiming he'd dropped his pants and made a pass at her while he was governor.

It was in January 1998 that the investigation had taken yet another turn as Clinton's involvement with Lewinsky became known. At that point, the central question had become whether or not Clinton had lied under oath to Jones's lawyers (and eventually a federal grand jury) about his relationship with Lewinsky, and whether he had urged her to lie as well as part of the cover-up.

This peculiar tale had unfolded as television news was moving into a new era — the era of round-the-clock coverage. As network audiences had gown smaller, the direct result of viewers having more channels to choose from, the network news departments came under intense new pressure to hold down costs. When a pie that was once split three ways, as CBS, NBC and ABC used to split the audience, is sliced into forty or fifty pieces, as the television audience is now divided, no broadcast organization, no matter how powerful, is going to attract as many viewers as it had when it had only one or two competitors. As the size of the audience shrinks, it becomes harder to attract advertisers.

With the new budget restraints, we had fewer resources to cover news, but faced more competition in gathering the news, and it was an intense contest that went on around the clock.

In earlier years, we might not have gone on

587

the air immediately with something like the Starr Report. But in the era of the twenty-four-hour news cycle, viewers had come to expect their news instantly. The cable channels were already on the air. To be competitive, to be thought of as a serious news organization, we believed we had to go on the air immediately when there was serious news to be told. When viewers hear of breaking news and turn to CBS and we are not reporting on it, they switch to another channel that is, and stay there.

Being the news organization that viewers depend on in times of crisis is how reputations are built, and is what all news organizations aspire to be, so at CBS News we made elaborate preparations that day to get the report first and get on the air with it.

As House Speaker Gingrich had planned it, all news organizations and the public would get the report at the same time over the Internet, the first congressional document to be made public that way. Since it had never been done before, we were dubious, and Mary Hager, the producer who had helped me cover Capitol Hill for many years, worked out a backup plan.

She arranged to get copies from several key members of Congress who would be receiving the first hard copies of the report. It was her plan that saved the day. Because the report hadn't been properly scanned electronically, it took much longer than expected to get it onto the Internet. An hour before that happened, Mary's source called to say the report had been delivered, copies just had to be Xeroxed. Waiting for a five-hundred-page report to be photocopied wasn't good enough for Mary. She raced to the office and grabbed the first few pages off the copy machine and delivered them to me in a Capitol office where we had set up a camera. Dan Rather was anchoring the broadcast from New York, and we were trying to think of pertinent things to say while we waited for the report, when Mary crawled up to me on hands and knees, below camera level, and handed me the pages, which enabled me to say, "Dan, I've got it. I've got the report."

As far as I know, we got it before anyone else (the other networks also had backup plans and were getting the report from other congressional offices).

We had the report, but the next question was, What to do with it? In another time, we might have waited until we had at least had a chance to digest a little of what was in it, but in the age of cable when our competitors were already on the air, viewers were seeing something they didn't usually see. We were not just reporting the news; we were allowing them to watch us gather it. If we had waited until we had a chance to digest it, our viewers would have turned away to another channel and we would never have gotten them back.

So I explained on the air that I had just been handed the first few pages, and started reading, skipping down to a section that read: "This information reveals that President Clinton lied under oath at a civil deposition while he was the defendant in a sexual harassment lawsuit, that he lied under oath to a grand jury." It went on to say that "he encouraged a witness to file an affidavit that the president knew would be false."

The report went on to suggest that it had all been done to cover up a relationship with "a former White House intern and employee, Monica Lewinsky."

Where all this was leading, we wouldn't know until we got deeper into the report, but this was serious stuff. The president of the United States was being accused by a federal investigator of lying to a grand jury and, possibly, obstructing justice.

When I finally asked Dan Rather for a break to catch my breath, he complimented me on my reading skills and quipped it just showed what a good education I had received in the Fort Worth public school system.

When Dan switched back to me a few minutes later, Mary and producers John Nolen, Dick Meyer and Evelyn Thomas had set up a relay from the congressman's copying machine to our camera position. It was like an old-time firemen's bucket brigade. As pages came off the copier, one of them would grab as many pages as possible and run to the next one and hand off. Eventually, one of them would reach the room where I was and, once there, he or she would sit on the floor out of camera range and scan the pages for items of interest. Then one would crawl over to where I was talking on camera and hand it up to me. As the afternoon passed, we had no idea if we had the pages out of order. I would just look them over briefly and try to make sense of what was there. My main concern was not to blunder into reading something that shouldn't be said aloud on television.

It was some of the gamiest prose I had ever encountered, and the more pages they handed me, the gamier it got.

I was there to report the news, but even on the police beat back in Fort Worth, I hadn't run across anything to match this. It just wasn't the kind of thing I was comfortable discussing when children might be listening.

For example, here is what a transcript of our broadcast reflects I said as I struggled through one passage in the report:

"While the president was on the telephone, according to her — 'Let me just read this to make sure we don't . . .' — he unzipped his pants and exposed himself and they had '. . . sex of a kind . . . ' [I couldn't bring myself to say oral sex. Where I came up with the term "sex of a kind" remains a mystery to me. I can't remember ever having said it before. It just popped out. I continued reading the report:] "Again, he stopped before . . . I would say . . . he was completed . . . I guess would be the way to put that.

"During the visit," I continued, "according to Ms. Lewinsky, the president told her he liked her smile. He also said, 'I'm usually around on weekends. No one else is around and you can come and see me.' "

It went on like that for what seemed like most of the afternoon. There was even confirmation of Lisa Myers' story about Clinton and Monica's games with the cigar. On that one, I wasn't about to go into detail, but I advised our viewers, "When folks get their copy on the Internet, they can look it up as they choose."

The stories laid out in the report were some of the most lurid tales I had ever tried to deal with on live television. This stuff made the sexual harassment allegations raised against Clarence Thomas during his Supreme Court confirmation hearings read like a Nancy Drew mystery.

But as more and more of the pages were handed to me that afternoon, I began to read the stories as more pathetic than pornographic. As the father of two grown daughters, I found the whole thing depressing.

This was the kind of story we had all heard before, a young woman — barely an adult —

who had fallen for a powerful, older, married man. It was clear that she had been a small part of his life, but he had become the central figure in hers.

According to the transcript of the broadcast, I said to Dan Rather at one point: "She says, in her recollection, the friendship with the president started to develop following their sixth sexual encounter — in other words, they started to become friends after having sex six times."

Until then, she told the prosecutors, he had really made no effort to get to know her. Even after having sex six times. (It was later reported that when Clinton had made his famous "I did not have sex with that woman, Miss Lewinsky" remark, the reason he had first called her "that woman" was that he had momentarily forgotten her name.)

Monica Lewinsky was not the first starstruck kid who fell in love with a married man who would use her for his pleasure. And, yes, she was something of a tart who brought much of it on herself.

But I felt sorry for the kid.

When the Senate finally acquitted Clinton in mid-February 1999, the people in the Washington bureau of CBS News did what reporters usually do when a big story ends. We repaired to the nearest bar. We had been covering this story and little else for well over a year, and as one who has been a reporter for more than four decades, I've been to a lot of post-big-story gatherings. This time it was different. For one thing, I had stopped drinking alcohol on Election Day, 1988, so I had only a diet Coke, but there was another difference as well. We all understood that we had covered a story that would wind up in the history books, but no one was talking about what a great story it had been.

Instead, the overwhelming emotion that night was simply a feeling of exhaustion, relief that it was finally over. No Woodward or Bernstein had emerged from the press on this one, no Clarence Darrow had risen from the lawyers' ranks. There was no Mr. Smith Going to Washington to take on the high-and-mighty.

The old story of the boss and the office flirt might have ended in another way in another office. Usually, the office flirt is forced out, and the powerful boss, because he is powerful, may or may not hang on. But this was not any office; it was the Oval Office, so it couldn't be ignored.

In the end, the system had worked. The president finally admitted it had all been his fault. The Senate heard the charges and concluded they were not serious enough to remove him from office.

But after what we had come to know about him, Clinton had no cause to celebrate. Nor did we. There had been no heroes on this story, we decided that night. It had diminished all who had touched it, Clinton, his pursuers, the government, the Congress and the media.

I never believed Clinton should have been impeached. To me, overturning the results of an election is the most extreme act authorized by our Constitution, and it should be reserved for traitors and those who would sell out the country, and Clinton was neither.

But he should never have been allowed to leave the presidency unpunished.

Clinton disgraced the highest office in the land, and as the tawdry details of his affairs became a part of the national conversation, he coarsened the culture of the people he had been elected to lead. That was his crime.

My rule about reporting on the private lives of public officials has always been that what they do in private is off-limits unless it interferes with their public duties. But Clinton crossed the line when he took advantage of a young intern in the Oval Office. He compounded the offense by making his loyal secretary, Betty Currie, drive in from her suburban home on her days off to clear Ms. Lewinsky into the White House grounds and required her to sit there and guard the door while they held their trysts. I always wondered what she must have thought as she sat there, waiting for them to finish.

When he was found out, he told the ranking women in his administration, Secretary of State Madeleine Albright and Secretary of Health and Human Services Donna Shalala, that the charges against him were false when he knew they were true, and asked them to put their own reputations on the line and defend him, which they did.

That the person who held the highest position of trust in the land would take advantage of those who worked for him in that way, never mind that he would risk having sexual adventures in the Oval Office at the very time he was being sued for sexual harassment, didn't add up to treason; it just stank of the worst kind of insensitivity and bad judgment. Clinton had been a champion of women's rights but he had shown himself to be a user of women who was not hesitant to take advantage of his friends when he found it necessary for business or pleasure.

I believe the episode had a profound and perhaps lasting impact on the country. Young people who had come to Washington to learn about government found themselves embarrassed to say they were interns. Parents found themselves confronting questions about oral sex from ten-year-olds.

Congress had an opportunity to censure him for those transgressions and would have, had it not been for Republican leaders who misread the national mood. To some extent, that was understandable. All of them came from safe, overwhelmingly conservative districts, where anti-Clinton feelings were the strongest.

"When I went back to my district, the only thing people said to me was 'Get the bastard,' " said South Carolina congressman Lindsey Graham, who was one of the House prosecutors when the case went to trial in the Senate. But Graham acknowledged that the view in his district was not the majority view across the country.

"For most people, it never got to the level of Watergate. People understand burglaries and that kind of thing. But to most people, this was just about a man who lied about having sex, and they are pretty forgiving in those kinds of situations.

"I have no regrets, I didn't want the children of the country to believe that anyone — even the president — could go unpunished if they didn't play by the rules, but by the time it got to the Senate, most Americans just didn't believe removing Clinton from office was warranted."

That reality was reflected in polls and especially among Senators. It was soon clear, even to the most casual observer, that the sixty-seven votes — two-thirds of the Senate — needed to remove Clinton were simply not there.

Former President Gerald Ford, who had

pardoned Richard Nixon, and even Bob Dole, the Republican standard-bearer who had been crushed by Clinton in the 1996 election, had warned Republicans that getting enough votes to impeach Clinton was not possible. Instead, both urged a strong censure and perhaps a fine, but the pleas went unheeded. Ford wanted Clinton to be called to the well of the House of Representatives for a rebuke.

Even after Democrats picked up House seats in the 1998 November midterm elections, at the height of the controversy, the Republican leaders did not read it as a sign to back off on impeachment. It is almost unheard-of for the party that holds the White House to pick up congressional seats in a midterm election, but with the economy growing even stronger, the Democrats had managed it.

In the beginning, the House Republicans had believed the elections would bring added pressure to impeach Clinton. Instead, it was House Speaker Gingrich who resigned. Earlier that year, Gingrich had survived an aborted coup attempt by some of his top lieutenants, and when the grumbling started again after the election, he stepped down. In a bizarre turn of events, his successor, Bob Livingston, resigned in a matter of weeks when it turned out that he had been involved in an extramarital affair. He was eventually replaced by Illinois congressman Dennis Hastert, a quiet onetime high school wrestling coach. Through the turmoil, the Republicans continued to press the case against Clinton, and in the days before Christmas — on a near party-line vote — they voted two Articles of Impeachment and sent the matter to the Senate.

The Senate is a different place, and there was an entirely different mood there.

Even the most anti-Clinton senators (and there was no shortage of disgust with Clinton among Democrats as well as Republicans) knew they couldn't get the votes, and several Republicans told me privately that their main priority at that point was to conduct the trial quickly and in a way that did not reflect badly on them and the institution itself, an effort that succeeded in large part.

That was also why the drive to censure the president ran out of steam in the Senate. House members fought censure because they saw it as a ploy by Clinton supporters to avoid impeachment. Senators feared that a debate over censure might turn into a partisan circus at a time when the public was tiring of the exercise and just wanted it over.

So it was that Clinton's remarkable ability to survive one crisis and go on to the next — the pattern that had marked his career from the beginning — held once more. With no penalty, he could again claim he had been the victim of political enemies — what his wife called "the vast right-wing conspiracy."

There was no question that some on the right had dogged Clinton since his days as Arkansas governor, and there were plenty of them. But it was probably too much to call it a conspiracy.

But to me, Clinton's enemies made the same mistake the cops had made with O. J. Simpson. Their piling on hurt, rather than strengthened, the case against him.

In August 1999, six months after Clinton's acquittal, I received an engraved card from Covington and Burling, one of Washington's oldest, biggest and most prestigious law firms. It announced that Lanny Breuer, who had been one of the president's lawyers, was returning to the firm. It was the kind of routine announcement Washington law firms make when a partner returns from government service, but what struck me was what the announcement said:

"During his tenure as special counsel, Mr. Breuer has represented the president and White House staff in presidential impeachment hearings and trial, four independent counsel investigations, a Justice Department task force investigation, and numerous congressional oversight investigations."

That was a concise summary of what the last two years had been like, and Lanny

Breuer was a good lawyer I had dealt with and come to like and respect over that time.

But to me, that engraved card carried an arresting and somewhat unsettling message: If you need a good criminal lawyer, get someone with White House experience.

END NOTE: Clinton's eight White House years ended in the same chaos and confusion that had marked most of his term. He had overhauled welfare and presided over a booming economy. But the midnight pardons that he granted to Marc Rich and the others during his last days in office were inexplicable, and the controversy over whether the Clintons had tried to haul away White House furniture that really belonged to the taxpayers was typical of the weird situations that he and his wife had confronted throughout his presidency.

The pardons set off the same kinds of questions about Clinton's integrity and judgment that had been raised in those early days when we first heard about Whitewater and sweetheart stock transactions and later during the episodes with Monica Lewinsky. But as had so often been the case during other episodes in his life, he remained fairly popular with the public as he left the White House.

I didn't see him again until July, six months after he left office. He was among the hundreds who had turned out for the funeral of

*Washington Post* publisher Katherine Graham. It had been a grand affair that had included everyone from Bill Gates and Warren Buffett to Henry Kissinger and most of official Washington, past and present. After the services, the family held a lunch at her home, and a buffet had been set up under a huge tent on the front lawn.

As Pat and I rounded the corner and headed into the Grahams' front yard, the first person we saw was Bill Clinton. He had positioned himself at the entrance to the tent and was working the crowd like someone who was running for sheriff.

He was tanned, relaxed and seemed in high good humor. He was just the way I had remembered him on that long-ago morning in 1988, the morning after he made that speech for Michael Dukakis — the speech the rest of us thought would wreck his political career.

# Twenty-six

## *Being Careful What You Wish For Is Still a Good Rule*

We have an informal tradition at CBS News. On the day before presidential elections, I put together a piece that sums up the election year for the *Evening News* broadcast. It's always a light-hearted piece, because what it really is is an excuse to string together pictures of some of the wacky events that took place during the campaign. Randy Wolfe, the producer who had covered the campaign with me, had squirreled away some of the best pictures ever that year and, melded together, they made for a whimsical look back at Campaign 2000. I've done four or five such pieces over the years, but never one as prescient as the one we assembled for the broadcast, the day before Americans went to the polls to decide if they wanted George W. Bush or Al Gore to be President.

It hadn't been the most exciting campaign

that I could remember, but it'd had its moments. John McCain had added some electricity during the early Republican primaries and Ralph Nader had tried to be a spoiler during the general election, but neither Bush nor Gore had been the kind of star to light up the night sky, and debates over who has fashioned the best lockbox for Social Security funds are not the kind of thing that kept us or the public on the edge of our seats.

Still, it had remained close right to the end. Usually, one candidate or the other breaks away during the final weeks of the campaign, but in 2000 neither candidate did. The final polls showed the race to be as close as it had been through the fall, and all of us who had been covering it were excited when we gathered in New York on the weekend before the election to prepare for election-night coverage. As the significance of the political conventions has faded, those of us at network news have come to see election night as the most important night of the year for us, the one time when we go head-to-head against the other networks, and the cable companies, as well.

I thought the election-night team that had been assembled that evening was as good as any I could remember. Dan was anchoring, Ed Bradley was handling polls, I was watching Senate races, and Lesley Stahl was covering governors' and House races. Back in the

1970s, CBS statistician Warren Mitofsky had invented the exit polling procedures that all the networks now used to call elections, and once again Mitofsky would be part of the CBS News team analyzing results.

Election night was shaping up as the kind of evening a political reporter dreams about, and I couldn't hide my enthusiasm on election eve.

Here is how I summed it up on the *Evening News* broadcast when Dan Rather turned to me for comment on that Monday before the Tuesday elections:

*"Dan, this is going to be so close, we may see one presidential candidate win the popular vote and lose the election because the other man gets the most electoral votes.*

*"And for the first time in a long time, who controls the House and Senate could also turn into a nail-biter.*

*"In a way, it is the perfect end to a campaign that had no shortage of weird moments.*

*"It seems like only yesterday that candidate Alan Keyes fell into that mosh pit in Iowa [the best picture of the campaign], and it turned out to be the most support he got anywhere.*

*"Gary Bauer fell, too, flipping pancakes, of all things [Bauer accidentally tumbling off a New Hampshire stage and disappearing from sight while trying to catch a pancake was the best sight gag of the campaign] and soon fell off the radar screen.*

"It was the year we learned about the power of a kiss. [Remember Al and Tipper going deep?]

"Virginia Senator Robb took it another step and kissed a dog, but we don't know if it got him votes. [It didn't. He lost to Republican George Allen.]

"Money was such a factor that a Kentucky state legislator trying to move up to Congress told her colleagues during a session of the Kentucky legislature:

"[LEGISLATOR:] 'Let's vote and get out of here. I've got a fund-raiser at six o'clock.'

"It was the year Al Gore got caught telling numerous tall tales. Once and for all, he did not invent the Internet. And who can forget George Bush helping his loyal running mate to get to know members of the press?

"[GOVERNOR BUSH:] 'There is Adam Clymer of the New York Times. Major League [Bleep].'

"[CHENEY:] 'Yeah . . . big time!' "

I closed off the piece by saying, "Whatever else the rest of us learned, we've all been wishing for an old-fashioned election night where we didn't know the outcome until early morning.

"Well, we may be about to get our wish, and I can't wait, Dan."

At that point, we had everything right. Unfortunately, our luck didn't hold. On the election-night broadcast the next evening, everything that could go wrong did go wrong.

I had been right on when I had predicted

that one candidate might get more actual votes, yet lose in the Electoral College. Full disclosure, however, requires me to confess that we thought it would be Bush, not Gore, since he was expected to get so many votes from his home state of Texas.

The election produced an even more closely divided Senate than I had predicted. We wound up with an exact split — for the first time ever, fifty Republicans and fifty Democrats.

As for a long and exciting night . . .

Our wish had been granted in a way we could not have imagined. We didn't get just a long night; we got more than a month of them. The thirty-six days and nights between election day and December 12, when the U.S. Supreme Court finally settled the election and made George W. Bush president, would be one of the most confusing, acrimonious periods in election history.

As every American who was not on a life-support system at the time knows by now, the election came down to which candidate won Florida's twenty-five electoral votes, and the two sides fought over them in the courts with lawsuits and countersuits, on television with a cadre of advocates who sometimes seemed willing to say anything to advance their respective causes. It had begun when Gore wanted a recount and Bush's people tried to block it, and the matter was argued up and down the legal system from Florida to the U.S. Supreme Court.

When the High Court finally stopped the recount in an obscure ruling handed down on the night of December 12, even the Court found itself accused of partisan politics. The justices who usually took the conservative side in Court arguments ruled for Bush. The moderate and liberal justices sided with Gore.

We can blame the candidates and their advocates for the white-hot, partisan atmosphere that marked those days leading up to the Court decision, but the confusion is another matter. Those of us at the networks must accept much of the responsibility for that.

We went into election night with a plan and procedures that proved faulty, equipment that didn't work and analysis that proved incorrect. Under pressure to get it first, we got it wrong. "Big time," as Dick Cheney might have put it.

We had no inkling of the trouble ahead as election night began, and things went smoothly enough early on. We expected Bush to take an early lead, and he did, with easy wins in South Carolina and Indiana. Shortly after 7 P.M. EST, Dan sounded the first warning that we might be in for a long evening and that what happened in Florida might be key to who won the election. He noted that even though the polls had closed there, we still didn't have enough data to call a winner. The race in Florida, he said, was "hot enough to peel off house paint," and it might be well into the night before we knew who won there.

Yet less than an hour later, at 7:49:40 EST, NBC called Florida for Gore. Thirty-one seconds later, Dan interrupted Mike Wallace. Mike had just begun an essay on campaign commercials and Dan said, "Mike, you know I wouldn't interrupt if it weren't important, but Gore has just won Florida." One minute and forty-nine seconds later, Fox called it for Gore as well, and ABC made the same call at 8:02.

Dan said winning Florida didn't mean Gore had won the election, but probably meant it was going to be a long evening. He got that right. At 10 P.M., he had the unhappy task of announcing why it was going to be so long. CBS was taking back the call and placing Florida in the undecided column.

"Computer and data problems," Dan explained. "We're going to redo all the mathematics, all the computer business, all the data business, and see how it comes out. Now, if you're disgusted with us, frankly, I don't blame you."

In a night when there were few honors to pass around, we could at least say we were first to admit we had made a mistake. It was a dubious honor, to be sure, but if the problems had stopped there, we might have gone on to have a good night.

It only got worse. As the evening wore on, it became clear that the Electoral College count was so close that the candidate who won Florida would be the next president. At 2:16 A.M. EST, the experts at Fox thought they knew who that would be. They called Florida for Bush.

One minute and thirty seconds later, NBC called Florida for Bush, we called it for Bush twenty-two seconds after that. At 2:20, ABC made the same call.

Dan Rather and I have been friends for forty years. We sometimes differ on issues or have a different take on things, but we've seldom had a cross personal word in all those years, certainly never on the air. But when he turned to me that night and asked why I thought Bush had won, he bristled at my answer.

I told him I thought it was impossible to know when a race was as close as this one.

"If we don't have to take back this call, as we had to take back Florida earlier in the evening," I told him, "I guess we can say he won because he got the most votes, but I'm not sure what else I would say here."

"Well," Dan shot back, "let's not joke about the calls for a second, okay? We — all of us — deserve to be the butt of some jokes, but let's put it in some perspective. Early in the evening, based on the models that held up over the years, and CBS News has the most dependable record for race calls by far of any network on presidential election nights, a call was made. It's Florida. I know of no one else in the business who didn't make the call."

I agreed with that. We had all missed this one.

One hour and forty minutes later, CBS again had the distinction of being the first network to admit it had been wrong.

At 3:57:49 A.M. EST, we put Florida back in the undecided column, ABC followed at 4:00 A.M., NBC at 4:02 and Fox at 4:05. Over on CNN, Jeff Greenfield had said, "Oh, waiter! One order of crow!"

By then, Bush's lead in actual votes counted had shrunk to 629. As Dan turned to me, I was shaking my head.

"Bob Schieffer just laughed because that's the only thing he knows to do," he said. I took that to mean we were friends again.

"Dan," I responded, "this is like . . . no longer an election. This is Alice in Wonderland. I mean, it just got 'stranger and stranger,' as Alice said . . . and she's as good a person to quote right now as anybody I know of."

Unfortunately, we could only quote Alice (or misquote her, since the phrase was actually "curiouser and curiouser"), we couldn't blame her for what was shaping up to be the most embarrassing night in the history of broadcast journalism. This one was right there with the *Chicago Tribune*'s famous "Dewey Beats Truman" edition.

We looked no worse than the other news organizations, but it was especially embarrassing for us, because CBS had more or less invented exit polling. The procedures that our statisticians had developed became the system that all news organizations used to determine winners, and over the years the process had proven remarkably accurate.

As Martin Plissner, the recently retired political director of CBS News, pointed out at a Princeton symposium, on only two occasions in eight previous elections had a state for president been called wrong. Yet we had to retract three presidential calls on election night 2000 — Florida, New Mexico and Washington state, along with the Washington Senate race.

So what went wrong? Almost everything. But the root cause can be traced back to growing pressures on all the news organizations over the last ten years to cut costs.

In the 1970s, all three networks fielded independent teams to conduct exit polls and call in actual vote totals and other information that statisticians use to determine voting trends and eventually winners. It is an enormous, expensive undertaking that involves a field force of approximately 40,000 people. To cut costs, the networks and several other news organizations formed a consortium to do the job in 1989. It was called Voter News Service (VNS), and the networks shared the cost.

Instead of three organizations conducting three exit polls, a combined force of field workers conducted one exit poll. The information was fed into one set of computers and compared with one common set of statistical models. All the networks got the same data, but each network then hired independent analysts to determine what the data meant. Thus, when one analyst called a race first, it wasn't because he had more information than anyone else; it was because he believed he saw something in the numbers that the others didn't.

Obviously, when the race is on to call a winner before your competitors do, the temptation to take risks can only increase. And when one network analyst called the key states on election night 2000, the other networks naturally followed. Everyone denies that it worked that way, but when you examine the minutes, sometimes seconds, that separated the calls, even I as a network partisan find that hard to believe.

In the days after the 2000 debacle, CBS News President Andrew Heyward ordered an in-house investigation to determine what had gone wrong. The panel of investigators was headed by CBS News vice president Linda Mason, and included CBS director of polling Kathleen Frankovic and Kathleen Hall Jamieson, chair of the Annenberg School for Communication at the University of Pennsylvania.

They concluded that the early call of Florida for Gore was probably unavoidable. It apparently resulted from incorrect data that had been fed into the computers. At one point the computers showed that Gore had received forty thousand more votes than he actually had. The investigators also discovered serious flaws in the statistical models that VNS had designed to compare the Florida vote to previous presidential elections. The absentee voting had been seriously underestimated and, inexplicably, the statistical model used to compare the vote to previous races had been based on an election for governor, not a presidential contest.

Bad data also figured in the later mistaken call of Florida for Bush. But incredibly, the investigators said that call might have been avoided — or at least delayed — had the CBS statisticians analyzing the data only heard what CBS correspondents were reporting on the air. In the minutes before the networks called Florida for Bush, the computers were showing there were still 179,713 votes to be counted. In reality, there were twice that many.

614

At the anchor desk, Ed Bradley had referred several times to Associated Press reports of voting irregularities and ballots still uncounted, and similar reports were coming from CBS News correspondent Byron Pitts in Florida. The call for Bush might have been delayed, Mason pointed out, had the analysts taken into account what Bradley and Pitts were reporting, and compared the vote totals they were receiving with those being reported by the Associated Press.

The Mason panel recommended that VNS had to be totally overhauled — new software, and hardware, more resources and better quality control — or replaced by a new data-gathering organization.

I would take it one more step. I believe it is time to change philosophy. The race to be first to call a winner should be stopped.

It's irrelevant if a person who happens to be tuned to CBS learns who has won a race a few seconds before someone else. The analysts are all working from the same data, and it is simply not worth the consequences when they are wrong.

Credibility is a news organization's most important asset. When we lose it, we cease to be.

That is why the charge leveled against us by the Republican chairman of the House Commerce Committee, Billy Tauzin, was so wrongheaded. He said we were slow to call states that Bush won narrowly, but called the similar states for Gore immediately. Mason and her team examined Tauzin's charges and concluded there was no statistical evidence to support them, but to me, that's not even relevant. The idea that network news organizations would spend millions of dollars to develop a process to beat their competitors, and then somehow enter into a plot with those same competitors to try to create an impression that one particular candidate was winning — that simply does not hold water.

The mistakes we made on election night resulted from competitive pressure and outdated equipment and procedures. They were not the result of partisan plots and conspiracies. Nevertheless, those mistakes hurt us badly and they hurt the country, because they raised questions about the credibility of the entire election process. We must never allow them to happen again.

For all the confusion of election night, Campaign 2000 had a promising start. It was clear from the beginning that Bill Bradley would be Gore's main competition for the Democratic nomination, and that maverick Republican John McCain would be the main challenger to George W. Bush on the Republican side.

It was the eighth time I had been assigned to cover a presidential campaign for CBS

News, and as I headed to New Hampshire for yet another primary there, it occurred to me that this would be the first time I had had something of a personal relationship with all the main contenders. I guess it's a sign of age, but I not only knew them all; I liked them. I had come to know Bradley during countless trips shared on the air shuttle between Washington and New York, in the days when he had been a New Jersey senator and I had been flying to New York on weekends to anchor the Saturday *News*. As a former professional basketball star and a Russian scholar, Bradley is one of the most fascinating people I know. He has views on almost everything, and I used to look forward to seeing him, especially on those flights when traffic delays left us sitting on the runway for hours before takeoff.

I had also come to know Gore over the years. I covered him in the Senate and, through mutual friends, Pat and I would sometimes find ourselves with Gore and his wife, Tipper, in various social settings. I have never known anyone whose off-camera demeanor was so different from what we saw on television. On TV, he seemed stiff and rehearsed, but off it, he was witty and interesting, and Tipper was natural and friendly. We knew them to be fine parents, and one of their daughters was a schoolmate of one of my daughters.

I knew McCain even better. We are about the same age, and since I am a little older than most of the reporters covering the Senate (actually, I'm considerably older), we came to see ourselves as a couple of geezers in a youthful crowd, and we have been razzing each other for years about who is actually the older. For the record, he is my senior by a couple of months. What I have always liked about McCain is not so much his politics, but his openness and independence. By his own admission, he is a rascal who will never be elected Miss Congeniality by his Senate colleagues, some of whom openly despise him — don't invite Trent Lott and McCain to the same dinner. But whether the news is good or bad, you can always find McCain. Most politicians are easy to find when they have good news to report about themselves, but they disappear when it turns bad. McCain is different in another way, as well. He seldom hides his emotions. When he's mad, everybody knows it. He also wisecracks at inopportune moments, is occasionally profane and, in short, acts like a normal person, which is a rarity in today's politics, where too many politicians won't say hello until they've checked the polls.

I first knew George W. Bush casually (no one ever called him George W. until the campaign) during his father's 1988 campaign, and first remember interviewing him on the floor at that year's Republican convention. But I came to know him better the next year, after the serendipitous chain of events by which my brother Tom became his partner in the Texas Rangers baseball club.

Tom had returned to Fort Worth to practice law, but he had remained active in Democratic politics and civic affairs. When reports circulated that the Rangers would be sold and might be moved to Florida, he and a golfing friend named Roger Williams put out some feelers about forming a group of investors to buy the team and keep it in Texas. What they didn't know was that Bush had already put together a group and they managed to buy the team before Tom's group could get organized. The Rangers play in Arlington, halfway between Dallas and Fort Worth, and draw their fans from both cities. Bush's investor group came mostly from the East and from Dallas, where Bush lived in those days, and to broaden the team's appeal, Bush wanted some investors from Fort Worth. Since most of the investors were Republicans, the Bush team also figured it wouldn't hurt to have a politically connected Democrat as part of their group. That's when someone remembered "that Schieffer guy from Fort Worth who was interested in the team."

Tom and I are both baseball fans, and when he was invited to invest in the group, he accepted, mainly because it sounded like fun.

My mother thought it was a somewhat frivolous idea, and told him, "I hope you're not going to let this interfere with your business!"

As it would turn out, baseball became Tom's main business. The other partners put him in charge of building the Rangers' new ballpark and soon named him president of the club. He ran the ball club for the next eight years, first with Bush and Dallas investor Rusty Rose, who served as co–general partners. When Bush became governor and put his interest in trust, Tom joined Rose as a general partner. It turned out to be a good management team. When they sold the club in 1998, the Rangers had become one of the most successful franchises in all of baseball, had gone to the divisional playoffs three times, and their stadium, The Ball Park in Arlington, had been called one of the best in modern baseball. Bush is a genuine baseball fan; we watched a lot of games together in those days, and there's no better company at a ballpark. In April 2001, Tom was on the verge of launching a new business venture when Bush asked him to serve as U.S. ambassador to Australia, an offer that stunned him since he had taken no part in the campaign. He was in a quandary about what to do, when his wife, Susanne, gave him the same advice she had given him when he had been reluctant about accepting his partners' offer to build a new ballpark for the Rangers. "This may be the only time in your life anybody will ask you to do something like this." He decided she was right, and several months later, was confirmed by the Senate.

At this point, the reader might conclude that being on such friendly terms with all the key players made it easier for me to cover the campaign. In fact, I did feel I had a good fix — the best fix I had ever had — on what kind of men the key players were. But for me, there is nothing harder than covering a news story that involves your friends — especially when they are on opposite sides.

To be absolutely candid about it, in the rough-and-tumble of a campaign, when all kinds of charges are being hurled about, it's easier to cover someone you don't like.

Americans like a good fight, and the fight that McCain waged against Bush in the early primaries brought out record numbers of voters. In New Hampshire, 100,000 more people cast ballots than had voted in 1996, twice as many turned out in South Carolina, three times as many in Michigan. Bush had cornered most of the Republican money early on, and McCain, with nothing but time on his hands, chartered a bus and began traveling the roads of New Hampshire. New Hampshire voters are a cantankerous lot who don't like to be taken for granted. McCain with his antiestablishment reform talk was their kind of guy. Bush and his people had been expecting a big win. After I interviewed him on *Face the Nation* on the Sunday before the primary, Bush told me, "We're going to win bigger up here than people think."

Instead, they got a bad surprise — McCain beat them soundly. But Bush had an advantage over McCain. Bush had enough money to go on even after a defeat; McCain had to win virtually every primary in order to raise the money to go on to the next one, and when Bush turned up the heat in South Carolina, it became harder and harder for McCain to keep the momentum going, and by the end of March, his campaign was over.

On the Democratic side, Bradley never really got going. The side of Bradley that I had seen on the Washington–New York shuttle, the thoughtful intellectual who had interesting things to say about almost everything, never came through to voters. Gore attacked every proposal that Bradley tried to lay out, questions were raised about Bradley's health (he has an irregular heartbeat), and with more money to spend, Gore stopped the Bradley campaign before it ever really jelled.

That I personally happened to like the main players in the 2000 campaign, however, did not mean that I liked what presidential politics had become. When I had talked to George McGovern during the interview for this book, he had told me he believed his campaign was the last one to be waged on the issues. He wanted to shut down the Vietnam War, and Nixon didn't. The issue was clearly drawn, and the voters sided overwhelmingly with Nixon.

Since then, he said, it has sometimes been hard to know what the campaigns have been about. I tend to agree.

There was no one grand issue such as Vietnam in 2000, but there were some real differences — gun control, abortion, campaign reform, foreign policy, gay rights and tobacco. Yet none of those issues proved central to the outcome of the campaign. As Gore and Bush argued around the margins of those issues, neither brought new converts to their positions, and it is fair to say the country remains as divided on all those questions as it was at the beginning of the campaign.

One reason for that, I believe, is that the candidates have shifted their emphasis from issues to image. As the campaigns have moved from the communities to the television screens, the candidates and their consultants have come to see image — the way they are personally perceived by voters — as the way to winning campaigns. We watched Jimmy Carter carry his own bags; we woke up to fuzzy, feel-good pictures of Reagan's "Morning in America"; and we saw the earnest young "Man from Hope" who was working for "people like us."

A campaign that stressed personal contact, such as Lyndon Johnson's helicopter tour across Texas that I had watched as a boy in 1948, is no longer considered cost-effective. The politicians can reach so many more people on television that campaign rallies have become a waste of time, except as backdrops for TV commercials. Candidates are not about to use television ads to lay out serious proposals; they need those brief and expensive seconds to burnish their images.

But here's the downside: The day that Lyndon Johnson came to our neighborhood in 1948 made such an impression on me that I still remember it. On the other hand, I can't remember any of the campaign commercials I saw during the last presidential campaign. Study after study shows that campaign commercials work in the short run, especially the negative ones, but they are quickly forgotten, in the way most advertising is forgotten. The human contact that once marked our politics has all but disappeared, and with it the zest and spontaneity that made it interesting and fun. Campaigns have become so dull that it is even difficult for me, a professional campaign watcher, to stay interested. Equally unfortunate, the shift to television has driven their costs into the stratosphere.

Fred Wertheimer, the longtime president of Common Cause, who now heads an organization devoted to campaign reform, told me one day in 2002 that he is beginning to see the outlines of an obvious but disturbing pattern. "Basically," he said, "the data show the people who spend the most money win."

In a way, that summed up the race for president in the year 2000. The candidates who spent the most won their party nominations. But as we get farther and farther from the rhetoric of that campaign, it is difficult to remember anything that any of the candidates said or did that would prove relevant to the problems that George W. Bush faced as president.

Yet, it was the most expensive campaign in history. Just as the campaign before it had been the most expensive, and the next campaign will be the most expensive.

It is what we have come to expect of our campaigns. We elect the person who spends the most. Only after he is on the job are we really able to know whether we have selected the best person.

It is hard to imagine a more unlikely end to a presidential campaign than what happened in Campaign 2000.

Until that bone-chilling December 12 night when the Supreme Court finally issued the opinion that settled it and made Bush the president, I thought the most difficult day I would ever spend on live television would be the afternoon I struggled to explain Ken Starr's report on Bill Clinton. But that was indoor work, and it was nothing compared to trying to decipher a sixty-five-page legal opinion in subfreezing cold on the marble steps of the U.S. Supreme Court.

Deciding when and how to release an opinion is something the justices do in private, so unless one of them reveals it, we will never know exactly why they did what they did that night.

As longtime Court watcher Linda Greenhouse would later write in the *New York Times*, "The justices who drove off into the night on Tuesday left behind more than a split decision that ended a disputed presidential election. They also left behind an institution that many students of the Court said appeared diminished, if not actually tarnished, by its extraordinary foray into presidential politics."

That conclusion is arguable, to say the least. But to those of us who struggled that night to determine exactly what the Court had wrought, it did seem the justices were not so proud of what they had done. From the way the opinion had been framed, you got the feeling that perhaps the justices wanted to disguise what the opinion actually meant. In essence, they had ruled it unconstitutional to have votes counted under various standards. But they had gone on to say that the ruling applied only to that particular election, because the issue was so complicated — a caveat that gave some legal scholars pause.

In many cases, the justices announce their decisions from the bench during public sessions, and the author of the majority opinion summarizes the main points. We had not expected that kind of guidance as we waited in the court pressroom the night of December 12. If the decision was to be made public that night, we expected no more than a printed copy of the opinion, and shortly after 10 P.M. we were alerted that it would be released shortly. As we would soon learn, it would not be in the format we had expected.

I spent a lot of time around the Fort Worth courthouse, so I know the basics of what a lawsuit is about and I can translate most legalese, but I hadn't been in the Supreme Court since the arguments over the Pentagon Papers back in the 1970s, and I was stunned by what we got that night. Significantly, so were the reporters who covered the Court on a regular basis, but I would only learn that later.

At CBS, we went on the air when we learned the opinion would soon be forthcoming. It would be another of those times when the viewers would be watching us figure out exactly what the news was before we reported it. I would soon have the opinion, but as had been the case two years earlier when I had been handed the first pages of the Starr Report, I would have no advance warning of what was in it. I wasn't particularly worried. Supreme Court decisions almost always begin with a "headnote," a brief summary of the majority opinion and how each justice has voted.

It was below freezing that night, there was a light wind, and when one of our producers, Deirdre Hester, ran out to the camera position and handed me the opinion, I had to remove my gloves to hold it. I was also flabbergasted. There was no headnote. I had been expecting to report immediately what the opinion had concluded and then take a breather, hand the broadcast back to Dan in New York, and read the entire opinion, so I would be able to return later in the broadcast with context. Instead, as David Von Drehle of the *Washington Post* would later write, while "all America watched, the correspondents began reading the sixty-five-page parcel, commenting as they went. Very quickly, they bogged down." Of course, there was no way I could have known then that the other network reporters were in the same fix I was. All I could think of was that somebody had figured this out and they were scooping me. I have never felt colder or lonelier or stupider than when I looked up from the report and told Dan Rather I would just have to plow through more of it before I could tell him what the justices decided.

As I would later learn, it was not just the missing headnote that made this opinion different.

It was not signed. Usually, the justice who writes the majority opinion in a case signs it. Instead, this opinion was issued anonymously, a practice usually reserved for unanimous opinions or opinions not considered important enough to identify the author.

Our CBS legal consultant for the evening, attorney Jonathan Turley, had flown to New York to be at Dan's side, and until a copy of the opinion could be faxed there, he had even less idea of what it meant than I did.

The court fights since election day had basically been about whether to accept that Bush had actually won Florida by several hundred votes, or to recount some or all of the votes. What the High Court did that night was to overturn a Florida Supreme Court ruling permitting the manual recount of some of the votes — but it did not say that until nine pages into the opinion. And even then, until you read the dissenting opinions, you could not be entirely sure whether or not the Court had ordered the lower court to come up with another remedy.

Linda Greenhouse had figured it out by the time she returned to her desk in the newspaper's Washington bureau, and she got the right story into her newspaper's main edition.

629

But at both Gore and Bush headquarters, they were not so sure. Bush's legal team held a lengthy conference before they were confident enough to tell Bush they thought it meant he had won. Gore's lawyers studied the opinion for more than an hour and a half, and it was not until the early-morning hours that Gore himself concluded that it meant the campaign was finally over.

On Wednesday, Gore finally conceded. When he had been Clinton's running mate in 1992, he had often taunted the Bush administration by saying, "It's time for them to go!"

As he conceded to the elder George Bush's son that Wednesday, he smiled and said, "And now my friends, in a phrase I once addressed to others, it's time for me to go."

I thought it was his finest moment of the campaign.

Bush was equally eloquent when he ended his victory statement by saying simply, "I will give it my all."

It had been long, and bitter and confusing, and the argument over the Court's decision would continue.

But the process ended as elections are supposed to end in America.

The winner was gracious in victory and, more important, the loser accepted the result.

# Twenty-seven

## 9-11

The attack on September 11, 2001, was unlike anything that any of us at CBS News had ever experienced. Each of us would have a story to tell about that day. For my friend New York producer Tom Flynn, the story began that morning in his Greenwich Village garden. Tom Flynn loved that little garden behind his house. He liked to have his coffee there and read the *Times* when the weather was good and the clear blue sky on the morning of September 11 held the promise of a fine day. An overnight rain had cleared the air and it was crisp and cool. The garden was where Tom Flynn liked to start his day, catching the last few minutes of quiet before he headed to work at CBS News in midtown Manhattan. It was never quiet there.

And then he heard it. Felt it, really. Directly overhead. The ear-splitting roar of an aircraft. It was so loud, it just surrounded him and shook the whole garden. It had come in so low and so fast that in the instant it took to look up from his paper, it was gone. But in a matter of seconds, he heard an explosion. He had no idea what it was, but he knew it was something bad.

From across the way, his neighbor shouted, "My God, what was it? A plane in trouble?"

It was a plane, but Flynn knew instinctively it wasn't in trouble. It was going full-bore. He knew from the sound that it had full power.

"I thought we were under some kind of attack," he said later, "I wondered if it had fired some kind of missile or had dropped a bomb."

He found his cell phone, got on his bike and pedaled hard toward where he had heard the explosion.

Melissa Valcarcel, twenty-three, the newest member of the *CBS Evening News* staff, on her first job out of college, didn't hear the explosion. She had been on the subway coming to work from the Bronx, where she lived with her parents. But she heard the sirens as she got off the subway, and as she walked into the lobby of the CBS News building on West Fifty-seventh Street, she knew something was wrong. Dozens of people were clustered around the television monitors in the building lobby. That was unusual. People who worked at CBS didn't tarry in the lobby. The only people who did were visitors waiting to be escorted past security, and there were never that many. Something was not right, she thought.

Then her heart jumped.

"They said a plane hit one of the World Trade Towers," she said. "That was where my father worked."

She began to shake and ran to her desk just off the main newsroom and called her mother.

"Oh, I was so happy," she said. "My mother said my father had just called and said he was all right, that the plane had hit the other tower. Then he told her he had to go, because he had to call the fire department and the police department.

"That was so much the way he was. He had polio when he was eight years old and had been in a wheelchair ever since. He was in the New York State tax office and they made him the office fire marshal because they said he would look after the people who had a hard time getting around. He laughed about it, but he took the responsibility seriously.

"I was so relieved. I talked to my Mom for a while and we were so thankful, and then I walked back out into the newsroom to see what was happening. That was when the plane hit the other tower, where my father was.

"We never heard from him again. When we called his cell phone, it went to voice mail for a while, and then we got nothing. That's all we know."

In the Washington bureau, Janet Leissner, the bureau chief, was talking to Jim McGlinchy, the Washington *Evening News* producer, about the day's schedule. The network morning shows were playing on the wall monitors, but the volume was turned down. They didn't realize what had happened when they saw the first pictures. It was just before 9 A.M. Janet went directly to the bureau control room two floors below. She would not leave her chair there for thirty-six hours.

Thus began the longest continuous coverage of any story in the history of CBS News, and it was a story unlike anything that any of us had ever covered. All of us had covered tragedy; that was part of being a reporter. But this time, we would find ourselves covering a story that was as much about us as it was about others. This time, it had been an attack where we lived. This time, it was not strangers, but our own families and friends, who were in danger. From 8:55 that Tuesday morning, when we broadcast the first reports of smoke coming from the tower, until 6 A.M. the following Saturday, we were on the air continuously for ninety-three hours and five minutes, nearly four days. During those hours, every one of the seventy-five CBS News correspondents in the United States and around the world, with the exception of Morley Safer of *60 Minutes*, got on the air at least once with a report related to the attack.

And Morley was on the air the following Tuesday with a profile of the New York City fire commissioner.

Marcy McGinnis, the executive who directed the coverage from New York, called it an amazing coming together.

"There were no dividers on this story," she said. "Usually, there is always someone who says, 'I don't do that kind of work,' but not on this one. From the first minutes, everyone knew this was a gigantic story, unlike anything we had ever covered, and everyone wanted to help. Hedy Gold from the finance office came in at one point and said, 'Give me something to do, I have to help.' I sent her off to find some medical help, some counselors. Some of our people were coming back from the scene in shock. I knew they were going to need some help and Hedy found what they needed.

"Because this was not a news story about other people. This was an attack on our homes and friends. Everybody knew somebody down there. People weren't just thinking about the story, they were thinking about the safety of their own families.

"One minute I was Marcy, the news executive, and the other minute I was Marcy, the human, worried about my mother, wondering if my boyfriend, who worked down there, was all right."

The reactions of the president of the

United States were much the same. He had flown to Orlando, Florida, that morning to make a series of speeches promoting his education reform plan. When he saw TV pictures of the first crash on television, he thought it was an accident.

"I remember saying that had to be one really fouled-up pilot," he told me in an interview for this book. "This guy must have been totally disoriented."

In a matter of minutes, he would learn otherwise. He had gone ahead with plans for a photo session with some students at an Orlando school, but had been in the classroom only a matter of minutes when his chief of staff, Andrew Card, approached and whispered to him there had been another plane.

"He told me we were under attack," Bush said. "My first reaction was, we must defend the country."

But as any American would, the president also wanted to know where his family was. As he returned to *Air Force One*, the Secret Service told him his daughters had been taken to a secure place. He located his wife, who had been on Capitol Hill preparing to testify before a congressional committee.

"She told me everything was fine," he said. "I wanted to make sure she got the dogs." (Not to worry, they had been taken to the bunker beneath the White House.)

As the day wore on, he worried about his

parents, because he knew they would be worried about him, and White House operators finally tracked them down late in the day.

"I said, 'Where are you?' " the president recalled. "And they said they were in Milwaukee in a motel on the outskirts of the town, and I said 'Why?' and they said, 'Because you grounded our airplane.' It was sort of funny."

Other presidents have told me there is always a point when the man elected to that office realizes the awesome responsibilities of the presidency. Bush knows now what they meant.

"For me, that moment came when Andy Card whispered in my ear, 'The United States is under attack.' "

Bush's first thought was to return directly to Washington, but those plans would be delayed as the government began to get itself organized and he flew first to an Air Force base in Louisiana.

Back at CBS, we were getting organized, too.

Bryant Gumbel and Jane Clayson of the *Early Show* handled the first hours of coverage. By 10 A.M., Dan Rather had taken over the anchor chair. He would stay there for the next sixteen hours, when he finally took his first break and slept for several hours. The overall coverage was being managed from the New York control room, and it was in chaos.

CBS News president Andrew Heyward, McGinnis and Al Ortiz, the executive who heads special-events coverage, had set up shop there. At the center of it all was Eric Shapiro, the director. In television, especially during nonscripted special-events coverage, the director is the key person. Producers control the editorial flow, deciding whom to interview, which parts of the story to pursue, but it is the director who pulls it all together. He positions the camera operators, coordinates the feeds coming in from numerous remote sites. He looks at a bank of several dozen monitors and chooses which pictures from which monitors to put on television. He is the one who puts the "supers" (the printed words that identify the person speaking), the maps and other graphics on the screen. But on that morning, Eric Shapiro was crying as he called the shots.

"I looked down there and there were tears running down his face," Heyward recalled. "I said, 'Eric, are you okay?' And he said he couldn't find his twenty-two-year-old daughter, Jennifer. He was trying to call her on the phone. She was just out of college and had just gone to work at Goldman Sachs and he knew her office was somewhere down there where the disaster was.

"I told him to give me some numbers, I would try to find his wife and see if I could locate her.

"I had come in there to direct coverage of the biggest story of my life, but I think that was probably the most important thing I did that day. It took me a half hour or so but I found his wife, and I'll never forget how he looked when I shouted to him across the control room, "Your wife says Jennifer is okay, they saw the whole thing from her office, but they got out and walked to Chinatown, and she is all right!"

In Washington, CBS News Justice Department correspondent Jim Stewart had been on the phone with an FBI source when tape of the first plane hitting the tower was shown. "Look at that," he remembers the FBI agent saying. "That sky is clear as a bell, that's no accident . . . gotta go." Stewart said four months passed before he ever reached the agent again.

Pat and I had just finished our breakfast that morning and I had gone to take a shower and to get dressed for work. Pat follows the stock market closely and had just switched the TV to CNBC and was watching analyst Mark Haines talk about what to expect that day on Wall Street, when the screen switched to scenes of black smoke billowing from one of the Trade Towers. Haines said there were reports a plane had hit there.

When she screamed the news to me in the shower, my first thought was that it was probably the Washington–New York air shuttle, which I had ridden for so many years. The shuttle often flies a flight path that takes it past the Trade Towers before it takes a right turn over midtown Manhattan onto final approach into La Guardia Airport. When the weather is clear, it makes for a spectacular view of New York. I grabbed a robe and we watched for a few minutes and then I returned to the shower. Pat went back to the TV and saw the second plane hit and came back to tell me. Like the rest of the world, we knew then, this was some kind of terrorist act. I dressed as quickly as I could.

She had an appointment in Georgetown that morning — an appointment she had made three months earlier to get a haircut — but as she came to the intersection of Thirtieth and M Streets facing the Potomac River in the heart of Georgetown, she saw a great cloud of black smoke boil up from across the river. She realized immediately that this was connected somehow to the crashes in New York and remembered saying to herself, What have they hit now? but before the light changed, she heard the reporter on the radio say, "We just got a report that a plane hit the Pentagon." She turned around and returned to our apartment, knowing that I was headed for the Capitol.

David Martin, the veteran CBS Pentagon correspondent, was on the Memorial Bridge, about a mile from the Pentagon, when he saw the same smoke.

"At first, it didn't occur to me that a plane had crashed into the Pentagon. I couldn't have imagined such a thing. I thought it must have been a tanker truck that had blown up on I-95, which runs beside the Pentagon. The place where I park is on the opposite side of the Pentagon from where the plane hit, and by the time I got there, they were saying it might be a plane.

"I had my cell phone, the smoke was really boiling out of the building, and as I rounded the corner it was so thick I couldn't see what had happened to the building, but there were all these bodies everywhere. I'm a little ashamed to say it, but my reporter training kicked in and I started counting them. I was trying to get a cell-phone call through to New York, but I didn't want to report that a plane had hit the building until I had some evidence. It was impossible to see into the building and I was looking for anything — a piece of metal, anything — and then I tripped on something in the smoke and looked down and there was a piece of the fuselage. There was no doubt that was what it was, so when I finally got a call through to CBS, I was able to report that it had been a plane. For some reason, all the cell phones had been knocked out and it would be awhile before I got another call out."

Donald Rumsfeld, the sixty-nine-year-old

secretary of defense, was in his office on the opposite side of the building when the plane hit. Ironically, he had just gotten a CIA intelligence briefing, but when he heard the explosion, he had no more inkling of what had happened than had anyone else. There had been nothing in the intelligence brief to suggest that terrorists had planned an attack that day, or that civilian airliners would be used as weapons. Rumsfeld had left his desk and run down the third-floor hallway until the smoke became too thick, then he went to a lower floor and outside. He helped in the early rescue efforts, and was lifting one victim's stretcher into an ambulance when aides told him he needed to go at once to the National Military Command Center in the heart of the Pentagon to help in managing the crisis.

I called in from my car, reached Janet in the control room and told her I was headed for the Capitol. She first said okay, then put me on hold and took another call. She came back on the line, and now she was shouting, "Don't go to the Capitol! They've blocked it off and told everybody to evacuate. They think another plane might be headed there."

"That was when I really got worried," Jim Stewart said later. "I had finally gotten through to a guy in the FBI Command Center. I could hear people shouting in the background, get everybody out of the Capitol . . . there's another plane out there. We think it's headed for the Capitol!"

"What worried me," Stewart said later, "was the tension I could hear in their voices. These were veteran law-enforcement officials and you could tell they were really upset."

In the Washington control room, Janet Leissner's first concern was for John Nolen, Evelyn Thomas and Kathy Mountcastle, the three producers who help me cover Congress. All three were already inside the Capitol that morning. She was frantically trying to reach them to tell them to get out.

Kathy had actually seen the Pentagon explosion from a window on the west side of the Capitol. John had been on the underground subway that connects the Senate and House office buildings with the Capitol, and Evelyn had just walked into a Capitol doorway, when she saw people running from the building.

Kathy remembered later that it was total panic. The police were not sure what the problem was; they just had orders to get people out as quickly as possible.

"What I remember as I ran out was all these women's shoes on the Capitol steps," Kathy remembered. "People were just throwing off their shoes or running out of their shoes — staffers, pages — there were shoes everywhere."

It is the hardest kind of a situation for a news executive. "You are trying to cover the story," Leissner remembered. "But you know your people are risking their lives to cover it. I wanted to make sure my people knew what the danger was, and I told John and Kathy and Evelyn to get out of there if they felt it was too dangerous."

By then, the three of them were on the lawn of the Capitol's east front and John finally said, "Look, Janet, we're not leaving until they make us go."

"No one really knew what to do," John said. "People were just wandering around the grounds — senators, staffers. The chaplain was leading people in prayer. I never saw anything like it. Finally, the police just cleared the whole area. When they told members of Congress to go to the capital police headquarters about a block away we all went down there until they reopened the Capitol grounds that evening. Only later would we learn that the plane that had crashed in Pennsylvania after a group of passengers overcame the terrorists was the one that officials feared was headed toward the Capitol."

Who can say where the plane was headed or how many of us owe our lives to those brave passengers? It is a question we asked many times in the Washington bureau as the months passed.

With the Capitol closed, I took a camera crew and went to the roof of the Chamber of Commerce building, a block north of the White House. We set up a microwave dish

644

that allowed us to broadcast live from there and, through the day, we used the spot to interview key officials. From there, I could look south past the White House to the Washington Monument and Jefferson Memorial and on to Reagan National Airport. To the right of the airport, I could see the smoke billowing from the Pentagon. It was an eerie sight. North of the Chamber building, the streets of Washington were teeming with people who had left their offices. But as I looked south, there was almost no one to be seen. The monuments had been closed to the public, the White House had been evacuated and aircraft all across the country had been grounded. I could see planes parked at the airport terminals, but nothing was landing or taking off. The only people I could see for miles were the snipers in black uniforms who paced along the flat White House roof.

By then, we were all running on adrenaline, but the news continued to astound us. At the Pentagon, David Martin had finally gotten through another cell-phone call to Dan Rather in New York

"I was looking right at where the plane had gone into the Pentagon, the smoke had cleared a little, and the fourth floor was beginning to crumble, that whole section of the building, all four floors were starting to collapse. That was Armaggedon to me, and then I heard Dan saying, 'David, we have to break away, we're getting reports that one of the World Trade Towers is starting to collapse.' "

In New York, Tom Flynn, who had ridden to the scene on his bicycle, got there before most of the firemen. He saw a man with a video camera and asked who he worked for. His name was Eddie Remy, and he said he did photo work for one of the investment houses. Flynn hired him on the spot to work for CBS News and they had spent those first minutes photographing the blazing towers and watching in horror as people had begun to jump from the higher stories.

"Most of the pictures we took were pictures you wouldn't want to see, they were just too tough to look at," FIynn said.

They were a half block away when they heard the roar and the first tower began to collapse.

Flynn said, "We turned to run and got separated. I looked around and there was another guy running beside me, and then I heard something and looked back, and the guy just wasn't there anymore. He had been hit by something and covered up. That was the part that television couldn't convey — the proportion of the debris that was coming down. Very few people were injured. The stuff was so big that if you got hit, you died; if you didn't, you got away unhurt." Flynn made it into a parking garage and remained there until the danger passed. Cameraman Remy took refuge in a deli. Flynn located him later and used some of the tape on our broadcast that night.

When I asked Flynn if he had been scared, he told me he really wasn't sure. "But I did think I was going to die," he said. "I guess that is a little different." When he made his way back to the CBS studios in midtown, he was covered in soot, but when he joined Dan Rather at the anchor desk, he gave a clear, crisp account of what had happened. "Being on camera is not my thing," he said. "I'm a behind-the-scenes guy, but I got through it. The hard part was that I had inhaled so much dust it was hard to breathe."

Marcy McGinnis believes he was in shock.

Everybody on the scene had close calls. Correspondents Mika Brzezinski and Byron Pitts had taken refuge in an evacuated school when debris had begun to fall. Correspondent Carol Marin was badly shaken. She had been pushed against a wall by a man who threw his own body on hers to protect her from falling debris she had not seen. The man disappeared before she could learn his name. Only later that night did Wayne Nelson, one of the *Evening News* producers, learn that his wife, who works for ABC News, had been trapped on a smoke-filled subway during the early hours of the disaster.

For Heyward and his management team in

New York and Janet Leissner in Washington, the hard part was trying to plan the coverage for the days ahead while covering what was happening at that moment. They knew they would be working around the clock, that this story was going to go on for a while. That meant that camera crews and correspondents on the scene had to be fed, extra tape editors and technical personnel had to be hired, hotel rooms had to be rented so that people would have places to get a few hours' sleep. People had to be rotated in to relieve those at the scene. In those first hours, they had to think days ahead. For example, it was decided that *Face the Nation* would be expanded to an hour and a half. Steps were begun to clear the change with our affiliate stations. A decision was also made to expand the *Evening News* to an hour until further notice. No one knew how long we would keep on with the continuous coverage.

"We didn't even think about going off the air," Heyward said. "That wasn't an option, and the corporate people didn't raise it either. They just said, 'Do what you have to do.' "

By noon, Heyward had worked out a detailed plan. Al Ortiz and his Special Events crew would run the coverage during the day; Jim Murphy, the *Evening News* producer, would direct coverage from 6 to 9:30 P.M.; Susan Zirinsky, the *48 Hours* producer, and

Jeff Fager, producer of *60 Minutes II*, would handle coverage through the prime-time hours. The correspondents had no schedule. We stayed on the job until we just couldn't go on (can till can't, we called it). I got home that night for a few hours. Some didn't.

"We also knew this went beyond news as we had come to know it," Heyward said. "Don Hewitt called me and said, 'This is the time to put aside your competitive instincts. You should call the other network news presidents and tell them that all of us should agree that if we come across something the American people really need to know or see, that we will all share it.' I thought Don was right about that, and I called the other guys and they agreed. We decided this was not the time to be trying for exclusives. It was just too important."

The president had remained aloft most of those first hours. After going first to the air base in Louisiana, he flew next to Offutt Air Force Base, the former home of the Strategic Air Command near Omaha, Nebraska.

On Capitol Hill, even in those early hours, some senators were saying the president should return immediately, that if he stayed away it would be a victory for the terrorists. New York mayor Rudy Giuliani had spent much of the day at Ground Zero doing everything but direct traffic, and that did not make the president look any better. The next day, I

649

ran into New York's new senator, Hillary Rodham Clinton, and asked her about it, but she refused to criticize him as others had.

"That's the Secret Service's doing," she told me. "Their job is to protect the president, and if they had their way, the president would never go outdoors, and if he did, he would travel by tank."

The president told me he had no regrets about his actions that day. His first thought had been to return to Washington to convene a meeting of top officials, but he said no one could be sure at that moment what was going on and he decided to follow a "continuity of government" plan that had been drafted for such emergencies.

"The person who gave me the strongest advice not to come back was Dick Cheney," he said. Bush said he was on the phone constantly for the rest of the day, determined to find out who was responsible for the attacks, and determined, he said, to bring them to justice. Shortly before nightfall, he was back at the White House.

With the president away, the White House had been evacuated during the first hours of the crisis, when officials had believed the White House was under attack, and the vice president had been hustled from his office to the fortified bunker beneath the White House.

Once the evacuation had begun, our White

House reporters, John Roberts, Bill Plante and Mark Knoller, were having a hard time getting information. With the president and his key advisors on *Air Force One* and other people in the White House dispersed to other places, there was no one to ask for information. Our most reliable information was coming from Stewart, who was dealing with his sources at the FBI and the Justice Department, and from correspondent Bob Orr, who covers the aviation beat. I worked the phones from my perch on top of the Chamber of Commerce, and from time to time I was able to pass on additional information. For all of us in those early hours, a major part of our job was knocking down false reports.

Orr recalled: "In the early part of the story, I spent most of my time checking out the bad information, so we could tell people it was wrong. Some of the cable companies were putting wild rumors on the air and the Internet was fueling a lot of it, but there was just a lot of bad stuff out there that had no basis in fact."

"I had it solid from the FAA that every civilian plane in the United States had been grounded, but we kept getting these reports that another plane was in the air. One story had it heading for the Sears Tower in Chicago, then we would get a report that it was a Delta plane heading to Atlanta.

"I had so many calls out to so many people

that I hesitated to go on the air with a story for fear I would miss a call back from one of my sources.

"Finally, I put a phone there at the Washington bureau anchor desk, and at one point I was on the air giving a report, when it rang. I did something I had never done before. I looked into the camera and said, 'Dan, I better take this call, so let me throw it back to you for a while . . .' Dan, understandably, was a little surprised, but it turned out to be a guy I had been trying to reach all morning, and when I hung up, I was able to go back on the air with fresh information."

By midafternoon, I had finally gotten back on the Capitol grounds, and the elected officials I found were stunned; some seemed a little dazed by it all. They didn't know what was coming next, but they were determined to get Congress in session the next day to show the terrorists — whoever they were — that they could not shut down the government. It was that night that more than three hundred members of Congress gathered on the Capitol steps and spontaneously began singing "God Bless America."

As I drove back to the Capitol the next morning, on my usual route past the Lincoln Memorial and the Washington Monument, I knew something was different, but it took me awhile to understand what. And then it hit me. There was none of the usual road rage. People were letting you pull in front of them, and waving when you let them by. It was also different at the Capitol. The panic of the day before was gone, but people were speaking to each other. It was as if we had all discovered there were others around us. Some just nodded and smiled. But you could see it in every face. We realized that we had all shared something we would never forget. Perhaps it had been a life-and-death situation. We could never really know, but we knew we were alive and had come through it together.

When the House and Senate convened, members were in a rage.

"This is war," Democratic leader Dick Gephardt stormed on the floor of the House. In the Senate, war hero John McCain sounded a grim warning: "I say to our enemies, we are coming. May God show you mercy."

In the next days, I would see Democrats and Republicans come together as I never had before. Within a week, they had passed more than forty billion dollars in emergency aid and passed it unanimously — something unheard of.

But it was the little things that I will remember longest: members of Congress lined up to have blood drawn in makeshift blood banks, American flags that suddenly appeared in the windows of most congressional offices.

When the Senate Democratic leader Tom Daschle and Republican leader Trent Lott walked to the microphones to announce that the emergency appropriations had been approved, it was a scene I had witnessed many times in the corridor off the Senate floor, but this time it was different. This time, Lott had his hand on Daschle's shoulder.

We had been through one of the worst days in all of American history, but it had brought out our best. In Congress, at Ground Zero — where rescue workers continued to search for the missing — and all across the country, people were telling each other, we will not allow this to stand. I was seeing the kind of America that I had remembered in the days before Kennedy's assassination, before the lies of Vietnam and Watergate had sapped our innocence and idealism and left us a cynical people, a people that had grown rude and all too often uncaring. We had been told in those years that the government was the enemy, but in the days after 9-11, we came to understand that the government was not the enemy — the government was just us, doing together what we could not do alone.

Some would say we are a different country since 9-11. But I am not so sure. I have been around long enough to believe we are again the country we used to be. The heroes of my youth — the soldiers, the firemen and policemen — are heroes again. In those days after 9-11, I think we came to realize that there is a difference between fame and heroism, a distinction that we had somehow forgotten. We realized once more what real heroes are, and that we need them, and that we need each other as well. The real heroes are those who are able to muster the know-how and courage in the face of danger to do what they would do in normal circumstances. We saw that over and over on September 11, and in the days that followed. People pulled together as they had not pulled together since World War II. Everyone wanted to help.

At the *Wall Street Journal*, whose headquarters building was across the street from the World Trade Center, the staff was evacuated from the building at 9:15 A.M., but the editor, Paul Steiger, was determined to put out a newspaper, no matter what the obstacles. He gathered whatever staff he could round up and assembled them at one of the *Journal*'s business offices in New Jersey. "People were asking what can we do, and we decided that what we knew how to do was put out a newspaper," he said.

When I heard that, it reminded me of what Eric Sevareid had once said: "Democracy requires more of its citizens than any other form of government."

It requires us to do what we know how to

do in times of crisis, and because millions of Americans recognized that responsibility to each other on 9-11, we emerged a stronger country, not a weaker one.

At CBS, we went on the air and stayed on the air. No one worried about cost (the coverage and lost revenue cost our parent company Viacom half a billion dollars, it was later estimated). Nor did anyone hesitate to cover the story because it was dangerous. Our job was to keep the information coming and our people risked their lives to get the job done. The attack on 9-11 was the hardest story that any of us had ever covered, but as I look back on it, I was never prouder to be a part of CBS News, to be a journalist, or to be an American.

At 6 A.M. EST, Saturday morning, we finally decided to end our continuous coverage. We had been on the air ninety-three hours and five minutes. An hour later we would go back on the air with the Saturday morning *Early Show*. It had been a crucial time for network news. People had been saying that the networks had become dinosaurs, that there was no longer a market for our kind of news. But viewers had done what they had always done in time of crisis: they had come back to the familiar, the news organizations they knew and trusted.

As Janet Leissner left the Washington control room that morning, she realized she had not been home in four days. After thirty-six straight hours in the Washington control room at the beginning of the crisis, she had slept for several hours in a hotel across from the bureau. She would return to the hotel from time to time in the early-morning hours, but never for more than two hours at a stretch. Nearly all of those four days had been spent in the control room. "I wasn't trying to set some record," she said. "I just couldn't find a way not to be there. I was really beat and drained of emotion, and then I turned onto the street where I live and I saw all these American flags, everywhere I looked. Not just on flag stands, but on porches and windows, everywhere I looked there were flags. That's when I just lost it. I hadn't been able to focus on the tragedy of it while I was working, but now we had taken a break in the work, and I started to cry. I thought about all those people who had died. But I was so proud of my country and I was proud of the job we had all done."

Six months after the attack, George Bush didn't have to be asked what was the hardest decision he had made on September 11. He volunteered that it was the decision to authorize the Air Force to shoot down other civilian airliners if it was determined that hijackers were trying to crash them into targets on the ground. He still thinks about it. And he still thinks about the example set by the passengers who overcame the hijackers on Flight 93 who lost their own lives when they forced that plane to crash.

"If history records it as it happened," he told me, "people will look back at that and realize that it was a defining moment in American history."

As spring of 2002 came to New York, Tom Flynn, the producer who had ridden his bike to Ground Zero on September 11 and nearly been killed, was looking forward to his daughter's graduation from Princeton. He still had the hacking cough he picked up breathing the dust from that day at Ground Zero.

The daughter that Eric Shapiro feared had been killed as he directed coverage during the early hours of the crisis was doing fine in her job as an investment banker. She went through a terrible period of nightmares, but they stopped after several months. She was still hesitant about flying.

Melissa Valcarcel, the young *Evening News* staffer who had watched her father die as the second plane slammed into the other tower, still knew no more about the circumstances of his death than what her family had learned in the first hours after the attack. But she was finally able to talk about it.

"Someone found his building ID card,"

she told me one afternoon. "But that's all we know. We don't even know where they found it."

Melissa's job at the *Evening News* is to track down videotape pictures from the CBS Archives, which means she has spent many hours combing through pictures of the tragedy that took her father's life. She returned to work two weeks after the attack and has been there since.

She was close to her father, and she told me that she thinks of him every day.

"There are so many things he won't get to see," she said. "I'm just so happy he saw me graduate from college. He was fifty-four and he planned to retire this year. He would look up from that wheelchair and tell us he was going to start a business when he retired — a ballet school."

She said that she and her sister had been interviewed by the FBI and asked if they would be willing to testify against Zacarias Moussaoui, the man charged with being one of those who planned the attack. She said the investigators wanted to put some of the families of those who died on the stand to help jurors understand the loss.

I asked if she understood that it might be dangerous, that the publicity could make her a target of the terrorists.

"Oh yes," she told me. "But we want to do it for our father. We have to do it."

I had been trying to console her, but she had made me feel better.

We have serious problems in this country, but if Melissa's generation is thinking that way, if enough of them share her values, they'll find a way to solve the problems.

I told her I thought her father would be very proud.

# Twenty-eight

## *End Piece*

When the Middle East blew up in April 2002, I got a call from New York. Dan Rather was headed to Jerusalem. Would I come to New York, and keep the anchor chair warm until he returned? Sure, I would. That's fairly easy duty, a job I have done many times over the years. Dan would report the developments from Jerusalem on the *Evening News* for the next week or so, and I would handle the "all else" section of the broadcast. Basically, I would be in New York as a backstop, to handle emergencies if technical problems developed, or if something went wrong at Dan's end. Or, in the unlikely instance that something happened in another part of the world, I would be available to anchor special reports.

Pat seldom travels with me when I go on assignment, but she decided to go along on this trip. Neither of us had been to New York since the terrorist attack, it was a chance to see our younger daughter, Sharon, who lives there, and both of us wanted to go to Ground Zero.

Early on a Friday morning, we took a cab downtown to the site. The cabbie let us out near a pier and showed us where the police handed out tickets to view the site. There was no charge, but a platform had been built at the south end, and to keep the size of the crowds manageable, tickets were issued which specified the hours spectators could go there. What struck me as I waited to go to the platform was that the people who had come there were not the usual sightseers. They were quiet, almost reverent, as if they were waiting to go into a cathedral or a holy place. There was a man and his wife who were from Denver there and we began to talk.

"I never lost a thing in this city," he told me. "I never had any interest in coming here, but after what happened, we just thought we ought to come."

I hadn't known what to expect, but I felt as I had when I had gone with Jimmy Carter to Normandy, and had seen the cemeteries where so many Americans were buried. I felt as I had when I had gone to the Vietnam Wall in Washington for the first time. The line to the viewing platform took us past walls where thousands of missing-person flyers had been posted. Each flyer gave vital statistics about someone, and there were pictures of the missing, but as we passed by them, we realized they all shared an unwritten message: These people are not missing; they are dead and they died in the expanse of rubble that suddenly confronted us as we stepped onto the viewing platform. The wreckage after the attack had been pulled down, only the flat gray rubble remained, sixteen acres of it, and it stretched for hundreds of feet before us. Only when we were able to see it with our own eyes was it possible to comprehend the enormity of what had happened. Beyond the rubble, and surrounding it on three sides, was the New York skyline, with its great skyscrapers, but we realized at once that the Towers had dwarfed all these buildings. But they were no longer there, only the gray rubble. It is as if we were looking at a photograph of something we had seen hundreds of times, only this time someone had erased part of it.

I looked down at Pat and she was crying. I realized that I was crying, too. I hugged her and told her how much I loved her and how glad I was that we had shared so much together, and she hugged me back.

Then my cell phone rang.

It was Wayne Nelson at CBS News headquarters.

"Hey, buddy," he said. "The president is going to make a big policy statement on the Middle East at 11 o'clock. We think he's going to send Colin Powell to Jerusalem. We're going to carry it live and we need you to anchor the broadcast. Can you get here by then?"

I glanced at my watch. It was 10:20 and the traffic was jammed. It would be close, but I told him I would be there.

I told Pat what I had told her so many times over the years. I told her I had to go to work.

"Just give me a minute," she said. She wiped away the tears, and then she said what she had said so many times when sudden assignments had forced us to postpone plans, or trips, or family outings: "You better get going, then."

We ran several hundred yards and finally flagged a cab. As we headed uptown to CBS, a hundred questions were swirling through my mind. Could I get there on time? What was Bush going to say? Why was he saying it now? What had he said before? They were the same kinds of questions that had always gone through my head as I had raced to hundreds of stories, the kinds of questions that had drawn me to journalism. There would be plenty of time later to contemplate our visit to Ground Zero, but now there was another story to cover and I had to get there, because I had told them I would, and because I was a reporter and that is what reporters do.

I made it with four minutes to spare.

# Chapter Work Notes, Sources, Afterthoughts and Observations

CHAPTER 1: *Oswald's Mother*. This chapter is written mostly from my own memories of those days. *Star-Telegram* colleagues Phil Record and Jon McConal helped me remember details. A brief account of my trip to Dallas with Mrs. Oswald is included in the Warren Commission Report. A fictionalized version of the episode also appeared in Thomas Thompson's novel *Celebrity*. Thompson was a writer for *Life* magazine and met the Oswald women that day at the Dallas police station after I had been "excused" by the FBI agent. He was later able to interview both of them. By coincidence, he was also a Fort Worth native. I didn't know him, but when I was a student at North Side High School, his father, C. A. Thompson, was principal of Polytechnic High School, our crosstown rival.

665

CHAPTER 2: *The Johnson City Windmill.* The first television I ever saw was in the window of an appliance store on Camp Bowie Boulevard in Fort Worth. The set had an eight-inch screen, and a movie starring Rex Harrison was being shown. The appliance store was next to a Mexican restaurant where we were going for dinner. We stopped to watch for a minute, but my father wasn't impressed. I remember he told us to move on because he was hungry.

Jake Pickle, Johnson's hat-catcher during the 1948 campaign, had come to Washington when Johnson was elected to Congress. Johnson found him a job working on the Capitol police force, but he spent part of each day working in Johnson's office. Eventually, he would be elected to Johnson's old congressional seat and he served many years on the House Ways and Means Committee. *Summer Stock* by Joe Phipps, published in 1992 by TCU Press, gives an excellent overview of the 1948 campaign across Texas.

CHAPTER 3: *Mississippi Burning.* For years, my memory was that I had seen Meredith enter Baxter Hall on the Sunday he was brought to the Ole Miss campus, but as I read accounts of that day in Richard Reeves's book *President Kennedy* and in Taylor Branch's *Parting the Waters,* the seminal work on the civil rights movement, it became clear to me that I could not have seen Meredith that day. On further reflection, I remembered the shirtless reporter walking beside him and I then realized I had not seen him until the next day, when he was escorted from Baxter Hall to the Lyceum Building for enrollment. Governor Barnett's "Which one of you is Meredith?" remark is taken from *Parting the Waters*, as are casualty statistics and other details about Meredith's stay there. Kennedy's secret conversations with Barnett have been reported many times since, and are from Reeves's book. The story line of Paul Guihard's play is taken from his obituary in the *New York Times*. The discovery of Henry Gallagher, the second lieutenant who led the first federal troops onto the campus, was one of those happy accidents. Bill Geoghegan, the Washington lawyer quoted in the chapter, knew I was writing this book and told me he had "run across a lawyer at a legal meeting who had been talking about being in charge of Meredith's security detail as a young officer." I called Gallagher and he gave me the details that solved the longtime mystery of why it had taken the troops so long to get to Oxford.

CHAPTER 4: *The Night Beat*. Amon Carter, who founded the *Star-Telegram*, was one of the great characters and promoters of the twentieth century. A wonderful account of his life can be found in Jerry Flemmons's book *Amon*, published by Texas Tech University Press in 1998, from which I drew some of the incidents in Amon's early life. Nothing fazed Amon. As Flemmons reported, he once told the *Saturday Evening Post* that to him, "No is just a word in the dictionary. I don't often consult the dictionary." It was his daughter-in-law who introduced me to Pat.

CHAPTER 5: *Courthouse Days*. This chapter is drawn mostly from memory and *Star-Telegram* stories from that period. In this chapter and subsequent chapters on Vietnam, I used Stanley Karnow's *Vietnam: A History*, published by Viking in 1983, for casualty statistics and an overview of the war. *The Military and the Media*, published by the U.S. Army Center for Military History in 1987, is also an excellent reference for those interested in the relationship between journalists and the military.

CHAPTER 6: *The* Star-Telegram *Goes to War* and CHAPTER 7: *"I Can't Never Tell What Happened to Me."* These chapters are based on clippings of stories that I wrote in the *Star-Telegram* from December 1965 to April 1966. I state in Chapter 6 that I interviewed 235 people in Vietnam. I arrived at that number by counting the names that appeared in the

*Star-Telegram* stories. All the quotes from U.S. military people are as they appeared in the *Star-Telegram*. Eddie Adams, the AP combat photographer who taught me how to take pictures, and often traveled with me, later won the Pulitzer for his photo of a South Vietnamese officer putting a pistol to the head of a prisoner and executing him, one of the best-remembered pictures of the war. Peter Arnett also wrote of the incident when the MP pulled a pistol on me in his book *Live from the Battlefield*, published in 1994 by Simon & Schuster. The Barry Zorthian quotes come from Peter's book. We have all remained friends over the years. Eddie, Peter, Horst Fass, Bob Poos, George Esper and Ed White of the AP Saigon bureau were already combat veterans when I got to Vietnam, and I will always be grateful for the help they gave me. Zorthian and I both wound up in Washington, where we became friends.

CHAPTER 8: *News at Six.* The history of Channel 5 is drawn mostly from Jerry Flemmons's book *Amon* and from conversations during my days at the station with Doyle Vinson, a longtime employee. It was Vinson who explained to me that the newsreel format for the newscasts had come about because the first employees had seen movie newsreels but never a television newscast. He said that unfamiliarity with television was also why the station's building was laid out as it was. The architects, who had never seen a TV station, modeled the physical plant on a school — offices around the outside of the building, with a huge studio in the middle where the school gym usually was. Bobbie Wygant, whose invitation to appear on her Channel 5 talk show led to my being hired by the station, is still associated with Channel 5 as I write this. Thanks, Bobbie.

CHAPTER 9: *1968.* Statistics on the numbers of security personnel deployed at the convention come from Theodore White's *The Making of the President, 1968.* Robert Strauss tipped me to the story about the possibility of the McCarthy–Connally ticket. James Reston, Jr., wrote about Johnson's aides feeling like "Charlie McCarthy sitting on Edgar Bergen's knee" in his book *The Lone Star: The Life of John Connally,* published in 1989 by Harper & Row, and all three aides later confirmed the story to me.

CHAPTER 10: *Washington.* Bill Small's remembrance of the day he hired me differs slightly from mine. He believes he told one of the underlings to have me write and record a five-minute newscast as a test, which was his usual habit when reporters applied for jobs, but I have no recollection of it. He does remember his deputy, Don Richardson, saying,

"You're not going to hire someone with that kind of accent, are you?" The story of Bob Pierpoint's ruined dinner party became legendary at CBS News. I had forgotten it until I ran across a clip of a story Phil Hilts had done about the bureau in the *Washington Post* Sunday magazine in April 1974. As one might expect, Pierpoint hadn't forgotten it when I talked to him in 2001. The "Sevareid and the ear trumpet" story also became part of the CBS legend, and Gary Paul Gates wrote about it in his fine history of CBS News, *Airtime*, published by Harper & Row in 1978. As I write this in April 2002, Helen Thomas is still covering the White House, still shows up there to cover stories on weekends and is still putting government officials in their places.

CHAPTER 11: *Nixon's War*. In his book *President Nixon*, Richard Reeves illustrates the good press reviews that Nixon got during his first months in office by pointing to the glowing assessments that CBS News correspondents gave in a CBS News special about Nixon's first one hundred days. I have examined the entire transcript of that broadcast and the assessments were even more positive than Reeves suggested. Only Dan Schorr had warned that night that it might be too early to draw conclusions. Bill Beecher's story of the secret bombing was one of the major scoops of that period and he was still the *New York Times* Pentagon correspondent when I covered the Pentagon. He was one of the most knowledgeable reporters I ever encountered, and later served in the Reagan administration in the office of the assistant secretary of defense for public affairs. In Dan Schorr's book *Clearing the Air*, published in 1977 by Houghton Mifflin, Marvin Kalb and others have written about the instant analysis that infuriated the White House after Nixon's speech. Magruder's memo, which has been published many times, is one of the many documents assembled in Corydon Dunham's book about Frank Stanton and is also among those in Eric Engberg's collection. Frank Stanton was well past ninety years old when I talked to him in the winter of 2001, but he had no trouble remembering any of what transpired in those days. He had been dealing with top government and White House officials for thirty years and still finds it all hard to believe.

CHAPTER 12: *The Puzzle Palace*. I had just begun to cover the Pentagon and wasn't thought to be well known enough to narrate a major documentary, so Roger Mudd was chosen to do the interviews and narrate *The Selling of the Pentagon*. However, when the controversy blew up over whether it had been a slanted, dishonest report, I drew the duty of listening to the complaints of Pentagon officials and interviewing congressional critics for a series of follow-up reports. It wasn't the happiest task I had ever been assigned, but it got me in the door to interview various people, including Armed Services Committee chairman F. Eddie Hebert, who would later prove to be valuable sources.

CHAPTER 13: *The Devious Dove.* Mel Laird was the kind of government official whom reporters dream about covering. He knew more about how the government worked than anybody in Washington, he was a key player and he was always up to something. Jim Schlesinger, who came after Laird at the Pentagon, said Laird once described his deputy David Packard as "the kind of guy who thought the shortest distance between two points was a straight line." Schlesinger said that told you more about Laird than Packard and it was what made the devious Laird so much fun to cover. If you listened closely, Mel Laird would always point you in the direction of a story. Al Haig's memoir *Inner Circles*, published by Warner Books in 1992, is an entertaining, very readable account of that era, and Haig was also quite candid in two interviews. White House documents cited in this chapter were made public by the National Archives over the years and came from the collection assembled by Eric

Engberg. Nixon's conversations in early 1972 with Haldeman and Colson in the hours after he had been interviewed by Dan Rather were discovered in a batch of tapes made available by the National Archives on October 26, 2000. They were found and transcribed by reporter James Rosen, who shared them with me for this book. For those looking for a basic reference book on the Defense Department and Defense budget statistics, I recommend George C. Wilson's *This War Really Matters*, published by CQ Press.

CHAPTER 14: *1972: Control and Chaos.* Most of this chapter comes from what I saw in Miami that summer and from interviews for this book with McGovern and his aides and George Wallace's then press secretary, Billy Joe Camp, but I also drew on Teddy White's reporting for the overview of the 1972 conventions. Much of the basic data in White's books (voter profiles, etc.) came from the CBS News convention handbooks prepared by CBS News political director Martin Plissner, who was also a source for this chapter. In his own memoir, Dan Schorr takes delight in recounting his convention scoop, obtaining the schedule of the Republican convention.

CHAPTER 15: *The Last Serious Campaign.* Early quotes from Jimmy Carter, McGovern and others come from a transcript of a *CBS News Special Report* broadcast after the Democratic convention. The account of George McGovern's secret meeting with Eagleton after his appearance on *Face the Nation* was first reported by Teddy White, but I confirmed it with McGovern. Eagleton no longer gives interviews about the campaign, but in a cordial series of e-mails he told me White's account of the campaign was generally accurate. Some of the people in Democratic politics whom I have known longest I met on the McGovern campaign. In addition to those named in the chapter, they include Sandy Berger, a McGovern speechwriter who went on to become national security advisor under Bill Clinton; Mike Barnicle, also a speechwriter and later a columnist; Mickey Kantor, McGovern campaign operative and later Clinton's secretary of commerce; Eli Segal; Anne Wexler; and Joe Duffey. Each of them gave me insight into McGovern in conversations along the way, as did Massachusetts senator John Kerry and his wife, Teresa Hines. As noted, McGovern himself gave me several long interviews for this book. In 1979, while anchoring the *Morning News*, I also interviewed George Wallace. Like McGovern, I came to believe he was sincere in the way he moderated his views on race. I was never able to get him to discuss his theories of who was behind his shooting.

CHAPTER 16: *The Nixon Endgame.* Woodward and Bernstein's *All the President's Men*, published by Simon & Schuster in 1973, remains the best reference for anyone researching Nixon's fall, but I also found the memoir of H. R. Haldeman, Nixon's chief of staff, quite candid and helpful. It is called *The Ends of Power*, and was published by Times Books. Both Dan Rather, who covered the White House for CBS News, and Tom Brokaw, who covered Nixon's last days, gave me considerable help in understanding how the White House operated during that time. Since those days when CBS was the "all Texas" network, Dan Rather and I have kidded each other in public forums about those "elite" institutions where we went to school. He'll introduce me by saying he's never had the pleasure of introducing a "horned frog" (the TCU mascot). I generally point out that Sam Houston State Teachers College was so far back in the woods, even the Episcopalians played with snakes during their services.

CHAPTER 17: *The Pardon* and CHAPTER 18: *Stumbling Along.* Arthur Taylor's disclosure that Nixon had actually pushed him in anger after the incident at the Houston press conference was news to both Dan and me.

Of all the public officials I have covered over the years, President Ford was the most genial and unassuming. He seemed to genuinely like people, sometimes more than Mrs. Ford appreciated, and he sometimes took a drink toward the end of long campaign days. During the last stop on one such campaign trip through Texas in 1976, he was greeted by the Kilgore Junior College Rangerettes, a marching team of several dozen glamorous coeds. Ford was so delighted to see them that he went down the line and gave every one of them a big kiss.

I have interviewed Ford numerous times in the years since he left office, but the most memorable encounter occurred in Rochester, New York, in 1980. Ford was making a speech there and we had rented a hotel conference room for the interview. We had set up our camera equipment, and as we waited for Ford to arrive, the Secret Service asked us to clear the room so a bomb-sniffing dog could be brought in to sweep the room for possible explosives. Such sweeps are normal security procedures, but when the camera crew and I were kept in the hallway for almost an hour, and security agents with worried looks on their faces began to file in and out of the room, I knew something out of the ordinary was going on. When we were finally allowed in, we were greeted by the overwhelming odor of disinfectant. After some prodding, a local policeman told me what had caused the holdup. The bomb-sniffing dog had entered the room, gone directly to the chair where the president was to be interviewed and proceeded to defecate. The conference room had no rest room, so the agents had been forced to clean up the mess and bring it through the hallway and take it to a men's room down the hall. Fearing we would poke fun at them, one of the agents had wrapped the stuff in a newspaper and put it in his pocket. Other agents had gone to a nearby grocery and bought the disinfectant, which explained the smell. I couldn't resist telling Ford about what the dog had done. The security people looked as if they could kill me for telling him, but he just laughed and said, "Well, everyone else has been dumping on me, why not the dog?"

CHAPTER 19: *Jimmy*. Carter's cousin Hugh Carter wrote a book with Frances Spatz Leighton called *Cousin Beedie and Cousin Hot*, published by Prentice-Hall in 1978. The family nicknames come from that.

Jody Powell, who was Carter's closest advisor, stayed on in Washington, as did Gerald Rafshoon, his ad man, and I have maintained contact with them over the years, but I didn't really reestablish contact with Hamilton Jordan until he wrote his recent book on surviving cancer, *No Such Thing as a Bad Day*, published by Longstreet Press in 2000. Hamilton has survived three bouts with cancer and I have come to admire the work he has done for those with the disease. He and his wife currently operate a summer camp for children with cancer. Most people who come to Washington get the kind of press coverage they deserve, but Hamilton deserved much better than he got from Washington. He was hounded by investigations into charges that proved groundless, and was the victim of more than one cheap shot from the press. Jimmy Carter's postpresidential accomplishments are well known and I have discussed some of them in this chapter, but as I have watched succeeding presidents grapple with the Middle East, I have come to appreciate more fully what he accomplished at Camp David.

All of us who lived in Plains during the fall of 1976 and the first weeks of 1977 owe thanks to Jimmy Murray, owner of the Best Western Motel. He put up with a lot and made us comfortable. We also remember the hospitality of the people of nearby Americus, Georgia. Bill and Dana Blair, whom I first met in those days when the people of Americus invited visiting reporters into their homes, have remained our friends through the years.

CHAPTER 20: *The* Morning Show: *A Time out of Time.* The move to New York in 1979 and my experiences on the *Morning News* were a difficult period and difficult to write about, but those years would be a turning point in my life. Gary Paul Gates, who was a writer on the *Evening News*, told me the "hand job" story and also included it in his book *Airtime*.

CHAPTER 21: *It Was All Foreign to Me*. A search of the CBS Archives revealed that I was able to file that first story from Argentina so quickly because of an accidental encounter. As I came off the plane in the Buenos Aires airport, I ran into Simon Winchester of the *London Sunday Times*, a reporter I had known from the days when he was based in Washington. He had been in the Falklands the day the Argentine army invaded, and gave me an eyewitness account. Later that week, Simon was arrested by Argentine authorities on trumped-up espionage charges and sat out the war in a Buenos Aires jail. He went on to become a successful author; his book *The Professor and the Madman*, an account of how the *Oxford English Dictionary* came to be, was a bestseller.

CHAPTER 22: *The New World Order: CBS in the 1980s*. Obviously I was a witness to and sometimes a participant in the turmoil that marked CBS News in the 1980s, and most of what appears in this chapter comes from my memory of that time and later interviews with others, including Larry Tisch. But I also used Peter J. Boyer's book *Who Killed CBS?*, published by Random House in 1988, to gain background, check my own memory and get a general overview of that era. I also used Peter's figures on budget cuts and layoffs. It is one of the best accounts of that time, and in drawing on it, I have come full circle. Peter's conclusions were his own, but I confess to being one of the sources for his book, sometimes on the record and sometimes not. To be sure, Ed Joyce's *Prime Times, Bad Times*, published by Doubleday in 1988, is Joyce's version of many of the events of that period, but I found it straightforward and helpful. Many of the events written about by Boyer and Joyce, including the incident with Rather's chair, have since been written about by others. So have several of the incidents concerning Phyllis George, but I was there and saw most of it as it happened.

CHAPTER 23: *Capitol Hill.* Some of the quotes from congressional officials in this section were included in stories I did for the CBS *Evening News* in the weeks after 9-11.

CHAPTER 24: *Sunday Services.* You never know where you'll find news, and the beginning of this chapter is a fine example. I called my competitor Tim Russert to see if he had really told an interviewer that he was a regular watcher of *Face the Nation*, and he told me the story of Walter Cronkite's becoming flustered and signing off a broadcast, "Thanks for joining us on *Meet the Press*." I had not been aware that Walter had ever hosted a Sunday show, but when I called him, he confirmed it and told me the story that begins this chapter. Brinkley himself and his wife, Susan, told me the story of how Roone Arledge created *This Week*.

When I say in the chapter that booking guests for the Sunday shows can be as complicated as negotiating a nuclear-arms agreement, the diplomatic metaphor is apt, as the following example illustrates: When the British turned Hong Kong over to China in 1997, we flew to Hong Kong to do the broadcast from there. The highlight of our broadcast was to be an interview with the U.S. ambassador to China, James Sasser, who by coincidence is a longtime family friend. Secretary of State Madeleine Albright left for Hong Kong at midweek to take part in the ceremonies and had already agreed to appear that Sunday on Russert's *Meet the Press*. On the day before we were to leave for Hong Kong, I got a call from Albright's plane. She had decided that Sasser would not be allowed to participate in our broadcast for diplomatic reasons. The State Department wanted to emphasize that Hong Kong would be treated separately from the rest of China, and therefore the U.S. ambassador was not the proper official to be speaking for the United States.

(Other State Department officials told me Secretary Albright simply did not like to share the spotlight with ambassadors.) Whatever the reasons, it left us in a dilemma. Russert was staying in Washington and interviewing Albright by satellite. We were going all the way to Hong Kong and had no American official to interview. In a series of phone calls, I proposed that Albright be on our show as well. No, I was told, she had promised Russert that the only sit-down interview she would do was with him. In desperation, I seized on the word "sit-down." I proposed that if she stood up instead of sitting she wouldn't break her promise to Tim. Several more phone calls later, I was stunned when an aide told me she had agreed. So it was that on that Sunday, Madeleine Albright walked into a Hong Kong hotel suite that we had rented, and as she stood there, I interviewed her for *Face the Nation*. Actually, it wasn't a bad interview. She thinks very well on her feet. When the show was done, Pat and I took a week off and flew to Beijing, had a delightful visit with Jim and Mary Sasser, and I finally saw the Great Wall, which I had been unable to see during working visits there, first with President Ford, and later with Secretary of State Shultz. On the way home, we stopped in Saigon, my first visit there since the war.

CHAPTER 25: *The Charmer*. I had remembered interviewing Clinton in 1988, but I had no idea what had been done with the interview or how much of it we had used in the report I did that night on the *Evening News.* When researcher Bonney Kapp found it in the CBS News Archives, we learned we had used only about ten seconds of it. The rest, as far as I know, has not been seen or published.

CHAPTER 26: *Being Careful What You Wish For Is Still a Good Rule.* The account of what happened on election night and all election-night quotes are from transcripts of our on-the-air coverage and from information compiled during the in-house investigation ordered by CBS News president Andrew Heyward.

The events of the night the Supreme Court ruled on the election have already produced a plethora of analytical articles and books, but the analysis that Linda Greenhouse wrote for the *New York Times* in the days after the court ruling remains the clearest and best explanation of what the court did, and is the one that most influenced my own conclusions.

CHAPTER 27: *9-11* and CHAPTER 28: *End Piece.* I was in the process of winding up the book when Marcy McGinnis asked me to come to New York and sit in for Dan while he was in the Middle East in the first part of April 2002. I had planned to focus the last chapter on what we had done that day in the Washington bureau, because that was the part I knew about, and because I had not been to New York since the attack. But when I got to New York, I realized that the events of 9-11 still hung heavy over CBS News headquarters there, and as I talked with my colleagues, I realized their stories as well as mine had to be a part of this book. It is a testament to their professionalism that the difficulties, and in some cases the near-death experiences many of them endured that day, had never been publicized. Their stories deserve to be told and I am glad that I have had an opportunity to do so.

"End piece," by the way, is what we call the last story in a television broadcast. "-30-" is the symbol newspaper reporters used in my day to mark the end of a story. In this case, it marks the end of this story; I'm still looking for the next one.